MW01618151

A Pre-Raphaelite Marriage

The Lives and Works of

Marie Spartali Stillman and William James Stillman

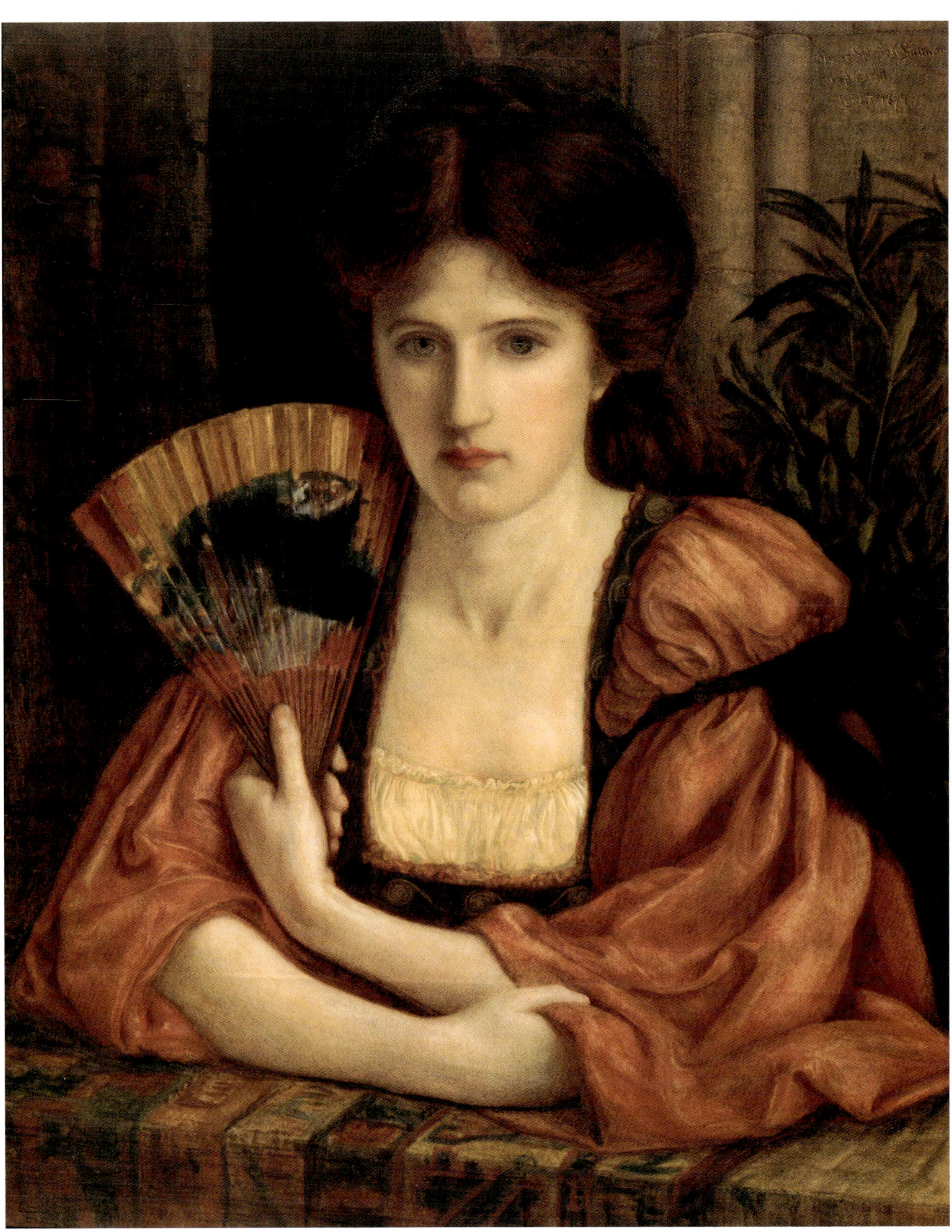

A Pre-Raphaelite Marriage

The Lives and Works of Marie Spartali Stillman and William James Stillman

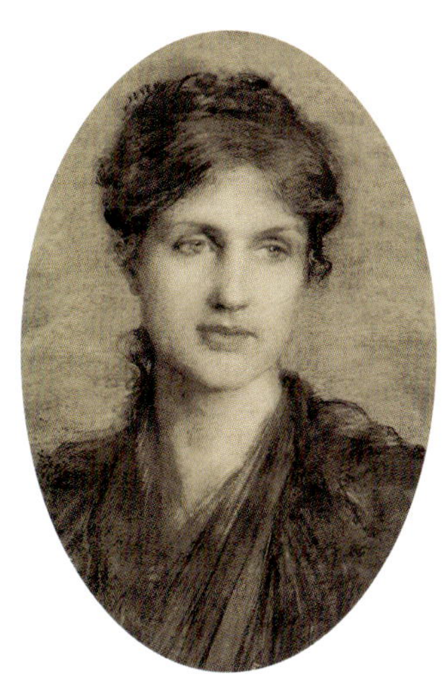

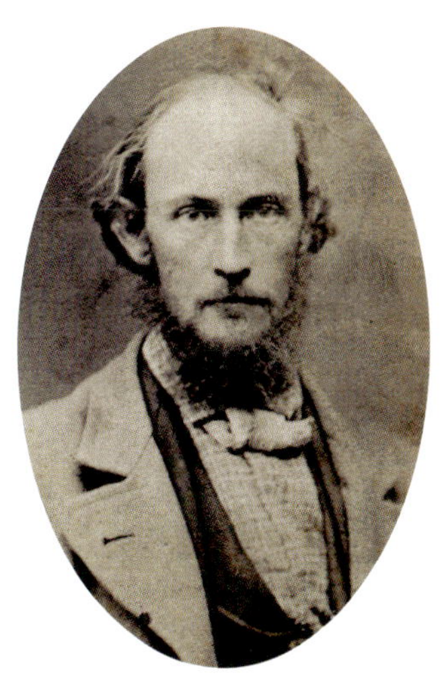

David B. Elliott

Antique Collectors' Club

First published 2006

ISBN 1 85149 495 2

British Library Cataloguing-in-Publication Data:
A catalogue record for this book is available from the British Library

Cover: Detail Plate 58
Marie Spartali Stillman
1889
The Enchanted Garden of Messer Ansaldo
Pre-Raphaelite Inc., London, by courtesy of Julian Hartnoll

Frontispiece: Plate 31
Marie Spartali Stillman
1874
Self Portrait
Watercolour on paper. 65 x 51 cm (25⅝ x 20⅛in)
Courtesy of The Maas Gallery, London

Designed by Sandra Pond
Text typeface 11pt Bergamo

Printed in China
Published in England by the Antique Collectors' Club Limited

Contents

Acknowledgements

My search for Marie Spartali Stillman – her story, her individuality and her work – was initially motivated by her 50 year friendship with my grandfather, Charles Fairfax Murray. They met and worked together in Dante Rossetti's studio in 1868 or 1869 and she was at his deathbed in January 1919. The quest shaped my next four years. Marie Spartali was notable for her charm and her beauty; yet she remains elusive, an intensely private person. The eldest child of a wealthy Greek family with deep roots in London and business interests throughout the Mediterranean, married to an American and thus an American citizen, her heart found its home in Florence. The greater part of her considerable output is in private collections on both sides of the Atlantic and my mission would have proved impossible without the generous and enthusiastic help I have received, both in England and the United States.

First and foremost, I must record my immense indebtedness to William Ritchie, Marie Stillman's great-grandson, and his wife Valerie for their hospitality over the last four years; he has lent family papers, traced pictures, translated from the Greek, answered innumerable questions, regaled me with family lore and introduced me to a host of Marie's far-flung Spartali and Stillman descendants. Of these I must particularly mention Mrs Genii Pell, the late Mrs Marion Stillman, Mary Sundra, Nancy Baumann, William Stillman, Pip Florance and Lisa de Quay who have contributed greatly.

Beyond the immediate family I have been greatly assisted by yet another William Stillman, the US West Coast keeper of the Stillman genealogy; still in America I have received generous help from academics and art historians, some previously unknown to me, others friends of some years, among them Gail Weinberg, Miriam Stewart, Rob Leith, Margaretta Frederick, Mark Samuels Lasner, Linda Merrill, Vineta Colby and Martha Vicinus.

In England the roll has been no less rich and rewarding. I have been fortunate in being able to exchange views and seek advice from Betty Elzea, Jan Marsh, Caroline Dakers, Fiona MacCarthy, Mary Bennett, Christopher Newall, Angela Thirlwell, Peter Faulkner, John Christian and Stephen Wildman. George Vassiadis, the genealogist of the 19th century Greek families in London, has been a mine of information on the Spartali family, their relations and on Greek politics. People at Christie's have been particularly helpful in tracing pictures. We have made strenuous efforts to find owners I have not met, and to any I have failed to contact I extend my sincere apologies for this omission. In Birmingham, the Pre-Raphaelite Society has been supportive throughout. I want also to acknowledge my debt to my Editor, Susannah Hecht, for her tireless enthusiasm, her eagle eye and her helpful comment.

For letters and diaries relating both to William and Marie Stillman I am indebted to the Trustees of the Victoria and Albert Museum for permission to make use of Ford Madox Brown's papers, to George Brandak at the University of British Columbia for letters and diaries in the Angeli-Dennis collection, to Ellen Fladger at Union College, Schenectady for extracts from William Stillman's papers, and to the Principal and Fellows of Somerville College, Oxford for Marie Stillman's letters in the Vernon Lee papers there. Other sources and quotations are recorded in the endnotes.

Lastly I wish to express my profound gratitude to the Paul Mellon Centre for Studies in British Art for their generous grant to me to continue my search for previously unpublished images of Marie Spartali Stillman's work. It has been a most rewarding task.

David Elliott
Harrow on the Hill

Introduction

"After ground frost overnight, the morning opened dull, finer towards noon & very fine after but cold," the *London Meteorological Observer* recorded.[1] It was as though Zeus and the Immortals had playfully devised a celestial allegory for the marriage of this unlikely pair of lovers.

Marie Euphrosyne Spartali, spinster aged 27, of The Shrubbery, Clapham was married by license to William James Stillman, widower aged 42, of 50 Sydney Street, Chelsea at Chelsea Register Office on the morning of 10 April 1871. The witnesses were Ford (transcribed incorrectly by the Registrar as Frederick) Madox Brown who gave her in marriage, and his daughter Lucy, Marie's close friend, painter and fellow pupil of her father. There were two other witnesses, Mr M Merrington, a colleague of the Spartali family's physician John Marshall, and his wife Margaret Merrington, a loyal friend of Marie.[2] The bride's parents were not present and the groom had no supporter. This was no run-away wedding nor a whirlwind romance, but the culmination of more than eighteen months of growing closeness between the two lovers amid acrimony, the opposition of the bride's father and her consequent defiance that tore at the heart of a close-knit family and left a wound that was slow to heal; and which dismayed Marie Spartali's many friends who thought it an unsuitable match. William Stillman's remaining family were three thousand miles away.

The choice of a civil ceremony was dictated both by the hostility of her family and the differing religious backgrounds the partners (though neither was notably observant): Marie Spartali came from a practising Greek Orthodox family, William Stillman from a zealously strict Baptist home. Civil marriages were fewer than one in ten in the 1870s, and were popular mainly in less affluent non-Conformist circles because they escaped the legal requirement for a Registrar to be present at weddings in Dissenting chapels, thus avoiding the difficulties, and cost, of arranging a religious service. Among the wealthier middle-classes, a Register Office wedding was generally regarded with patronising distaste; "... a prosaic, almost sordid ceremony – civil marriages are not conducted with much dignity and seem rather to suggest a certain shadiness in the contracting partners."[3] Marie Spartali was defiantly turning her back on her wealthy and socially-conventional parents and on an arranged marriage within the Greek community, rejecting the established values of the family she was born in to, and marrying for love.

The couple spent a short honeymoon on the Isle of Wight in a house owned by her father, Michael Spartali. Their first night as husband and wife was not without its problems as William Stillman wrote to Madox Brown next day from Christchurch: "We have got here alright, some the worse for wear – M was excessively fatigued and feverish but today she seems calm and stronger – the rain which considerately kept off for the wedding follows us here and shuts us indoors, while the landlord having a previous order for our room insists on turning us out. In the dilemma we go to Bournemouth by the next train. We went this morning to see the church which is interesting and I gave M a lecture on Gothic architecture which, if neither profound nor technical, was I think useful tho' M says she didn't take it in. I cannot say that on the whole I like the town – the hotel I certainly do not – which makes the incivility of the landlord a godsend as an excuse for seeing nobody and so saving a shilling... We shall stay at Bournemouth until the rain stops and then go over to Freshwater. A beastly band has drawn up outside the front door and makes music worse than drawing teeth."[4]

The joylessness, the conscious avoidance of emotion, that flawed so much of William Stillman's life is startlingly evident in these chilly lines. Against the opposition of her father, he had won the heart of a vital, strikingly beautiful young woman who was without exception loved and admired by all who came within her orbit. Dante Gabriel Rossetti spoke for her friends: "She is a noble girl – in beauty, in sweetness and in artistic gifts, and the sky should seem very warm and calm above, and all ill things left behind forever, to him who sets out on his life's journey, foot to foot and hand in hand... I warmly hope that happiness is in store for both of them. She is a pearl among women, and there are points in Stillman's character of the manliest and truest I know. His prospects are at present very uncertain."[5] The battle won, he could at last enjoy her warmth and her enthusiasms, and find with her the peace in which to rebuild the young family which had been shattered by his first wife's suicide and the fatal decline of his young son. On this happiest of days he remained as dour and isolated as before.

Unpromising though the marriage seemed to all who looked on, it lasted the 30 years that remained of William Stillman's lifetime, and at the end Marie Spartali Stillman wrote poignantly of her loss of "this dearest of all companions and friends".[6]

Chapter One

The Greeks in London

In the middle years of Queen Victoria's long reign the Phanariot Greeks in London formed a close-knit, wealthy banking and trading community comprised of a number of powerful families concerned for the most part in shipping, commodity trading and commercial finance. In the 40 years between 1854 and 1894 successive heads of the Spartali and Ionides families represented Greek business interests in England as Consuls General. Both senior members and their wives in the 1850s were descended from expatriate refugees from religious extremism in the Ottoman Empire who became patriotic subjects of the Queen.

Generations of the Ionides had been prominent members of the Greek merchant community in Constantinople where they traded in cotton and silks until they were forced to seek refuge from Muslim religious persecution that culminated horribly in their great-grandfather's death, crucified on his own front door. They left their possessions behind to the mob and eventually found their way to Manchester where Alexander Constantine's father established the English branch of the family firm.

The Spartalis were expatriate Greeks who had generations earlier put down roots among the Greek community in Bursa on the southern shore of the Sea of Marmora in Turkish Asia Minor, operating at the margin between Europe and Asia. Their relations, the Laskarides were established residents there. The Spartalis had later moved to Smyrna, trading in the flourishing market for grain and dried fruits there, until they too were forced to abandon their home and business and make their way north by way of Trieste to find asylum in London. Michael Spartali was 9 months old when the family fled Smyrna. He was educated in Switzerland, following his parents to England at the age of twelve in 1832. By the 1840s the family were the senior partners in the respected London firm Spartali & Laskarides, bankers and grain merchants, with interests in shipping and branches in Marseilles and Alexandria. Michael Spartali, who was appointed Greek Consul General in London in 1866 in succession to Alexander Constantine Ionides and was succeeded by Alecco Ionides in 1884, never visited his native land.[1] His wife, Euphrosyne Valsami, came from an expatriate Greek merchant family in Genoa.

At the time of Marie Spartali's birth on 10 March 1844, the Spartalis and the

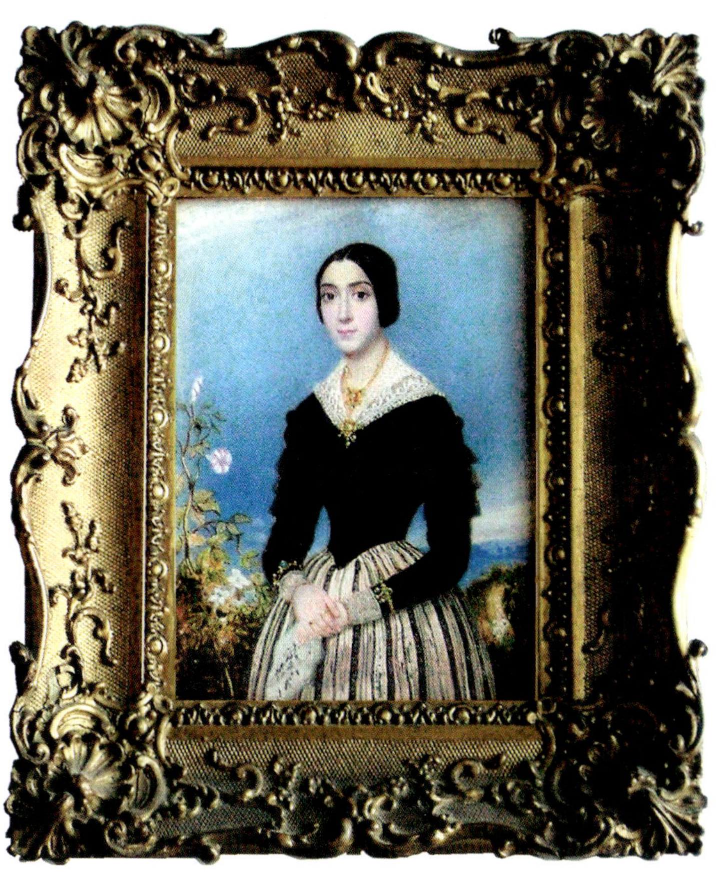

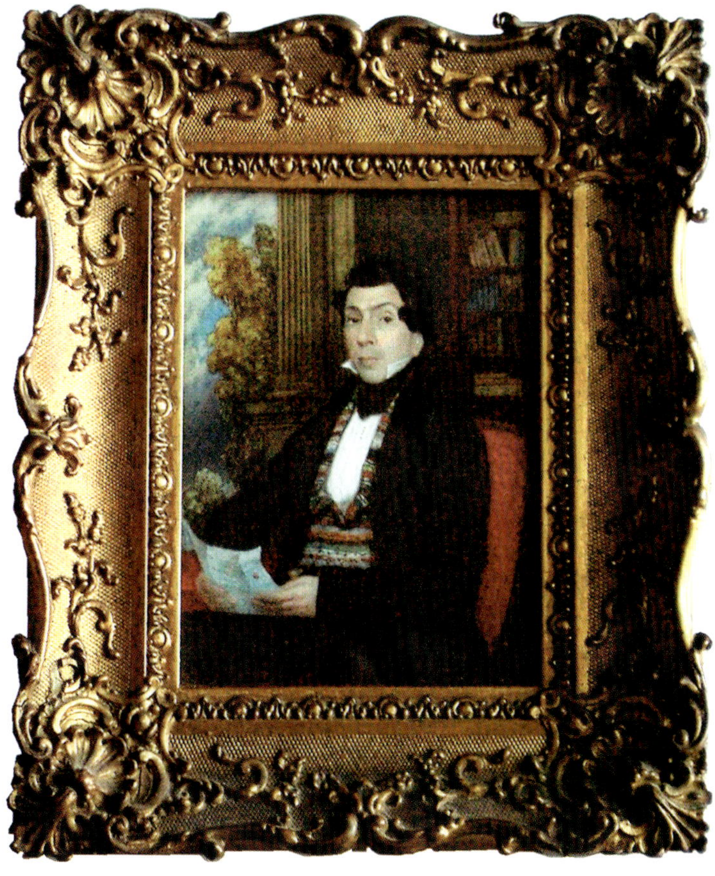

Plates 1 and 1A
c.1838
Portrait miniatures of Michael Spartali and Euphrosyne Valsami exchanged between them before their engagement to be married
Watercolour on paper mounted on panel. 18.5 x 11.25 cm (7¼ x 4½in)

Ionides were among the wealthiest of the Greek trading houses and they enjoyed a familiar relationship. Alecco – Alexander Alexander – Ionides (1840-1894) gained his early business experience with the firm of Spartali & Laskarides of 38 Finsbury Circus; Ionides & Co., Turkey Merchants were housed at 9 Finsbury Circus. The two families were not, however, blood-related, nor did they share inseparable social lives and interests. They lived on opposite sides of the Thames at the distant fringes of suburban London, north and south, until the mid-1880s.

As the first children of their respective families reached adulthood, Michael Spartali was noticeably a more traditionally parental figure than Alexander Constantine Ionides, a gregarious, cultured man who loved and commissioned the best of contemporary art. Ionides had first commissioned George Frederic Watts as a young unknown artist to copy a portrait of his father in 1837, and the younger artists who would become the towering figures of the mid-Victorian art world were welcomed in to his home and indeed in to the homes of the next generation of Ionides. Michael Spartali and his gentle, nervous wife, Euphrosyne Valsami, the daughter of a Genoese Greek family whom he had not met before their betrothal and marriage, enjoyed a more traditional, less outgoing style of life. (Euphrosyne chose Spartali among four pressing suitors from a portrait sent by his father; the arranged, dynastic marriage was happy.) The relaxed social manners that George Du Maurier noticed in the Ionides household – "The women will sometimes take one's hand in talking to one, or put their arm round the back of one's chair at dinner, and with all this ease and *tutoiement*, or perhaps because of it, they are I do believe the most thoroughly well-bred and perfect gentlefolks in all of England"[2] – would have been out of place in the Spartali home. The Spartalis brought up two extremely beautiful daughters in an age of strict social custom when young women stayed close to their parents' side or were allowed out only in approved circumstances accompanied by a vigilant chaperon.

Spartali's comfortable, conservative values were those of the wealthy man; he was never happier than when he was tending the perfect grapes that he grew in his heated glass-houses. He owned extensive properties, both in London and on the Isle of Wight, but he chose to decorate his houses in a lighter, late-Empire manner rather than the 'mediaeval' taste of Morris, Marshall, Faulkner & Company, then at the height of fashion, favoured by the Ionides. Under the influence of James Abbott McNeill Whistler, Spartali came to appreciate the lighter taste for *japonaiserie,* and the main house on the island was, according to the diaries of Jeanette Marshall,[3] "most tastefully furnished... with the most exquisite artistic papers (designed by Walter Crane) that I ever set eyes on. All the doors are blk. & gold, the mantel-pieces the most lovely marbles, and the fire-places inlaid with Minton's tiles. Windows over the fire-places, and the bed-room furniture in blk. & gold." The floors were covered with matting and the furniture stained light blue and dark green, "very artistic but pretty". He collected Henri Fantin-Latour still-lifes, though he later he ceased to buy them because he thought his work was becoming repetitive.[4] He maintained a credit balance with the 21-year-old Fairfax Murray to buy and sell on his behalf – they split any profit, a boon to the young artist – which yielded a painting by the 16th century Netherlandish artist Maerten van Heemskerck and a fine Teniers.[5] Marie good-humouredly described her father's way of thinking as: "...typical of the London Greeks (apart from the Ionides) who chose the most expensive portraitists as high prices would appear to validate their abilities."[6]

In 1855 Whistler had settled in the *quartier latin* of Left-Bank Paris where he studied under Charles Gleyre, Monet's teacher, and later worked alongside Henri Fantin-Latour and Alphonse Legros; they formed a partnership they called the Society of Three to help one another in finding patrons and outlets for their work, although Whistler's legendary capacity for making enemies saw to it that the uneasy friendship did not long survive. Alecco Ionides who was studying at the Sorbonne, and his brother Luke who visited him in Paris, also became friendly with Whistler; their sociably unpretentious natures and their generosity, ensured that they were universally welcomed. Whistler's brother William married Helen Ionides, the cousin of Luke and Alecco.

George Du Maurier, Edward Poynter and Thomas Armstrong were also studying painting in Paris at this time. With Alecco Ionides, the four became life-long friends, celebrated in George Du Maurier's novel *Trilby,* the story of an artist's model, Trilby O'Farrell. In the book, Ionides was renamed Poluphloisboiospaleapologos Petrilopetrolicoconose, on the grounds of his real name being too long for day-to-day use. Whistler, whose apparently easy-going manner concealed his industry, lively intellect and litigious temper, was portrayed as the fictional Joe Sibley, the idle apprentice. Prickly at the best of times, he took it ill, and threatened to sue Du Maurier.

Whistler and his mother moved back to London in 1860 and, through his friendship with Luke Ionides, was drawn in to the circle of Greek patronage, at first as a printmaker and soon as a painter. Ion, Alexander Constantine, commissioned a portrait of Luke and one of the early paintings of the Thames, *Old Battersea Bridge,* that year.[7] With George Du Maurier, Whistler was a lead player in a theatrical evening at the Ionides's on 14 January 1861 for which Du Maurier designed the programme, and Marie recalled that Whistler dined at the Spartalis's "as often as he was invited". Marie, then 17, and her younger sister Christina, were as frequently at the Ionides's as the younger generation of the Ionides family were at the Spartali's house. In the spring of 1863, Alphonse Legros was introduced to "une coterie de Grecs" who included, in addition to Alexander Constantine, his sister Madame Cassavetti, Madame Cavafy, Madame Laskarides and the Spartalis together with their daughters. Euphrosyne Cassavetti, the imperious mother of Maria Zambaco who was widely known as 'the Duchess', was fondly remembered for her patronage at a time when commissions were in short supply following the collapse of Overend & Gurney, the London secondary bank, which brought down many prominent patrons. Legros was particularly grateful for her discerning commissions.[8] It was Whistler – by turns witty and amusing, dedicated to his work, sardonic and adversarial – who first gave Marie a glimpse of a world of ideas and creativity, though she was to wait four more years before her father consented to her having professional art lessons. Fantin-Latour's sought-after flower pieces were another source of inspiration giving rise to many distinguished examples of the *genre* from her brush in later years.

Another regular social visitor was the rising surgeon and anatomist, John Marshall,[9] who numbered the Spartalis among his wealthy and distinguished patients. Marshall was the medical adviser, physician and friend of a wide circle of artists since the days that he had been a neighbour of Madox Brown in Mornington Crescent when they were both at the bottom of the ladder. Through this connection Marshall was consulted by Dante Gabriel Rossetti, Walter Deverall, William Michael Rossetti, the Burne-Joneses, William Cave Thomas, F G Stephens and Maria Zambaco among many. His dinner table conversation can only have served to stir Marie's longing to see the painters at work and measure her own developing artistic talent. He was the trusted conduit for news and gossip about the second wave of Pre-Raphaelites in the formative years during which Marie Spartali turned from adolescence to maturity.

In keeping with Michael Spartali's patriarchal outlook both Marie and her sister Christina were educated at home; so that almost nothing is known of their childhood. In addition to her perfect English, Marie was fluent in French and German (and later in Italian, which she loved though she deplored her accent); with her parents she spoke Greek. Their friends were largely confined to the children of the Greek community, and they lived in some seclusion in Hornsey, then a leafy suburb north of London; Marie was already twenty years old when the family moved to Clapham Common in 1864. Christina at eighteen was a pianist of near-professional standard. Marie was a gifted singer who studied under Manuel Garcia, the son of the greatest tenor of the time.

Conservative though he was in family affairs and in his taste in portraiture and painting, Michael Spartali was no rich philistine. A man of wide-ranging intellectual interests and radical political sympathies, his Sunday gatherings attracted an unorthodox group quite unlike the self-conscious cream of aesthetic London patronised by the Ionides that revolved around the Prinseps at Little Holland House, or the social and political élite who frequented Mrs Adelaide Sartoris's Thursday *salons.*[10] Charles Hallé, painter and later the manager of the Grosvenor Gallery, knew this different world: "I confess that I often played truant from Little Holland House on a Sunday afternoon to spend a few hours at the Shrubbery, Clapham Common.

This was the house of Mr Spartali, whose wife and two daughters surpassed in beauty any three women I have ever seen. I have often wondered why it is that a man may say that he has travelled a thousand miles to see a famous painting, a landscape, or a waterfall, yet he raises a smile if he confesses he has turned a few yards out of his way to see a beautiful face... The Shrubbery, apart from other considerations, was very interesting through the men Mr Spartali liked to gather around him. Here it was that I met Mazzini, Herzen the Russian conspirator and Muller-Strübing... he also had been a great conspirator; the scene of his operations was Prussia. What he did was so little to the liking of the authorities that he was tried and condemned to death. The sentence read out to him was to be broken on the wheel. He made up his mind to submit with the best grace possible... however, he was reprieved and put in charge of the prison library, and eventually made his escape to England..."[11] Professor Muller-Strübing taught Marie Greek philosophy; it was his enthusiasm for Greek mythology and the feminist heroines of Athenian democracy that fired her imagination and influenced her early choice of subjects for her painting.

Michael Spartali's pride in his origins and his dedicated interest in Greek democracy and freedom were not restricted to Sunday afternoons in Clapham. Though he never visited his mother country he was actively involved in revolutionary politics, and his support for the Greek communities labouring under the Ottoman yoke in the Levant, Crete and Egypt was not confined to commiseration. Through his trading partnerships throughout the Middle East he gave the Greek minorities practical assistance, which included the dangerous business of procuring arms for the Cretan insurrection of 1867. This public-spirited commitment led ultimately to two deep personal crises, the cause of incalculable sorrow to him and his wife, even though both were overcome and eventually put behind them. The first of these was the introduction of William Stillman in to his household through their mutual association with Stavros Dilberoglue, a native of Smyrna and a relative, possibly a cousin, of Michael Spartali, and the friend of William Michael Rossetti. Dilberoglue was persuaded by Stillman to attempt to raise funds among the Greek community in London for the relief of the appalling hardships of the Cretan Greeks after the failed insurrection. The second was Spartali's business failure in 1886.

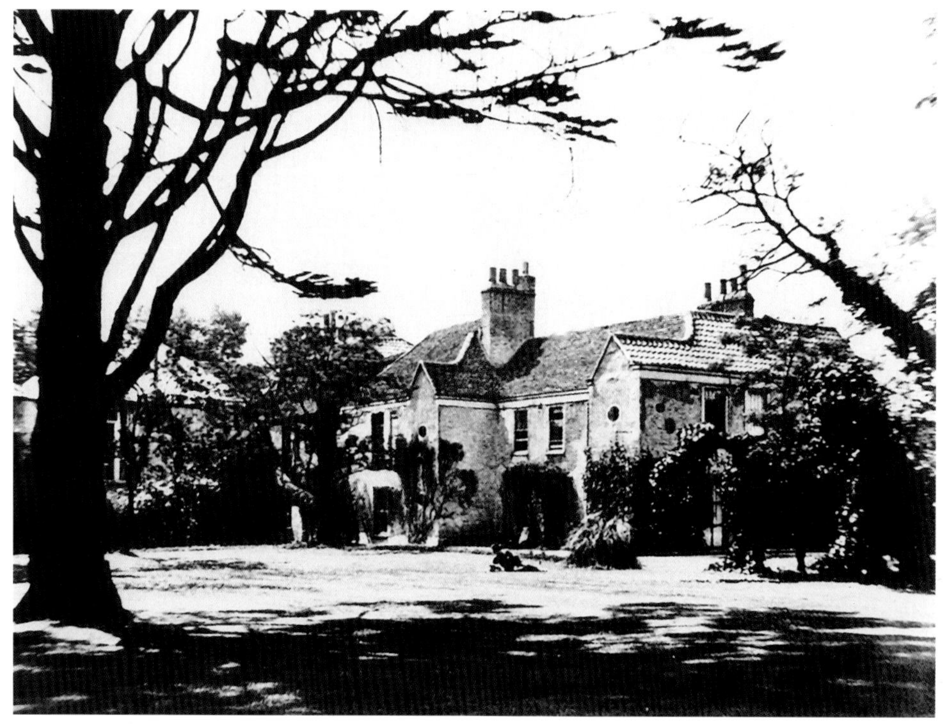

Plate 2
Little Holland House, demolished in 1875, in the 1860s

CHAPTER TWO

LITTLE HOLLAND HOUSE

Alexander Constantine Ionides and his son Alecco were habitués of the Little Holland House, the home of Sara and Thoby Prinsep, the retired Chief Secretary to the Government of India and a Director of the East India Company, long before they moved nearby. Great collectors and generous supporters of contemporary art, the Prinseps were patrons of George Frederic Watts, who lived with them ("He came to stay for three weeks, he stayed for thirty years"), and later of Rossetti, Burne-Jones and Morris as they too were gathered in to Aunt Sara's fold.

In the late summer of 1864, Alexander Ionides and his family – Alecco, Luke, Aglaia, and Chariclea (together with his widowed sister, Euphrosyne Cassavetti, her daughter Maria Zambaco and her son Alexander) – moved north of the Thames from the grand house on Tulse Hill to 1 Holland Park, drawn by the cultured and engaging circle of writers, painters and their patrons and the need to realise a costly asset, having lost heavily in the banking crisis.[1] In October, Michael Spartali too moved his family, from Muswell Hill in the north to The Shrubbery, 2 Lavender Gardens, Clapham

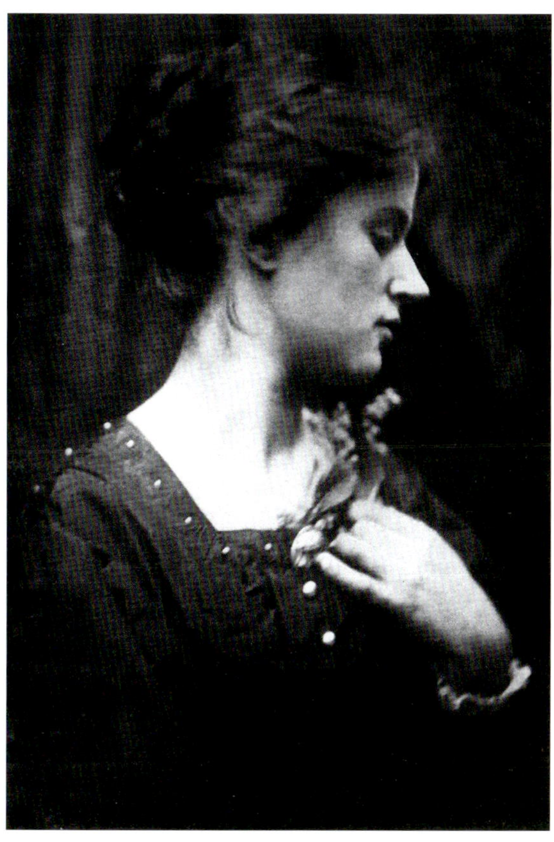

Plate 3
Julia Margaret Cameron
1868
Cabinet card photograph of Marie Spartali
Private Collection

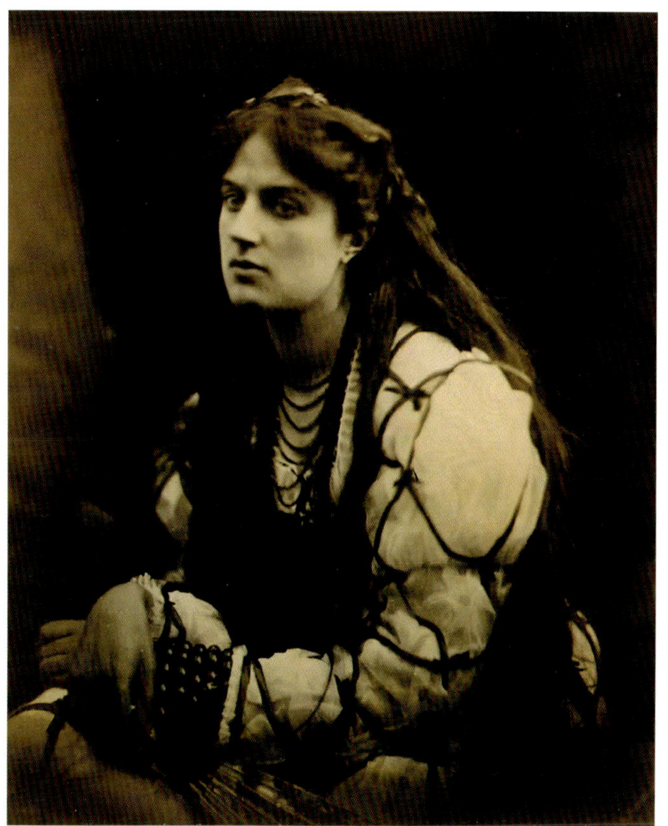

Plate 4
Julia Margaret Cameron
1865
Marie Spartali as Hypatia from Charles Kingsley's 1853 novel about Hypatia of Alexandria, 5th century mathematician, astronomer and feminist
Private Collection

Common, south of the river, bringing the two households closer together, although the Thames still intervened. Marie Spartali, the Ionides's married daughter Aglaia Coronio and her cousin Maria Zambaco – formed an artistic link between the two families, collectively admired in the Holland Park circle as 'The Three Graces'.

The photographer Julia Margaret Cameron, Sara Prinsep's sister, also had a part in drawing the Spartali sisters closer in to the *milieu* of Aunt Sara's artistic and literary *salon* at Little Holland House. Michael Spartali had frequented the Isle of Wight since 1837, first with his parents, and then with his wife, taking extended summer holidays there with their children as they came along. When in later years he acquired three substantial properties on the island, the first being Rylstone House near Shanklin in 1866, the Isle of Wight was already a kind of Little Holland House-on-Sea.

Julia Margaret Pattle had married Charles Hay Cameron in 1838 in Calcutta, and they had returned to England on his retirement from the Supreme Council of India in 1848, living first in Tunbridge Wells and then in London; when, in 1859, Cameron

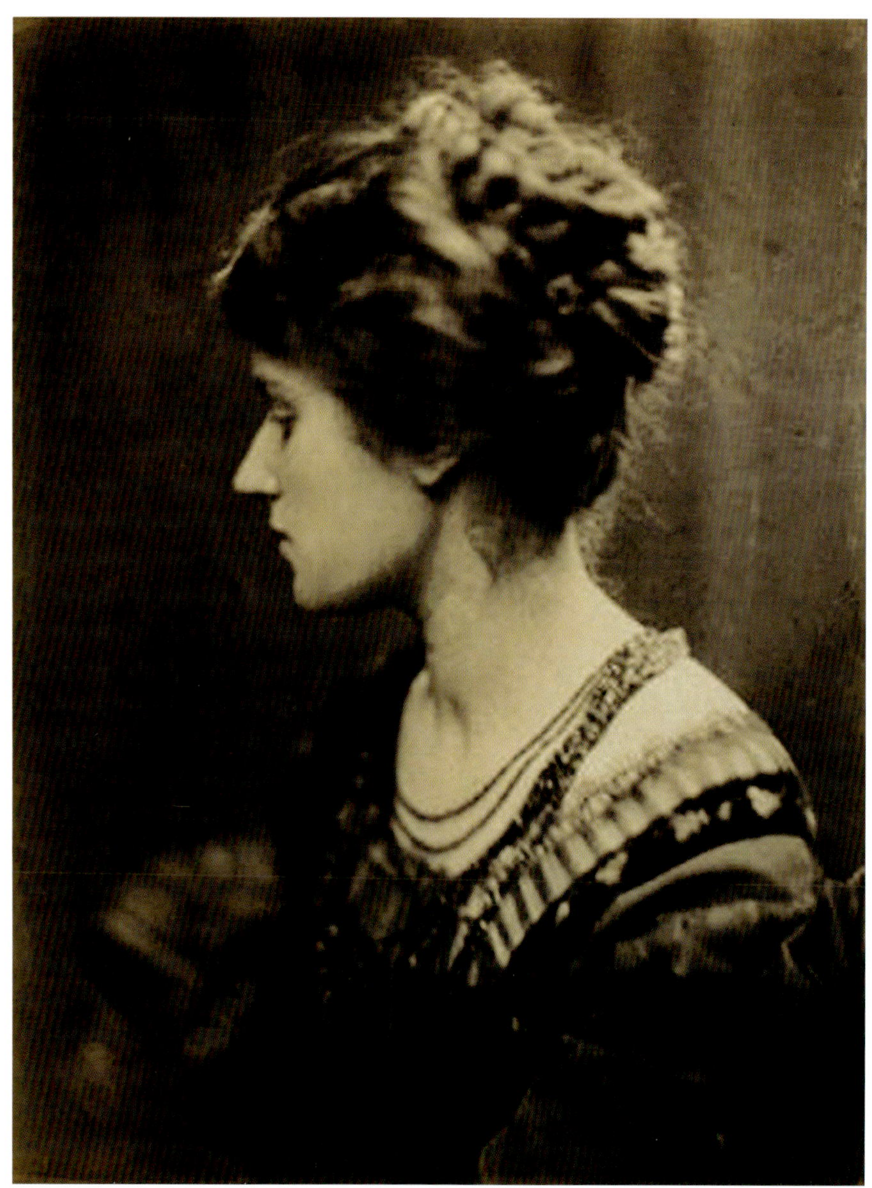

Plate 5
Julia Margaret Cameron
1865
Marie Spartali
Cabinet portrait

returned to Ceylon to inspect his coffee estates as he did every few years, Julia went to stay with Alfred and Emily Tennyson at Farringford, close to Freshwater Bay. Early in 1860, on the cliff edge at Freshwater, she spied two cottages, which she bought and joined together by erecting a castellated tower between them to create an eccentric Victorian seaside villa. This she named 'Dimbola' after one of her husband's plantations in Ceylon. The attraction of Freshwater was closely related to the lure of her sister Sara Prinsep's circle of literary lions; apart from the Tennyson's estate, the Isle of Wight was the preferred summer residence of G F Watts (who spent the honeymoon of his disastrous, short-lived marriage to Ellen Terry there),

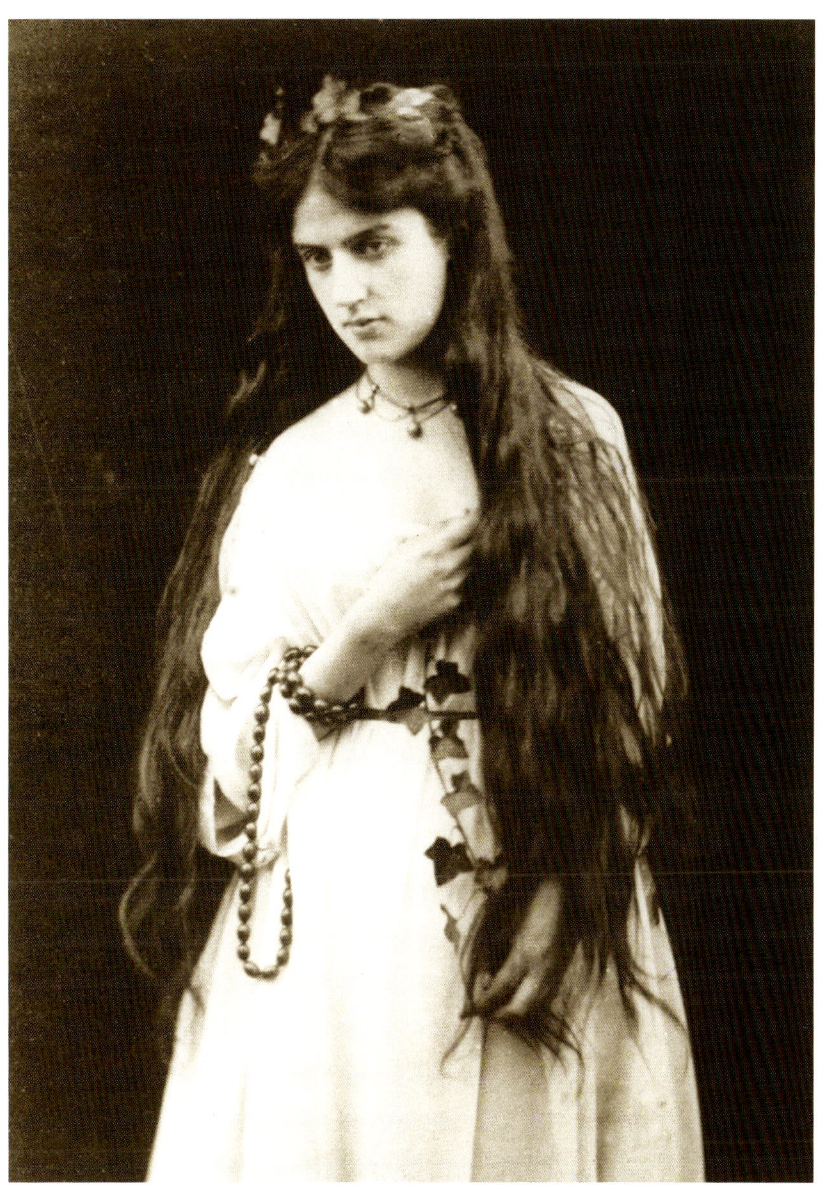

Plate 6
Julia Margaret Cameron
c.1866
Marie Spartali as Mnemosyne, the goddess of memory and mother of the nine Muses

of the younger Prinseps, and of a host of visitors, including the Thackeray daughters, Anne and Minnie (close friends of Marie), Benjamin Jowett (the Master of Balliol), Anthony Trollope, Charles Darwin and Edward Lear.

Julia Margaret Cameron took up photography only in December 1864, the same year that Marie Spartali started to take lessons with Ford Madox Brown. Like everything else Julia did, she went to it with ferocious energy; sitters were commanded and an endless stream of negatives was produced and printed on albumen paper, despite the grave technical difficulty of the wet collodion process that she employed.[2] Photography was the routine occupation every morning. Marie

Spartali was an early subject. In 1866, at 23, Marie was photographed as Mnemosyne, the mother of the Muses and goddess of memory: she is dressed in a flowing white gown, her hair loosened and her head crowned with ivy, a pensive image quite unlike Rossetti's last, confident representation of Janey Morris in the same rôle. In the following year, Marie Spartali was portrayed as Hypatia (of Charles Kingsley's novel) in a muslin dress banded with ribbons reminiscent of *Sidonia von Bork* in the young Burne-Jones's painting, three years later, of the Sorceress of Meinhold's gothick tale. An untitled portrait of Marie dates from the previous year; the last known was made in 1870. Marie also sat to Valentine Prinsep, in 1869; her qualities as model were not only readiness and beauty, but also a deep involvement in the work and the artist, whether it was Madox Brown, Julia Margaret Cameron, Val Prinsep, John Roddam Spencer Stanhope or Rossetti.

Despite the elegance of his *bon môt* that Marie Spartali was "so to speak, Mrs Morris for Beginners,"[3] W Graham Robertson, as he later conceded,[4] missed the acumen that underlay the lovely exterior; hers was indeed "a lofty beauty, gracious and noble; the beauty worshipped in Greece of old, yet with a wistful tenderness of poise, a mystery of shadowed eyes that gave life to what might have been a marble goddess; a beauty which would seem to possess much of that marble's eternity." "When I myself in due time came to know... Mrs Stillman," he wrote, "I could not conceive that she had ever been more beautiful. Nature was loath to spoil her wonderful work, and the years crowned it with added perfection." Yet her distinctive beauty lay as much in the "lively glance, penetrating, interested in the world about her, and not a little quizzical: her features classically defined."[5] It is only in the ravishing, idealised beauty in Rossetti's paintings – the 'beautiful women with floral adjuncts' as William Michael Rossetti bluntly described the later works – that the distinctive looks of the two women are merged in a Pre-Raphaelite version of the truth. Marie Spartali's ancient beauty, the knee-length auburn hair plaited and piled up on her head, the sweet but impish mouth and long straight nose, above all the calm but resolute character, are evident in Julia Margaret Cameron's photographic portraits rather than in Rossetti's paradigms; here Cameron achieves her ideal of "sacrificing nothing of truth by all possible devotion to poetry." Marie Spartali is revealed as a young woman of strength and grace. Her intelligence and gently acerbic wit are conspicuous, in no way hidden by her beauty and standing in no need of comparison.

Marie Spartali was just twenty-one when – the story goes – the sisters first caught a glimpse of the uninhibited and irreverent world of Whistler and Rossetti, as guests of the Ionides at a garden party at Tulse Hill, the last before their move to Holland Park. In the familiar description of the scene, Whistler, Dante Gabriel Rossetti, Edward Poynter, Thomas Armstrong, Alphonse Legros and George Du Maurier were enthralled by their beauty and charm.[6] Lamont in his *Memoir* of Thomas Armstrong gives a more accurate account, also at secondhand. Alecco Ionides – who was actually there – described Marie as very nervous, "dressed in muslin and a satin sash".[7] The *dramatis personae* of this legendary occasion are the subject of some confusion. Dante Gabriel Rossetti, who (so the ever-reliable William Michael remembered) had only recently become acquainted with Whistler as their near neighbour in Chelsea through their mutual friend the poet Algernon Charles Swinburne, was not in fact present; nor is it certain that Whistler, who was in reality already well known to the Spartalis, was himself there on that occasion, although the rest of the artists who tumbled out of their four-wheeler comprised the cast of *Trilby* reunited once again.

Impressionable, warm, creative and intellectually educated well beyond the general level of attainment of girls of her position, Marie Spartali's experience of the world outside was gleaned largely through her father's friends, from the strictly-regulated balls with their ever-vigilant chaperons, and the social round of selected families on which they called and in turn entertained. She looked out beyond the confines of the house in Hornsey to the freedom of ideas and expression that characterised the artists and their *metier,* and what she saw excited her imagination. She had reached – and passed – the age at which young girls of her class were expected to take a husband after their first season and, following the accepted rule, to establish their own and their husband's social environment before settling down to bearing as many children as their husbands chose to father. In the 1860s some one in three women of marriageable age was 'left on the shelf', a failure that carried the drastic social consequences of spinsterhood: the inescapable obligations of keeping house for aging parents, and the genteel pursuits of needlepoint, reading improving literature and touring the department stores.[8] At 21 Marie was as willing as Evelyn Pickering to exchange the enforced idleness, the tedium of drawing room conversation and constant changes of dress that Pickering noted in her diaries, for something of lasting value.

Among the wealthy middle-classes, marriage for love occurred less often than an arranged partnership of perceived 'suitability', which inevitably included financial considerations. In Marie Spartali's instance there was the added pressure that her parents expected her to look for a partner of accomplishment, prospects and standing from among the prosperous but circumscribed Greek community, the Ionides and Cassavetti families, the Cavafys, the Dilberoglues, the Laskarides (Margeta Laskarides was Marie's godmother), the Rallis and Mavrogordatos. Demetrius, her brother, would marry a Ralli, Eustratius married the daughter of a close business partner, Sir John Antoniadi of Alexandria.

Nevertheless, half way through the century the accepted conventions of the marriage market were under increasing strain; evidence in the Norton affair, in which a brutal husband had sued Victoria's Prime Minister, Lord Palmerston, for damages arising from 'criminal conversation' with his wife Caroline Norton – only to have his case thrown out by a jury that took just one minute to reach its verdict against him – had highlighted the legal plight of women trapped in loveless marriages. After years of gerrymandering, Parliament had passed the Matrimonial Causes Act of 1857, which offered wronged wives a glimmer of hope, but it would not be until 1888 that the Married Women's Property Act would give a divorced or separated wife any claim on the marital estate or to her children. As the position of women as chattels slowly eased, the movement towards their taking up careers, inside or outside of marriage, swelled. George Eliot – Marian Evans – who scandalised society by living openly with G H Lewis (who was already married to someone else), was both famous and fêted as the author of *Middlemarsh,* and could not be ignored. Elizabeth Garrett Anderson combined her assertion of women's right to a career with a pioneering approach to women's medicine.

Marie Spartali was as strong-willed as she was beautiful. Encouraged by Luke Ionides, she was at length able to persuade her reluctant father that she was determined to become an artist of stature and not a Sunday-afternoon watercolourist. Michael Spartali was perhaps not so much opposed to her wish to paint as to any interruption of the customary transition from girlhood to married woman, and to the lifestyles in artistic circles, which he deplored, knowing something of their ways from Whistler and quite well able to imagine more. However, he acceded to her decision to study under a professional painter.

Marie had first wanted Dante Gabriel Rossetti to be her mentor, though she had not yet met him. Rossetti – the close companion of Luke Ionides – was then at the height of his reputation, an eligible widower following the death of his wife Lizzie Siddal (though he would never marry again, as he told his friend the Irish customs officer-turned-poet, William Allingham.) Tales of his splendid new establishment in Cheyne Walk with its menagerie of exotic animals, of the patrons who gave him large advances on the pictures they would wait years to receive, with Fanny Cornforth in residence and Alexa Wilding sitting to him must have sounded like a wonderland to the cloistered 21-year-old. These were the years of *Bocca Baciata,* the *Blue Bower* and of *Venus Verticordia* – the nude head and shoulders that so dismayed Ruskin, painted from a cook that Rossetti met in the street – and that marked the beginning of the series of the half-length studies of idealised 'stunners' for which he is chiefly remembered. Next year, Jane Burden Morris would return to London after the Red House was abandoned, bringing with her an altogether deeper relationship with Dante Gabriel Rossetti. He had always refused to take pupils, being better aware than most of his technical limitations. Gently declining to take Marie as his pupil, he suggested to Luke Ionides – who had once nurtured hopes of becoming a painter himself – that he should talk to Ford Madox Brown.

The ever-generous Dante Gabriel Rossetti thus once more procured a valuable introduction for a member of the circle of artists that he dominated. "I send you this from Ionides..." he wrote to Madox Brown,[9] enclosing a note from Luke Ionides that read: "My dear Rossetti – thank you for your kind letter. I have already communicated its contents to my friend Mr Spartali and hope to be able to call on Mr F M Brown. Ever yours, Sincerely, Luke A Ionides." As Madox Brown, who was notorious for mangling names or forgetting to whom they belonged, had not met Ionides, Rossetti took the opportunity to coach him: "Ionides, which name (not Jonydese) please fix in your mind...", he began; while a paragraph from *The Times*, which read: "Erratum; In a case at Lambeth Police Court yesterday the name of the prosecutor was erroneously given as Colnaghi. It should have been Mather," prompted the thought that Madox Brown might perhaps have reported the case.

Marie started her formal training under Ford Madox Brown almost immediately, first at 14 Grove Terrace, Kentish Town and later at 37 Fitzroy Square, the grander establishment where the Madox Browns gave "unreasonably open-handed" parties and Emma kept doves in an imposing cage on the window ledge: "It had, as it were, a private compartment for the children."[10] They both understood that painting under his direction was the first step towards a professional career.

How little Michael Spartali appreciated his daughter's determination to make her way as a professional painter can be gauged from his seemingly innocent instruction to her, six years later, to make Frederick Leyland the gift of a picture he wanted to buy from the Dudley in 1870. Rossetti was horrified and wrote to his patron, Leyland: "I had already heard with some consternation from Miss S of her extraordinary decision. However, it is not hers but her father's. She was delighted beyond measure with your wish to buy, as old Brown (who first reported it to her from my report) told me before she got your letter. However when she showed this to her father, he said that the compliment on your & my part (considering the fine works you possess & my flattering opinion) was so great that he could not think of any other course but her offering the picture as a present & and it was he who caused her to do this very much against her own conviction. Indeed she was very uncomfortable afterwards & said she really feared that you might consider it almost in the light of an impertinence.

"I must explain to you that she really does sell her works and is quite bent on adopting art as a serious profession, and that her father takes this view most entirely. Only in the present instance (being an impulsive man) he seems to have felt so flattered by the incident as to have been driven to this extraordinary course. My own impression is that your best course is to write a very serious letter to the lady, thanking her duly, but saying you really feel awkward and uncomfortable at so unexpected a result, and must venture to press her extremely to view the matter as you intended & accept the price of the picture, for which Brown has I believe advised her to ask 40gns."[11]

Not only had Michael Spartali failed to appreciate either the talents or the ambitions of his daughter, after five years of Madox Brown's training, but Marie thought it unfitting to question his decision. Her subsequent intransigence was equally painful to both.

CHAPTER THREE

MARIE SPARTALI AND THE ROSSETTI CIRCLE

Two months after he had made Marie Spartali's introduction to Ford Madox Brown, Dante Gabriel Rossetti had yet to meet this new stunner who had suddenly burst upon them. Arrangements were, however, in hand with Luke Ionides. Rossetti had recently discovered that Ford Madox Brown's new pupil was none other than the beautiful maiden of Tulse Hill: "I hear now that she is one and the same with a marvellous beauty of whom I have heard so much talk. Just box her up, and don't let fellows see her, I mean to have first shy at her in the way of sitting. She will be coming here soon to see the crib and appurtenances."[1] Marie's cousin Chauncey recorded that at the age of 81 she would still recall the sleepless night before she was due to meet Rossetti.

Rossetti was gifted with immense charm and a wholly genuine interest in those around him, which evoked a warm response from all who fell under his spell. He went out of his way to help people he knew. Though he could be outrageously selfish and even cruel to his friends, almost to a man they returned: "It is no good asking me to criticise him. He was such a great man – a man who gave the impression of greatness, of genius... and of such irresistible generosity and kindness,"[2] Fairfax Murray wrote later. William Stillman characteristically emphasised the opposite view: "He had been so spoiled by all his friends... that none rebelled at being treated in his princely way... for it was only with his friends that he used it. He dominated all who had the least sympathy with his genius."[3] Both views are essentially just and it is not difficult to imagine that a starry-eyed young woman who was ready to devote her life to her painting might imagine herself a little in love with the image of an artist she had not previously met; she certainly held him in an almost reverent awe, which matured in to a fond friendship between them.

Although she sat to Rossetti on many occasions in the years that followed, it was Ford Madox Brown who captured both Marie's beauty and her air of reserve, even of shyness, that is intensely appealing in a particularly fine likeness, *Marie Spartali at her Easel*. Her younger sister Christina was, however, first to sit as a model: to

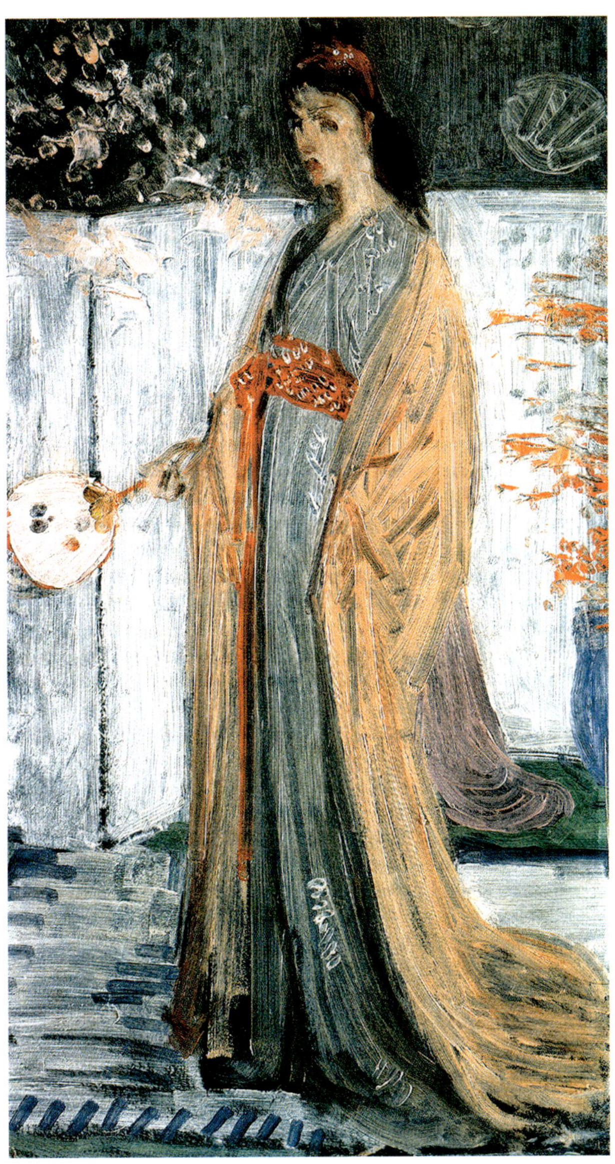

Plate 7
James McNeill Whistler
1863-4
Sketch for the portrait of *La Princesse du Pays de la Porcelaine*
Oil on paper mounted on panel. 62.8 x 34 cm (24¾ x 13½in)
Worcester Art Museum, Massachusetts

Whistler, interminably, for *La Princesse du Pays de la Porcelaine.* By October 1864, Du Maurier was writing to Thomas Armstrong in Manchester describing "a large picture with the smallest Miss Spartali in it as a Chinese."[4] There is a small oil sketch painted the previous year in Paris from his model, muse and mistress Jo Hiffernan that shows he had perfected the idea before he found his model.[5] Indeed, Marie later recalled that Whistler had arrived with the picture meticulously worked out together with the properties and the gown.

Marie Spartali who chaperoned her sister recounted that "at first the work went quickly, then it began to drag. Whistler rubbed it out just as she thought it finished, and day after day she returned to find that everything was to be done over." The two sisters went to the studio twice a week, and this continued through the winter. She described Whistler's method of placing his easel beside the model, walking back the length of the room to contemplate sitter and painting together, before rushing forward to dab at his canvas and returning to look again. Their parents tired of it and eventually sought to dissuade them from going to the studio; but the girls shared Whistler's enthusiasm (which was all to the good; Whistler was pitiless with his models.) The head of the *Princesse* gave him most trouble, and he kept Christina Spartali standing while he worked on it, never letting her rest; she must keep the entire pose, and she would not admit her fatigue, until she was at last taken ill with peritonitis. Chariclea Ionides took her place for a time. When Christina was getting better, Whistler made a pencil-drawing of her head, but she did not sit again.[6]

The sisters wanted their father to buy the wonderfully original and atmospheric work, but Michael Spartali objected to it as a portrait of his daughter. He was unable to make the leap of imagination from the familiar dark-brown portraiture of a thousand Victorian drawing-rooms. The full-length figure portrays Christina in a flowered kimono, the elongated figure curved backwards in imitation of the *lange lijzen,* the 'long ladies' of blue-and-white Chinese porcelain, her manner tentative with eyes downcast. This is an intensely personal characterisation of a beautiful young woman that captures an essential melancholy in her nature, the same air of resignation that Julia Margaret Cameron revealed in a characteristic photograph taken the same year; outwardly so like her sister Marie in her looks, yet so unlike her in an inexpressible and private pain. The same sweet sadness is visible in Marie Spartali's early 'self-portrait' painted around this time, which is almost certainly actually that of her sister.[7]

Michael Spartali having declined to acquire *La Princesse du Pays de la Porcelaine,* it was eventually sold to Frederick Leyland, in whose house in Princes Gate it later became the centrepiece of the Peacock Room, decorated with Whistler's fantastic *chinoiserie*. (The story of this wonderful room, and of the falling-out between Whistler and Leyland, is a tale in itself.[8] When in 1875 Whistler was bankrupted by the cost of winning – he was awarded the derisory sum of one farthing – his libel suit against Ruskin over criticism of his *Nocturne in Black and Gold*, the Japanese screen that was the *mise en scène* to Christina's portrait went to Charles Augustus Howell in a sale of Whistler's assets.)

Through the hours spent with Whistler, Ford Madox Brown and Dante Gabriel Rossetti, Marie had entered an exciting new world beyond the formal drawing room on Clapham Common and the hushed aestheticism of Little Holland House; what she saw made her hungry for more, anxious to be free; the stifling patriarchal

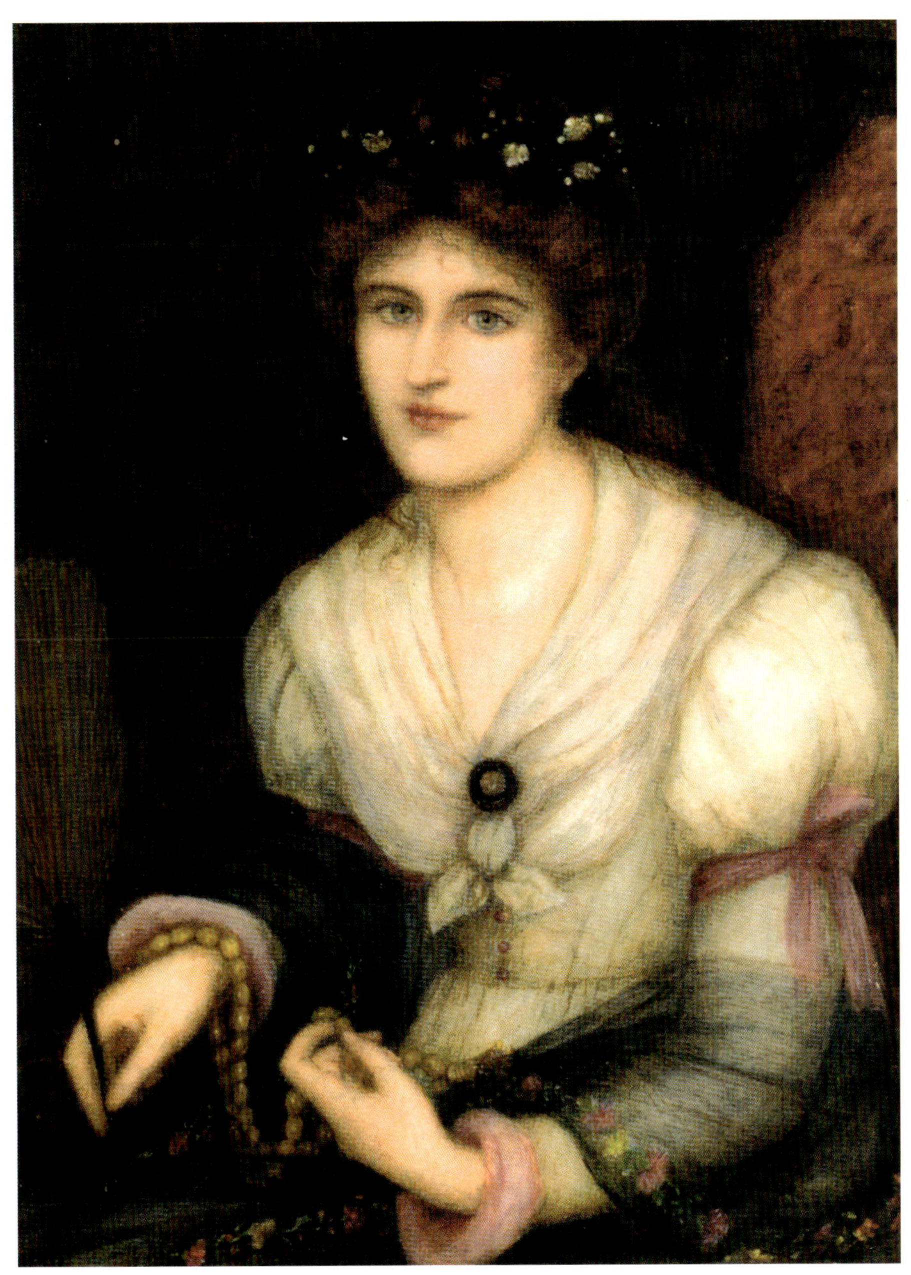

Plate 8
Marie Spartali Stillman
c.1867
Portrait of Christina Spartali
Pencil and watercolour with gum arabic heightened with white.
69.8 x 52.1 cm (27½ x 20½in)
Private Collection

dictates of their father contrasted starkly with the liberal education the sisters had received, and he would reap the reward. Her watchful father was keen to know Rossetti and form his own opinion: "Mr Spartali called on me on Sunday last and pressed me very kindly to go and see them. They have asked me on many special occasions and I have never been, so I think one must make the effort. Would you come?... is Sunday a good evening? Perhaps you could get a hint from the young ladies if you see them," Rossetti wrote to Madox Brown.[9]

Towards the end of the 1860s Marie Spartali's name was being linked with that of Lord Ranelagh, with whom she was said by William Holman Hunt to have had an unhappy love affair. This was to the great disapproval of her father, who put an end to her seeing him: "... He must be of a discontented disposition for they say that he actually broke off an intended marriage with Lord R which the beauty had set her heart on and which his Lordship too had condecended [sic] to agree to..."[10] While Holman Hunt is the only authority for this affair, it is unlikely that he fabricated the story. Michael Spartali would certainly have had wind of Ranelagh's reputation as a womaniser. Thomas Heron Jones, Lord Ranelagh, the 7th Viscount (1812-1885) was well-known in Pre-Raphaelite circles. A former officer of the Life Guards, he commanded the 2nd South Middlesex Rifle Volunteers, formed to repel Napoleon III's threatened invasion in 1859; the 38th Middlesex (Artists') Rifles Volunteer Corps (which mustered Frederic Leighton, William Morris, Dante Gabriel Rossetti, Ford Madox Brown, George Price Boyce, G F Watts and William Holman Hunt among many others) met regularly to drill in Hyde Park, and trained together with the 2nd Middlesex and other units on Wimbledon Common. Ranelagh was a member of the Hogarth Club, a favourite Pre-Raphaelite dining circle.

In 1854 William Holman Hunt had set out to paint in the Holy Land, leaving the luscious, illiterate Annie Miller, his model, mistress and intended wife, in the care of F G Stephens, with £200 for her education and support; Annie however felt that there was more to life than learning and she was soon to be seen dancing at the Cremorne Gardens with Stephens and William Michael Rossetti. She might also on occasion be found sitting to George Price Boyce, when not more energetically engaged with him; or modelling for Dante Rossetti, who also enjoyed her abundant and available charms, despite his engagement to Lizzie Siddal. She became the

---

Plate 9
James McNeill Whistler
1864-5
La Princesse du Pays de la Porcelaine
Oil on canvas. 199.9 x 116.1 cm (78¾ x 45¾in)
Freer Gallery of Art, Smithsonian Institution, Washington DC: Gift of Charles Lang Freer

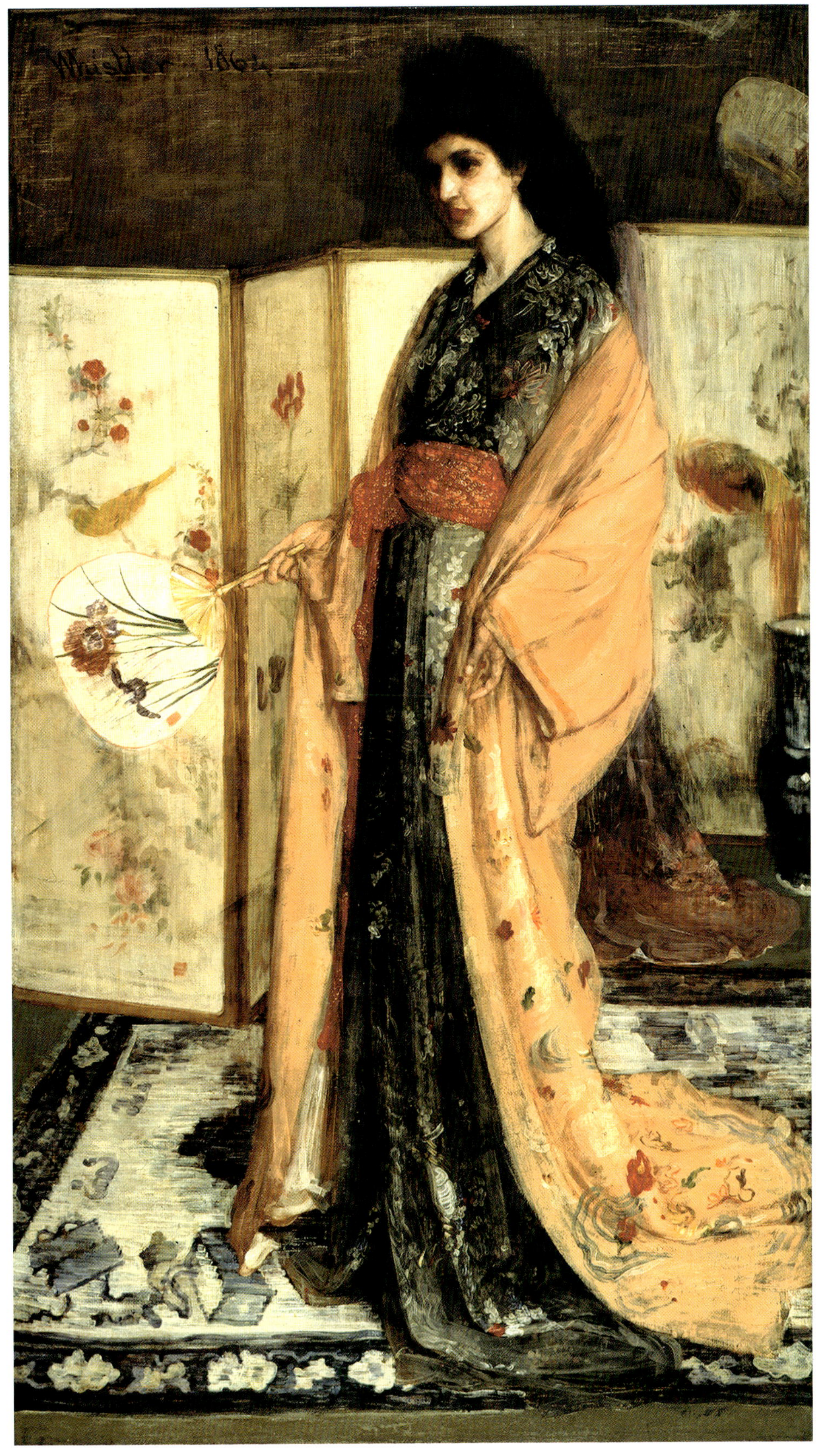

mistress of Lord Ranelagh, who abruptly dropped her on Hunt's return in 1856, and eventually she married Ranelagh's cousin. When confronted by Holman Hunt, Ranelagh readily conceded that Annie had been one of many mistresses, remarking in aristocratic astonishment that he "could not at all understand a man writing passionate letters to a whore."[11] More recently, in August 1868, Ranelagh had been involved as a witness in a lawsuit in which one Mrs Borrodaile sued 'Madame Rachael' who sold cosmetics in Bond Street and 'provided other services to gentlemen,' for the return of £1000. She alleged that Madame Rachael had told her that Lord Ranelagh, who frequented her establishment, was in love with her, but that in order to become the wife of a nobleman she must be 'enamelled' and made beautiful for ever, for which she paid £1000.[12] Although the court found that Ranelagh was not party to the fraud, Michael Spartali could in no circumstances have accepted him as a son-in-law.

Marie may simply have been naive; probably this was her first serious affair of the heart. The rakish, charming Ranelagh, a man of means who was 56 in 1868 and a confirmed bachelor, would have been unlikely to have had any real intention of plunging in to marriage with a 24-year-old girl – wealthy, beautiful or otherwise – however attractive she might have been on his arm or in his bed. When Marie married William Stillman, Holman Hunt recalled her earlier hopes of marrying Ranelagh: "Stillman's a lucky fellow to get such a wife... Spartali père deserves no commiseration, for I heard that when the young lady once wanted to marry the beautiful Lord – he was not even then satisfied with the proposed son-in-law."[13] The comment seems curious in the light of his own experience of the 7th Viscount.

It was only in mid-Summer of 1869 that Marie Spartali first sat to Rossetti. Keeping Janey Morris informed of news from London as she underwent a spa cure in Bad Ems, Rossetti wrote of *Dante's Dream*: "I wanted much to get the little Beatrice I was doing from you finished, but the hands are in the way as I think I *must* alter them and all the models have such vile hands. I have an idea I may ask Mary Spartali to sit for them..."[14] and a few days later added: "Val has also done a sketch of Mary Spartali which seems like a faint reminiscence of Watt's feeblest portraits of his mother. I said so to the lady, and found her an entire sympathiser as to the nature of Val's art. She said that he was about 4 hours doing it (it looks like 20 minutes' work) and that her maid said afterwards that she supposed that when that gentleman drew heads he liked to have one sitting 'for company's sake like'."[15]

The tone of these letters, of which only Rossetti's now remain, suggests that Marie and Janey, who would later be the closest of friends, knew one another by this time, but not well. It is impossible to be certain when or where they first met; but it seems most likely to have been in 1865. There was a memorable gathering at Rossetti's in Cheyne Walk in April 1865 at which William and Janey Morris, Bessie Burden, Algernon Swinburne and forty or more others including the Burne-Joneses were present, and another glittering party that Georgiana 'Georgie' Burne-Jones later recalled, the last party before the Madox Browns moved from Kentish Town to Fitzroy Square in December 1865, with William and Janey Morris, James Whistler, Alphonse Legros and Dante Rossetti among the guests; Marie would most likely have been of the company, and she would in any event have been found with the Madox Browns once or twice a week at that time.[16] Georgie also recalled "a very noticeable introduction to a part of the Greek colony" that occurred at Little Holland House in 1866, her one, delphic mention of Maria Zambaco: "...before this we had had the pleasure of meeting the beautiful Miss Spartali and her sister,"[17] she noted. Marie and Janey might have met, or met again, at another lavish party in Fitzroy Square in November 1867 and at the "huge party of Greeks" that William Bell Scott described to Alice Boyd in November 1868.[18] However, when Marie stayed at Kelmscott Manor in September 1872, in company with Dante Gabriel Rossetti, Alexa Wilding and the Heuffers, Janey was in London.[19] Their friendship bloomed only in Florence in 1881; the focus of their affection, as it had been all along, was the failing Dante Gabriel Rossetti.

"I am thinking of making a drawing of Mary Spartali if she can sit to me one or two days next week. I began one in the fag end of the 2nd sitting for the hands (which I have got done) but it was not satisfactory and I shall begin another if she can sit. She is very difficult, but putting her against the light as you sat for the Pandora, I found the expression and character perhaps the finest and want to make the drawing in that way. I have been doing one or two other drawings to raise the wind – drawings from models. Brown has begun a second drawing of Mary S. It is much prettier than the first, but somehow does not seem to have the amount of likeness which that had in spite of its want of beauty,"[20] Rossetti wrote to Janey in August 1869; later in the month he added "... I hoped on getting the hands put into your picture from Miss S that I might be able to take it up and get it out of hand; but other things have come in the way and it sticks as it was since then... since she sat for the hands Miss Spartali has given me two more sittings and I have made 3 chalk heads of her. The last I think is not unsuccessful, though the 2 first were completely so. I find her head about the most difficult I ever drew. It depends not nearly so much on real form as on a subtle charm of life which one cannot recreate. I think it would be hardly possible to make a completely successful picture of her, and feel a great deal humbler now when I look at other peoples' attempts."[21]

In the same vein Rossetti wrote to Kitty Howell from Penkill of the portrait: "Several people have recognised it spontaneously, though I cannot say it seems to me a striking likeness. Miss Spartali who was sitting to me lately, did not recognise it at first, yet ultimately thought it a successful portrait." Marie Spartali's image, her head and shoulders in black, white and red crayon on light green tinted paper, were ultimately to be used as model for the Attendant on the right in the oil version of

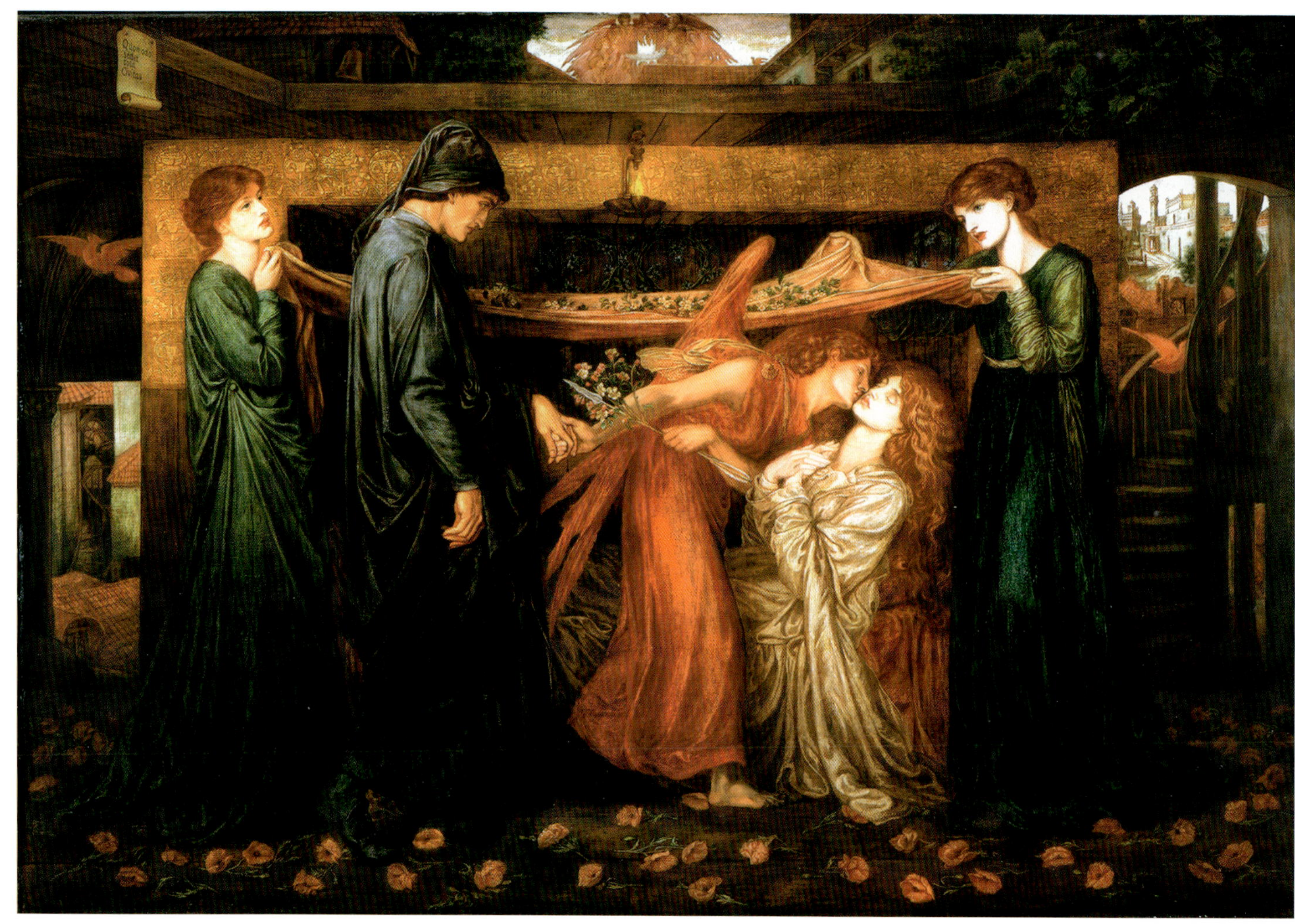

Plate 10
Dante Gabriel Rossetti
1871
Dante's Dream
Oil on canvas. 216 x 312.4 cm (85 x 123in)
National Museums Liverpool (The Walker)

Dante's Dream at the Time of the Death of Beatrice in which Janey Morris is Beatrice. Dante Rossetti completed it for William Graham in 1871; its size, 7 x 10.5 feet (2.13 x 3.2m), proved too great for Graham's setting, and it went in 1873 to the solicitor, Leonard Rowe Valpy who in his turn sent it back when he moved to a smaller house; it was sold in the end to the Walker Art Gallery in Liverpool in the last year of the artist's life: "Things have gone better for the arts in London for some time past. The good folk of Liverpool have just bought my big picture (3rd time of sale!) and I am beginning to wonder whether increasing age will admit of my tackling another large canvas..." he wrote to Fairfax Murray in Florence.[22]

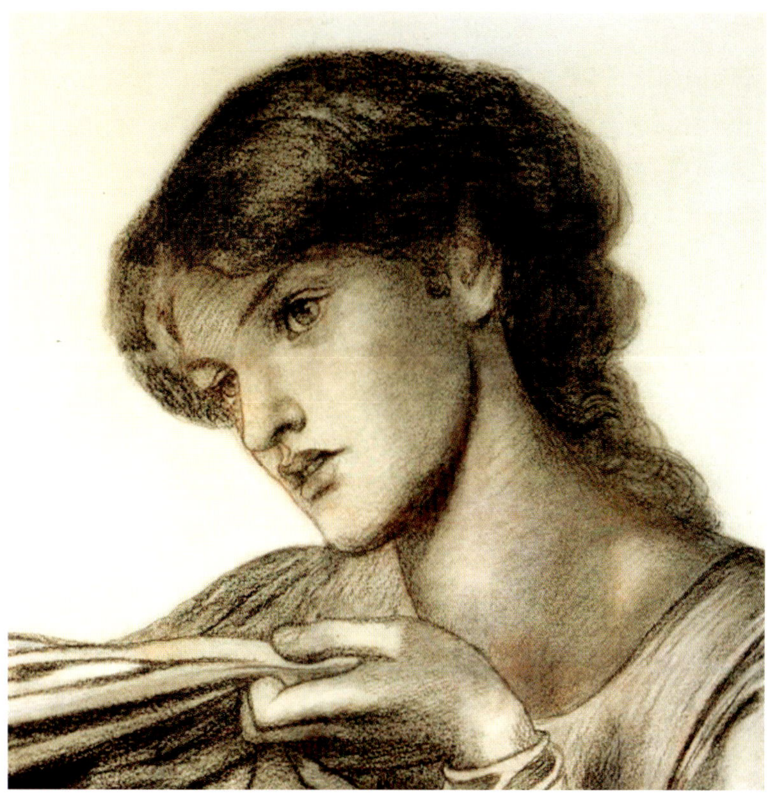

Plate 11
Dante Gabriel Rossetti
1874
Study for Pall Bearer, for *Dante's Dream* (detail)
Red, black and white chalks on green paper
Whitworth Art Gallery, University of Manchester

Marie Spartali was unusual for an aspiring woman artist in not being the daughter or sister of an established male artist, as for example were Joanna Boyce, Emma Sandys, Rosa Brett and Rebecca Solomon. Her resolve to paint and her dedication to her art were entirely her own. In Lucy Madox Brown – yet another artist daughter of an artist and Marie Spartali's closest early confidante – the pursuit of art was closely linked to her determination to better the lot of women in the Victorian social pattern. For Marie Spartali, it was the plunge in to the art world, rather than any strong sense of social mission, that took hold of her imagination and opened her eyes to the liberated world beyond the clipped box hedges that enclosed The Shrubbery.

Chapter Four

William James Stillman, Childhood and Youth

William James Stillman, artist, critic and writer, came from a long line of dissenting Baptist expatriate English farmers and West Country landowners, whose home had been in America for almost 150 years.

George Stileman Pickering might well have lost his head after the Bloody Assizes at Taunton, where Judge Jeffreys – the most infamous of all English jurists – sentenced more than 200 men and women to be hanged, 800 or so more to be transported and hundreds more to be imprisoned or flogged following the failure of the Monmouth Rebellion. The exiled Duke of Monmouth, Protestant pretender to the throne of England and the bastard son of Charles II, landed a small force at Lyme Regis in Dorset in June 1685 and was proclaimed King at Taunton. Despite sympathy for his cause among the West Country gentry, few were actually inclined to provide men and arms. Monmouth, ill-equipped and outnumbered, was crushingly defeated at Sedgemoor, taken and publicly beheaded in London on July 15. Among Monmouth's supporters was George Stileman, the elder son of a landowning family from Steeple Ashton in Wiltshire. His wife, Jane Pickering, was the daughter of Sir Gilbert Pickering, a strict Puritan, who had been Lord Chamberlain to the Lord Protector Oliver Cromwell. Jane and her husband, now George Stileman Pickering (he added his wife's name to his own in the custom of the time) were immediately apprehended and it was only through wealth and influence that they escaped the fate that many others suffered at the hands of Judge Jeffreys. Pickering was allowed to set sail from London for the American Colonies in late 1685. He left behind his wife, Jane and their children, George and Samuel, who were to follow. Jane Pickering did not live to see her new homeland. She had eluded Jeffreys only to die in childbirth at sea on their journey to America.

The widowed George Stileman Pickering settled in Hadley, Massachusetts, where he dropped the married name of Pickering and adopted the alternative spelling Stillman. There he prospered in trade with England and the West Indies; he became a Selectman for Hadley, entitled to the courtesy of being addressed as 'Mr', and was doubtless satisfied when, in 1688, the Protestant William of Orange was invited to take the throne of England.

George Stillman remarried, to Rebecca Smith of Hadley, the granddaughter of one of the Pilgrim founders of Wethersfield, Connecticut. Relations between the colonists and the indigenous people were always uneasy at best. When King Phillip's War – the inevitable American Indian rebellion against continuing Puritan encroachment into native lands – threatened his property, wealth and family, Stillman moved to Wethersfield, where he served as a Selectman and, from 1698, as Representative at the Court of Massachusetts. He died a wealthy man in 1728.[1]

His son Dr George Stillman Jr practised medicine and served as Clerk of the First Seventh Day Baptist Church in Newport, Rhode Island for more than 30 years. The Seventh Day Baptists professed the first Baptist principle of baptism by total immersion; it was their growing conviction of the strict scriptural basis for doctrine and practice that led them to a distinguishing belief in the literal interpretation of the fourth Commandment, which forbade all work on the Sabbath as an inescapable requirement of Christian observance. Their Sabbath, Saturday, was that of the Old Testament; the prohibition of any work, including domestic duties such as cooking and lighting fires, was that of the orthodox Jewish faith. Their stern system of belief, their sense of example and civic responsibility, and their evangelical intensity put them among the most exacting branches of their faith.[2] The second of Dr George Stillman Jr's eight children was Deacon Joseph Stillman; of his thirteen children the eighth, born in January 1779, was Joseph Stillman III.

Joseph Stillman III, known in Rhode Island simply as 'Old Honest Joe', was William James Stillman's father. A ship builder and inventor, Joe learned the trade of ship's carpenter in Westerly, on the Connecticut – Rhode Island border, close to the whaling port of Mystic at the head of Long Island Sound. William's mother,[3] Eliza Ward Maxson, from Newport, Rhode Island, was descended from John Maxson, a Baptist who had been driven out of the Massachusetts community by the Puritans for his Sabbatarian beliefs.

Early in the 1820s Old Honest Joe designed a fulling machine for the cleaning and processing of woven cloth, set aside his trade as a shipwright and made his temporary home in Schenectady, an important Dutch settlement in upper New York State a little to the north of Albany with significant trading links to the untamed West. Here Joseph Stillman found a ready market for his invention, and he entered in to partnership in Westerly to manufacture it. The venture failed due to his associate's dishonesty, leaving Joe with debts and the threat of bankruptcy; his capital lost, he fled back to Schenectady to avoid his creditors until he might restore his family's solvency and repay his debts, this time taking with him his struggling family. William Stillman's mother bore the penury and near starvation of the move west to Schenectady with unshaken religious faith: "...guided by profound belief in the good intentions of Providence... the ghastly Hebrew conception of God,"[4] as William Stillman was later to describe it in his autobiography.

It was in to this long-established New England family that William James Stillman was born on 1 June 1828 in Schenectady; in London, Dante Gabriel Rossetti had been born two weeks earlier. William was the youngest of nine children; the eldest, Professor Thomas Bliss Stillman,[5] 22 years his senior, was a marine engineer who played a prominent part in the American Civil War and was appointed Supervising Inspector of the Revenue Marine – the Coast Guard of the day – by Abraham Lincoln. Two older brothers became doctors. Another, Alfred, was the author of a treatise on 'The Steam Engine Indicator and Improved Manometer Steam and Vacuum Gauges'[6] and who died, with unhappy irony, in a boiler explosion on a Mississippi stern-wheeler.

At the age of seven, William was sent to New York where he was enrolled at a New York free school, which was run by the Public School Society and funded by non-sectarian benefactors, and looked after by his eldest brother whose wife saw to it that he was provided only the familiar spartan regime of essentials for his maintenance. One early memory he had was of the catastrophic fire in 1835, which destroyed a large part of the city below Canal Street, as a result of which William was returned to the financially-stricken home in Schenectady. The following year he was moved once more, now to a Sabbatarian boarding school in De Ruyter, New York State run by his fifth brother, Dr Jacob Davis Stillman. There he stayed until he was past fourteen. De Ruyter was, in those days, at the dark heart of an unsettled forest wilderness west of Albany, bounded on the north by the Mohawk River at Syracuse, and was barely coming to life as the railroads drove west. Buffalo, at the end of the line 150 miles on, at the edge of Lake Erie, was the Wild West of legend.

The frontier life, the intense relationship with nature and the constant instruction in the wonders of God's creation, was deeply impressive to the sensitive young William Stillman. He learned to enjoy the solitude of lonely expeditions in the wooded country, even to depend on the stillness of nature to offset the harshness of his life at home, a childhood spent forever between the rock and the hard place. When William was eleven he was baptised by total immersion, among the ice floes, in the river in thaw at Wethersfield. Old Honest Joe was mercilessly strict. William's relationship with his father was one of unremitting severity, of fearing God and telling no lies, and of practical skills learned in the workshop, punctuated by flogging for any imagined infringement.

At the age of seven William Stillman, an intellectually precocious child, had suffered a bout of typhoid fever and the capacity to enjoy learning and to absorb knowledge seemed to desert him. Old Honest Joe, who placed practical experience ahead of textbook learning, expressed the loving side of his nature by diligently passing on his knowledge and skills of the outdoors, plants and animal life during long walks on Saturdays (since he would not attend church on his day of rest.) William's mother was devoutly, unquestioningly pious, and he would later recall his religious education being, "of the severest orthodox character... Hell and its terrors were always present to me."[7] It was not a joyous upbringing for a young child of a delicate constitution.

At fourteen, the question of his further education arose. He showed a talent for painting, which he matched with careful observation and passionate commitment, and he dearly wished to enter art school and make a career as a painter. While his father remained resolutely opposed to any higher education his mother was no less insistent that he should go on to university and, finally, her will prevailed. Though the argument raged back and forth for more than a year, William, the supposed beneficiary, was not consulted: "I was diverted from the only career for which I had a recognisable calling and ultimately drifted in to journalism," he wrote at the end of his life.[8] William was sent to the Lyceum in New York to prepare for entrance to Union College, Schenectady, the senior university after Harvard and Yale at that time.

William Stillman graduated from Union College in 1848. His friendship there with the Principal, Dr Nott, would later have an important impact on his future career, but he lacked both ambition and a goal as he left the university: "Before entering College, art was a passion but when at the age of twenty the release gave me the opportunity to throw myself in to painting, the finer roots of enthusiasm were dead and I became only a dilettante, for the years in which one acquires mastery were passed..."[9] This, too, was autobiography as the last opportunity to set the record straight, to justify his failure, as he saw it, to pursue the life and career of an artist.

For a time Stillman explored the rules of perspective with John Wilson, an English portraitist who had made his home and a successful career in St Petersburg before moving to the United States to become a travelling teacher of shorthand (invented by Isaac Pitman in 1837.) He worked with Samuel Sexton, a shoemaker by trade with a natural talent as a painter, who taught him the rudiments of painting in oils.[10] Stillman next proposed himself as a pupil to Asher Brown Durand (1796-1886), the elder-statesman of the New England landscape painters, who proved too modest to take pupils. Stillman's fitful search for the way ahead reveals an unwillingness to accept the formal disciplines of training in technique and composition, trusting to talent rather than study.

In the winter 1848-9, however, William Stillman was still eager to pursue painting, and he studied under Frederick Edwin Church (1826-1900), the precocious and strikingly talented *en plein air* landscape painter who became a leading figure in the Hudson River School in succession to his mentor, Thomas Cole (1801-1848), the first of the great American landscape painters, who had died that year. The distinctive qualities of the vastness of wholly unspoilt nature inspired Thomas Cole, an Englishman by birth who had migrated to America as a boy, to develop the concept of wilderness paintings as epitomised in his series *The Course of Empire*, not simply as pictorial record but as social, moral and religious commentary. In so doing he captured the conflict at the heart of the white expansion towards the west: the creeping industrialisation, the subjugation of the indigenous people and the destruction of nature. Within his vision he encapsulated for the first time the message and ideals of a distinctive American school of painting that owed little to its European forbears.

The completion of the Erie Canal in 1825, linking the Hudson River north of Albany in upper New York State by way of Schenectady and Syracuse to the Great Lakes below Niagara Falls at Buffalo, opened up measureless tracts of untamed wilderness of great beauty that were soon to be laid waste by commercial interests. Church set out to record the awesome beauty of the vanishing wilderness. A gifted colourist and fine draughtsman, he was only two years older than William Stillman, but he had already reached an early maturity and he would be celebrated long before the outbreak of the Civil War a decade later. Stillman was his first pupil, and Church's way of working – travelling, camping, hiking and sketching through the summer months, returning to New York to work up his sketches and notes in to finished canvasses in the winter – appealed strongly to the younger man as they ranged through the Adirondacks, though characteristically he later wrote: "I learned nothing from him that was worth remembering."[11]

Early in 1850, the restless young artist sold a picture for $30 at the American Art Union, the *salon de dernier resort* in New York and, flush with this windfall, set out for London in pursuit of his long-held ambition to meet John Ruskin. In the event, their first encounter that summer was by chance, in the gallery run by Griffiths, James Mallord William Turner's dealer. He was introduced to Effie Ruskin and warmly invited to visit at Park Street, where the reluctant spouse had rented a house for the season in order that his young wife – much tried though frivolous – could enjoy the social life of Mayfair while he toiled in seclusion preparing *The Stones of Venice* for the press. Although acquaintance turned to friendship, and William Stillman long remained Ruskin's admirer and follower, the seeds of doubt were sown early: "Differences came to me reluctantly for my reverence for the man was never to be shaken, while my study of art showed me finally that however correct his views on the ethics of art might be, from the point of view of pure art he was entirely mistaken."[12] William was troubled by a "serious perplexity as to the accuracy of Ruskin's perceptions of Nature," the cornerstone of his belief in Ruskin's dicta. Ruskin it seems had failed to notice that Turner's *Juliet and Her Nurse* in the Holford collection, its sky filled with dazzling fireworks, was an impression of a moonlit night.

William Stillman returned to New York in the autumn, without any clear idea of the direction his life would now take, nor any keen ambition. The spur to any decision was temporarily removed by an accident: he was innocently involved in a street gang fight in which a snowball, with a solid core of packed ice, missed its intended target and hit him hard in the mouth, smashing his upper jaw and cheekbone, breaking the teeth on one side of his face. The damage was serious, and long to mend. While he was convalescing, he occupied his time studying the issues of the day in the art world, in social affairs and on the European political scene, which he had found to be of consuming interest during his visit to England as The Year of Revolutions trailed away into instability in France, Italy, Hungary and the Balkans.

Lajos Kossuth (1802-1894), the Hungarian patriot and revolutionary who had fled to Turkey in 1849 when an uprising failed to free his country from the Austrian yoke, was touring the United States to raise funds for another attempt to overturn Austria's rule. William Stillman fell heavily under the influence of this charismatic, impractical revolutionary and volunteered his service to Hungary's cause. Funded by Kossuth he travelled to Europe once more, via London, where they met clandestinely in a Bayswater hotel to plan the great adventure.

Kossuth initially allotted Stillman the task of assisting in an abortive design to help Giuseppe Mazzini (who had in March 1848 attempted a war of national liberation in the Veneto against the occupying Austrian forces) by preventing Hungarian troops in the service of Austria from firing on Italian insurgents in a second revolutionary attempt planned for the following Spring in Milan. Stillman was to carry posters proclaiming the liberation, and ensure that they were displayed. As the partners – Kossuth and Mazzini – exchanged enciphered messages it became apparent that Kossuth was not yet ready with his grand design for a simultaneous rebellion in Hungary, while Mazzini was determined to press ahead. The co-operative scheme was dropped, and with it Stillman's involvement in the uprising in Italy. Instead, travelling in the guise of a tourist, Stillman was ordered to proceed, by way of Paris, Brussels, Berlin, Dresden, and Prague, to Vienna to establish a new communications network among dissident Hungarians, the old cell having been penetrated and the participants apprehended. His bungled attempts twice led to his imminent arrest by the Austrian secret police, who had all those concerned under routine surveillance.

William Stillman moved on to Pesth, charged with a key involvement in the delicate assignment of rescuing the Hungarian Crown of St Stephen from a secret hiding place near Budapest, where Lajos Kossuth and a fellow conspirator named Szmere had buried it. Stillman was to act as courier, his whimsical mission being to smuggle the Crown out of Hungary by way of Constantinople concealed in a pot of plum conserve, thence to be delivered in Boston to Dr Samuel Gridley Howe. Stillman carried half of Kossuth's coded secret instructions – to be matched with those of his contact – in the hollowed heel of his boot. Szmere had meanwhile gone over to the Austrians and with him went the Crown. Stillman's heel was by now worn out thereby exposing his instructions; he threw the pair of boots in to the

Danube and made his way back to his hotel barefooted. The following day he left for Paris. Forty years later Stillman commented: "A very stupid and impractical individual I must have been... as a habit, the realization of my danger only came to me when the danger itself had gone by, and then I was frightened." Nothing in this period of his life was too unlikely to be undertaken with the utmost seriousness. Lajos Kossuth, he realised, was a very poor organiser of conspiracies. He had, however, seen most of Europe.[13]

While awaiting Mazzini's revolution (which failed once more in the Spring of 1853) Stillman spent the winter of 1852-3 in Paris, studying painting under Yvon, the Director of the Ecole des Beaux Arts, who took private pupils. Here he met Delacroix, Ingres and the landscape painter Théodore Rousseau, the central figure of the Barbizon school. He returned home in the Spring of 1853; his fractured maxilla was now a serious and painful problem, and while his doctor brother's able reconstruction removed the infected bone he was left with a slightly disfigured face. The early summer he spent alone, painting in the Connecticut and Housatonic River valleys, though he was dissatisfied with the landscape, which he found "too trim". He moved on to "months on end" in the wilderness around Pittsfield, in the densely wooded slopes of the Berkshire Hills that divide Rensselaer County NY from Massachusetts.

William Stillman's years at Union College had been a time of religious exploration. At that time Union was one of the few major universities not under denominational control. "My dogmatic theological education had been entirely incidental, for my Mother never discussed dogmas or doctrine, but the simple duties and promises of religion," he recalled. He had contrived to conceal from his mother his doubts about the literal truth of the Bible, and increasingly thought about the Swedenborgian 'internal sense' of the Bible, the search for spiritual truth and the immortality of the soul. To the end, Stillman believed deeply in the immortality of the souls of animals. In the extreme solitude of the backwoods of New England William Stillman pondered the spirituality of nature and man's relationship to God until he reached a point of hearing illusory voices. He listened to processions of marching footsteps, and the calls of imaginary hunting parties. It was, he wrote, "...illusion as unaccountable as spiritism, sometimes more real than physical facts." Aware that this might easily lead to insanity, he fastened his attention on painting to preserve his balance.[14] Winter came, and he set out with his brother Paul, an evangelising Swedenborgian, distributing tracts among the backwoods communities. The year had been spent on a spiritual odyssey that had led him far from the fundamental Christian beliefs of his mother, his father and his communal background.

Chapter Five

The Critic and the Seeds of Journalism

On his return to New York, William Stillman took up his first serious journalistic appointment, a short spell as Fine Arts Editor of the *New York Evening Post* under William Cullen Bryant; and he continued to paint. Stillman was self-taught as a critic and this was his first opportunity to air his strong, Ruskinian views on the significance of the emergent school of truly American art. The wilderness painters were not without individual success, but the notion of a wholly American school was slow to gain critical understanding and attempts by the artists themselves to promote the school to a wider public had been largely unsuccessful.

As Frederick Edwin Church's pupil, William Stillman came to know a wide circle in the art world and he saw the opening for a magazine devoted to the arts and the ideas that he was burning to disseminate. In January 1855 he founded *The Crayon* with John Brown Durand, Asher B Durand's son. Financed by Stillman's eldest brother, Thomas, and John Durand equally, this was not the first American publication devoted to the fine arts. The most important of its predecessors was the *Art Union Bulletin*, a narrowly nationalistic bi-monthly sponsored by some of the artists concerned with earlier attempts to promote the Hudson River school; it ceased publication in 1848.

The merit of *The Crayon* lay in its wider compass and an unswerving dedication to the Ruskinian credo of fidelity to natural truth in art. "We believe that it will be scarcely possible that any Art should arise here of which Ruskin and his ideas should not be a large component." There were letters from John Ruskin and William Michael Rossetti, *The Crayon's* London correspondent, who was appointed on the advice of Ruskin, in February: "A word from Ruskin will do more to attract notice to merit, as yet unadmitted, than anything else whatever," the latter shrewdly observed. *The Crayon* was a critical success and a valuable addition to the art resources of the day. Poet contributors included James Russell Lowell, Thomas Bailey Aldrich and William Cullen Bryant, Stillman's editor at the *New York Evening Post,* while Stillman wrote most of the art criticism himself.

There is no doubt that *The Crayon* under Stillman's editorship reflected the intellectual climate of the time. Nathaniel Hawthorne voiced the view that

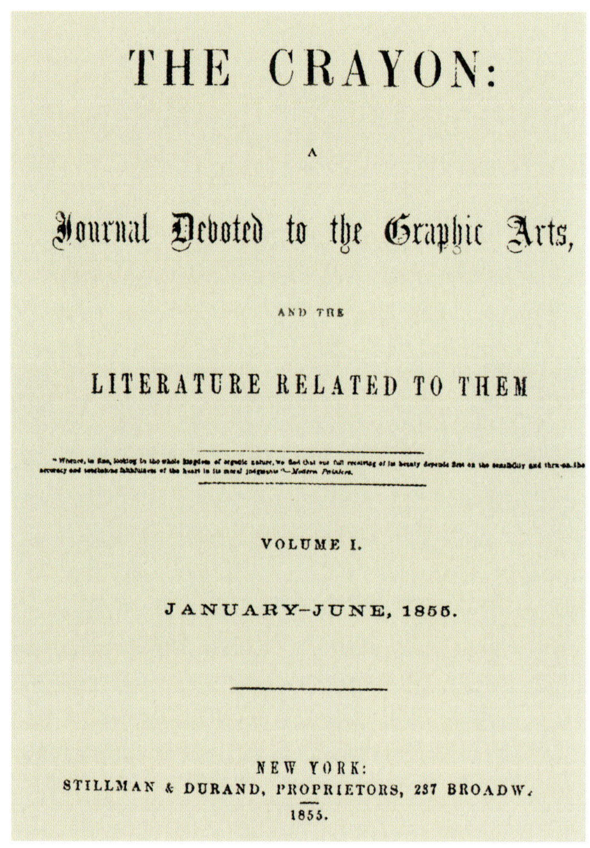

THE CRAYON:

A

Journal Devoted to the Graphic Arts,

AND THE

LITERATURE RELATED TO THEM

VOLUME I.

JANUARY–JUNE, 1855.

NEW YORK:
STILLMAN & DURAND, PROPRIETORS, 237 BROADW.
1855.

Plate 12
The first issue of *The Crayon*, January-June 1855, edited by William James Stillman

Cimabue and Giotto "might certainly be dismissed henceforth and forever without any detriment to the cause of good art." The American school of naturalist painting was beginning to make headway and there was widespread agreement among academic opinion-formers that the young country should foster its own style to reflect the nation's aspirations.

During the year William Stillman honed his journalistic style and his taste for controversy, indulging himself in the first of a number of judgmental polemics against James Jackson Jarves, a modestly wealthy American collector who lived in Florence in poor health. Jarves was a pioneering connoisseur who outran his inherited income in acquiring a notable collection of paintings, mainly of the Italian *trecento*. It was his intention to build a collection that should remain together on public display in a suitable gallery in the United States. The importance of this early instance of an American collection of Italian primitives did not, however, achieve the recognition it merited without a struggle. The aim behind the collection was diametrically opposed to the concept of the supremacy of a modern American school. Stillman, a practicing artist, an American Ruskinian and a fervent disciple of painting the truth in Nature, disapproved strongly of Jarves's intention to bring the early-Renaissance art of Italy to the attention of the American public.

The Crayon was soon in the field against the notion of "such a startling novelty as a large collection of Italian paintings," as the *New York Tribune* dubbed it.[1] There was a strong element of personal dislike for Jarves in Stillman's headstrong attack on what he unedifyingly described as "pre-Giottoesque ligneous daubs... which should be burned." An evangelist thirty years ahead of his time, Jarves shared the fate of another American collector of early European art, Thomas Jefferson Bryan, whose collection was formed in Paris. It too failed to find a public home in New York and was eventually given to Philadelphia in 1864.

In 1855, Jarves sold two paintings to a pretentious New York lawyer by the name of John Neal, who had achieved success as a popular novelist. These were a painting of the *Roman Campagna before Sunrise* by Claude Lorraine and a *Danaë,* supposedly by Titian; hugely satisfied with his purchase, John Neal wrote a self-congratulatory letter to *The Crayon* to advise them that these eminent works were now on American shores. This raised the hackles of the intemperate editor who, nevertheless, published the announcement in the issue of 21 July 1855. With Durand he forthwith examined Neal's two pictures. Jarves meanwhile had written from Florence to say that he had personally discovered the 'Titian', fearing that his contribution to the nation's culture might otherwise be overlooked.

Stillman seized the opening thus presented: "Since our publication of the letter by John Neal we have had the opportunity to see these pictures and we are quite satisfied that the *Danaë* is not by Titian... [it is] full of errors both in linear drawing and modelling, errors so gross that we are sure that if Titian had, by any misapplication of his senses produced such a piece of work, he would have destroyed it instantly that he recovered the right use of his eyes..." The Claude he considered to be genuine. Dismayed, Jarves wrote to Ruskin – whose reply was brutally final: "I entirely agreed with The Crayon in all it said about your 'Titian'... I was truly grieved that such a picture should go to America as representative of Titian. But, I never said a word to the editor of The Crayon."

Stillman's broadside had a serious effect on James Jackson Jarves's reputation as a connoisseur and, more importantly, further reduced any latent enthusiasm for buying his collection. The public were 'more amused than edified' by 'this extraordinary collection' said the *New York Times* when it was exhibited at the Derby Galleries in 1863. Charles Eliot Norton failed to persuade Boston or Harvard to buy the collection as a whole, and it languished at Yale, the victim of "popular indifference, mis-understanding, misliking and even hostility", the hostage for a loan that Jarves had been forced to take out. He was now in financial straits due to the cost of bringing the pictures from Europe; unable to redeem his loan, more than half the collection passed in to Yale's possession in 1871.[2] The remainder was purchased in 1883 by Liberty E Holden, the silver mining magnate and owner of the

Plain Dealer of Cleveland, where it now forms a substantial portion of the Museum of Art's fine holdings. Stillman's attack ensured also that Jarves's book, *Art Hints, 1855* – a guide to European art intended for aspiring American collectors – was unfavourably received. *The Crayon* relentlessly put the case for a purely American School: "We need only men who will... stand with their brows bared and their eyes and hearts open before Nature and tell us honestly what they see and what they feel without any reference to any previous Art..." For all *The Crayon's* prejudices and its pamphleteering editorial style, the magazine made a lively contribution to the developing awareness of a home-grown School, distinct from the European tradition of artists like John Singleton Copley.

It was a short-lived achievement. In June 1856 William Stillman was forced to retire from the editorship by a nervous collapse brought on by the strain of writing, editing and publishing the greater part of the first 18 months' issues single-handed.[3] He gifted his share to Durand, but the fall in editorial standard was immediately remarked on by Clarence Cook – the gadfly art journalist and charter member of the Association for the Advancement of Truth in Art who would later edit *The New Path,* the Society's journal. *The New Path* took up the crusade at the point that Stillman left off, and the Society's Manifesto was virtually identical to the earlier published 'Aims of *The Crayon*'. There was much truth in William Stillman's assertion that *The Crayon* "had a considerable public sympathetic with its sentimental vein, readers of Ruskin and lovers of pure nature – the circle larger perhaps for the incomplete state of art education in our community."[4]

In Boston, James Russell Lowell introduced William Stillman to a circle of intellectuals with interests in the arts including Henry Wadsworth Longfellow, R H Dana, Charles Eliot Norton, John G Whittier, E P Whipple, Charles Sumner, Harvard's eminent geologist Prof. Louis Agassiz, the Unitarian priest turned poet Ralph Waldo Emerson, Oliver Wendell Holmes's brother John Holmes, and Judge Ebenezer Rockwood Hoar.[5] He met also Barbara Leigh Smith Bodichon and her husband Dr Eugène Bodichon. In 1857 an ambitious exhibition of contemporary British art, mounted in New York by Captain Augustus A Ruxton and Ernest Gambart, failed to attract buyers in a depressed economic and financial market. Ruxton however insisted, against Gambart's advice, on adding Philadelphia and Boston to the tour. *The Crayon's* recent contributor, William Michael Rossetti was Secretary to the enterprise and, with William Stillman's aid, he was able to ensure a more receptive audience in Boston. Among works shown were Ford Madox Brown's *King Lear,* Arthur Hughes's *Sailor Boy,* William Holman Hunt's *The Light of the World,* and Frederic Leighton's *Reconciliation of the Montagues and Capulets over the Bodies of Romeo and Juliet.* Three of John Brett's Swiss landscapes, the *Wellhorn,* the *Wetterhorn* and *Glacier at Rosenlaui* were particularly praised for their feeling and accuracy by the glaciologist Prof. Agassiz.

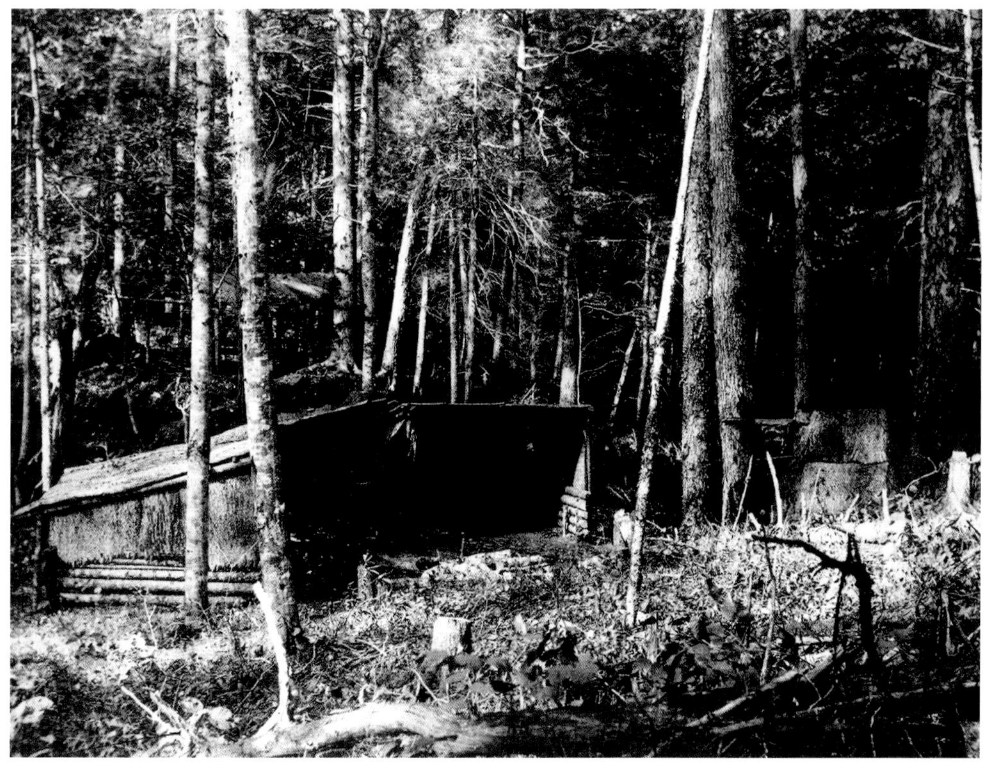

Plate 13
William James Stillman
1859
'Hut in the Adirondacks', from *Photographic Studies, Part 1, The Forest*; possibly the shelter built by Stillman and the Adirondack Club
Private Collection

In the autumn of 1857, following savage bouts of pneumonia and pleurisy, William Stillman travelled to Florida, where he intended to continue his studies in photography, with the generous financial assistance of Charles Eliot Norton. Here William Stillman saw slave life at first hand on the St John's River: "Kindliness to the slaves was universal... the negro was a better appreciated element of social life than in the north."[6] While many slaves in the South were permitted to own small-holdings, and Southern freed Blacks often became blue-collar craftsmen – painters, carpenters and boot-makers – their brothers in the North remained economically and socially at the bottom of the ladder without so much as the remote prospect of a foot on the first rung. The North, Stillman saw, had no monopoly of respect for the dignity of the individual and he reluctantly concluded that freedom for black Americans might not be an unmixed blessing. There was a spirit of ethical and scientific enquiry abroad among New England intellectuals. Alexis de Tocqueville's *De la Démocratie en Amerique* had exposed the racial implications of slavery. "Northerners frequently talk about slavery because they have nothing directly to fear from it. Southerners do, thus their silence," de Tocqueville observed. Despite his reservations, Stillman's sympathy was with the abolitionists; Louis Agassiz, however,

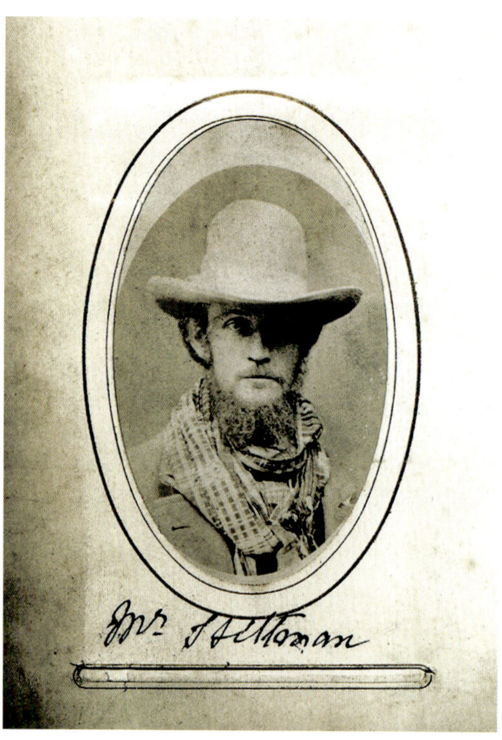

Plate 14
William James Stillman dressed for The Philosophers' Camp
c.1865
From Cathy Heuffer's photograph album, annotated in her hand
Private Collection

remained a staunch anti-Evolutionist who thought Darwin was wrong and that black Africans were a distinct species and he campaigned in the South in favour of slavery.

The essential immorality of slavery, whatever extenuation there might be, could no longer be denied. Among the dominant abolitionist voices in Congress and in the universities were those of Wendell Phillips of New York and William Lloyd Garrison of Massachusetts. They spoke movingly of the rights of man, and of Toussaint l'Ouverture, the African freedman of absentee American slave-owners who had fought to rid Haiti of the Spanish and the English 50 years before and had been betrayed by Napoleon; Toussaint died in a dungeon at Fort-de-Joux, in the French Jura, where his heroic life and tragic death made him a symbol of the fight for liberty. (Garrison's son, named Wendell Phillips for his father's co-worker in the abolitionist cause, was later the Editor of *The Nation* and contributor to another journal, the *Century Quarterly*, in both of which Stillman would afterwards publish many of his articles.)

As he recovered his health in the following 18 months, William Stillman retreated further in to the study of nature, intent on mastering landscape painting, working hard but without guidance or any real sense of direction. Much of the time he was

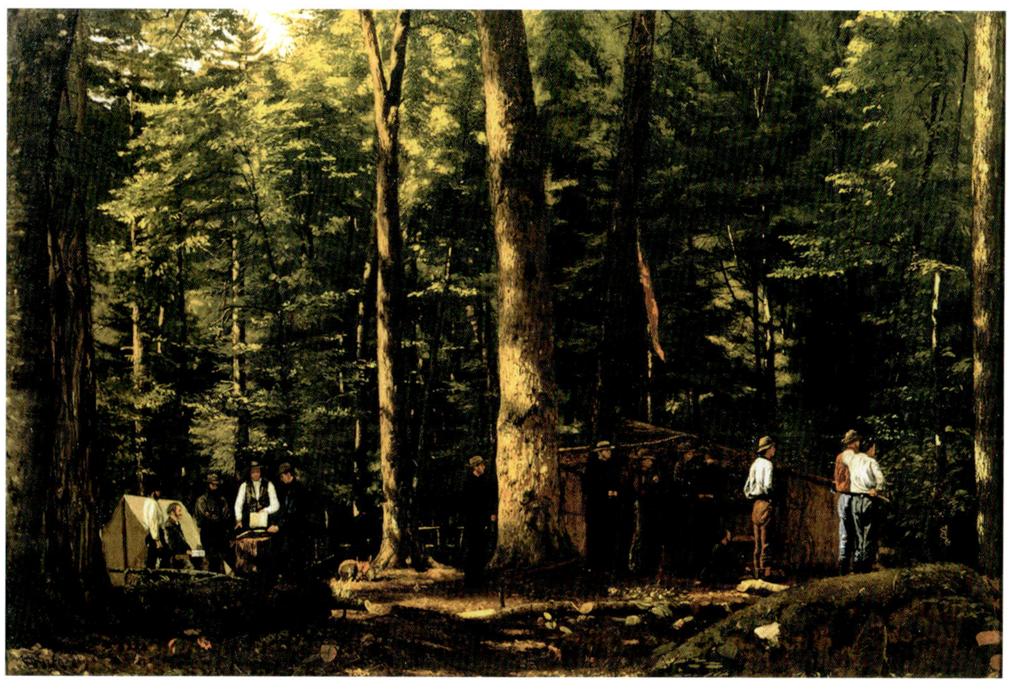

Plate 15
William James Stillman
1858
The Philosophers' Camp
Oil on canvas. 51.1 x 76.2 cm (20 x 30in)
Concord Free Public Library, Concord MA

alone in the remote countryside at the head waters of the Raquette River and around the Saranac Lakes: "Here the morbid passion of solitude grew on me,"[7] he commented. In the Summer of 1858, Stillman, now 30, founded the Adirondack Club whose members sought to try their hands at the simple life in the wilderness. Among the early participants were Louis Agassiz, Prof Jeffries Wyman, the poet James Russell Lowell, Dr Estes Howe (Lowell's brother-in-law), Judge Hoar, Ralph Waldo Emerson, Dr Amos Binney and Horatio Woodman. The camp, in temporary quarters at Tupper's Lake (often referred to as the "Philosophers' Camp" after Stillman's painting of that name) was a great success with the band of wits, poets and professors who built their quarters, hunted and fished for food, chopped wood for their fires and drew their water from the lake under William Stillman's firm direction.

Returning to Cambridge in the autumn, William Stillman became engaged to Laura Mack, the daughter of a prominent lawyer, David Mack; he had lodged in the Mack household while painting at Waverley.[8] There were Baptist connections between the Macks and the Stillman family; David Mack was a member of the utopian Northampton Association, which was distinguished by communal ownership of their resources. William Lloyd Garrison, the father of Stillman's closest friend, Wendell Phillips Garrison, was among the community's supporters, and others of Stillman's later friendships – including Henry James and Ralph Waldo Emerson – were visitors there. In the manner of the times the betrothal was probably something of an inevitable union rather than a love match. The call of the wild still echoed. During the winter, Stillman negotiated the purchase of Ampersand Lake and 1000 acres of forested land for $600, for the use of the Adirondack Club. Wendell Phillips Garrison recalled William Stillman "...in those wild-wood days. Tall he was then, of course, and slender, and of a build that seemed to warrant the prediction of an early death from consumption, while in truth he possessed a wiry constitution and a remarkable vitality. A wealth of long, brown hair framed a handsome, smooth-shaven face, with broad, intellectual forehead, large eyes and a well-shaped mouth, of which the smile was something to be remembered."[9] Despite avoiding an early grave he was particularly prone to bronchial weakness throughout his life, and his later wanderings as diplomat and journalist were punctuated by acute phases of pleurisy and physical exhaustion.

The Adirondack Club summered enjoyably at their new camp at Ampersand Lake in 1859 but, in December, William Stillman's "uneasy and thriftless spirit" drove him once more to England with letters of introduction from Charles Eliot Norton to the poet Arthur Hugh Clough, who had "a fatigued way of looking at great subjects";[10] and from Lowell to Thomas Hughes, the author of *Tom Brown's Schooldays* and the founder, with Frederick Denison Maurice, of the Working Men's College. Through his contacts with William Michael Rossetti, Stillman was already a welcome visitor to the Rossetti family in Albany Street. He greatly admired Christina for her "noble serenity and dignity, the spiritual exaltation that dominated her and made her above all other women of whom I know anything, the poetess of the divine life." Dante Gabriel Rossetti, who now lived with Lizzie Siddal in what was to be the last year of her life, called on Stillman at his digs in Charles Street; Stillman had brought a canvas with him, *A Bed of Ferns,* a landscape in which a hunter posing over the dead stag he has killed occupied a prominent position in the composition. John Ruskin criticised the inclusion of the stag in characteristically intemperate terms and told him to remove "that carrion". Rossetti, when he saw this done, said angrily: "You have ruined your picture." Stillman destroyed it.[11]

William Stillman's respect for Ruskin remained despite the contretemps. In the spring of 1860, he leapt at the invitation to visit Switzerland for a painting holiday as Ruskin's guest. Stillman was awed by the natural beauty, the light and colour of the Alps but he did not find the scene a congenial subject for his brush. Both men were moody and out of sorts. This Ruskin later attributed to his error in starting their expedition in Chamonix: "We made a great mistake in spending half our time in Chamouni which is not a place for sulky people by any means," he consented, blithely ignoring the effect of his choice on his companion who had started out on a career as an aspiring painter from nature and was one of his devoted American disciples. Ruskin, instead, roundly criticised Stillman's half-hearted efforts to paint the views before them in a manner he deemed satisfactory, making one another, Ruskin said, "reciprocally miserable to an amazing extent"[12] and further resulting in William Stillman's loss of confidence in his skills as a painter. Whatever part the Professor played in this abrupt abandonment of his hopes, it is apparent that Stillman had already reached the turning point in his art some time before. He also suffered a sudden impairment of his eyesight in Switzerland, perhaps from eye-strain but quite probably from a nervous reaction, from which he did not recover for two years. Inevitably, there followed disenchantment with Ruskin's advice, and the temptation to blame him for the outcome.

"[Ruskin is] fundamentally wrong on all practical questions, and his advice and direction the worst thing a young artist can have," William Stillman confided later to Charles Eliot Norton. Ruskin, he added, had "dragged me from my old methods and given me none to replace them. I lost faith in myself, and in him as a guide in art."[13] They had differed root and branch on a central question of technique, Ruskin demanding that Stillman achieve the effect he sought by laying in his finished colour a stroke at a time, while Stillman's preferred method was to build the body of colour he wanted by a gradual reworking – blending his pigment on the sheet, which produced a result of great fidelity akin to a photograph. A sepia reproduction of his painting *The Philosophers' Camp*,[14] of the Adirondack Club at work, chopping wood and cooking over an open fire under a canopy of tall firs, Emerson in a white slouch hat and blue hunting shirt, was indeed mistaken for a photograph. Many of his American scenes, such as *Mount Chocarua, New Hampshire* which dates from this period, display this flat, literal quality. There was some justice in Ruskin's criticism of a lack of power or emotion; he could not, however, fault Stillman as failing to "go to nature in all singleness of heart... rejecting nothing, selecting nothing, scorning nothing," as he had famously prescribed in *Modern Painters*[15] and the consequence was anger and confusion. Time did not heal the wound. Thirty years on, ranging far beyond questions of technique to the fundamental thesis of *Modern Painters*, Stillman wrote of Ruskin: "His art criticism is radically, and irretrievably, wrong. That which makes art what it is, *as art*, has absolutely nothing to do with the phenomena of nature."[16]

Parting from Ruskin in Switzerland, Stillman moved on to Paris but he could not settle to serious painting; instead he decided to join Garibaldi's expedition to Marsala to overthrow the Kingdom of the Two Sicilies, and he was on the point of leaving Paris for Italy when a letter came from his fiancée's father to say that his bride-to-be was extremely sorrowful at the continued absence of her betrothed and that "her perplexities and distress of mind over our marriage" had so increased that they "feared for her reason if she were not set at rest",[17] an unhappy presentiment of

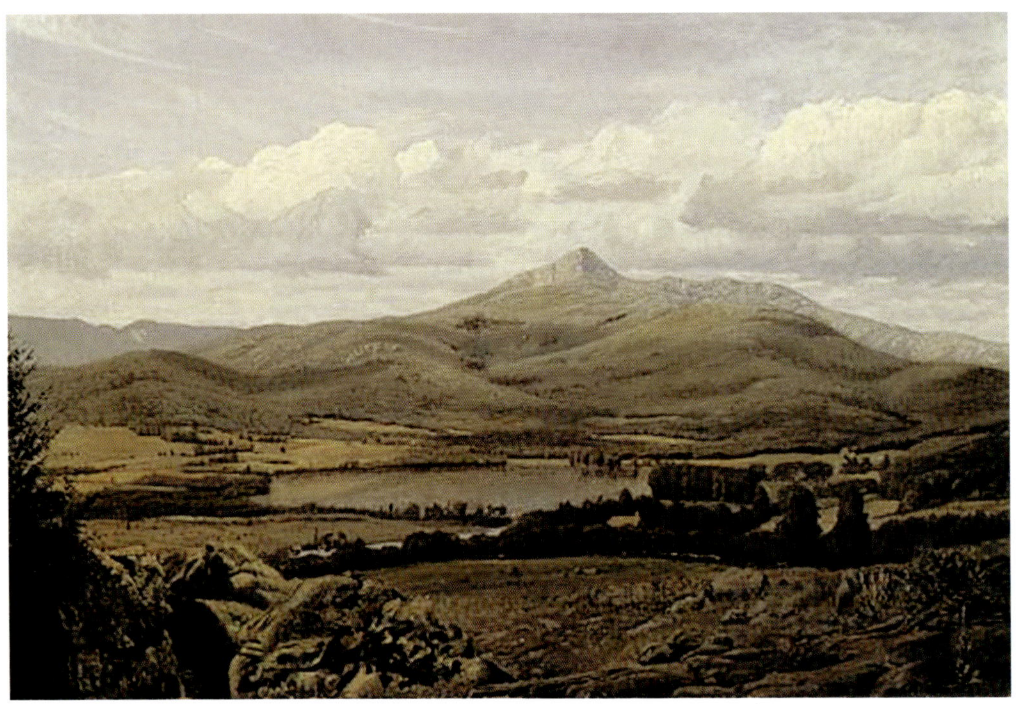

Plate 16
William James Stillman
1856
Mount Chocarua, New Hampshire
Oil on canvas. 30.8 x 45.6 cm (12⅛ x 18in)
Smithsonian American Art Museum, Washington

her later breakdown and suicide. Stillman embarked for Boston on the next available ship. He married Laura Mack two days after his arrival, on 19th November 1860, and returned with her to Europe by the next sailing. In the light of his subsequent behaviour as a marriage partner, it is difficult to conclude that this casual negligence was anything other than a portent of his complete self-absorption in his personal activities throughout his life. It was perhaps the result of a solitary childhood.

They did not remain in Paris for long. During the winter they had met Robert Browning senior, the poet's father, who was living there with his daughter in order to escape the financial consequences of a successful breach of promise action brought against him in Italy. A projected summer stay in Fontainebleau, together with the younger Browning and his wife, had to be abandoned because of Elizabeth Barrett Browning's death. In the United States, mistrust and the irreconcilable political and cultural differences between the slave-owning South and the European-oriented, industrial North made conflict inescapable. The election of Abraham Lincoln to the Presidency in 1860, by a narrow margin in a four-way contest, and the secession of South Carolina from the Union, touched off the Civil War – the Southern Rebellion as it was known in Federalist circles – of 1861-65. On 12 April 1861 the bombardment of Fort Sumter in Charleston Harbour by Confederate troops under the command of General Pierre Gustave Toutant Beauregard heralded the commencement of hostilities.

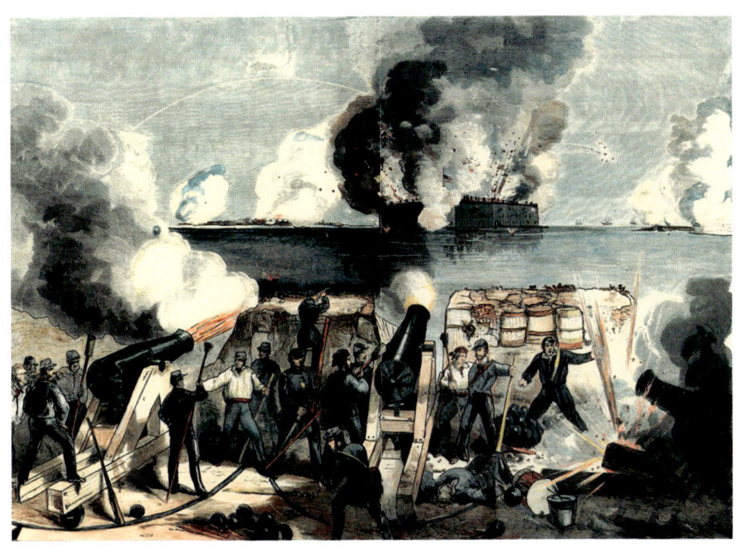

Plate 17
A contemporary aquatint of the bombardment of Fort Sumter on 12 April 1861 by Confederate forces under General Beauregard that marked the beginning of the American Civil War of 1861-5

Chapter Six

Diplomacy

William Stillman hastened back to Washington with his bride to enlist in the Federal service. Rejected for the army on medical grounds, his early mentor Dr Nott of Union College secured him the appointment of consular officer at the Vatican, Stillman having applied for Venice. Among his new companions in the diplomatic service was the poet William Dean Howells (who, having applied for Dresden, found he was posted to Venice.)[1]

Going on ahead of his wife Laura, William Stillman moved to Rome in January 1862: "My unfailing capacity for getting in to hot water was not to find an exception in Rome," he remembered. 'Russie', their son John Ruskin Stillman, who was to die at the age of 13 after years of suffering a painful bone condition, was born in America.

William arrived in the Holy See at a critical juncture in the development of Italy as a major European nation. The long struggle for independence from France, Austria and Papal Rome remained to be fully resolved. In October 1850 Count Camillo Benso di Cavour had set about the formidable task of the unification of the independent states that comprised mainland Italy. In January 1860 Garibaldi, with a threadbare army of volunteers, 'The Thousand', achieved the liberation of Sicily from the French, the expedition that just two years earlier Stillman had himself wanted to join. The little force, swelled by local volunteers to some 5,000 men, quickly captured Palermo, which was defended by 18,000 Neapolitan regular troops.

When, in March 1861, the Kingdom of Italy was proclaimed under Victor Emmanuel II, it united Parma, Sardinia-Piedmont, Lombardy, Romagna, Modena, Lucca, Tuscany and the Two Sicilies. Rome, occupied by French troops, and the Papal States comprising the greater part of central Italy, remained outside the Kingdom, protected by Napoleon III. The Veneto was still part of the Hapsburg Austrian Empire.

William James Stillman had recently presented his accreditation to the Vatican when, on 22 August 1862, Garibaldi crossed the straits of Messina back into Calabria at the head of his volunteer army, with the new war-cry, "Rome or Death". To permit him to pass unchecked would have meant certain war with Napoleon, and the undoing of all that had been achieved; Victor Emmanuel reluctantly proclaimed Garibaldi an insurgent, while Pope Pius IX continued to obstruct the cause of an united Italy by whatever political means came to hand. The Papal cause was managed by the astute and princely Cardinal Giacomo Antonelli. He was an imposing man, tall, with the Levantine appearance of many southern Italians – the aquiline nose and gaunt face, the heavy brow shading dark

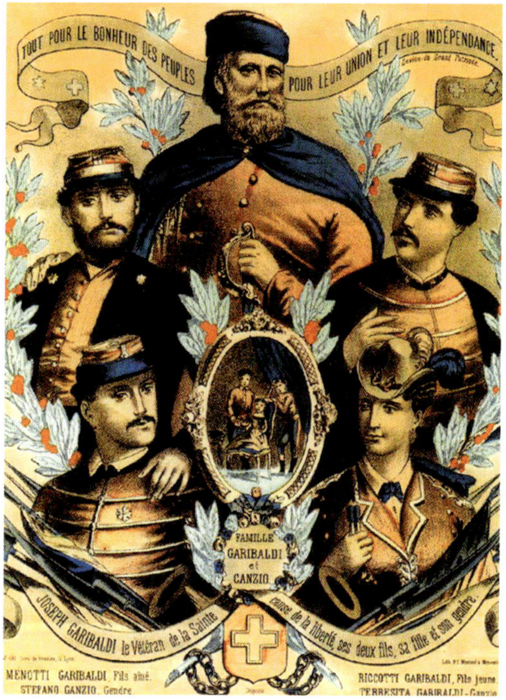

Plate 18
Giuseppe Garibaldi (1807-1882), the hero of the Sicilian campaign of 1860 for the unification of Italy, and his family, celebrated in a contemporary popular print

eyes and a penetrating glance. It was Antonelli's consummate diplomatic skills in the office of Secretary of State that kept the Papal interest alive, while Pius followed his religious obligations. Antonelli's word was law in the Holy City.

Antonelli's rise to power, his dismissive response to praise and criticism alike and, above all, his dedicated and rigorous pursuit of the Church's privileges and prerogatives aroused widespread animosity. He was accused of venality and personal aggrandisement. He was charged with concupiscence inappropriate in a prince of the Church. (In truth, Antonelli was not a priest, but a lay Cardinal who started his climb to the pinnacle as a jurist, having been first appointed to be Apostolic Delegate to the province of Orvieto, rising to become, successively, Minister of the Interior, Treasurer of the Apostolic Camera, Cardinal, Minister of Finance, president of the Council of State, and Prefect of the Sacred Palaces, in which innocent-sounding office he became the virtual ruler of Rome.) Antonelli was a determined paladin, whether as diplomat, dictator or gallant; he was the true heir of Machiavelli's Prince. To Stillman, Antonelli was "the very impersonation of unscrupulous and malignant intellect, subtle with all the Italian subtlety and as unscrupulous as any of the brigands of the community in which he had his origins."[2] The wiles of this vulpine prince of the Church deeply offended the idealistic East Coast American. Stillman was careful to exclude Pope Pius IX, whom he regarded as a good man and a reformer from within, from his anathemas. Pius, however, became an arch-conservative in his last ten years in the Papacy; he proclaimed the doctrine of papal infallibility at the First Vatican Council in 1870, saying: "I am the Church and I am tradition." He was also blatantly anti-Semitic and once compared the Jews in Rome to "howling dogs".[3]

It is remarkable that William Stillman, who had played a walk-on part in Italian revolutionary politics in Milan ten years before and who knew at first-hand something of the rivalries and the opposing policies of monarchists and republicans at this critical moment in Italy's history, should have found space in his autobiography only for two main topics of comment on more than three years in consular office in Rome: first, Antonelli's amorous proclivities and the wider moral failings of the Church of Rome and, secondly, Stillman's difficulties with his superiors over his dealings with Antonelli on consular matters. He was in post to represent the policies of his Government and not to pursue an agenda of his own, and the inescapable conclusion is that he was wholly unfitted by temperament or conviction for diplomacy. Instead, he regarded his rôle as that of the egalitarian observer, criticising his political masters in Washington with the same scorn that he poured on the Vatican. So little did he care for the diligent exercise of his consular duties that William Bell Scott and William Michael Rossetti were able to join him in Albano for a cultural excursion in May 1862, just a few months after his arrival.[4]

Protestant worship was prohibited within the walls of the Vatican City. Provocatively, William Stillman rented a house within sight of St Peter's, put up the Seal of the American Consulate, which afforded him diplomatic immunity, and turned the drawing-room in to the Consulate's chapel. He was already embarked on another crusade, against the State Department in Washington. Returning briefly to America to consult with Secretary Seward, William Stillman arrived the day after the decisive battle of Gettysburg. Seward had appointed Governor Randall of Wisconsin to head the legation in the short term as 'bed-warmer' for his crony General Rufus King "against the time that he should wish to give up soldiering." William Stillman made his disapproval clear, emphasising his view when back in Rome (accompanied by his wife Laura and Russie), by turning over his duties to Mr Brown, the consular agent in Civitavecchia, and setting off once more to paint in the hills outside Rome.

The smouldering antagonism between the Consul and the Holy See occasionally flared in to open disagreement but, in the main, it was a three-sided battle of wills. By 1865 General King was free to take up his appointment as head of the US Legation in the Vatican. William Stillman promptly protested at arrangements King made with Antonelli concerning the issue of passports to Confederate Southerners, which he regarded as "illegal" since this was the province of the Consul and changes had been made without consultation. When, in the ensuing controversy in Washington, Secretary Seward refused to recall General King, Congress "struck out from the consular appropriations the appropriation for the Legation in Rome"; William Stillman was a deplorably short-sighted diplomat who had succeeded mainly in abolishing King's and his own post.

High-minded, even priggish, ethical positions were a recurrent feature of his career, frequently to his cost. Thirty years on he produced an elegant summary of the Italian political landscape in the 19th century – *The Union of Italy 1815-1895* – which testifies to keen observation combined with powerful reportage. Yet as a journalist he habitually carried a torch for causes he judged to be right, albeit with great honesty, and he made little pretense of even-handedness; nor was he above using the public prints, who paid him for the privilege, to carry on vendettas or to excuse his own lapses of judgment. In this, he had more of the character of an eighteenth-century coffee-house pamphleteer than that of a correspondent.

His hopes of re-posting to Paris were now frustrated by the antagonism of Seward despite the intervention of his friend Judge Hoar. Instead, his appointment to the post of Consular Officer in Crete was signed by Abraham Lincoln on 14 April 1865, possibly the President's last act in office before his assassination by John Wilkes Booth at Ford's Theatre in Washington later that day. In the autumn, William Stillman bade farewell in Rome to his wife Laura who was carrying their first daughter Lisa, and set out for Crete. Delayed in Syra by quarantine restrictions because of an outbreak of cholera in the Levant, he made the acquaintance of a retired British Army officer who offered to carry Stillman on his yacht to Canea, the capital of the island, to take up his new appointment. They arrived as the Cretans were on the eve of a fresh revolt against their Turkish overlords. The terrible history of this episode can be studied in Stillman's account of *The Cretan Insurrection,* a graphic description of the horrors of a conflict in which he had no part beyond human sympathy for the cause of the insurgents, and risking his life for them. "His complicity with them consisted in nothing more than being a sort of postman between them and Europe,"[5] to which must be added his unbending Christian beliefs. Diplomatic colleagues were greatly reliant on the American Consul for the information that they transmitted to their governments and he in return ensured that they worked to mitigate the plight of the helpless victims of Turkish reprisals exacted against the civil population in revenge for the activities of the militants.

Eliza (Lisa) Ramona Stillman, Laura and William's second child, was born in Rome on the 23 December 1865 and, the following January, Stillman made the difficult return trip to Rome to collect his wife, his son Russie and the tiny baby, just a few weeks old. They travelled unhurriedly by way of Florence and Ancona to Crete, arriving after a perilous journey on 27 January. "My temperament and the habit of my life had always prevented me from anticipating trouble," William Stillman wrote in his autobiography. It was a mantra oft repeated throughout his career.[6]

Once settled in Crete the outspoken Stillman soon came to be regarded on all sides as a principal figure in the rebellion: by the insurgents who took comfort and inspiration from his personal stand against the atrocities committed by the local government, by the Greek government who regarded him as their voice in a subjugated territory, and by the Turkish authorities on the island who regarded him as a dangerous *agent provocateur*. One shining result of his strenuous efforts was that the non-Greek Christian population, who had suffered miserably at the hands of the Muslim Ottoman authorities, were at last taken off the island by foreign warships, with the predictable effect that the insurrectionists were freed to resume their vicious war of liberation. William Stillman bore the brunt of the authorities' displeasure, justifiably to the extent that he was, at the same time as he carried out his consular duties, striving to raise funds in London to arm and supply the guerrillas, an enterprise that was certainly inconsistent with his posting as a representative of the United States government. His house was stoned and windows broken by a paid Turkish mob; William and his family lived under constant threat of having their home torched. A virtual prisoner in his own house, Stillman was finally compelled to transfer his family, and the consulate, to a yacht.[7]

Throughout 1867 William Michael Rossetti acted as Stillman's point of contact with the outside world, seeing to the publication of his letters to the *Daily Telegraph,* meeting the new Greek minister Sir Peter Brailas at Alexander Ionides's invitation, and informing the London Greek community of the day-to-day situation on the island.

Bella Helena Stillman was born 14 June 1868 in Canea as Ottoman Turkish reprisals against the rebellion reached their brutal peak. Laura Stillman had endured a difficult pregnancy under conditions of extraordinary privation – short of food, in daily fear of her own life and without any means of protecting her young family beyond the rifle that William kept by him. The birth of another daughter served only to add to the weight of oppression that she felt for her own family, and for the innocent victims of the failed uprising. From post-natal depression she slipped slowly in to utter despair and finally to complete nervous collapse. William Stillman was left with the responsibility of a baby of only a few months, Lisa who was just a toddler, Russie who was now six, and his unfortunate wife who was sinking towards insanity. The consular post was poorly paid and Stillman faced the further dilemma that the Ottoman government in Constantinople had at last perceived that the simple way to remove the unashamedly partisan American representative was to complain to the Secretary of State that he was making trouble between their two countries. Secretary Seward, who had crossed swords with Stillman over the mismanagement of the Rome legation, readily agreed to his removal from office. Suddenly unemployed and without any financial means, William Stillman was compelled to sell his few possessions and borrow from supportive colleagues in order to pay for their passage to Athens.

They reached the safety of Athens too late to save Laura Mack Stillman. She committed suicide there in a state of religious exaltation; "insanity accompanied by religious delusions,"[8] wrote William Stillman describing her unhappy end. She was buried in Athens's First Cemetery beneath an impressive memorial erected to her memory at the expense of Greek admirers of the Stillmans's stand against Turkish brutality in Crete.

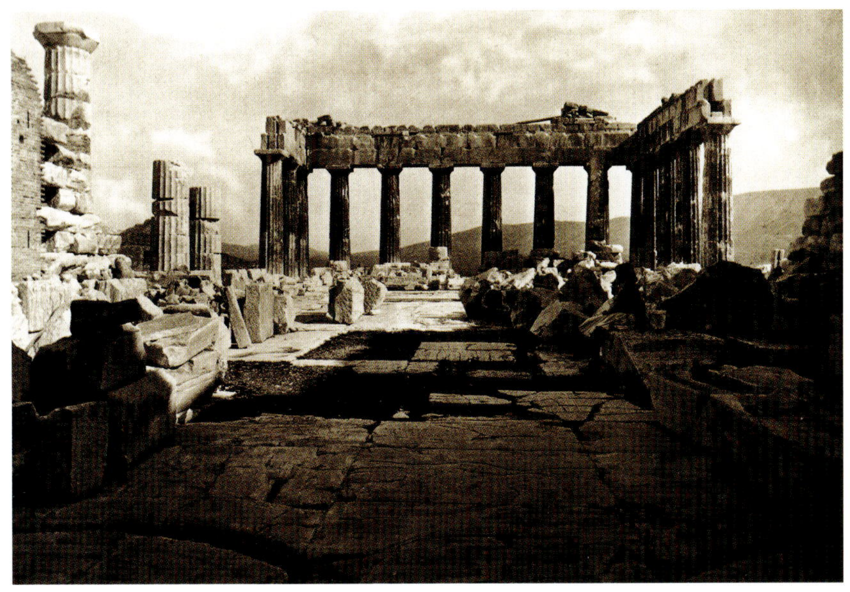

Plate 19
William James Stillman
1869
'The Parthenon looking east', from *The Acropolis of Athens,* published by Ellis & Elvey, London, 1870

The column bears the inscription, in Greek 'Laura Mack, American, wife of W J Stillman, American Consul in Crete. To the eternal memory of her love and good deeds unhappy Crete in grateful mourning dedicates this pillar.' Stillman was heavily in debt over the expense of their escape from Crete, with no immediate prospect of any remunerative employment. Ignoring this he travelled to Constantinople to meet face to face the Ottoman ruler A'ali Pasha, whose representatives in Crete he had strenuously opposed for the last four years, on a brave personal mission to persuade A'ali of the immorality and futility of treating his unwilling Cretan subjects in so harsh a manner.

Stillman's family's practical streak remained strong in him. A photograph that he had made in the 1850s from a landscape painting of his was warmly praised and led to a semi-professional interest in photography; he devised an improved swing-back for his Kinnear camera, which was later marketed in London – "He sent [it] me over from Crete 3 or 4 years ago... he thinks of patenting or at least registering this invention,"[9] Rossetti noted in his diary in 1867 – and Stillman passed on his technical knowledge in *An Amateur's Photographic Guide Book, Being a Complete Resumé of the Most Useful Dry and Wet Collodion Processes.* Now he made use of his creative talent as a photographer, making "the noble series of plates, partly architectural, partly picturesque of the Acropolis of Athens that he published in 1870... the astonished Greeks saw him clamber to a windy perch on the top of the Parthenon, for the sake of that plunging view, which shows the only portion of the sculptured frieze *in situ*, together with that convexity of the horizontal lines of their temples in which Stillman sees a subtle intention of the Greek architects to exaggerate the perspective."[10] William Stillman made his way to London in the September of 1869.

Chapter Seven

William James Stillman in London, 1869

From the time of his arrival in Crete, William Stillman had been actively soliciting funds from the Greek community in London for the armed support of the Cretan Christian population in their struggle against their Turkish overlords. William Michael Rossetti and his close acquaintance Stavros Dilberoglue were Stillman's principal conduits to Greek contributors to the doomed uprising; Michael Spartali, the Greek Consul General in London, chaired the Committee for the relief of the Greek community of Crete. In 1868, Rossetti recorded a visit to the Spartalis's in his diary: "Went with Stavros Dilberoglue to the Spartalis. Many photographs of Miss S lying about... only one, so far as I notice, goes pretty near to doing her justice. Miss S showed me a watercolour she is engaged in of a young girl by a window, looking out over a Venetian lagoon."[1]

Arriving in London with his three children early in September 1869 William Stillman once more set about his personal mission to secure help for the Greek inhabitants of Crete. Within days of Stillman's arrival William Michael Rossetti again visited Michael Spartali, "to meet there Stillman and Stavros Dilberoglue"[2]; also, this was to be the first encounter between William Stillman and Marie Spartali. Moved and excited by the gaunt and tragic figure with his tales of the suffering Greek community, of the death of his wife driven to madness and of his three motherless children, Marie soon came to feel the force of his uncompromising opinions and to experience a flood of sympathy for his and his children's situation.

Her parents were soon aware that she and William Stillman were meeting away from the watchful eye of chaperons, and that sympathy, shared interests and intellectual compatibility were turning rapidly to love. Michael Spartali and his wife were appalled at the developing situation and sought to prevent the affair from going further. Their opposition served only to rouse Marie's determination to see Stillman, and strengthen her tenacious resistance to being denied her right to choose her partner for life for a second time. She was 24 years of age, beautiful, eager to spread her wings and in love; and perhaps she feared too that she might otherwise remain forever at home, painting to while away the hours. Seeing that his efforts to limit their meetings were doomed, her father called a truce. "As my daughter asked permission to occasionally See the party & as our house is her house it was agreed that instead (of) meeting at friends' houses & causing remarks of scandal, she was to receive him at her own house, once a week & it was her own proposal & wish to avoid meeting elsewhere as my daughter is as free as the air, in her movements. I thought the proposition a very proper & fair one. During his visits to her the House is my daughter's, not mine,"[3] Michael Spartali curtly informed Madox Brown when he tried to ease the tensions.

As a result of his 15-year association with William Michael Rossetti, Stillman gained immediate entrée to the circle of artists. He met Algernon Swinburne at a dinner arranged by Dante Gabriel Rossetti, and dined with John Ruskin and Charles Fairfax Murray before he left for a brief visit to his family in America.[4] "Stillman left for New York on 17 November but expects to be back here for a while before winter is out,"[5] wrote William Michael Rossetti. Two evenings before Stillman sailed for the States, Rossetti "dined at Brown's with Miss Spartali, Stillman and Gabriel. Gabriel read his Lilith ..." at the request of Marie Spartali, who was sitting at the time to Ford Madox Brown for the central character of *Don Juan found on the Beach by Haidée,* his illustration for the Moxon edition of Byron edited by William Michael Rossetti.[6] (Stricken by grief and an uneasy conscience at the time of his wife's death in February 1862, Dante Gabriel Rossetti had placed his manuscript of poems beside her body in the coffin. Repenting of his dramatic gesture seven years later, he had wanted them back to edit and publish.) The *Poems* had been exhumed from Lizzie Siddal's grave in Highgate Cemetery less than six weeks previously – an event that Rossetti, in the grip of guilt and fear of the consequences if the story should leak out, insisted be treated with the utmost secrecy (though the prospect of an appreciative audience proved sufficient to overcome his doubts; Rossetti had read the poems to George and Rosalind Howard after dinner with the Burne-Joneses at the Grange a few evenings earlier.) Marie and William were in that exhilarated state of heightened awareness that lovers share. Madox Brown had been party to their secret for some weeks. William Michael Rossetti, Stillman's closest friend in England played a hand in the subterfuges by which they could be almost alone; and the couple met often under the blind eye of a mutual friend, Mrs Jeannie Hughes Senior, a close friend of George Frederic Watts and widow of Oxford's Professor of Political Economy, Nassau William Senior.

In the light of his sincere doubts about their engagement in the New Year, it seems unlikely that Dante Gabriel Rossetti furthered the match in any positive way; his own affair with Janey Morris now entirely pre-occupied him. "R's being so fond of Mrs Top,"[7] as William Bell Scott put it to Alice Boyd, had been the gossip of the day for more than twelve months – indeed Whistler had passed comment as early as 1863, two years before the Morrises left the Red House[8] – and Janey had recently returned from Bad Ems.

Nor had Rossetti any desire to supplement his affair with Janey Morris by a liaison with Marie Spartali. One evening fifteen years later, Dante and William Michael Rossetti looked back at those days; Rossetti recorded in his diary that there had been, "...a good deal of conversation about Mrs Stillman. It seems tolerably clear that when G first met her as Miss Spartali [in 1864], she was very graciously disposed towards him and would have accepted an offer from him had he made it, which circumstances of the time prevented. And Spartali, during the courtship of Stillman assured G in most express terms that he was himself in favour of such a match, and would from the first have promoted it. I remember he said the same to me at the time, about myself."[9]

It was the influence of Dante Gabriel Rossetti's deep love of the poetry of Dante and Boccaccio that informed the development of Marie's affinity with the culture of early Renaissance Italy, the stuff of her finest work, just as Ford Madox Brown's training was the foundation of her technique. And when in despair Michael Spartali turned to Rossetti in the hope of using his influence to persuade Marie against marrying William Stillman, it was as to an equal as a man of the world that he wrote with disarming sincerity: "I dreamt once that you had thought her worthy to be your companion in life."[10]

Chapter Eight

The Engagement

William Stillman became engaged to marry Marie Spartali on 15 January 1870; they had known one another for barely five months, two of which he had been in America: "There is nothing to me in the range of human interest like a husband and wife who grow together in intellectual sympathy and aspiration, and show the divine in them shining through the weakness of the human and transfiguring it to the true, angelic humanity. This is the glory and beauty of [love?] the world cannot comprehend and rarely sees, for such are not content to live in it, but to enjoy the divine life which art and poetry and true worship and wisdom create." In this exalted state of mind he went to see Michael Spartali: "10pm. The terrible meeting has passed and I have come out about as I went in. I have not compromised our future in the least, have given no promises save what I was ready to give..." William Stillman wrote to his beloved.[1]

Dante Gabriel Rossetti carried the news to Ford Madox Brown at midnight, and they stayed up all night talking. Neither could find it in them to welcome the marriage in prospect. Both wished Marie well but feared for the outcome; both were dismayed that she should have thrown away her prospects on William Stillman, less from any strong personal distaste for him than from grave doubts about his situation and his future.

Whether Ford Madox Brown nursed a hopeless yearning for the love of his pupil has been a matter of intense debate. The suggestion stems from an exercise book containing a dozen or more sonnets expressing a secret and unrequited devotion.[2] The identification of Marie Spartali as the object of Madox Brown's unpublished poem addressed 'Je te salue, Marie plein de grace' is scarcely in question,[3] while his deteriorating relationship with his wife Emma at the time provides a persuasive backdrop.[4] Emma had first sat to Madox Brown as a model in her teens, and had remained at his side during hard times to become his second wife; but as their fortunes improved and their daughter and her stepdaughter increasingly took on her rôle of model, she felt excluded and sought refuge in alcohol; she was often drunk.

The question is how closely do these verses mirror reality. They express the romantic essence of a Pygmalion relationship: the artist in love with his creation. The poetry of courtly love, the celebration of the exquisite pain of a remote and chivalric worship of an unattainable beloved, was a quintessentially Victorian art form; it was one in which

Madox Brown delighted (though Rossetti uncharitably remarked that his verse "contained a few obscurities"). Sonnets, the appendage to many a Pre-Raphaelite picture-frame and *predella*, were as much a tool of his trade as his palette and maulstick.[5] He taught his son Nolly to use the form. It seems fruitless to conflate his fatherly, protective affection for Marie and his fussy persistence in her training, with the poetic fiction she undoubtedly inspired. To construe the poetry as a factual expression of repressed longing strains one to believe that Marie Spartali could work alongside the sighing Madox Brown, twice a week for nearly five years, without feeling any disquiet. He gave her away at her wedding and the wedding breakfast was held in the house in Fitzroy Square. Moreover, he was infinitely patient and caring for Emma; she recovered.

He took as close and fatherly in Marie's work as in that of his own children, Cathy, Lucy and Nolly, all of whom he taught the elements of technique. Lucy Madox Brown was Marie's greatest friend; spending the summer of 1869 with the Spartalis on the Isle of Wight, her father wrote to Lucy "…ask [Marie] from me not to forget to work entirely but to meditate her subjects while at Rylstone, for I think a great deal more of what you four are going to produce in the next few years than of my own work …"[6] Marie Spartali returned his fondness with gratitude and tender respect, which she extended to the family, not least to Emma. She remained on close terms with them until his death more than twenty years later.

Nevertheless, Ford Madox Brown was profoundly shaken by the news of Marie's engagement to William Stillman, brought to him in equal distress by Dante Rossetti, though both were already well aware of the closeness between the lovers. They stayed up late in to the night, sharing their incomprehension and sadness; it may also be that Madox Brown sensed the latent hostility towards him that William Stillman manifested after the wedding. It seemed to be the end of an era, the ambition he held for his pupil dashed; but both were determined to defend Marie's right to choose her partner for life against the wishes of her parents.

On 18th March Marie warned Madox Brown: "He knows you take a different view to his and does not wish to be convinced at present... I feel sure now that any remonstrance would be useless and might prevent my being allowed to come to your house as usual – I saw Mr Stillman yesterday and he naturally insists on things remaining – so far as he is concerned – in exactly the same position and I suppose he will not be allowed to come again, for after he left Mama had a serious nervous attack from which I feared she would never recover... I am afraid she is very ill."[7]

Michael Spartali was incensed at the engagement, to which he had refused his consent. It was a further blow to his authority as the head of his family. Christina Spartali had eloped the year before with Comte Edmond Cahen d'Anvers, a wealthy Jewish Belgian who was head of the Paris branch of his family's bank. His Papal title had been purchased by his father, Joseph Mayer Cahen, a commodity trader and merchant in Antwerp. Christina and Edmond had married abroad in the face of Michael Spartali's veto. The pervasive anti-

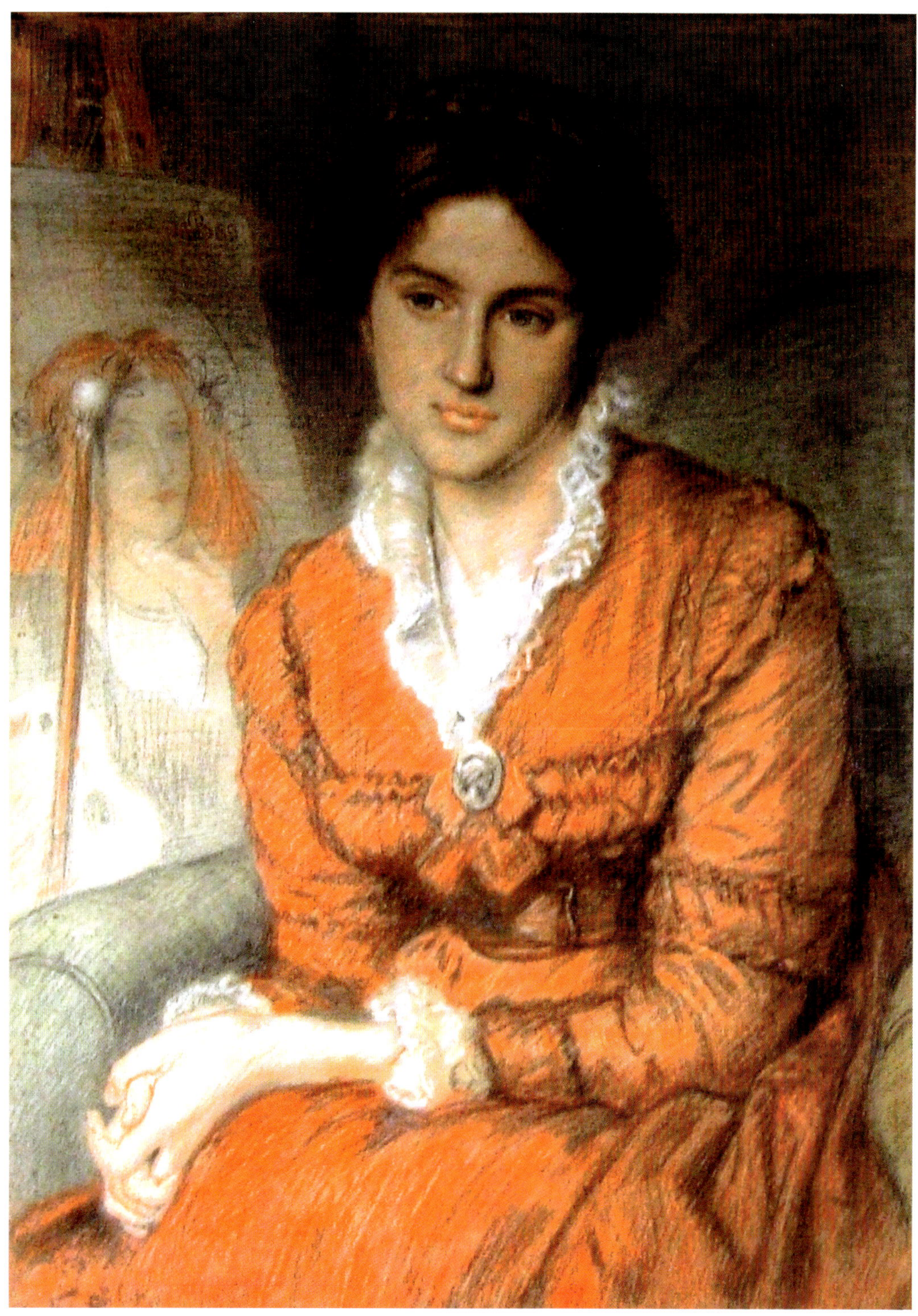

Plate 20
Ford Madox Brown
1869
Marie Spartali at her Easel
Red, black and white chalks on paper. 73.5 x 54.6 cm (29 x 21½in)
Exhibited: Royal Manchester Institution, 1879; Delaware Art Museum, 1976
Private Collection

Semitism of the time may have played a part in his opposition to their match, but no less important was the cultural mind-set of the close-knit Greek community.

Now he placed his hopes of parting Marie from her paramour on the artists he knew personally to have earned his daughter's respect. Unwisely he attempted to enlist Madox Brown's support with a legitimate but untimely payment: "In thanking you sincerely for continuing to guide my daughter in her artistic pursuits, and with more than parental interest and zeal, permit me to beg your acceptance of the enclosed cheque for the disbursements you have been put to during the past twelve months..."[8] The cheque was returned with Madox Brown's kind but firm refusal to intervene. Michael Spartali tried again, this time by appealing to Madox Brown's understanding as the father of one of Marie's closest friends, but with barely concealed anger: "I regret the unwholesome adulation my daughter the paintress receives from a narrow circle of friends – you who are behind the scenes ought to discourage it. As to the consolation you render, I receive it in all kindness but, from a father of family – with much regret. I have yet to learn that because you hold a man in honour & regard – it follows that he is the most fitted in the world (physically, socially, & intellectually etc) for the hand of your daughter... marriages under such conditions are celebrated over the corpses or graves of parents... May you good Mr Brown never, as a father, have to regret your no doubt well-intentioned remarks – this is my sincere warmest wish. I was in hopes that my daughter might have heard really parental advice from your lips... I know the interest you take in her & the great influence you have over her."[9]

It is easy both to understand the father's despair and to sympathise with Madox Brown's situation in the midst of this impossible dilemma. Marie was coolly, sadly determined. Madox Brown offered to go to Michael Spartali to plead her case. "I cannot thank you sufficiently for your kindness," she wrote, "I feel there is nothing that can be done at present to help us, and my Father would <u>not</u> take a better but rather a worse view of the case – I suppose he cannot change his nature any more than I can change mine, and I feel that if he insists on the sacrifice I must make it at any cost."[10] Her mother, who had asked Madox Brown to visit her, wrote too: "After you left I again thought the matter over and find it useless for you to write to my husband as I had proposed. He does not agree with you on any point, therefore the less he hears on the subject the better it will be. I thank you for your kindness warmly, Yours sincerely, E Spartali." In this heavy

---

Plate 21
Marie Spartali Stillman
1868
Mariana
Watercolour on paper. 38 x 27.5 cm (15 x 10¾in)
Exhibited: Dudley, 1868; Oehme, New York, 1908
Private Collection

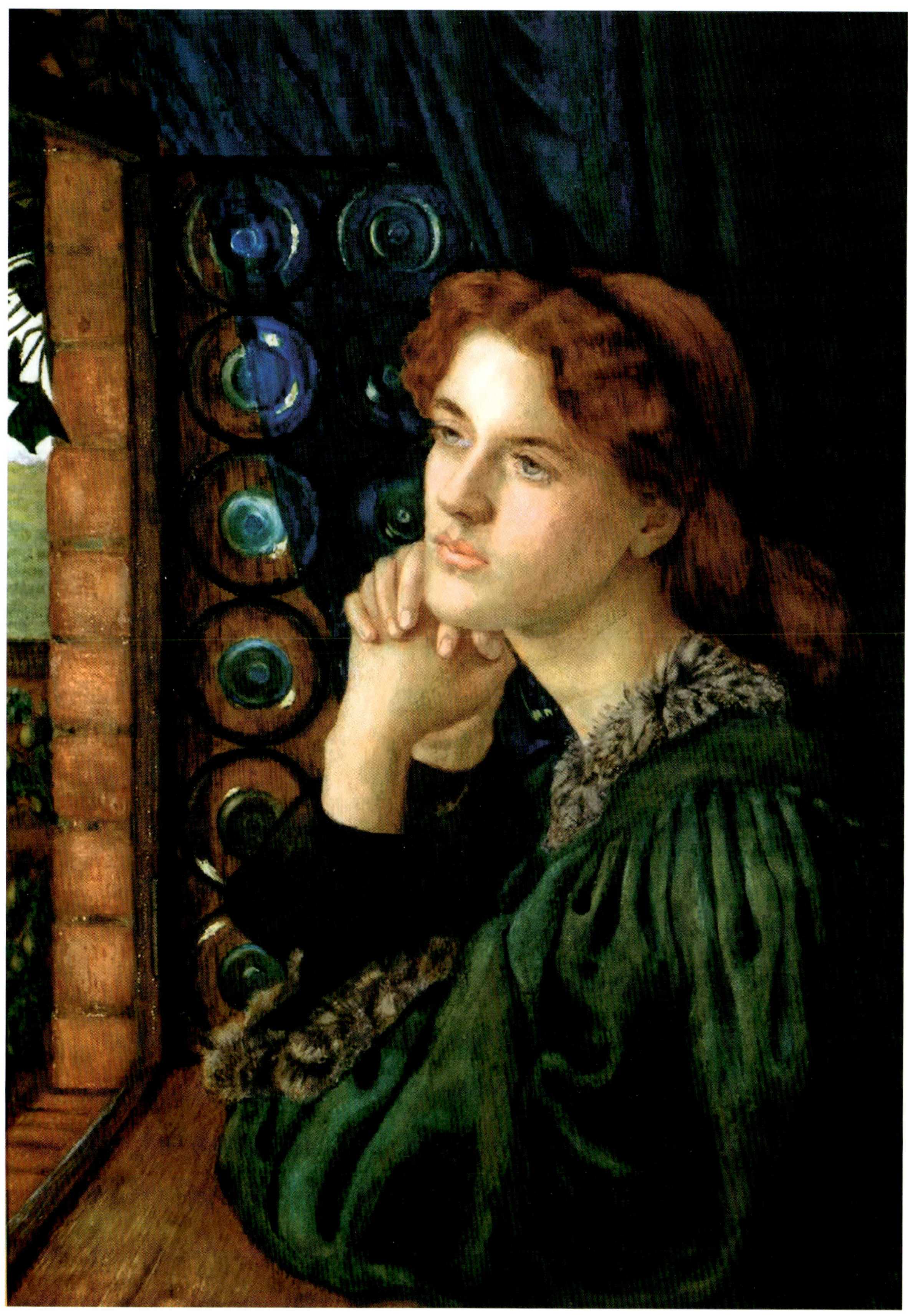

atmosphere William Stillman removed himself to the country, hoping to ease the situation, to 'recruit his health' and to give Marie time to consider the force of her father's resistance to their marriage, which he continued bitterly to oppose.

Dante Gabriel Rossetti, whose health and eye-sight were precarious, was also in need of rest and country air. He put the question to Janey Morris for her approval: "I have received an invitation again from Mrs Bodichon to go down to her cottage near Hastings, and really incline to think it will be the best thing to do. Only now unluckily it has been lent to Stillman and he has been asked to try and still get me to accompany him. I wish I had taken it when first offered and had it myself."[11] Nevertheless they went together, Stillman travelling with Rossetti's man servant the previous day and missing the train by looking it up in an out-of-date timetable. He spent March, from the 11th, and much of April, with Dante Gabriel Rossetti at Scalands on Barbara Bodichon's family estate near Robertsbridge in Sussex, while Rossetti awaited the publication of his *Poems*, which included those recovered by Charles Augustus Howell from Lizzie Siddal's grave, sharing expenses with him. Rossetti soon wrote enthusiastically to his hostess: "Good, quiet Stillman is the best of accommodating companions... and walks with me, talks with me and avoids me with the truest tact in the world... he has fallen to work a little on painting but has some pre-occupations of a kind which are apt to interfere with art..."[12] To Janey he added: "He's a wonderful example of an American. I met him spasmodically years ago, but now I see him more and I like him very much. This Johnnie is a thoroughly discreet person, who will leave me completely alone with myself..." To Allingham he described his companion as "an utterly unobtrusive man..."[13] Characteristically, he also wrote to his publisher, Frederick Startridge Ellis, commending Stillman's Athens photographs.[14]

With his habitual disregard for the likely consequences and by now a little bored by his eremitic companion, who insisted on healthy walks, regular mealtimes and early to bed – the house being candle-lit – Rossetti invited Madox Brown and Emma to join them, without consulting his comrade; they were succeeded by the Morrises. William Morris had an excellent appetite and enjoyed a bottle of claret with his meals. Stillman, who shared the expenses with Rossetti, soon found his frugal budget perilously overstretched. He followed William Morris back to London, while Rossetti remained until 9 May, Janey Morris visiting from nearby Hastings. "Stillman says that Mrs Bodichon, himself and others, are thinking of entering in to a pact – to include as many people as they can prevail upon – to keep up a simple, economical style of living – as, for instance, to limit dinner to three courses..." William Michael Rossetti noted: "I told Stillman it would be a waste of faith to suppose Gabriel will ever deny himself any expenditure he feels disposed for."[15]

His letters to Marie from Scalands show that Stillman himself could scarcely believe his good fortune that Marie had agreed to marry him: "You seem to me so gentle and confiding that I cannot understand how it is that you have not long ago found it necessary to lean on some arm and give yourself up to some over-ruling influence. How can it be except that God has some purpose in bringing us together as He did!"[16] In another letter he wrote: "I take shame to myself for having believed that I knew you when I contemplated so faintly the fullness of your love and its worshipful abandon. I sit thinking and wonder how it can be! and I almost tremble lest I shall have done something to jar on your utter, unselfish and undeserved devotion of yourself to me… there were moments when I doubted the absoluteness of your love – if it would endure absence and want of luxury and loss of your coterie who 'call you the goddess' – if you could love me enough to go and be with me and for me alone… what am I, Oh my love, poor creature of folly and falsehood, weak and worthless as the worms of the dust, to be worthy of such a love and such a soul."[17] William Stillman's surviving letters from this time speak of his fragile health, of sickness and his apprehension while awaiting the postman, of sleeplessness, of elation and despair in quick succession; the tone goes well beyond the literary note of a Yankee at the Court of King Arthur and the flowery conventions of the time, elevated by the spirit of courtly love that touched the small circle of poets and painters.

Wrestling with lofty invocations of the Virgin Mary, addressing a woman brought up in Victorian England in the Greek Orthodox faith as "my Mary", borders on blasphemous. Hoping to convey turbulent emotions he did not himself fully understand, he sought to resolve his own doubts by representing them as hers. There is an element of self-delusion in the suggestion that God would provide for them, the very belief that had sustained his mother in her times of tribulation, but here distorted in order to rebut Michael Spartali's substantial concern about Stillman's financial situation. The impression lingers that he was a little unbalanced by his recent difficulties.

Marie remained calm and resolute. Sympathy for William's plight had turned to deeper love; the question of why she was so determined on the match no contemporary observer was able to answer. While William Stillman was prostrating himself – "Dear Soul, how is it that this poor life and nature, so unfruitful of happiness even to myself, can promise you so much – how can I bring you life who am at times almost ready to abandon life myself…"[18] – Marie was at home with her parents, helpless to ease the pain she knew she had caused them. She was ready if necessary to turn her back on wealth and comfort for love though she had no experience by which to judge the realities of the life she would lead, and probably misjudged the harm her decision would do to her family. Rossetti, Stillman said, had "fallen in to the trap and gives one much good advice & counsel about being precipitate & looking well to a sufficient income before we move a step. In fact all the set seem to regard it as inevitable that I must provide you with a certain amount of luxury before marrying because of the style you have been brought up in and you are 'a great lady.' Yet it seems to me that a woman who has an intellect capable of occupying itself with anything that offers, a heart capable of loving with a full and pure love, art to occupy all her energies, music and a love of poetry, is surely the woman above all others capable of living without the empty attributes of artificial life."[19] The doubts of her friends provided handy ammunition in this battle of wills.

Stillman and Madox Brown remained on civil terms, if only for Marie's sake. Indeed, writing from Scalands, Stillman maintained: "I hope she will never be separated from your advice & direction & that the ties which bind her to your family may never be weakened. I hope & believe that you will always be most true to what you believe to be her true interest."[20] (However, he also found it necessary to write to Madox Brown telling him to disregard any reports he heard of his criticisms of his teaching methods. This followed some injudicious comment on Marie's developing talents. His remark, he said, was that Madox Brown should help Marie to be more selective in her choice of subjects.)

As a critic of some substance, and a minor painter with practical understanding of the craft of painting, William Stillman's private estimate of Madox Brown's work was at odds with this stilted and patently insincere compliment: "The predominance of the intellectual powers in him was so great that the purely artistic was impossible to him..." Stillman wrote in his autobiography, continuing the hostility beyond Madox Brown's death in 1892 to the edge of his own grave. "The telling of the story was, in his estimation, the highest office of art; so that while his drawing was bad in style and his execution was scrappy and amateurish and deficient in breadth and co-ordination, his compositions were often masterly, fine in conception and harmonious in line in the pen-and-ink study. But the want of ensemble and the subordination of insistent detail generally made his work less imposing when it was on the canvas..."[21] There is no reason to think that this stinging critique, written years later, was any less charitable than his view at the time. He pointedly contrasted Madox Brown with William Morris, "the largest all-round man of the group", and added dismissively of Burne-Jones that he saw little of him at that time, as "he was still working out his artistic problem", a tasteless reference to his affair with Maria Zambaco.[22] Possibly his comment that Madox Brown had been "carried away by youthful enthusiasm for art out of his true occupation, which was history" was intended kindly; it seems unlikely. There remained an undercurrent of antagonism between them. The respect in which Marie held him was salt in the wound.

When Dante Gabriel Rossetti's *Poems* were published in May, Marie Spartali was among the first to receive a copy. "I was waiting their publication with the greatest impatience shared by so many others. Having heard some made me naturally all the more anxious to be able to read them continually. Will you also allow me to thank you for your great kindness and sympathy for us in moments of extreme perplexity... it has been a great consolation to me to know that Mr Stillman was with so kind and indulgent a friend,"[23] she wrote to him. Talk of the engagement was on everyone's lips. Edward Burne-Jones thought her the most beautiful of the Three Graces, an opinion he maintained sixteen years later in a letter to F S Ellis: "... And so constant of heart am I that I think so still – she is a Greek and married to a husband – women often are – I never know why."[24] William Morris wrote to Janey that he had been "to Holland Park;

and it seems that they had heard of Stillman's affairs, and were rather full of them. I went to Aglaia's yesterday afternoon and saw both the ladies, who were still on the subject."[25] The topic had quite replaced that of Maria Zambaco and her lover.

On learning of the engagement, Euphrosyne Cassavetti – Alexander Constantine Ionides's sister and the widow of Demetrius 'Hadji' Cassavetti, a wealthy Greek merchant in Alexandria – commissioned Edward Burne-Jones to paint her daughter, Maria Zambaco, as a wedding gift to the Stillmans. Known to all as 'The Duchess' for her uninhibited and forthright ways, Euphrosyne Cassavetti saw nothing singular in choosing her daughter's lover – notwithstanding the very public scandal of just a year before – to paint a full-length nude figure of the striking, sensual woman he so much desired. Nor was Burne-Jones reluctant to undertake the commission. He portrayed her as *Venus Epithalamia.* (When Mme Cassavetti saw the picture she rather coveted her gift and commissioned a gouache copy, heightened in gold, from Fairfax Murray. It passed to Maria Zambaco when her mother died.)

At Scalands, William Stillman introduced Dante Gabriel Rossetti to chloral as a remedy for his chronic insomnia. In his autobiography, published in the year he died, Stillman wrote: "I recommended him to try chloral, then a nearly new remedy, that I had used by prescription with excellent effect on my own sleeplessness... I gave him twenty grains dissolved in water to be taken in three doses but, as he forgot the first two nights, he took the whole on the third, and complained to me the next day that it made him sleep stupidly for a few hours, and then made him so wakeful that he was worse than without it... nor did he at that time, or as long as we remained in touch with each other, venture another trial of it..."[26] Stillman had published an earlier vindication, *Dante Gabriel Rossetti and Chloral,* in the *Academy* magazine sixteen years after Rossetti's death: "...taking it on the prescription of a physician which he had made up at several druggists simultaneously as the amount did not satisfy his craving, he fell in to the habit of using it to his great injury, from the want of self-control... between my prescription and the habit of misuse there was no connection whatsoever."[27] Stillman lived under that cloud to the end of his life and it cast its shadow over his companionship with William Michael Rossetti who noted that his brother was "one of the men least fitted to try any such experiment with impunity."

Two years before the stay at Scalands, Ford Madox Brown had, on Stillman's advice, recommended chloral to Rossetti's friend, the Manchester artist, Frederick Shields who quickly became seriously addicted.[28] The sensitive and deeply religious Shields was enslaved by the drug and freed himself only by an uncommon effort of will in 1874; "Chloral gives only death-like stupefaction without restorative power... no friend had the same experimental sympathy with Gabriel as I had," he later wrote.[29] William Stillman was already well acquainted with the drug. He continued to use it throughout his life and admitted within the family circle that he was often unable to sleep without it. It is not unreasonable to infer that he too was chloral-dependant, at least to some degree, wittingly or not. His manic-depressive changes

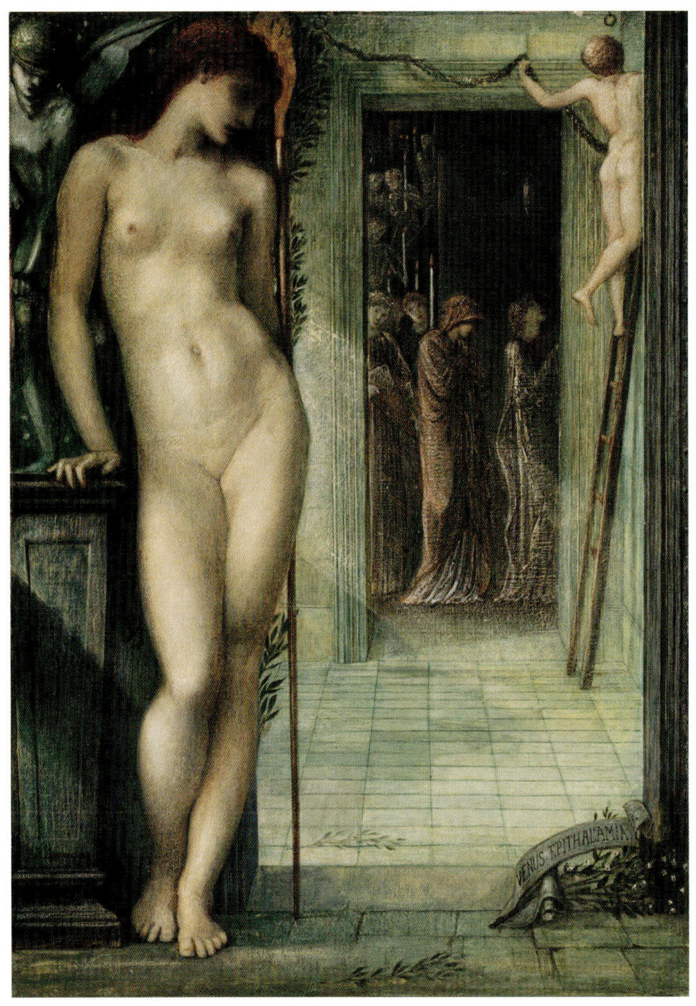

Plate 22
Edward Burne-Jones
1871
Venus Epithalamia
Watercolour & gouache, metallic gold paint with chinese white.
37.5 x 26.9 cm (14¾ x 10½in)
Fogg Art Museum, Harvard University, bequest of Grenville L Winthrop

of mood and antagonistic relationships are consistent with this conclusion.[30]

With their engagement now public, William Stillman arranged that his three children should be put in the care of relatives in the States for the time being, and it was thus unavoidable that he must be away for a considerable period, which, in the event, extended from June until the following February. The lingering doubts that all would be right in the end, and the urgency of their unexpected, distracted love is evident in the rambling, passionate letters that William Stillman wrote before he left England once again: "I have been very happy and buoyant all day and more than happy since I saw you... it seemed as if some cloud had cleared away, as if you had come to some clearer understanding of yourself and decided something which you had not yet been decided about... and this in the face of my going away – I don't understand it in myself or in you."[31] Their future would be one of harmony and shared artistic fulfilment: "Yes, I must paint and you must paint and we shall find time pass... we should both do so much more and so much better work if we were together, and have the happiness thrown in..."[32] an idyll in which they would work at their art side by side, empowered by one another's creative energy. He worried that efforts would be made to persuade Marie to break off their engagement in his absence: "I cannot lose sight of the hostility of your friends and the probable crusade which will be organised as soon as I am gone."[33] With William Stillman no longer allowed to visit her at the Shrubbery, the lovers relied on sympathetic friends for places to meet in some degree of calm and privacy: "...if you do not find me at 6 go to Mrs Senior and wait fifteen minutes and if I am not there by that time you may be sure I cannot come..." There were melodramatic assignations: "I shall go to the South Kensington Museum tomorrow unless you write me something different... if you want me to go with you anywhere it will be enough that you drive up to the walk in front of the house and show a veiled face at the cab door... or a gloved hand on the open glass..."[34]

Nevertheless he proposed an armistice during his absence in America: "I suppose that if your father accepts my proposition he will insist that our correspondence shall be restricted... and that I shall abstain from any approach to your feelings and comport myself simply as a friend and keep my letters at the dead level of familiarity at best... I shall not promise him to hide my feelings but I am willing to promise not to make any appeals to stimulate yours..."[35] William Stillman was at last able to recognise that Marie was a loving daughter who would not long endure repeated criticism of her father despite their difficulties: "In these days of comparative calm I have thought a good deal about your Father and his opposition and I feel that I have done him an injustice – not so much as he has me but more than I should if I had not been irritated beyond the power of judging justly. I have said harsh and bitter things of him which I should not have said and which I see were not deserved, but nothing so bitter as I have heard from others or as he has said of me. If I die without coming to an understanding with him, tell him this..."[36] he added bathetically.

There was something of the preacher deep in his make-up and it found its way in to every passionate declaration to Marie: "It always gives me new life when you talk in [your] earnest, faithful tone and I see that you are learning to accept the will of God which is the only assured way... I have most earnestly desired for you that you might see God in all things and understand that in Him is the highest, truest life and that... I may know that I have not stirred in vain the depths of your heart and taught you to love."[37] Or, from another letter: "The world may think what it will of our folly and improvidence, we are His children not the world's and we will ask His blessing and protection."[38] It might be inferred that Stillman was a dedicated, practising Christian, but he phrased his high-minded sentiments in the language of

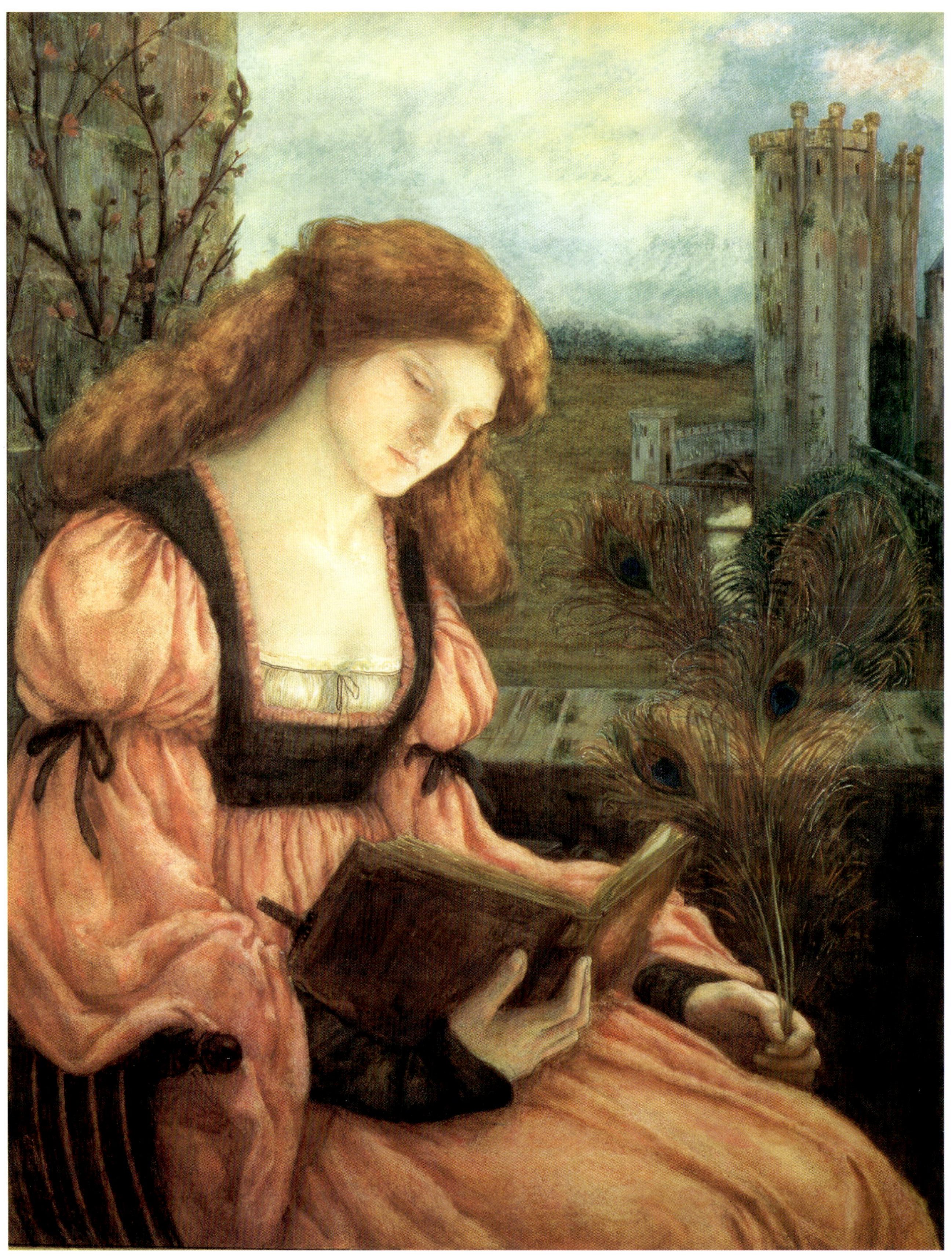

a creed he had rejected; if his beliefs had a label, he was a Swedenborgian. Rather, the language was the habit of a lifetime, the product of his Seventh-Day Baptist childhood. From that background too came his keen conviction of a calling to instruct, to expound his opinions and promote his personal beliefs as principles, and to assume command of the verities. This was the mainspring of his approach to life, to art and art criticism, and to his work as a diplomat and later on as a journalist, which never lacked a central purpose. Honest and outspoken, valiant for truth – his truth – and without fear, William Stillman could also be unforgiving, priggish and judgmental. No humour coloured his happiness. Even in this moment of unanticipated joy he displayed an air of dour superiority; yet he was dogged throughout his life with a sense of failure.

Leaving his few effects in the care of William Bell Scott at Belle Vue House on Cheyne Walk, William Stillman and his three children sailed for New York from Liverpool early in June.[39] He was anxious to see his mother whom he had not seen for 7 years and who was now dreadfully frail. There was another cause for great concern: while he was in Istanbul after his wife's death, his son John Ruskin, Russie, had fallen heavily and bruising to his hip had resulted in the onset of the tubercular bone disease that would eventually lead to his early death. They were met on the quay in New York by William's brother Charles who told him that their mother had died just two weeks before. Their elder brother Thomas, on whom William had relied for financial help on several occasions, had died on 1 January 1866 while William was still in Crete. There was a small legacy, but William Stillman would have no regular income again until he was salaried by *The Times* in 1886, sixteen years later.

In spite of the emotional upheavals that prevailed on all sides, it was for Marie Spartali a fruitful and creative time. She emerged as a talent in her own right, a fully-fledged member of the circle that ebbed and flowed around Rossetti and Madox Brown; no longer was she the rich man's daughter with artistic pretensions. During July, she sat for her portrait to Henry Treffrey Dunn, Dante Rossetti's studio assistant. Treffrey Dunn was at this time sitting as a model to Marie; the reciprocal arrangement was Rossetti's idea.

Marie herself painted *St Barbara (*known also as *The Girl with the Peacock Feather,)* a story from *The Golden Legend* with poignant autobiographical undertones. St Barbara,

---

Plate 23
Marie Spartali Stillman
1870
St Barbara (The Girl with the Peacock Feathers)
Tempera on paper. 69 x 54 cm (27¼ x 21¼in)
Exhibited: Royal Academy, 1870
Courtesy of The Maas Gallery, London; Bridgeman Art Library

an important figure in the Greek Orthodox calendar, was the beautiful daughter of Dioscuros who shut her up in a golden tower to discourage her many suitors. When she embraced Christianity, Dioscuros denounced her to the authorities who ordered her father to have her put to death. As she died he was struck by lightening and reduced to ashes.[40] In the picture, St Barbara sits quietly reading from her missal; the tower (her attribute) looms behind her. By the October Dante Gabriel Rossetti was hard at work on *Dante's Dream at the Time of the Death of Beatrice*, his eyesight much improved; his earlier drawing of Marie served as his model for the attendant on the right of the picture. Marie Spartali exhibited *Procne in Search of Philomela,* Catalogue 131 at the annual exhibition of the Society of Women Artists. (There is no record of her continued membership; the picture is now unlocated.)

In America, William Stillman received a landscape commission from J M Forbes of Boston, but taking up his palette he was compelled to confront his loss of vocation as a painter and the picture was never completed. He returned to journalism, writing for Dr Holland of *Scribner's*, and he was offered a permanent position on this influential publication. "The biggest business mistake I ever made was in leaving," William Stillman wrote in the last year of his life; it was a summing up of his fortunes in the next thirty years. For a time, better fate attended him in England. His photographs of Athens, dedicated 'To the esteemed Miss Maria Spartali, native of this country' and published by Rossetti's friend and publisher, F S Ellis, under the title of *The Acropolis of Athens*, earned him $1000. This, together with a legacy of $500 from his brother Thomas's estate, enabled William to pay off his debts and to regard his married future with some optimism. Rossetti was rather less sanguine.

No sooner had Stillman returned to England than Michael Spartali renewed his efforts to break the engagement, which doubtless he hoped would have foundered on nine months' separation. His own arranged marriage had brought both him and his wife great content and four fine children, and he considered that daughters of Greek families should follow this tradition, which had lent strength and homogeneity to the Greek diaspora. Understandably he felt that the impoverished William Stillman – whatever his qualifications as a friend of Greek emancipation – a widower in poor health, with three young children and no income or prospects, 15 years older than Marie and a sceptic in religion, was a conspicuously unsuitable husband for the most beautiful young woman of her circle, the eldest daughter of a wealthy and highly regarded family. In a last anguished attempt to prevent the marriage he called for help from Dante Gabriel Rossetti. His letters are an eloquent mixture of flattery, affront and despair that compel sympathy for the bewildered father met with a resolute daughter. By the standards of the day, Michael Spartali had every reason to feel aggrieved by his daughter's defiance: "... as I understand my daughter is calling on you tomorrow to sit, it may be a favourable opportunity for your opening the subject of her unfortunate & misplaced attachment... it would be presumptuous in me to suggest the best way to succeed, as you are so superior in tact, fertility of resources, knowledge of the human heart, etc... I can only assure you that if the dreaded event takes place it will be her death & mine & perhaps my wife's, & that you are the only person on earth that can save her & prevent it ... she looks up to you (& rightly so) as a superior being & she so admired your character, your art & your poetry, that I dreamt once that you had thought her worthy to be your companion in life (Excuse pray the admission).

"You are the apostle of the purest poetic love & adoration & you know best how to make her understand its highest & purest aims... you might think it not out of place to add, that, if the love is to have reasonable chance of lasting, that the loved one should have some great distinguishing merit: either as a great Poet, Artist, Warrior, Statesman, Scientific Man, Historian, etc. or excel in Chivalry, Courage, Beauty, etc. But if the Sir Lancelot is a toothless commonplace everyday nonentity – as soon as the Spell is broken, he who was considered Sublime, becomes ridiculous & hateful & the disenchantment of a high spirited woman who has Sacrificed herself & everything else, duty, honour, parents, friends & defied public opinion – is terrible... You alone can save this poor, deluded girl. Pray keep this & the whole matter strictly entre nous & above all, do not take Mr Brown in to your counsel."[41] Madox Brown remained unforgiven for his earlier attempt to put Marie's case to her parents.

Without incurring the wrath that Madox Brown had so evidently brought upon himself, Rossetti succeeded at least in conveying to Spartali that, despite his understanding of a father's concern, he could not conscientiously attempt to persuade the lovers to renounce their chosen future together. Perhaps because Rossetti shared his own reservations – "...the ultimate result of their marriage is as anxious a problem," – Spartali's reply is noticeably free of the sterile blandishments of his first letter and is altogether more balanced in tone and genuinely respectful of a differing point of view: "I have to thank you for a most wonderfully kind letter... no one wants her to break her pledged word. If their best friends consider (as they do) the engagement an unfortunate one & cannot avoid deploring that she should not have chosen a more suitable man... it would only be doing both a real service to quietly discuss the matter, with each of them separately & put it in the proper light... the best advice his friends can render <u>him</u> personally is to prevent his marrying at all. He is ailing & not in a fit state of health & has not been for years (tho' he has been taking medicines & has been trying to recruit his health for 16 months)... let him take all the time necessary to obtain permanent good health & let him settle down to some permanent work before he thinks of marrying if they cannot be induced to give it up altogether)... this advice is quite consonant with your wise opinion of not interfering in any way in their most intense love for one another... be assured that if you can in any way either prevent or postpone their marriage, you will be their real friend & benefactor."[42]

Chapter Nine

Marriage

Michael Spartali's earnest wish was not granted: neither Marie's conviction nor her courage wavered. Marie Euphrosyne Spartali, spinster aged 27 of The Shrubbery, Clapham was married by special license to William James Stillman, widower aged 42 of 50 Sydney Street, Chelsea at Chelsea Register Office on 10 April 1871.

The couple spent their honeymoon at one of the Spartali properties on the Isle of Wight and returned, after three weeks, to London. William Michael Rossetti noted: "Stillman and his wife are back in London; she means to get over the two girls forthwith from America – the boy being too ill to be moved."[1] Russie's condition had deteriorated sharply in the six months since his father had left for England. The outlook worsened during May: "Stillman receives bad news of his boy in America: the hip-joint is ankylosed (sic) and likely to remain moveless for life; and his general condition is very low. Stillman proposes to go over shortly to America with his wife: not very sure whether they will return,"[2] Rossetti recorded towards the end of May that year. Marie and William sailed for Boston on 6 June in to an Atlantic storm, and they remained in the States for six weeks, visiting William's relatives and visiting the museums and galleries of Boston and New York, Marie for the first time. "I had a letter from Stillman loud in proclaiming his wife's enchantment with American people and things. They're coming back this month by sailing-ship. I suppose you heard of their dreadful journey out..."[3] Dante Rossetti wrote to William Bell Scott at the time.

A few days before the Stillmans sailed, Fairfax Murray accompanied William Morris to Faringdon, "lunched at Lechlade and drove over to Kelmscott to look at a house and returned in the evening."[4] Bowing to the inevitability of Janey's relationship with Rossetti but still anxious to avoid the mounting scandal surrounding her, Morris took a joint lease on Kelmscott Manor with Rossetti in order that Janey and Rossetti could plausibly be together without arousing comment, well away from the public gaze. The irony of Spartali's laboured compliments must have struck Dante Rossetti, the apostle of the purest poetic love & adoration.

"I find now that Brown has a very good opinion of Stillman in his matrimonial relation,"[5] William Michael Rossetti noted in June. He was to be disillusioned. As soon as they married William Stillman displayed the other face of his depressive tendencies by switching briskly from supplicant to dominant male, attempting to oust Ford Madox Brown. Talk of painting together before God ceased abruptly. He did little to encourage her painting and was, if anything, jealous of her acceptance by

Rossetti, Madox Brown and her circle of artist friends, of her social connections and perhaps even of her strength. He did, however, sit to Lucy Madox Brown for Cornelius Agrippa, the necromancer and savant in her picture *The Fair Geraldine*.[6] Ford Madox Brown had invested his hopes and his experience in the lovely pupil for whom he saw a glowing future – in which they both believed – as a painter. If ever he had pictured himself as her courtly artistic champion, the illusion had been shattered by the arrival of this alien and remote American.

Marie and William returned to England in the third week of August 1871; William Michael Rossetti noted in his diary: "Stillman and his wife have been back from America these last few days, bringing the three children over with them. Mrs Stillman is staying with her mother at Shanklin: her father ignores her, and, on meeting her lately at a railway station, gave no sign of recognition. Stillman is looking out for a house in which to settle. His son it is now thought may prove curable so far as the hip is concerned; but of late a serious enlargement of the liver has come on, causing some anxiety."[7] Stillman had had a wheeled wire cage constructed in America to surround Russie's lower body so that he could be moved about without causing him undue pain, and he carried him in his arms throughout the journey.[8] Christina Rossetti and her mother took great interest in his care, Christina taking him to the zoo, while Princess Mary Ouroussoff, the wife of the Russian diplomat in Rome, sent him squirrels in a cage to entertain him. William Stillman had now to weigh his opportunities for a successful career in America against the ties of Marie's home and background in London. Many of his contacts were in America but Europe seemed to offer more opportunity. He decided that his place, at least for the time being, was in England and the family moved to a rented house at 100 Clarendon Road, Notting Hill.

He soon came to the attention of the publishing fraternity in London. "Stillman has been writing to *The Times* etc., on the question of Anglo-American copyright. He considered the chief obstructives to be the English (rather than the American) publishers – who fear lest, if English authors are entitled to copyright in America, the American publishers would bid higher for their works than the English, and thus the latter would have to pay higher also than they now do,"[9] Rossetti recorded. In *The Times* of 27 September 1871 a letter signed 'A Traveller' and headed 'American Piracy' complained that American publishers reprinted English books without giving their authors any remuneration. With his habitual lack of thought for the consequences, William Stillman replied, that "i) American authors have no more rights in England, ii) that no English author recently published in America goes under the same arrangement as that made for American authors in England, and iii) English publishers chiefly oppose an Anglo-American copyright treaty because some authors would get considerably more for their work published in England than they do now." The controversy rumbled on; the immediate outcome of his entry in to the dispute was that William Stillman lost his regular freelance assignments with the *Pall Mall Gazette* and the *Daily News*, which

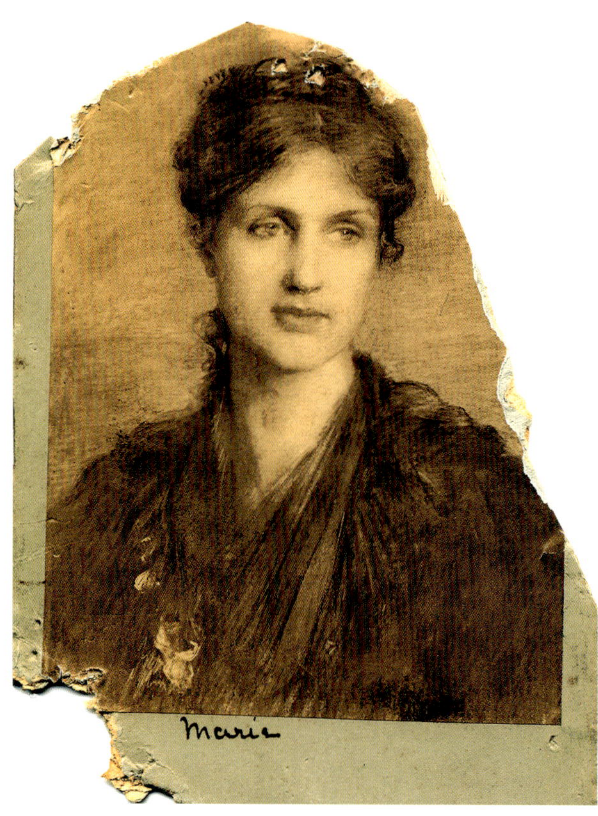

Plate 24
Marie Spartali
c.1872
Cabinet portrait photograph over-painted by hand and copied
Private Collection

published an editorial condemning him as 'The Friend of Piracy', and he was virtually blackballed by the English media. Stillman and Marie, who was now pregnant, reluctantly concluded that they must after all make their life in the United States.[10]

William Michael Rossetti took a sympathetic interest in their difficulties, noting in his diary: "Stillman feels that his campaign (in *The Times* etc) against English publishers, in their relation to authors and American publishers, has set the former class against him, and will trammel his career as a writer for publication here: and I fear this apprehension to be too well founded."[11] London's literary world was close-knit and influential.

William Stillman had returned to London with a letter of introduction from James Russell Lowell to Sir Leslie Stephen, the first editor of the *Dictionary of National Biography* to which he contributed over 400 entries. His London literary circle was the counterpart to Boston's Adirondack Club. Stephen was a familiar of Little Holland House; his wife, Hariet 'Minnie' Marian Thackeray was a daughter of the novelist William Makepeace Thackeray and a close friend of Marie Spartali. (On Minnie's death in November 1875, Stephen would marry Julia Duckworth, who would give him two daughters: Virginia Woolf and Vanessa Bell).

Stillman was undoubtedly unwise to be drawn in to the argument on American

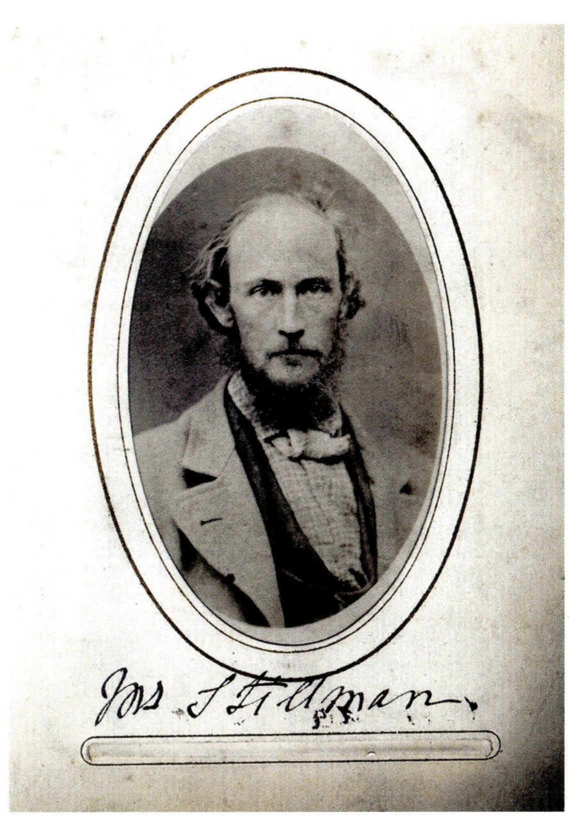

Plate 25
William James Stillman
1871
Carte de visite from Cathy Heuffer's photograph album, annotated in her hand

publishing and copyrights at a time when he might have counted on the Stephens's extensive contacts and goodwill. Ever the Yankee, pugnacious, opinionated and convinced of the rightness of his cause, he would never come to terms with the English distaste for those who rocked the boat. The door closed and was not re-opened to him for a decade.

Marie had another, more personal cause of anguish: "Stillman called... His wife found her mother, when she visited her last Friday painfully cold and unsympathetic; this had so distressing effect on poor Marie that she cried incessantly till past midnight. Stillman thinks that the father is now coercing the mother in to this harsh line of conduct, and that total alienation may probably ensue: I fear he has some good reason for his opinion,"[12] Rossetti recorded. Ten days later, Rossetti noted another crisis that had arisen within the Spartali family – Demetrius, Marie's brother had broken the news "... of a very dangerous illness of his sister Christina, now at Naples; Demetrius and his mother are starting off today to see her."[13] In the middle of December, William Michael Rossetti wrote in his diary: "Stillman called. His wife's sister Christina is again very ill (a cataleptic habit); and this and other matters weigh heavy on poor Marie, making her very miserable at times: her cough also persistent and severe. Mr Spartali, it seems, under these afflicting circumstances has written to Christina, and that quarrel may be considered in course of healing: I should hope that the quarrel with Marie, much less well-grounded in its essence, may also be healed at no distant date."[14]

This delphic understatement testifies to William Michael Rossetti's delicacy; almost certainly, he was aware that at 26, headstrong, unhappy Christina's "cataleptic habit" was a symptom of her acute dependency on chloral.[15] Demetrius Spartali brought Christina back to Paris where she and her husband Edmond Cahen d'Anvers had their principal residence. "I am unexpectedly obliged to go to Paris," Marie wrote to Madox Brown, "Christina is very unwell and we shall all be anxious if I am not there to try to amuse her."[16] Lodged in Paris, Marie wrote to Madox Brown once more from the Ave. des Princes, Boulogne sur Seine – the mansion in the Bois – about her work on *Antigone,* and about Paris: "My brother-in-law drove Strati[17] and me to Robinson's this afternoon where people dine up in the trees and draw things up in a basket... I quite understand that the place could be delightful in congenial company, but the fact of Mr Cahen's presence makes me feel as gay as if I were at a funeral – it was a different thing

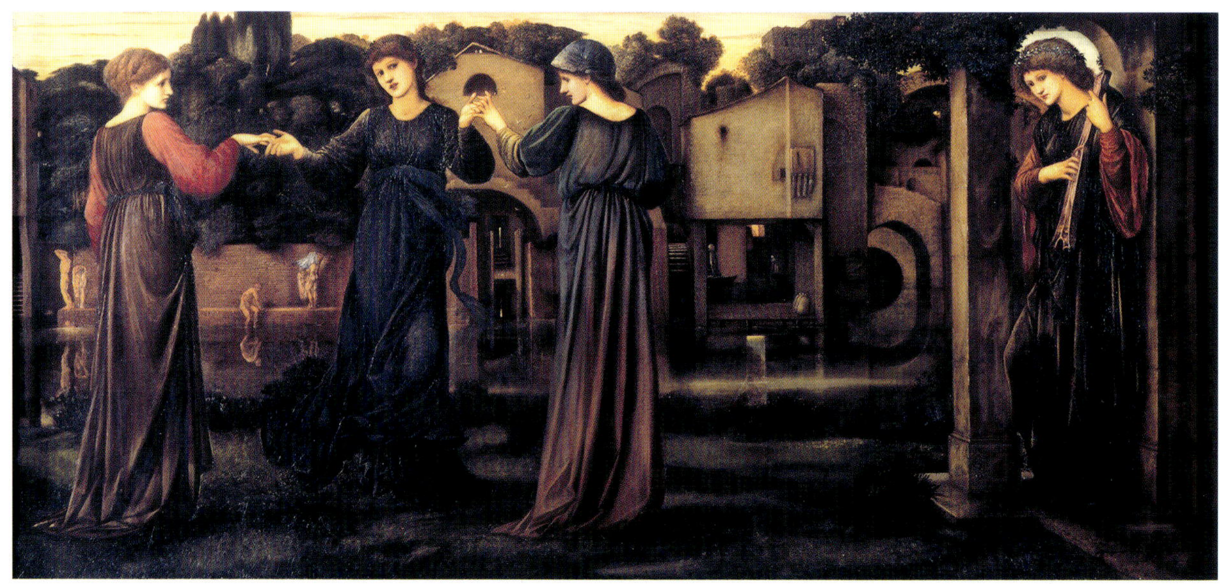

Plate 26
Edward Burne-Jones
1870-82
The Mill
Oil on canvas. 90.8 x 197.5 cm (35¾ x 77¾in)
Exhibited: Grosvenor Gallery, 1882; New Gallery, 1892 and 1898-99
Ionides Collection, Victoria & Albert Museum
The dancers are Aglaia Coronio, Maria Zambaco and (on the right) Marie Spartali, the Three Graces

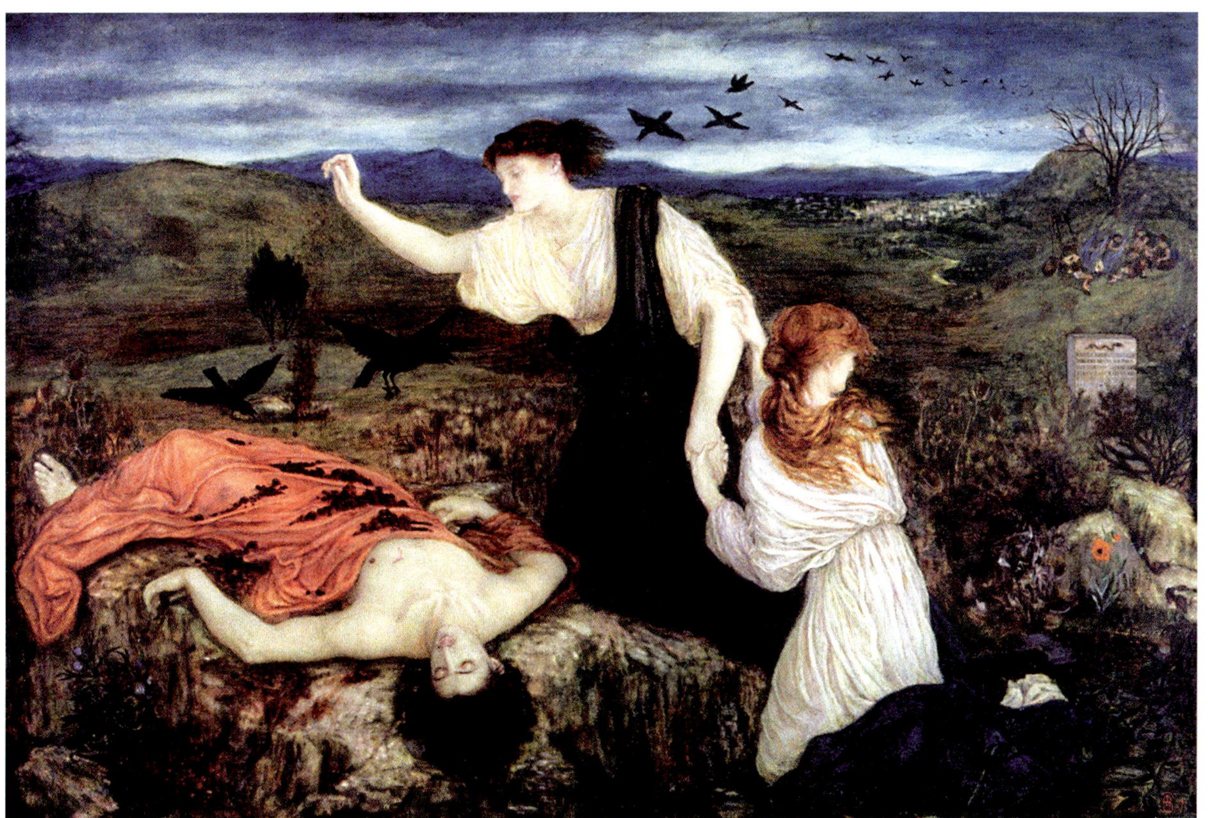

Plate 27
Marie Spartali Stillman
1871
Antigone and Ismene Burying their Brother Polynices on the Battlefield
Oil on canvas
Exhibited: Dudley, 1871
Simon Carter Gallery, Woodbridge, Suffolk

last year before we were related and I could laugh at him as much as I liked. Christina has been much better ever since last week, but I can scarcely believe the improvement will last, she has had so many relapses."[18] Marie was in the final weeks of her pregnancy but somehow she rose above the problems around her. In the closing days of 1871, William Michael Rossetti noted: "[The] youngest child Bella has shown some signs of brain-disease lately, which of course adds to his anxieties."[19] Marie Stillman's first year of marriage was indeed a testing time of unhappiness and uncertainty.

In spite of it all, it had been another productive year for the painters. Marie Spartali sat for Dante Gabriel Rossetti in February; this may have been for *The Bower Meadow*, which was painted during the Spring and Summer of 1872 at Kelmscott.[20] Marie Stillman is the model for the figure on the left, with Alexa Wilding to the right; her idealised likeness was afterwards completed from sketches that Rossetti made in 1870, while the background was itself painted years earlier and was originally intended for a Dante subject. Edward Burne-Jones, putting aside the depression that gripped him following his climactic affair with Maria Zambaco and the outcry over the nude male depicted in his *Phyllis and Demophoön* when it was exhibited at the Old Water Colour Society in the previous May, commenced *The Mill,* in which the Three Graces, Aglaia Coronio, Maria Zambaco and Marie Spartali were, it is said, the models for the dancers. The sketches at least were probably made in 1870. Marie herself exhibited *Antigone and Ismene Burying their Brother Polynices on the Battlefield* at the Dudley and painted a fine self-portrait.[21]

On 8 January 1872, her daughter Euphrosyne (Effie) Stillman was born after a difficult labour. Marie had hoped for a boy but Effie's birth brought reconciliation with her father closer, though William Michael Rossetti noted cautiously: "It is not even yet clear however that he will be on affectionate terms with her henceforward – still less with Stillman."[22] Her mother had already forgiven her. Writing to Madox Brown from Rylstone, in reply to his invitation to Cathy Madox Brown's wedding, Marie Stillman described the problems of employing a wet-nurse: "I have been very much agitated on little Effie's account – the nurse became so intolerably insolent that we had to accept her offer to leave on the spot so poor baby has to be weaned suddenly and Mama and I watch her night and day with intense anxiety, although she is very well and drinks her food out of a glass like a grown-up person."[23] William Michael Rossetti recorded in his diary that William Stillman had had some unusual experience of the effects of nurse-milk on infants: "He knew in Crete a girl who, having been reared by a goat, had the jumping habits of a goat, and was so shy and skittish as to fall in to convulsions on going in to company; also a young man reared by a cow that wholly consorted with cattle, and never with sheep."[24]

According to Rossetti's diary, towards the end of January, Marie's father had "now relented so far as to have two interviews with her, which passed off satisfactorily. Mrs Spartali is very urgent that the Stillmans should come and live in a vacant house abutting upon the 'Shrubbery' grounds. Stillman has written a conciliatory letter to Spartali, and there seems a fair prospect of his replying in such terms as to make some sort of intercourse between them possible henceforward. Assuming this, the projected house-taking will be effected – Mrs Spartali furnishing all or some of the funds for the requisite furniture, etc., Stillman in his letter expressly said that he would not under any circumstances expect nor even accept a dowry or any form of provision for Marie. Spartali is very kind to Stillman's two girls who have been staying at the 'Shrubbery' ever since the confinement began."[25]

By March, the Stillmans were comfortably installed at 8 Altenburg Gardens at the rear of the 'Shrubbery'. William Rossetti recorded: "Mrs Stillman seems quite reconciled to her father again... There seemed to be no strain or distance between them. Stillman tells me that he is as yet not on any confidential footing with Spartali; but they meet on terms of mutual tolerance and concession... Euphrosyne seems a more than commonly well-looking and well-grown infant... Stillman's book about Crete is all in print.[26] The English publishers are Smith & Elder... now the reverse of cordial towards him – the copyright controversy in which he lately took part having had the effect of seriously hampering their sale of advance sheets in America, as (following the advice given by Stillman) the authors themselves are now put in the way of securing the profits in this form."[27] Stillman later wrote that the four-year delay in publication resulted in an almost complete lack of interest in his contemporary account of a forgotten episode. Sadly, Russie had now developed dropsy and there seemed very little prospect for him save death after a lingering illness.

Dante Gabriel Rossetti suffered a complete mental breakdown in June 1872 as a consequence of Robert Buchanan's attacks on "the Fleshly School of Poetry" and his guilt over the removal of his *Poems* from Lizzie Siddal Rossetti's Highgate grave. His life was despaired of during the summer, but by September he was writing to his brother William Michael that, "wherever I can find peace, there I shall assuredly work; but all I now find by experience, depends on my not being deprived of the prospect of the society of the one necessary person..."[28] He returned to Kelmscott Manor on 25 September, accompanied by George Hake as his attendant. His return there was much resented by William Morris who told Aglaia Coronio: "Rossetti has set himself down at Kelmscott as if he never meant to go away; and not only does that keep me from that harbour of refuge (because it really is a farce our meeting when we can help it) but he also has all sorts of ways so unsympathetic with the sweet, simple old place..."[29] It was in this tense situation that William Michael Rossetti proposed to his brother that William Stillman should stay with him, perhaps to relieve George Hake. Memories of Stillman's regime at Scalands resolved Dante Rossetti firmly to dismiss any such suggestion: "I don't know that it would be much use Stillman's coming here just now. I am fully occupied and, seeing no-one, having nothing to talk about..."[30] he replied with greater decision than he had shown of late. He was in any case working hard and successfully; the months spent back at Kelmscott produced *La Ghirlandata* with Alexa Wilding as the model; and *Proserpine,* the reluctant wife of Pluto, Emperor of Hades, biting in to the pomegranate by which she forfeited her promised return to Earth, with Janey Morris as his sitter. The message of the picture once again is of a woman trapped in a loveless marriage.

Later in the year, Marie was once more obliged to return to Paris: "Christina is worse and still alone and I am the only person who has some influence over her..." She brought her sister back to The Shrubbery. William Stillman, she told Ford Madox Brown, was leaving shortly for the United States.[31] William Michael Rossetti noted in his diary: "Stillman finds no real outlet for his energies here and thinks he may soon be going to America, to see about a projected Journal of Art of which he would be appointed Editor. He would go alone but if the scheme takes shape would settle in America and take his wife and family over."[32] Michael Spartali settled £400 pa – some £15,000 today – on Marie and the editorial proposition lapsed. This income was to be the Stillmans's lifeline for the next 15 years.

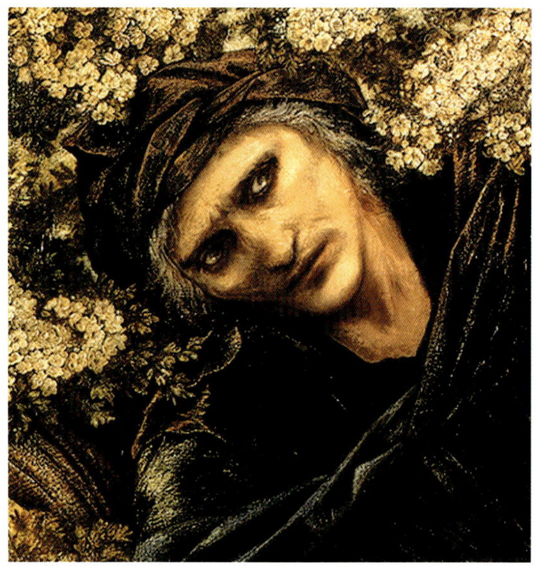

The New Year of 1873 opened to an uncertain outlook. William Michael Rossetti's diary records: "The infant Euphrosyne (just about a year old) recognised the other day, as 'Papa' and Mama', the crayon portraits that Gabriel did three years or so ago of the parents: this must I think be an act of considerable precocity... Stillman now mixed up in a row going on at the Photographic Society."[33] He seemed unable to touch anything without causing controversy, in this instance by involving himself without invitation in a dispute between two fellow members. Marie continued to be preoccupied with her sister: "Christina takes up a great part of my afternoons and my baby has been unwell..."[34] she told Madox Brown; her painting suffered.

Early in the year, William Stillman obtained a freelance assignment to cover the American section of the international Vienna Exhibition for the *New York Tribune*. He soon uncovered evidence of corruption in the United States Commission in awarding concessions, which the *Tribune,* and their competitors, the *Herald,* were reluctant to publish. Stillman instead exposed the scandal through diplomatic channels and the entire Commission was dismissed. Recognising Stillman's resourceful reporting, the *Herald* offered him a permanent appointment as their correspondent in Europe. Characteristically, he adopted a moral tone and refused; he was, he said, employed by the *Tribune.* The *Tribune* dispensed with his services.

Towards the end of July 1873, when William had returned to England, a sudden squall blew up between Marie Stillman and Ford Madox Brown. Since the birth of Effie, Madox Brown had been in the habit of making regular visits to the Shrubbery to continue Marie's instruction and advise her on the progress of her work; she remained as serious in her intention to paint professionally as she had been before her marriage. Without warning, Marie informed Madox Brown that she must give up painting for a while because of her health. The prickly Madox Brown interpreted this as a deliberate snub from William Stillman; it is hard to disagree. The latent dislike between them flared briefly. Madox Brown held back for some days before he wrote to Marie: "I need scarcely tell you I was rather taken aback by your informing me the other day that you were considered too weak to paint now & that moreover you and your husband agreed in thinking that my visits to Clapham were a sacrifice in time such as you could no longer acquiesce in... my object in writing is not to urge you in opposition to the wishes of your husband... as I may have misunderstood you and you may have misunderstood me, I think it right to make it clear that I have never considered attending to your painting as a trouble and have never wished it to be thought so... I shall continue to consider your work in my care

Opposite: **Plate 28A**
Detail from Edward Burne-Jones's *The Beguiling of Merlin* for which William James Stillman was his model

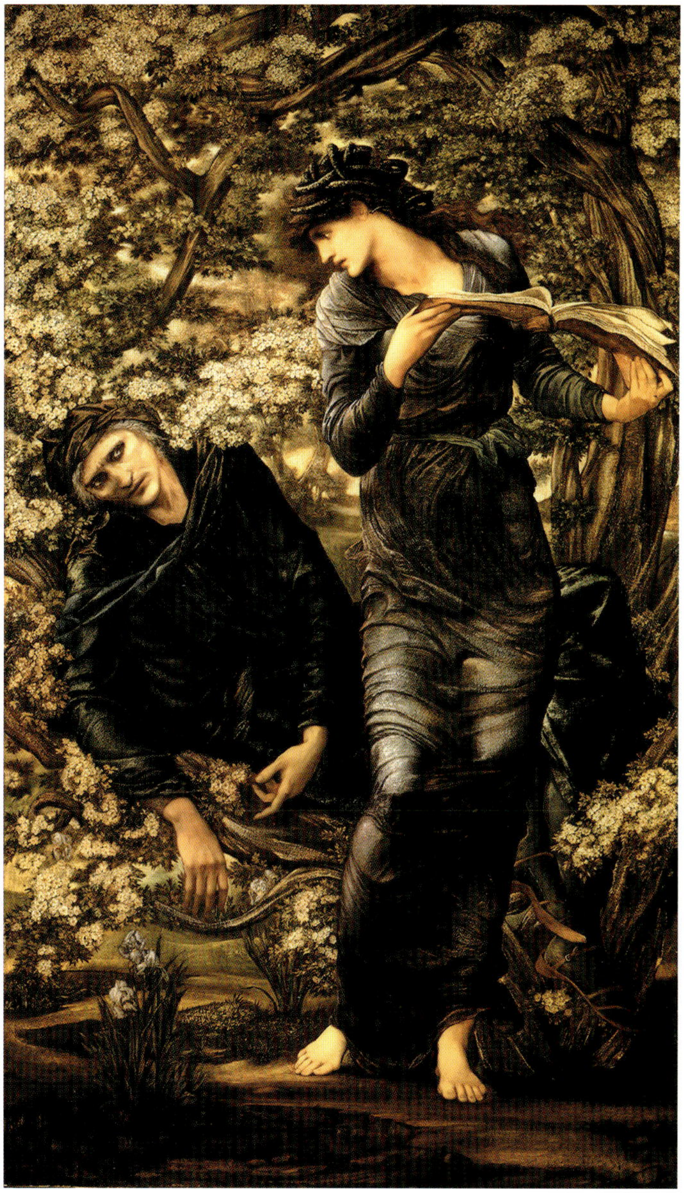

Plate 28
Edward Burne-Jones
1873-4
The Beguiling of Merlin
Oil on canvas. 186 x 111 cm (73¼ x 43¾in)
Exhibited: Grosvenor Gallery, 1877;
Paris Exposition Universelle, 1878;
New Gallery, 1892 and 1898
National Museums, Liverpool (Lady Lever Art Gallery)

(in the way best suited to our mutual convenience) whenever you may think it fit to resume it. Remember me to your husband."[35] Marie Stillman hurried to mollify his feelings: "I must have explained myself very awkwardly... I have not the slightest intention of giving up painting – what I meant to say was that for a few weeks my husband wishes me to rest because after working a very short time my eyes see nothing distinctly and my head swims, and the consequence is that what I paint carefully one day I have to wash out the next, and this makes me quite dispirited and unhappy, and so nervous that I am unable to do anything – this has been the case while I have been painting Christina and you see the result is by no means satisfactory. I have felt so anxious all summer about my sister that I long for a change of scene, and it is possible that William will take me with him to Antwerp when Christina leaves England... what I wished to say about coming to Clapham was that we both feel it is too great a sacrifice of time on your part."[36]

Only three years before, William Stillman had written lyrically of a life in which they would paint side by side. Never from the day they married had reality matched this vision. Stillman resented the continuing influence of Ford Madox Brown over his wife's work and her continued tutelage. First among the causes must have been a strong measure of jealousy. On a personal level, Stillman resented the deep affection in which Dante Gabriel Rossetti and Madox Brown continued to hold his wife, while extending him a more formal friendship as her spouse. Further, he deeply disapproved of Rossetti's morals, of Morris's acquiescence in his relationship with Janey, and of Ned Jones and Maria Zambaco – a genuinely principled if somewhat priggish stand that embraced the whole circle and further contributed to his alienation. He would dearly have liked Marie to turn her back on her closest friends. Whilst she continued to develop her creative talent and gain public recognition, he was in poor financial straits, unable to make headway as a journalist in the arts, or as an author; while his aptitude as a painter had been severely checked by Ruskin's criticism and his own realisation of the limits of his skill. He did nevertheless make some effort to pick up the brush once more, one example being his *English Wild Flowers*,[37] which is inscribed 'WJS to Mrs WPG 1876'. (William Stillman was in the Balkans for the greater part of that year, and it is likely that the work dates from 1873. 'Mrs WPG' was the former Lucy McKim, the wife of his friend Wendell Phillips Garrison.)

Edward Burne-Jones resumed his painting *Merlin and Nimuë* for Leyland after a problem in an earlier version – he would push his materials beyond their indicated uses to create stunning but often unstable effects; as Robertson commented: "Like the old man of Thermopolye, who never did *anything* properly, whether working in oil, in water colour in pastel or pure line, he appeared willfully to ignore the possibilities of his medium and put it to uses for which it was never intended... when he turned to oil he would shun the richness of *impasto*, drawing thin glazes over careful drawings heightened in white; if he used pastel, it was to imitate oil."[38] Unable to find a suitable model for the magician Merlin he consulted Rossetti who recommended William Stillman's battered countenance. "I really think that Stillman would do for me, but how can I ask him! ... I don't think I *can* ask him, knowing him so little and the pose being torture," Burne-Jones replied.[39] Nevertheless, it is William Stillman's agonised gaze that looks up at Maria Zambaco's beautiful likeness in the face of Nimuë. The picture was an outstanding and acclaimed exhibit at the Grosvenor Gallery in 1877.

Despite the burden of looking after her sister, Marie managed to find some time to paint: "If you can come, any day will suit me if you can let me know what time. I am often with Christina and very seldom out in town," she told Madox Brown.[40] James Abbott McNeill Whistler's first one-man show in London opened at the Pall Mall Galleries in June 1874. Marie Stillman described the setting: "The walls were grey, the pictures were well spaced, there were palms and flowers, blue pots and bronzes, and it

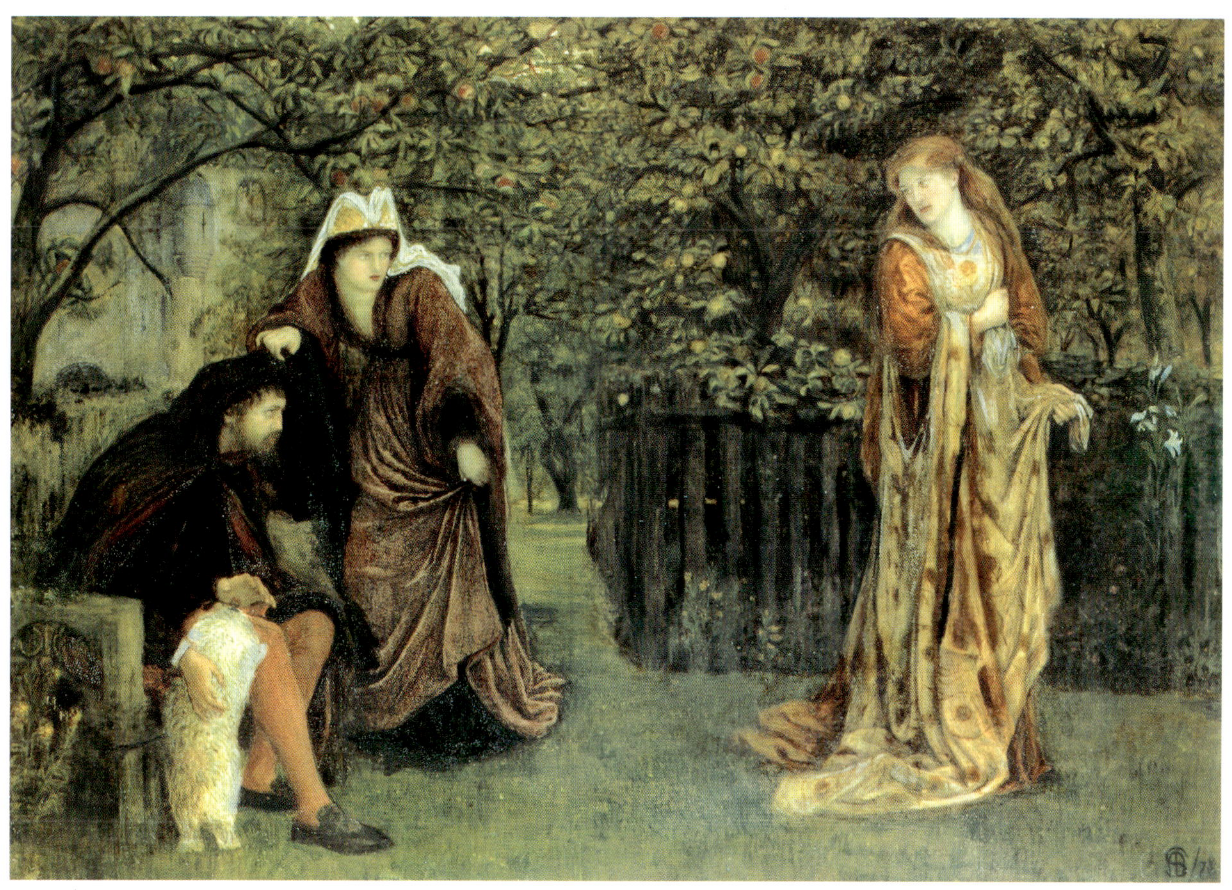

Plate 29
Marie Spartali Stillman
1873
Sir Tristram and La Belle Iseult
Watercolour heightened with bodycolour. 53 x 76 cm (20 9/10 x x29 9/10in)
Exhibited: Royal Academy, 1873; Philadelphia Centennial, 1876; Liverpool, 1877
Private Collection

was all very beautiful." It was, she said, "The first time in London that anyone had ventured to show that a picture exhibition could be beautifully arranged." Standing out from its muted surroundings was Christina's portrait, *La Princesse du Pays de la Porcelaine.*[41]

Towards the end of July, William Stillman sailed once more for America, taking Russie with him in a desperate last attempt to restore his strength. John Marshall[42] had proposed to operate to free the joint but the boy was now too ill to risk surgery without a significant improvement in his general condition. Brave, unlucky Russie was eager to seize the chance of release from the continual pain of his disease; so it was decided that he should spend the summer gaining strength in the sun and fresh air of Maine before the operation. By October it was evident that there would be no improvement. Back in Clapham in December 1874, Stillman wrote to Ruskin; "... it is sad in what it tells me about your poor son..." Ruskin replied and, suddenly distracted by thoughts of Rose La Touche, "There are many of them [friends] who

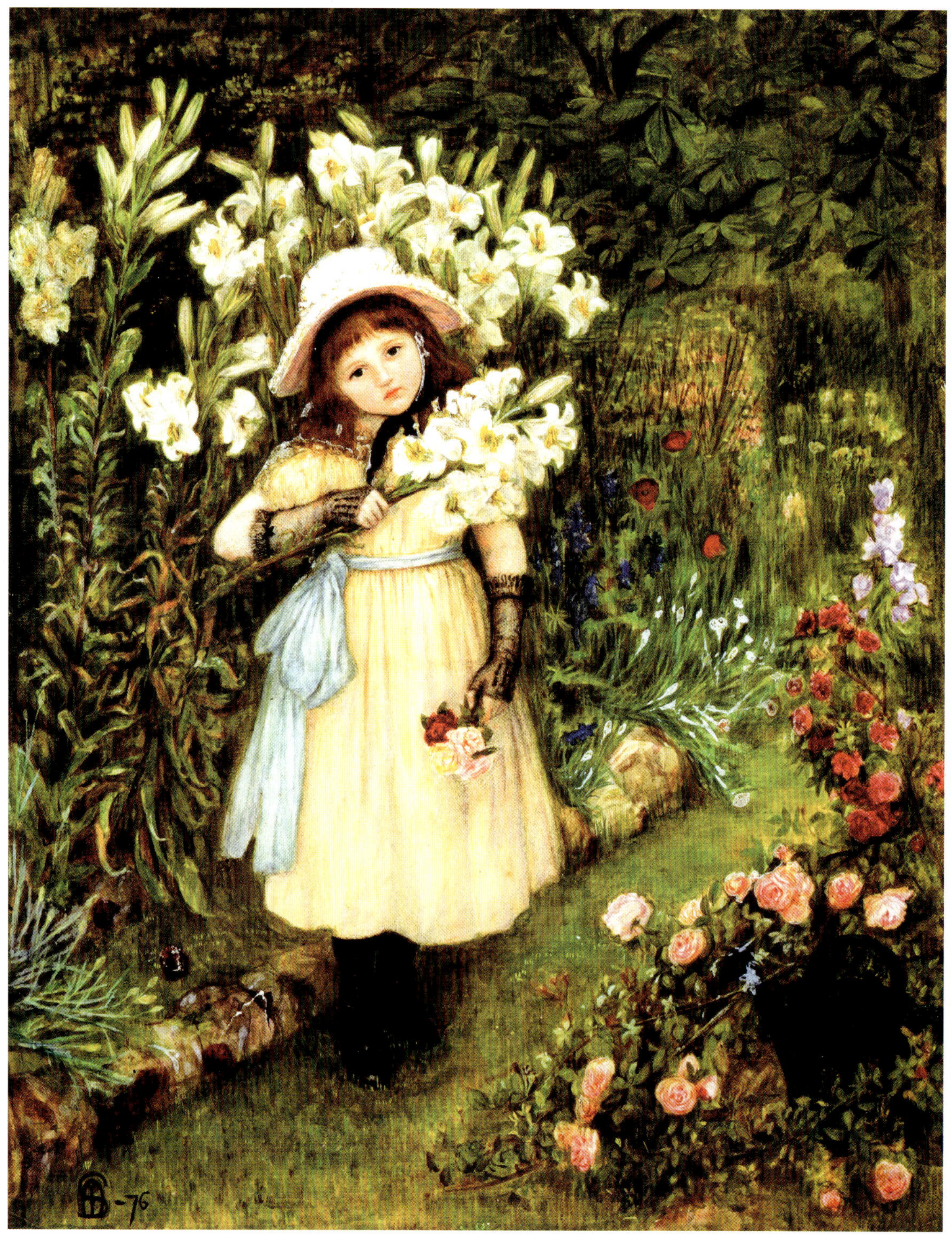

Plate 30
Marie Spartali Stillman
1876
Consider the Lilies - portrait of Effie Stillman, 3
Watercolour and bodycolour heightened with gum arabic. 47 x 36.8 cm (18½ x 14½in)
Exhibited: Royal Academy, 1876; Exposition Universelle, Paris, 1878
Private Collection

say pleasant things to me and when I am gone, pity me for a madman."[43]

While he was in the United States, Stillman published an American edition of his book *The Cretan Insurrection,* and an article in *Atlantic Monthly* entitled *Two European Schools of Design,*[44] in which he drew an unfavourable comparison between the aims and teaching methods of the Government Schools of Design, and in particular that attached to the South Kensington Museum, with the Academy school in Antwerp (where Madox Brown had once been a pupil). He was in Montenegro when the controversy erupted in London the following year. Marie was left to smooth ruffled feathers: "... He did not of course intend to reflect on Poynter who did not institute the SKM system."

Early in 1875 it became clear that Russie's end must be near. Michael Spartali offered William Stillman a cottage on his estates on the Isle of Wight where they might share Russie's last days in privacy and quiet. Marie remained at Altenburg Gardens preparing her pictures for exhibition. Stillman and his boy put up for a few days in a private hotel until the house could be readied. There Russie developed convulsions, and with his death clearly a matter of days or even hours, Stillman took him in his arms by train the twelve or so miles to the Spartalis's house. He died there almost as they arrived, on 3 March 1875 and he was buried at Arreton, near Newport on the island. "I have never been able to find a consolation for that loss, for it carried with it the future and its best dreams," Stillman wrote in the last year of his life.

In the spring Marie Stillman exhibited *Elaine Finding Sir Lancelot Disguised as a Fool* at the Dudley, together with several flower pieces and a number of her works were shown at the American Society of Painters in Water Color exhibition "Galaxy", at the National Academy in New York. Ellen Clayton, the authoress, asked her for information to include in a new book, *English Women Artists.* Marie's innate reserve came immediately to the fore: "Perhaps she might be inclined to mention my work critically without touching on personal details – I think it bad taste to write of living people personally even when remarkable, and the very little success I have had makes it ridiculous to do so," she wrote, asking advice of Madox Brown.[45] The anodyne critical comments published next year scarcely justified her concern. "It is a little strange and somewhat mortifying to find that so few of our lady artists are of direct English descent..." Clayton began.

The aimlessness and uncertainty of William Stillman's life, crushed by the death of Russie and with no regular income since his marriage, continued to exasperate his father-in-law. Taking matters in to his own hands Michael Spartali arranged an interview for him with John Delane, editor of *The Times* from 1841 to 1877. Delane had allowed his personal hopes of keeping England out of any involvement in the simmering conflict in the Balkans to dull his journalistic antennae, and the rival *Daily News* was running regular reports on preparations for war, days ahead of *The Times*. In May 1876, Murad V deposed his uncle, the Ottoman Sultan Abdul Aziz, and was in turn ousted three months later by his younger brother Abdul Hamid II; the turmoil in Istanbul was the signal for a Bulgarian uprising against their Turkish overlords, much as the Cretans had risen 10 years before. In June, Serbia declared war on Turkey and, in July, Montenegro followed.

The Times was in urgent need of able representation on the battlefield. Delane offered Stillman an open-ended freelance assignment to report on the war from Herzegovina. Any correspondence printed would be paid by *The Times*. Michael Spartali undertook the payment of Stillman's travel expenses, and it is not difficult to imagine a degree of satisfaction on his part when the arrangement was concluded. Stillman, as was usual following crises, took to his bed. "...plans uncertain on account of William who is unwell. He has been persuaded to go abroad and will probably go to Herzegovina,"[46] Marie wrote to Madox Brown. Once there "[Stillman] proved able and trustworthy... beginning a long service to *The Times*, [which] despite bouts of ill-health brought many abuses to light and guided public opinion."[47]

William had left London in August 1875 for Trieste and travelled by sea and on horseback to Cetinje close to the Adriatic coast of Montenegro. He was to spend in all nearly three years in the Balkans reporting for *The Times*, writing occasional pieces for the *New York Herald,* and returning to London during lulls in the fighting; this was the first of a series of long absences from Marie and his children. Stillman's account of his travels, often in conditions of great personal danger, shows him to be wholly without fear of what might befall him, innocent of false modesty and uncompromising in his opinions.

In little more than four years since her marriage, Marie Spartali Stillman had seen the promises of a joyous union in which they "should both do so much more and so much better work together, and have the happiness thrown in"[48] to be hollow in the event. She had instead found her friendships criticized and, at a low point, she had been pressed to give up her painting for a time. She had endured the rejection of her father and mother and won back their love. Stillman having no regular income, she depended on the financial support of her father and the proceeds from the sale of her paintings, managing her family of six in a house her father had had to provide, just as he had forewarned her.

Despite these pressing difficulties she had borne a lovely daughter, cared for the dying Russie and secured the lasting deep affection of her three remaining step-children, often alone; her husband had been out of the country for more than a year of the four they had been married. Although he would now be absent for the greater part of another three years, much of which she would spend isolated on the Isle of Wight with only the three small children for company, there is no hint of any disillusion in her choice of marriage partner or her situation, for example, in the detailed record of William Michael Rossetti's diaries or her letters to Madox Brown. It is testament to her remarkable strength of character that she continued to paint and pursue the undeviating path that she had set her heart and mind to ten years earlier. "Of all the women who elicited Gabriel's admiration, Marie Spartali was probably the most gifted intellectually. Of an ancient and noble race, austere, virtuous and fearless, she was not lacking in a caustic wit and a sharp tongue..."[49] Her dedication was her refuge and her salvation.

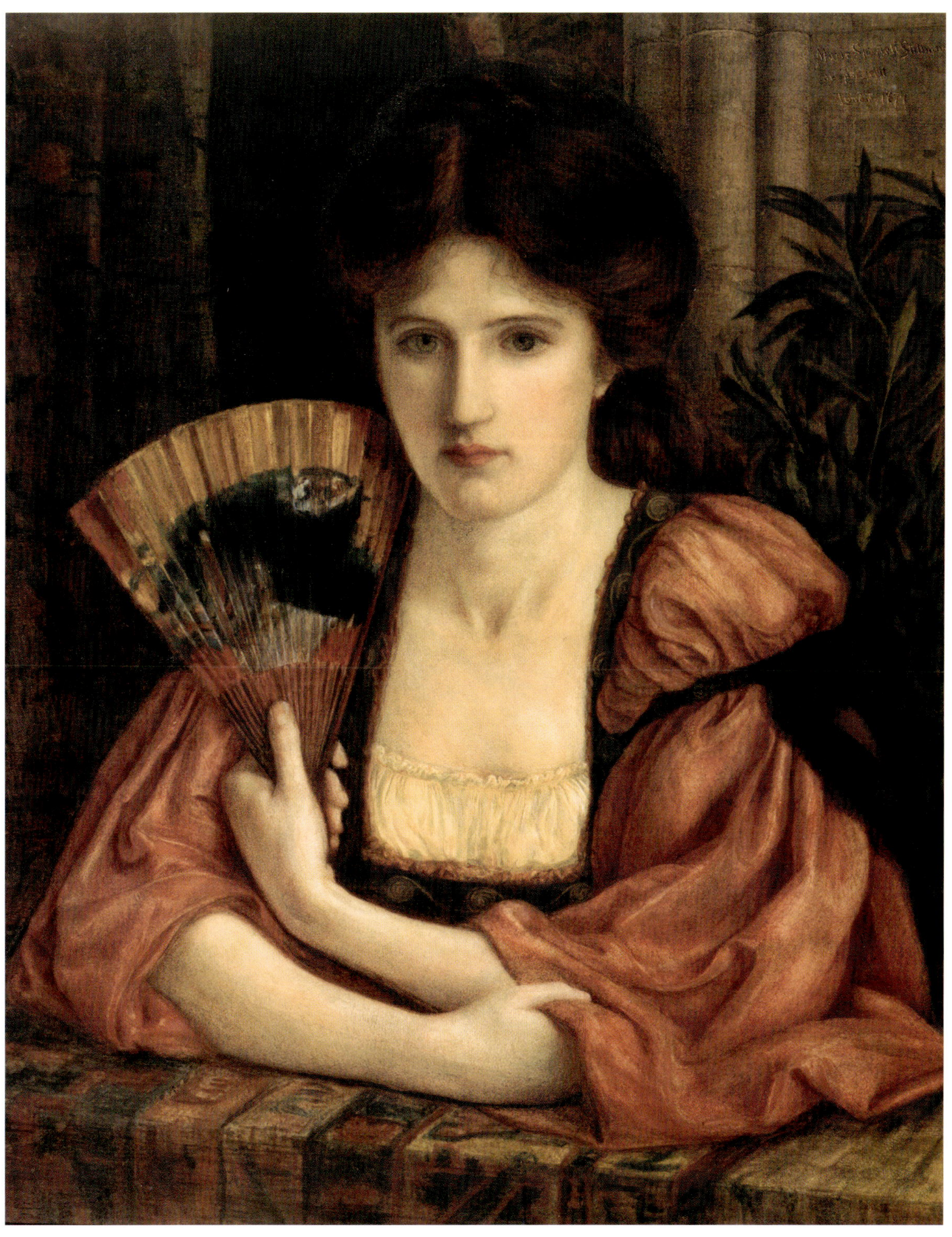

Plate 31

Marie Spartali Stillman

1874

Self Portrait

Watercolour on paper. 65 x 51 cm (25⅝ x 20⅛in)

Courtesy of The Maas Gallery, London; Bridgeman Art Library

Chapter Ten

Corfu

William Michael Rossetti married Lucy Madox Brown on 31 March 1874. Lucy was 32, William Michael was 46. Olivia Frances Madox Rossetti, Lucy and William Michael Rossetti's first child, was born in September 1875. Marie Stillman wrote to Ford Madox Brown, who was finishing *Rose d'Infante,* his portrait of Effie: "I am glad to hear that Lucy is progressing favourably – neither you nor Mr Rossetti offer any description of the baby; so as I am not an enthusiast for that early stage I shall suppose it to be somewhat monotonous in colour and uncertain in outline. William has left Montenegro and is going to Herzegovina for a few days – there is no fighting in Montenegro-Servia so he will then go to Olympia where some Germans are fighting. This last few weeks with Christina have been most trying as she cannot make up her mind what she wishes or means to do, and one goes through the most intense excitement day after day all for nothing. She has just made up her mind to go to Rome with her husband who is there now..."[1] "I have no fixed plans as yet as I hear very little of William who is travelling about in Montenegro, and do not know if he thinks the war will last long or what he wishes to do..." Marie wrote to Emma Madox Brown.[2]

In September the Serbs were routed at Alexinatz and the Bulgarian insurrection was crushed: Montenegro, a mountain Principality ruled by the 25-year-old Nicholas I, Prince of Tsrnogorsk, became the last Balkan country to remain in the fighting. An armistice was concluded in October. Stillman returned to London at Christmas, via Venice, which he later recalled in his autobiography: "I beheld the city for the first time early in the morning as we were coming by boat from Trieste. Accustomed as I was to the colours of Turner, it seemed to me that what I was seeing from the ship was the ghost of Venice, pale, faint, in faded colours which were hints only of the colours of Turner. But it was still beautiful in its decline, with an impression more moving than that which the explosive palette of the great English painter gave it. My wife was waiting for me at the ship, and we went home, making short stops because I was too exhausted to endure a long railway journey."[3] They spent the following three months together on the Isle of Wight. William Stillman's longer-term plans for his family remained unclear. Marie as usual confided in Ford Madox Brown, Christina was ill in Paris but intending to go on to Rome: "You do not say whether you will require any more sittings for Effie... we may all go to Florence a little later on. William is busy with a book on the insurrection and innumerable letters to the newspapers on the subject. We are always in a state of excitement over the newspapers tho' I am glad not to be obliged to read The Times assiduously now..."[4]

In March 1877 Stillman made a brief trip to London for consultations with *The Times*; William Michael Rossetti recorded in his diary: "Stillman called at Somerset House. He expects to be off again in a day or two as Times correspondent to Montenegro and to be away perhaps a year..."[5] In April Russia, taking advantage of the distracted situation of the Turks – who were weakened despite their recent successes – declared war and marched in to Bulgaria. Disraeli's administration sided with the Turks because Russian success in the Balkans might threaten Britain's trade routes to India by way of the Suez Canal, which he had secured in November 1875 by borrowing £4 million overnight from the Rothschilds. Being of Jewish parentage, Disraeli was also profoundly offended by pogroms in Russia. The Eastern Question was a greatly divisive issue: of the Stillman's many friends William Morris, Edward Burne-Jones and many like them took Russia's part with the aim of avoiding Britain's being drawn in to the conflict; William Morris became Treasurer of the opposition Eastern Question Association; the evolutionist Charles Darwin, John Ruskin, W T Stead (the campaigning editor of the *Northern Echo*), Robert Browning and Anthony Trollope were all among the founders. Gladstone came out of retirement to add his weight in opposition to Disraeli's policy.

In Montenegro, Nicholas I continued the fight against the Turks from his mountain Principality and Russian troops joined his outnumbered force. William Stillman, now *The Times'* Special Correspondent (but still freelance), reached Montenegro in May, writing to Marie from the coast before joining the Prince's army once more: "I don't suppose that I shall send or receive letters henceforth with any kind of regularity... [Lowell] is right in a limited sense about my liking to rough it – I do, only not too much and for a few weeks at a time. I stand the roughing it here very well so far, though I fear I am looking like a wild man and very brown – I begin to realise that I am getting old, dear, and to think it a great shame that your life should be wasted on such a wreck as I am... if only I could be sure to keep you happy as long as you live or even as long as I live I shouldn't so much regret the fruitlessness of my life... but sometimes I am much saddened by a fear that I rather marred your life than otherwise & that perhaps if you had not seen me you might have found a truer life elsewhere."[6] With that he once more took the dangerous trail high in to the mountains, among people who had never seen a foreigner and without a word of their language, to Nicsic where the retreating Turkish army were under siege from Russian and Montenegrin troops. They were routed in the subsequent battle during which Stillman came under fire.

It was another lonely summer for Marie Stillman, with three small girls to care for. Most of it she spent on the Isle of Wight. William Stillman too found time weighing heavily on him. Early in July he wrote to W J Stebbing, the Manager of *The Times*, "...the more I see of the people the more I am convinced that there might be the making of a people which would rally round it the whole south Slav race but the more I see of the Prince in trying times and situations the more I feel that he is utterly wanting in the qualities of organiser and discipliner necessary to educate a people..."[7] In the autumn he again brought up the question of his return, discussing whether the winter suspension of hostilities would allow "even the temporary throwing off the mantle", complaining about the effect of the climate on his rheumatism, the monotony of the same sphere for two years and the consequent strain on his sympathies. He had been in the Balkans for 18 months with only one short break. He wanted to be nearer to his family and his thoughts turned to their leaving England for somewhere closer to his accreditation and further from Marie's watchful parents. "I cannot understand yet where we are going as William sends a fresh suggestion in every letter and leaves it to me now and then. I think it will be Corfu after all tho' for many reasons I should prefer Florence, but as William would like to be near Albania & Montenegro it might be too far and he takes so lively an interest in the war it would be unfair to keep him away,"[8] she told Madox Brown.

Marie was back at the Shrubbery in September and Dante Gabriel Rossetti quickly took advantage of her return, getting her to sit for *A Vision of Fiammetta*; "The first thing I began from Mrs Stillman," he told his brother William.[9] The question of the Stillmans's domicile was settled. Writing to Janey Morris who was spending the winter with her daughters on the Italian Riviera at Oneglia, Dante Gabriel Rossetti related the progress of his work and kept up the flow of incident to amuse her: "I have been very busy beginning a picture from Mrs. Stillman, as she is on the point of leaving England for the winter. Her husband is to meet her and the children at Turin, and they are to proceed to Corfu for the winter. I have misgivings that they will settle there. I am becoming most unfortunate in my models. She is the only person who wd in any degree have suited me for ideal subjects now that you can hardly be hoped for as a sitter; and now she must needs take herself off, with the best will in the world to sit if

---

Plate 32
Dante Gabriel Rossetti
1878
A Vision of Fiammetta
Oil on canvas. 146 x 88.9 cm (57½ x 35in)
Exhibited: Royal Institute, Manchester, 1882; Rossetti Exhibition RA, 1883; Guildhall Art Gallery, 1897; New Gallery, 1897; Royal Academy, 2003
Courtesy of the Andrew Lloyd Webber Art Foundation

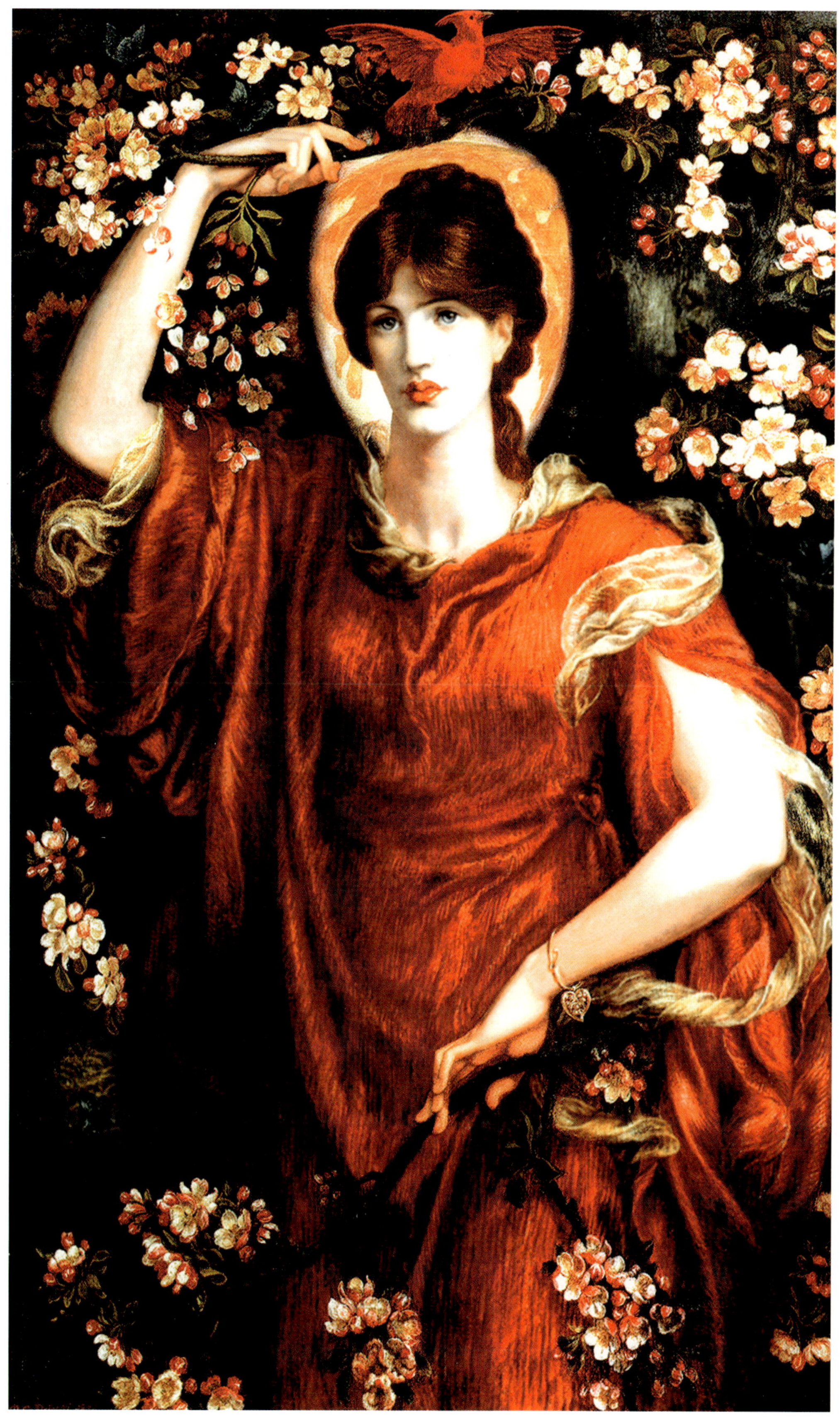

she were only staying. I have finished the head of the picture – Fiammetta, from Boccaccio's sonnet on his last sight of her – and it is far better than I ever painted from anyone but yourself. She has given me the sittings most kindly under great difficulties, her own little girl having had an accident and broken her collar-bone: however it is going on quite well... Bye the bye, Mrs Stillman told me of calling in Paris on poor Mary Z. who it seems must be dying of consumption. She was very pale, very ill-dressed, and (added Mrs S.) 'she must be very ill, for her hair was quite black.'"[10]

A few days before Christmas Rossetti wrote again: "I saw the last of Mrs Stillman on Monday. She came here with the three girls and was to start next day for Turin where Stillman is to meet them. He must have had a narrow escape when the Prince of Montenegro's house was blown up – he is almost always there – and would probably have lost his life if he had not already started on his way... I was most charmed with little Effie who will be extremely like her mother, she is a charming, dreamy looking girl, almost as tall as Mrs Stillman now: and Bella is engaging through her extreme intelligence, and comely though the only one of the three who is not beautiful. They all draw and design no end, Lisa has quite settled to be an artist; she is a lovely and lovable creature... [Mrs Stillman] showed me two of her latest watercolour pictures – life-sized half figures with a good deal of elaborate and sometimes excellent imitative painting in the floral accessories but, I am sorry to say, I found them disappointing, they are not nearly as good in the higher sense as some things she did before her marriage."[11]

Rossetti's creative engagement with his models is nowhere more clearly stated than in this letter to Janey: "I have hung the drawings of you in the studio now and finished the one of Pandora which before looked undraped. I want to start an important picture of this, full length to the feet, as soon as possible. It has certainly occurred to me sometimes to try and work out some of these drawings as pictures, using any nature at hand for the mere surface and light and shade of the flesh and adhering in all respects to the drawing as a guide. All my models of value – to wit, 2 only, yourself and Marie S. – are leaving me in the lurch, and I may be forced on this alternative. Pictures from common models people will not buy from me..."

William Stillman was met by Marie and his family, and they travelled on together to Corfu where he had finally decided they would spend the rest of the winter. She had few ties to keep her in England. In six years of married life she had been denied a home of her own, and she wanted to put down roots for her family. For William Stillman, a home was an obligation that he had never previously undertaken; whether in his parents' house, at boarding school, at University, in the backwoods and lakes of the Adirondacks, with the Macks, in Paris, Budapest, Vienna, Rome, Crete, London or Montenegro, he had always been a guest, a tenant, a camper or a lodger, a life-time habit of 50 years of mostly solitary existence, living within himself; almost six months more would pass before the Stillmans at last set up house in Florence.

The Russo-Turkish War ended. On the first day of the New Year 1878, Prince Nicholas I decorated William Stillman with the Order 3rd Degree of Prince Danil I, the highest civilian honour he could confer, for his services to Montenegro. An armistice was signed at the end of January and, on 15 February 1878, a British Fleet anchored in the Sea of Marmora opposite the Golden Horn to focus the attention of the Sublime Porte on the decisions of the Great Powers. In March the Treaty of San Stefano gave independence to Romania, Serbia and Montenegro; and the Congress of Berlin in July further dismembered the Ottoman Empire. With the peace, William Stillman was once more without regular employment. He had once again displayed his capacity for vivid and influential reporting, his resourcefulness, his fierce discrimination against injustice; and no less, his isolated irresponsibility, placing himself in great danger without question or consideration of his family. This was Stillman the solitary man, who enjoyed testing his will against hardship, physical danger and poor health. Motivated perhaps by his need to earn his family's bread, he was driven by the same self-absorption in a search for his inner self that had marked his solitary days in the Adirondacks twenty years before.

Dante Gabriel Rossetti had still heard nothing of Marie by the end of February 1878, as he wrote to Janey who was staying with the Howards in Oneglia: "... I also am anxious about Mrs Stillman. She has never written to me but did answer a letter of Lucy's. She was then at Corfu after spending some time in Venice and elsewhere. Her husband is reported very well. I cannot help fearing that there is every risk of her being integrated in to a harem along with the 2 girls and the baby who wd be brought up as a first-class odalisque."[12]

In April Marie Stillman found time to write: "I have been meaning to write to you for weeks but our plans have been so uncertain. I have been feeling so very weak and unwell... people here do not remember so severe a winter. It is only quite lately that I have begun to paint again <u>in</u>doors – there are very lovely landscapes here with blue and purple distances of every depth and colour, grey olive plantations and orange groves – I shall be very sorry to go away with no sketches or studies. I shall have no pictures at the Grosvenor this year – I worked so continuously at the picture I hoped to send, but at the last before leaving England Mr Brown advised me to give it up for this year... we have been having a good deal of political excitement here and an ill-managed insurrection in Epirus which was organised in Corfu. I was so glad to leave the town and come with my cousins Peter and Ralou Laskarides and her husband to Gasturi, a little village on a hill, where all is quiet and the air is pure... William has been absent in Dalmatia but is now here..."[13]

When the Stillmans moved to Florence at the end of April, Marie was again pregnant. William took up painting once more; but he soon admitted to himself that "the pencil found less attraction than the pen".[14] He had finally resolved the conflict between painting and writing as a livelihood.

Chapter Eleven

Florence 1878-1883

Florence was the city most closely associated with the artists and poets of the early Renaissance, who were dear to Marie's heart; it was convenient too for William Stillman's freelance work, whether on Roman and Greek antiquities or the political situation in Greece and the Balkans. Christina, who divided her days in an unhappy marriage between great houses in Paris and Rome, was now frequently under Marie's care and Florence was more easily accessible.

There were problems at first, as Marie Stillman described to Ford Madox Brown from their apartment at 56 Vialle Principessa Margherita: "We have been here more than three months but it seems hardly possible to realise the fact as we have been so constantly and entirely occupied with Christina... (she) has been very ill and has required the constant attendance of someone having some kind of authority over her and I was chosen as the most likely to succeed in breaking her of taking chloral – by constant watchfulness and ruse I was partly successful but the heat of Florence was too great for her and she left on Friday with William who will see her as far as Paris. William went the rounds of the studios with his Californian brother and strongly advised me to refrain from indulging my curiosity... Effie has been improving in appearance lately and promises to be a good model for me in time, Lisa has fortunately stopped growing and Bella has caught all the Italian gesticulation without obtaining any fluency in the language..."[1]

Dante Gabriel Rossetti was an entertaining correspondent: "... the picture's owner [W A Turner, a Manchester manufacturer had bought *A Vision of Fiammetta*] saw it yesterday together with his wife and both were delighted though it still needs work which I am delaying until the arrival of the frame. I had a [illegible] with the apple blossom which is all over the picture. By some freak of nature the blossom came out full everywhere in a day whereupon it was immediately blighted by an east wind, and all we could get after this was such belated bits as appeared after their time... I have since begun a new picture of Mrs Morris founded on one of the old cartoons which Stillman will recollect my doing at Scalands and the subject of which is to be La Donna della Finestra from the Vita Nuova... I judge you may possibly now be either in Florence or Paris... Burne Jones is, I understand, the lion of the English section in Paris, and it is to be hoped sure of a first-class medal; this would do him good with this benighted country. But if he is expected to go for it like a good boy I suspect he will

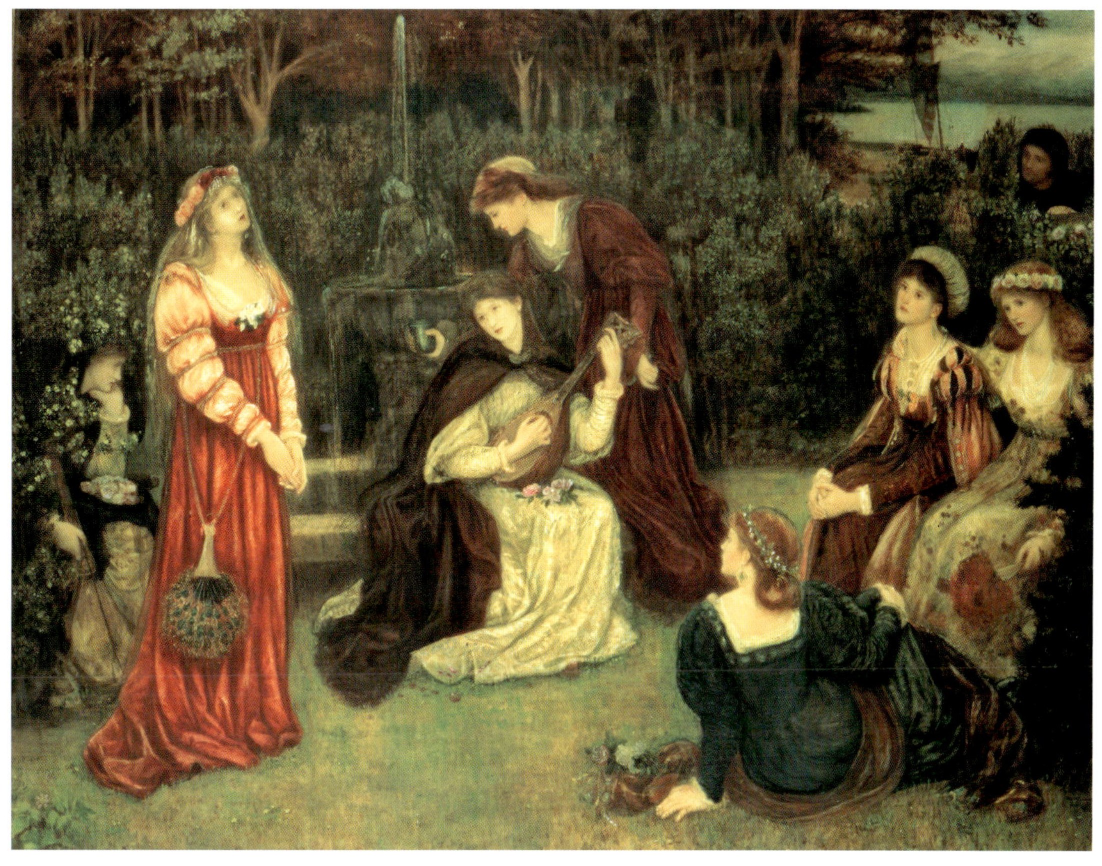

Plate 33
Marie Spartali Stillman
1879
Fiammetta Singing
Oil on canvas
Exhibited: Grosvenor Gallery, 1879
Pre-Raphaelite Inc., by courtesy of Julian Hartnoll; Bridgeman Art Library

leave it where it is like his Oxford degree... I am sorry (and feel guilty too) as to your not getting your picture at the Grosvenor. I do [believe?] the curse was your extreme goodness in giving time to those last sittings..."[2] His private opinion, however, he expressed in a letter to Frederick Shields: "I fear they may not be her best..."[3] William Michael Rossetti was measured in his enthusiasm for his brother's picture, writing to Lucy: "Gabriel was very lively, and his *Fiammetta* (Mrs Stillman) is now finished, or all but; you remember the head which we both like much – the red tint of the drapery is also very successful. I don't myself think that the picture in other respects is one of Gabriel's best."[4]

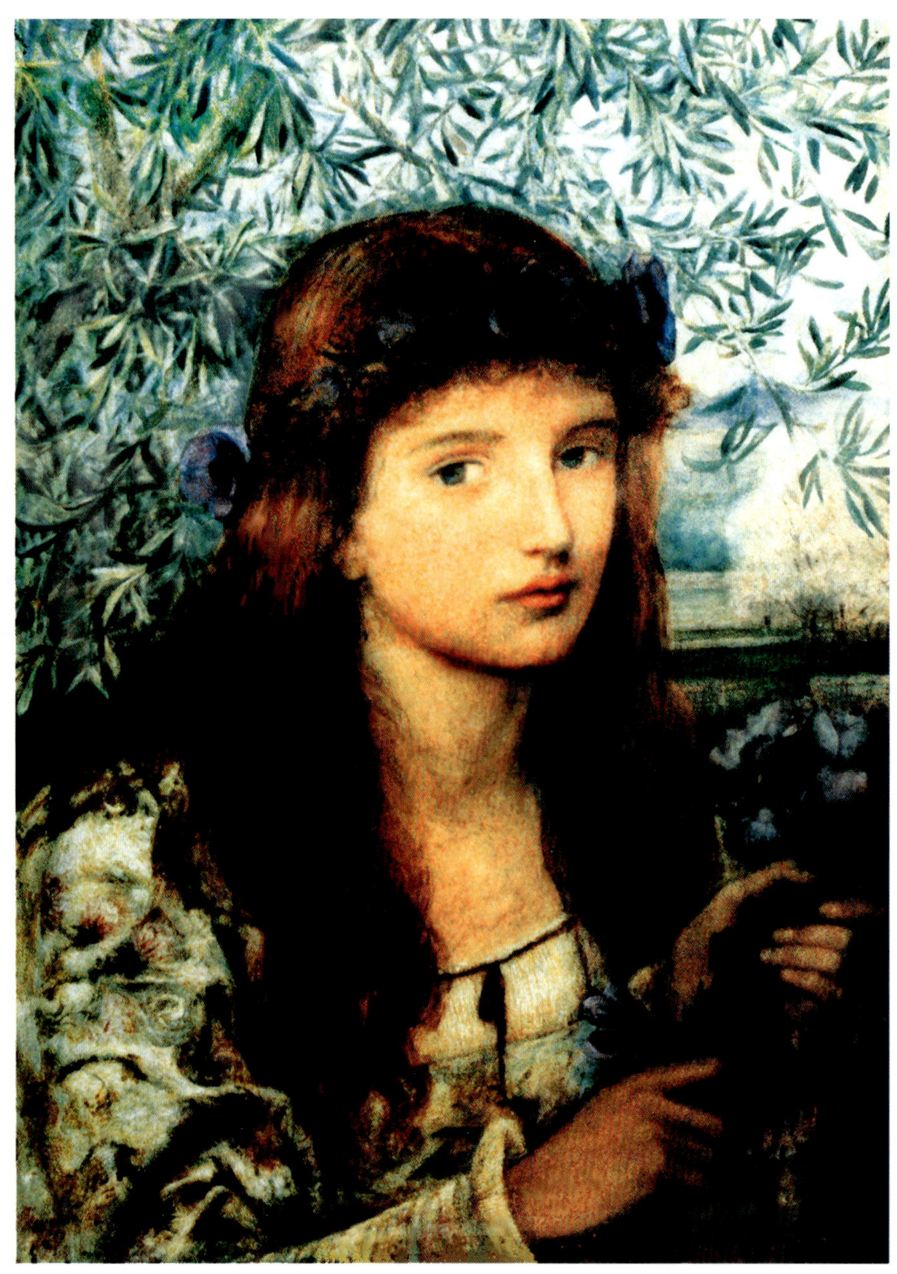

Plate 34
Marie Spartali Stillman
1880
Among the Willows of Tuscany
Watercolour and gouache on paper
Exhibited: Grosvenor Gallery, Winter 1880
Private Collection

In August, William Stillman was briefly back in London, having escorted Christina as far as Paris, while the family stayed on in Florence. William Michael noted in his diary: "Stillman called on me at Som. Ho. and got me to dine at the Spartalis. He returns to Florence tomorrow and thinks it possible that he and his may remain there for some years... he thinks the Peace of Berlin illusive and that the Turkish Empire will continue to be subjected to a series of shocks, crumbling it at last in to nothingness...", an astute prediction.[5]

Pausing briefly with his family, William set off for Montenegro, while Marie Stillman went about creating a home for the children; she was never happier than in Florence. Writing from the studio she had rented on the Lungarno degli Acciaiuoli, overlooking the Arno between the Santa Trinita Bridge and the Ponte Vecchio, she confessed to Ford Madox Brown: "I have never looked out of the window so much." Here she resumed her painting, which flourished under the inspiration of Dante, Boccaccio and Rodolfo Ghirlandaio while she awaited the birth of her second child.

Marie sent Madox Brown further news from Florence in the last weeks before her confinement: "Lisa has so much facility and so little perseverance... the three children are delighted at the prospect of a new baby, I am far less so as I find three children..." The rest of this letter is missing but it is not difficult to complete the sentence.[6] Michael Spartali Stillman, known always as Mico to family and close friends, was born in Italy on 28 October 1878.

Despite Rossetti's forebodings, the years in Florence that followed were perhaps the most fulfilling of Marie Stillman's long life. She was now 35, and the estrangement from her father resulting from her marriage to William was forgotten; she had a lovely daughter, her baby son and two delightful step-daughters whom she loved and who loved her dearly. She delighted in the art and culture of Italy, in Florence itself, which quickly became her preferred city of all, in the clear skies of summer and the relative warmth of the winters – she hated the English winters, which affected her badly – and she enjoyed a circle of friends drawn to her by her beauty and held captive by her unassuming charm and accomplishment, and on whom she could rely for help when it was needed. Marie was the mainstay and manager of their family throughout her years in Florence. Her husband, working alone in the Balkans, Greece or the United States, was as often absent as on hand to support her.

From London, William Michael Rossetti, Lucy, Dante Gabriel Rossetti and Ford Madox Brown kept her informed of everything that passed among the circle. William Michael in particular remained in close contact with the Spartali family: "We went round to the Spartalis and stayed for dinner, the eldest son Demetrius having just got married. We were introduced to Eustratius's wife... Mrs Stillman is expected over in England towards the beginning of June with the children and possibly tho' not certainly her husband. Wd be in London a little while and afterwards in the Isle of Wight whither Mrs Spartali invited Lucy and the children," he noted in his diary in April 1879.[7]

Marie Stillman travelled to London in late May 1879 for her first visit in a year, to see her parents and to escape the furious heat of summer in Florence. In June Fairfax Murray wrote to Dante Rossetti: "I think you will have heard from Mrs Stillman that her spouse did finally notify her that he was still in existence..."[8] In July, Marie was joined by William for three months. Dante Rossetti continued his reports to Janey Morris: "Mrs Stillman came in yesterday with the divinely lovely Effie. The Mama says she is thinner herself every day and that her bones are coming through. Certainly she and her husband must weigh less than any such tall couple in the world."[9] The Stillmans were an imposing sight out for a walk together and became known to their neighbours in Florence as 'la famiglia lunga e magra.' They were indeed long and thin; William was 6'3" tall, Bella a modest 5'9", Marie, Lisa and Effie in between; Mico as an adult topped them all, at 6'4". Stillman referred to his daughters as '18ft of longitude.'

Stillman returned to Florence in September and travelled up to Cortina to meet Gladstone who was holidaying there. Weighing opinions and formulating the policies on the Eastern Question that would carry him back to office as Prime Minister the following year, Gladstone again sought Stillman's first-hand opinions of Prince Nicholas and Montenegrin institutions: he was always worth listening to.

Marie stayed on in England. She remained on the Isle of Wight until the end of August and was back at The Shrubbery in September; "I think I told you that Mary Stillman is to sit to me, though whether this picture or any other will sell nowadays, heaven knows,"[10] Dante Rossetti wrote to Janey Morris. Janey's response reveals the extent to which the passion that once inspired their relationship had cooled to friendship: "I am most glad that you have got M. Stillman to sit to you again, you will make a beautiful picture of her – who would have thought a year back when I appeared so much the stronger woman that she would be sitting to you when I am becoming a mummy? So much has Happiness done for one and Misery for the Other."[11] "I am still expecting Mrs Stillman to get about my Desdemona picture from her. I have it all in my head and shall make it a good one,"[12] Rossetti replied in

---

Plate 35
Marie Spartali Stillman
1883
The Childhood of St Cecily
Watercolour. 102.3 x 75 cm (40¼ x 29½in)
Exhibited: Grosvenor Gallery, Liverpool, 1883
Courtesy of Peter Nahum at the Leicester Galleries, London

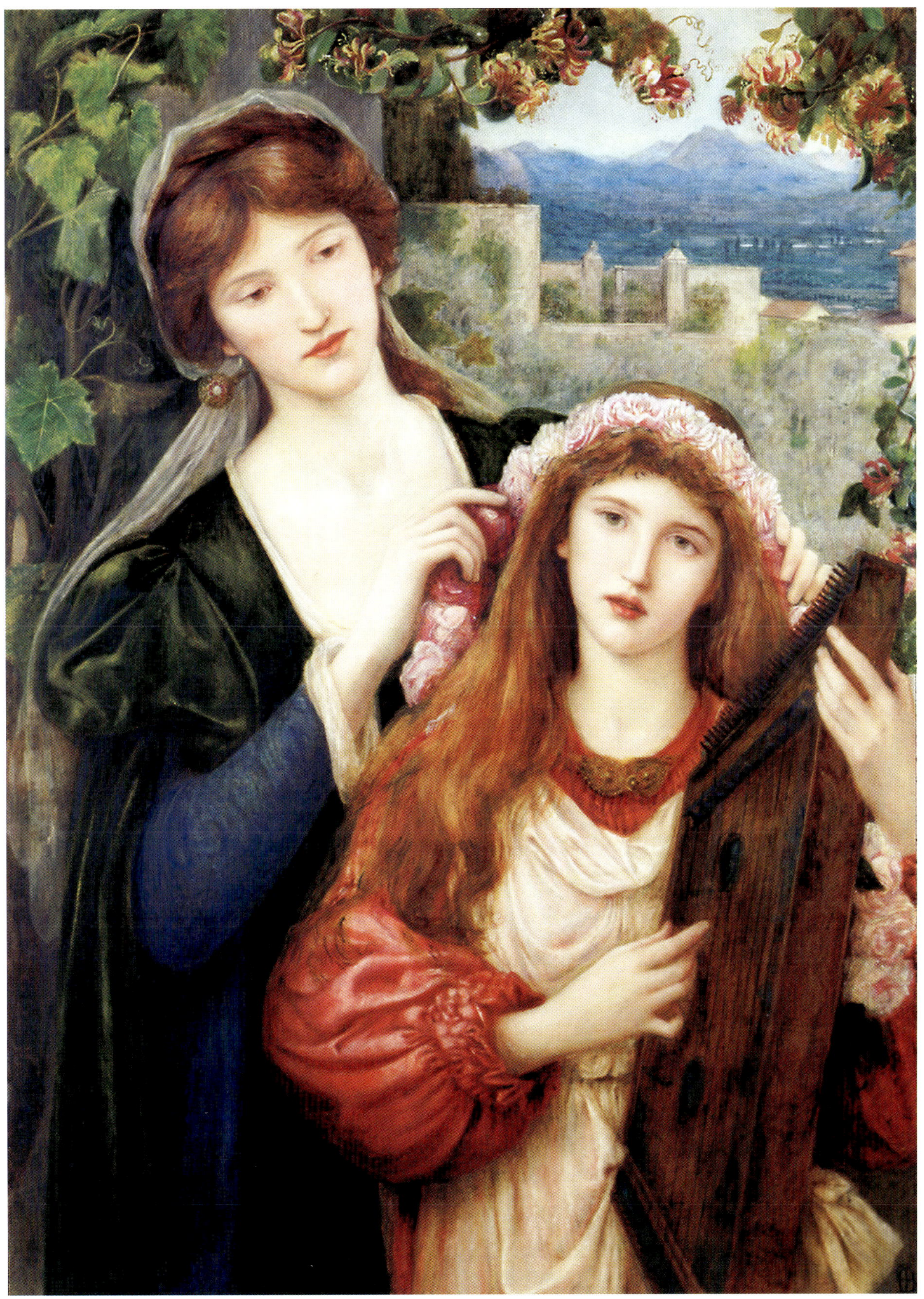

August. However, it was October before Marie went to Cheyne Walk, as he wrote to his sister, Christina Rossetti: "Mrs Stillman began her sittings to me today which last up to 5 hours at a stretch (necessarily) and leave me rather wearied in my weak state. She is graciousness itself and received with cordial return the remembrances you sent..."[13] The painting, never completed, was intended for Alecco Ionides: "Ionides has closed my offer and would evidently have paid more. Pazienza!"[14] Rossetti wrote to a friend. It was found one day, forgotten, in a cupboard at William Michael Rossetti's house in St Edmund's Terrace by his daughter Helen Rossetti Angeli. Some twenty years had passed since Dante Rossetti's death; William Rossetti gave Helen the finished painting of the head and arms, and she had the canvas cut down.

As ever, Marie had spent the last few weeks of her visit to England painting. "Mrs Stillman was here with two portraits of her brothers; she expects to be back in Florence before the end of the month and settle there, & does not contemplate ever taking up residence in England again on the grounds of expense,"[15] William Michael Rossetti recorded in his diary. Dante Rossetti urged Janey Morris, who was staying at Westward Ho! with Crom Price,[16] to make a winter visit to Florence for her health when Marie returned there: "I am sure the Stillmans would be very attentive and you know others there too... shall I ask Mrs Stillman about it? I made a drawing of Mrs Stillman and have got the head on the canvas. She sits again on Saturday. Her gracious good nature is inexhaustible... it seems that Stillman is still subject to woeful despondency, and sits in complete collapse with his head and arms hanging. Just fancy, when a wife like that is to hand. He is now at Cadore painting a large landscape of which Marie does not seem interested in the details. His two daughters are with him."[17] Janey's weary reply, from Kelmscott House, was full of resigned self-pity: "...I should like to see Mary Stillman again, but suppose she is nowhere within my visiting distance..." It was only in 1881 that they met once more, in Florence.

William Stillman was never robust, as Michael Spartali had disparagingly observed. He had suffered from childhood with respiratory weaknesses ranging from bronchitis to pleurisy, and he was prone to disabling rheumatism. He came,

---

Plate 36
Marie Spartali Stillman
1879
La Pensierosa
Pencil, watercolour and bodycolour, heightened with gum arabic
Exhibited: Grosvenor Gallery, Summer, 1880
Elvehjem Museum of Art, University of Wisconsin-Madison
Courtesy of Christopher Wood

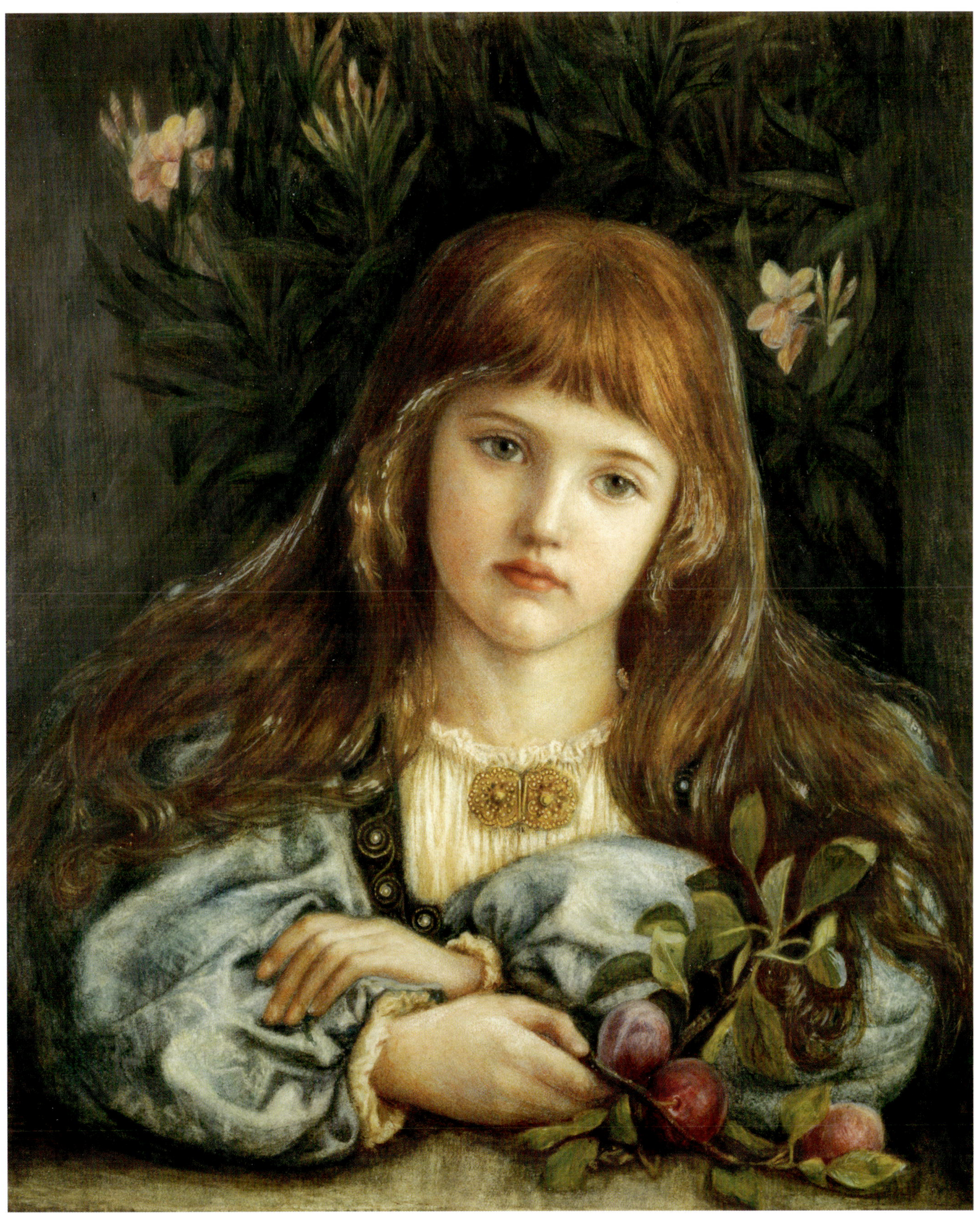

moreover, from a family background of harsh discipline and fervent religious conviction that had left a searing mark on his personality, which inclined towards the heavy-laden; from his earliest days he knew only a wrathful God and the stern imperatives of truth and duty as he had been taught them. This unbending outlook led inevitably to conflict between his convictions and the realities of day-to-day living; he was creative, highly intelligent and perceptive, which increased the tensions within him. One outcome was that he was a poor sleeper. For this he regularly took chloral hydrate, the drug that he had confidently recommended to Dante Gabriel Rossetti as harmless. The physical effects of chloral abuse include severe respiratory depression and very low blood pressure, the 'cataleptic habit' that William Michael Rossetti described in Christina Spartali,[18] and that he recounted as inducing in his brother "deep melancholy and weakness of will".[19] It is more than a coincidence that William Stillman, a confirmed user with severe depressive indications, was prey to bouts of immobile despair. He was always under the strain of an uncertain income and a family he was unable fully to support; he appears simply to have been unaware, or supremely confident that he had control, of the psychological effects of the prolonged use of chloral on a vulnerable temperament.

"I heard from William the progress of your Fiammetta, and from my sister of its completion, knowing how severe a critic you are of your own work it is all the greater privation to me to have no chance of seeing it at present... William is in the Maremma and after a short time with us here will start for a two month journey to the east. I suppose it will be good for him, but I am sorry he will be away just when everything is lovely here..." Marie Stillman wrote to Dante Gabriel Rossetti in November 1879.[20] William was already planning his return to the Aegean, this time to record and photograph a dig in Crete for the American Archeological Society. He had secured a commission from the New York journal, *Scribner's,* to undertake a series of articles that were later collected and published as *In the Steps of Ulysses, with an Excursion in Quest of the so-called Venus of Melos*, the subject of which he believed was "not properly a Venus but a Nike Apteros".[21]

The trip was not a complete success. The ketch he chartered – the same boat on which he had escaped from Crete 11 years before – came perilously close to shipwreck in a terrible gale off Crete: "... we had all the antique love of adventure and indifference to danger," he recalled contentedly. Once there, the Turkish authorities refused Stillman their *firman* to excavate the site; further, the local inhabitants had taken advantage of ten years of relative security to dig up any artifacts of value, offering them for sale to every passer-by. Stillman however spent an isolated three months, happily exploring parts of the island he had been prevented by the insurrection from visiting in 1869. He was back home late in December. "... I got a longish letter from Stillman yesterday," Rossetti told Janey Morris, "he writes from

Florence where they seem quite settled. The baby boy seems an ideal, and Lisa has grown 2 inches taller than her stepmother! I don't believe it, she wd be as tall as her father... I wish I had any more news – for instance such tidings as Ruskin was hanged or something equally welcome. But I haven't so it's no use going on."[22]

On his return Stillman took up the cudgels again, this time against William Morris and the newly-formed Society for the Protection of Ancient Buildings in the angry war of words over the restoration of San Marco, asserting that if necessary works had not been undertaken (they had in fact been under way for forty years before William Morris raised hue and cry) San Marco would have long since fallen in to the Piazza, and the Doge's Palace crumbled in to the lagoon. The credit that William Stillman gained in Italy by this intervention in what had become a major diplomatic rift was balanced by the odium he incurred in London, particularly as he was identified with *The Times.* "Mr Stillman has lately done some good work for us [SPAB], but he is at the same time the correspondent who gave erroneous information to *The Times*," Philip Webb was to comment a couple of years later.[23] Stillman's unpopular position over San Marco was, however, forgiven in England when he launched a blistering attack on the 'restorers' of the Duomo whom he found were cleaning the green and white marble exterior "with acid and with chisel". His furious denunciation was published, unsigned, in the *Cornhill Magazine* and caused consternation in Florence. 'High quarters' in the Ministry of Public Instruction approached William Stillman to ask for his help in defending the city's officers against the 'insolent Englishman' who was libelling them in the *Cornhill.* Pasquale Villari, their close friend in Florence, who was himself later appointed Minister of Public Instruction with responsibility for Italy's art heritage and who went on to become President of Italy in 1896, was blissfully unaware of the identity of their trenchant critic.

That accomplished, Stillman set off again. "Mrs Stillman is anxious about Mr Stillman who had not been heard of for 3 weeks – he had gone on a mad expedition with a young painter who has been spending his honeymoon in Italy & Mrs Stillman has had this gent's wife on her hands – she says Mrs Paget[24] has been ill moreover, I think it is too bad I must say – Mrs Stillman is very cheerful however,"[25] Fairfax Murray reported to Dante Gabriel Rossetti . Rossetti, had also received a letter from Marie, which he forwarded to Janey Morris: "I enclose a letter from Mary Stillman – showing what a Monster her William is. I have told her in reply that he should encounter Scylla and Charybidis, Polyphemus's cave and everything else and find no Penelope when he gets back... Poor Mary Stillman does not mention that Stillman went wandering off with another Yankee, leaving said Yankee's sick wife on her hands... she really is too great a fool to him."[26]

William Stillman left Florence for Athens in February 1881 to cover the Greek national elections, a further temporary appointment on similar lines to his correspondence during the Balkan insurrection; *The Times* had a regular representative in Athens (he was later assassinated) but Stillman had unique access to Charilaos Tricoupis, the opposition leader who was about to win his third term in office. Tricoupis had lived for 14 years in London where his father was the Greek Ambassador; both the Ionides and the Spartalis were close personal friends. William spent the greater part of the year in Athens, accompanied by Lisa while Marie remained in Florence for the next 3 months with the other children.

James William Stillman, the short-lived infant Giacomino, was born at the Shrubbery on 13 August 1881 and baptised at the Greek Church on London Wall on 25 September; his godmother was his aunt, Strati's wife, Olga Spartali. In his last letter to Fairfax Murray before his death six months later, Dante Gabriel Rossetti wrote: "It is centuries since I heard from you in any shape... no doubt you know that the cares of the charming Mrs Stillman have been increased by another baby..."[27] In reply, Fairfax Murray confessed to his astonishment: "With your letter came one from Mrs Stillman announcing the new arrival. I was much surprised as although I saw her immediately before she left here [Florence] she betrayed no sign of double life..."[28]

William Stillman was still in Greece when their second son was born. He wrote to Marie from Athens on 21st August: "I have just got back from my trip and got your letters and Christina's with details of the baby's birth. I have only a short time to write as the mail leaves at noon... I have written a letter on the trip which you will also get by this post and have nothing to add. Of course, Lisa may go to Smalleys and much more safely than with the Morrises for you know I don't like the moral views of the Morris and Rossetti set, but I suppose as she will not be there in the atmosphere long it won't do her much harm. I am writing to McDonald[29] by this post to insist on a leave of absence for a month at least as the heat here is such that I am fit for nothing and shall be fit for nothing all winter if I am to stay without a complete change of climate, Your Will."[30] There is a eerie absence of any expression of pleasure at the birth of his son, or of any congratulation or concern for his wife; while the authoritarian manner of his communications concerning his children contrasts with his leaving Marie to fend for them from day to day.

A month later Marie wrote to Ford Madox Brown, thanking him for his note of congratulation "on the birth of my little son." She continued: "I am expecting William this evening and he found the heat of Athens and the malaria very trying and at last has a holiday after nine months absence from home... my baby is very strong and good looking for his tender age and I am glad to have another boy as the longer I live the greater I find the difficulties in a woman's way of doing anything well if she has others to look after and care for."[31] Once more, Marie put family responsibilities before her calling as a painter. She had been alone for the full nine months of her pregnancy and had borne her confinement without her husband's support.

Returning from Athens to London by easy stages, William Stillman stopped off in pacified Montenegro, where he received a princely welcome. He was in London at the end of September; "Stillman called, will soon return to Athens as correspondent, leaving en route his wife and family in Florence,"[32] William Michael Rossetti noted in his diary. The journey home had not been without alarms. William Michael Rossetti wrote to his brother: "Did you hear of the rumour of Stillman's being murdered by Arnauts? Promptly disproved for us, by Lucy's going round to the Spartalis."[33] The report had reached Stillman in Venice on his journey back, prompting a flurry of telegrams to Marie, Michael Spartali, the Foreign Office, *The Times*, and to Charilaos Tricoupis who had recently become Prime Minister of Greece for the third time, succeeding Alexander Koumoundouros. Koumoundouros, who died the following year, was succeeded as opposition leader by Theodor Deligiannis, a personal as well as political enemy of Tricoupis, who would pursue his vendetta by involving Michael Spartali in a series of bureaucratic delays to the payment of the considerable debt owed him by the Greek government.

"[Mary Robinson] says that Mrs Stillman's infant suffers from bronchitis and gives some anxiety,"[34] William Michael Rossetti noted in his diary early in March 1882; on 1 May, James – Giacomino – died, aged 9 months. Dante Gabriel Rossetti, the artist whom Marie Stillman admired above all others, had been buried in the churchyard at Birchington just two weeks earlier. Marie had long been "in perpetual anxiety" about unexplained feverish illnesses that had regularly overtaken them, which in particular afflicted their children. Contamination of the city's water supply by waste water seeping from the Arno in to wells was beginning to be suspected. It was reluctantly decided that the risk of their remaining in Florence during the summer was too great. Too late to save Giacomino who was buried in the Anglican cemetery in Florence, Marie Stillman returned to the Spartali home in Clapham with Bella, Effie and Mico.

Spending the summer in her parents' house on the Isle of Wight, Marie Stillman remained anxious to return to Florence: "I long to get back to Italy and to some independent home, it is so difficult being on a visit with such a large family. We are going to Florence next month... My husband will meet us and we shall try to settle ourselves down for a certain time. My sister is here... Our relatives from Alexandria have been perfectly wild with excitement at the war news,"[35] she wrote to Vernon Lee in September. General Sir Garnet Wolseley had decisively defeated an Egyptian nationalist army at Tel el Kebir, and established British suzerainty in Egypt and the Suez Canal Zone, thereby freeing the Greek expatriate community of Alexandria – who included many Spartali relatives – from Ottoman control. Sir Garnet Wolseley was something of a hero in Greek eyes.

Although many of the companions of her later life were friends from her time in Florence, Marie's time there was far from carefree. She faced the problems of daily life, of bringing up and educating a small tribe of children on a precarious budget, while continuing to follow her chosen career as a painter. William was in the Balkans reporting on the wars there for *The Times,* or digging in Crete, for the greater part of the family's five-year residence in Florence. She suffered the anxiety of a shortage of money due to the uncertainty of William's income. Despite these obstacles, surrounded by kindred spirits, Marie Stillman flowered intellectually in the climate of cultured exchange, as education passed in to experience. There was no backward glance to the comfortable life she had let behind. Florence marked the beginning of a new chapter, in which her innate strength of character triumphed.William too spoke of finding in Florence "an intellectual life and a serenity non-existent elsewhere, surrounded by the noblest art of the Renaissance and by an intellectual atmosphere which could only with difficulty be rediscovered in any other Italian city."[36]

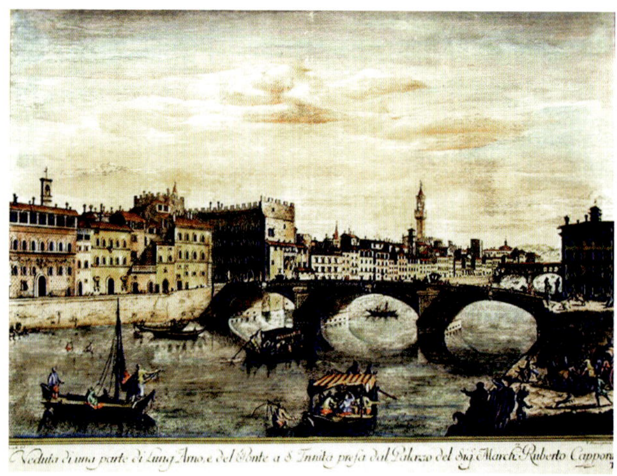

Plate 37
A contemporary view of Florence from the southern bank of the Arno in the 17th century

Chapter Twelve

Expatriates, Friends and Visitors

The longest-standing of the Stillman family's friends in Florence was Charles Fairfax Murray. Murray had known Marie Spartali since 1867 when, as the young studio assistant to Burne-Jones and part-time amanuensis and copyist for Rossetti, they were often together in the studio in Cheyne Walk; they remained on terms of close affection and she was at his deathbed 50 years later – a life-long understanding. At the time of her marriage in 1871, Fairfax Murray was already living in Pisa, and by 1875 was himself married with a young Italian wife, Angelica Colivicchi. In the autumn of 1878, a few weeks after the Stillmans's arrival, he had moved his family – his wife and three infants – from Siena to Florence and they now resided at 108 via de Serragli. During the years that the two families shared in Florence, Fairfax Murray was something of a surrogate father to Lisa Stillman – Marie's older stepdaughter – and Effie, the youngest of the three girls, in William Stillman's absences; Bella, the last of the children of William Stillman's marriage to Laura Mack was more reserved, more down to earth and self-sufficient. A child of just a few months old when her mother committed suicide, Bella was temperamentally closer to her father than were her sister and step-sister, less the artist and more the practical thinker, though no less a loving step-daughter to Marie; she regarded herself as "a Yankee" and although she was not the eldest, she was the manager among the children.

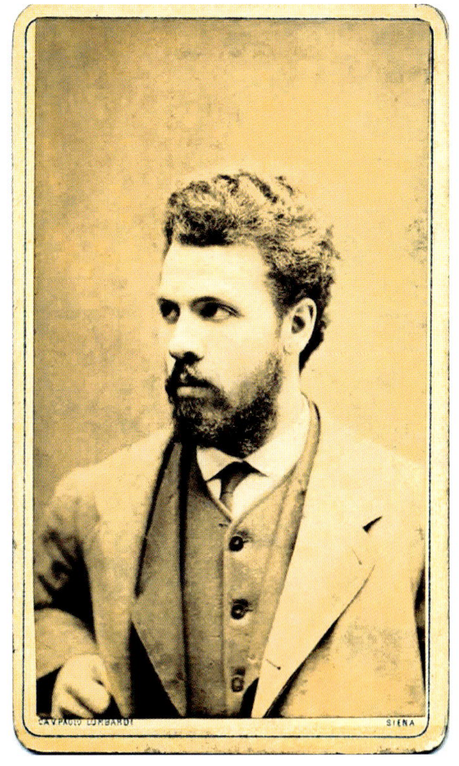

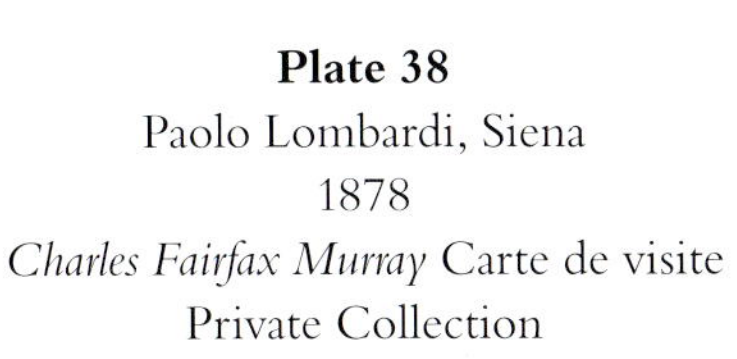

Plate 38
Paolo Lombardi, Siena
1878
Charles Fairfax Murray Carte de visite
Private Collection

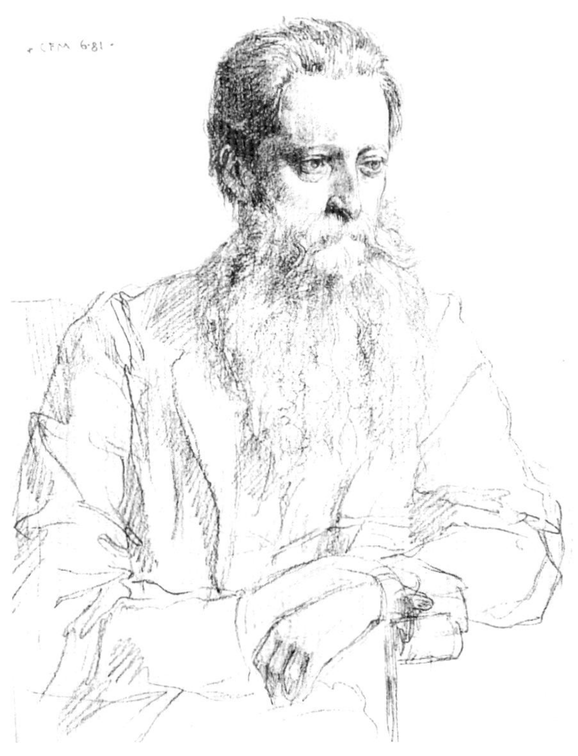

Plate 39
Charles Fairfax Murray
June 1881
William James Stillman, 53, Florence,
Pencil portrait, signed and dated
Private Collection

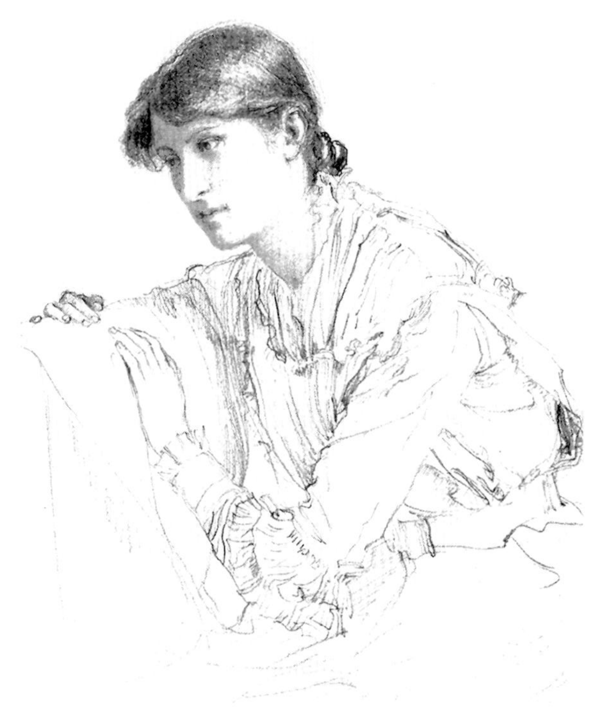

Plate 40
Charles Fairfax Murray
1882
Lisa Stillman
Pencil. 31 x 23.5 cm (12¼ x 9¼in)
Private Collection

Fairfax Murray took a close interest in the family's artistic and professional development. He gave both Lisa and Effie regular drawing lessons, drew delightful portraits of the three young girls and kept Rossetti in touch with news of his beautiful model until his death in 1882. Murray's diary notes lessons continuing in London in 1889. Marie for her part kept a watchful eye on the welfare of Fairfax Murray's young family during his prolonged absences in search of pictures for the London market. The Stillman family stayed annually with Angelica Murray at their holiday villa in Poggiarello and shared the domestic trials and satisfactions of two mothers with absent husbands and seven young children between them. It was part of Marie Stillman's charm that she was as much at ease with the docile Angelica, who aspired to nothing greater than keeping house for Fairfax Murray and their children, as with the opinionated intellectual Vernon Lee.

The most influential milestone in Marie Stillman's intellectual life in Florence was her meeting the controversial writer Violet Paget (1856-1935) – twelve years her junior – who wrote under the *nom de plume* of Vernon Lee, the name by which she is generally known. The separation of the two, Violet Paget – unfeminine, opinionated, lesbian – from Vernon Lee – the probing, inventive bluestocking – reflected two distinct aspects of her character. Paget's capacity for passionate intimacy with other women (though ardent by nature she had a horror of physical relationships) was often

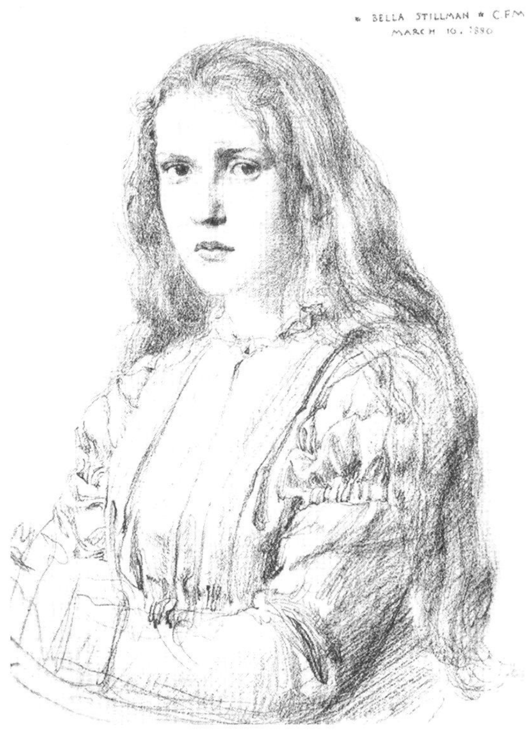

Plate 41
Charles Fairfax Murray
March 1880
Bella Helena Stillman, 12, Florence
Pencil portrait, signed and dated
Private Collection

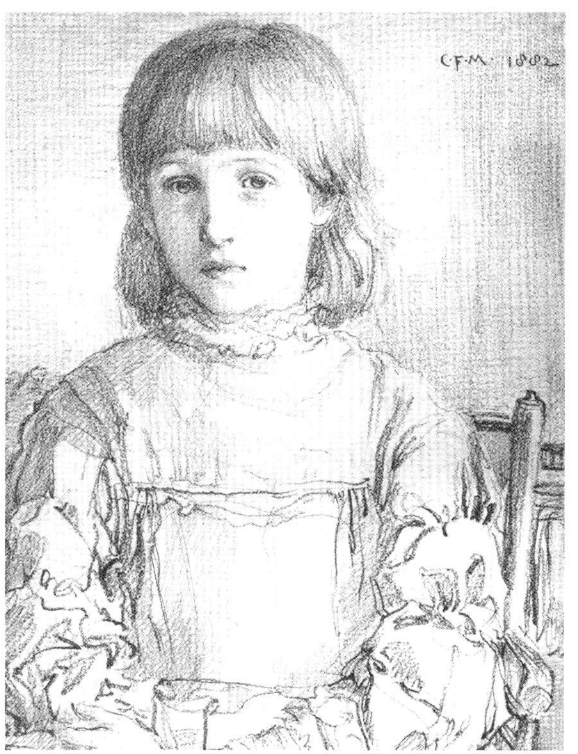

Plate 42
Charles Fairfax Murray
1882
Euphrosyne (Effie) Stillman
Pencil portrait, signed and dated
Private Collection

at odds with her critical and intellectual disposition. Vernon Lee became Marie's close friend and confidant soon after the Stillmans arrived in Florence, and she remained closely attached to Marie for the rest of her life, a strong bond of sympathy that lasted more than 40 years and survived several of Lee's unacceptable social lapses. "I feel so very glad that we are returning and one reason is that I am so very happy to live near you for I love you very much dear Vernon,"[1] Marie wrote on one occasion when she was away from Florence, early in their acquaintance.

It was, perhaps, a sign of Marie's isolation that Vernon Lee, who was generally disliked by women other than her platonic *amoureuses* and frequently resented by men, should engender so strong an emotional response in Marie Stillman. In the social mores of the day, passionate relationships between women were neither uncommon nor condemned, whereas to form a close friendship with one of the opposite sex would be to invite certain censure. Marie had long attracted swooning glances from men of all ages, which served only to emphasise her natural reserve; she was not unaware, and indeed was a little afraid, of the effect she produced and this further denied her any closeness with men. She responded as a fond older sister to the *gamine* waywardness of Violet Paget, cloaked in her *alter ego,* the cerebral Vernon Lee. Lee was unblushingly egotistical and, as she said of herself: "I like people as I

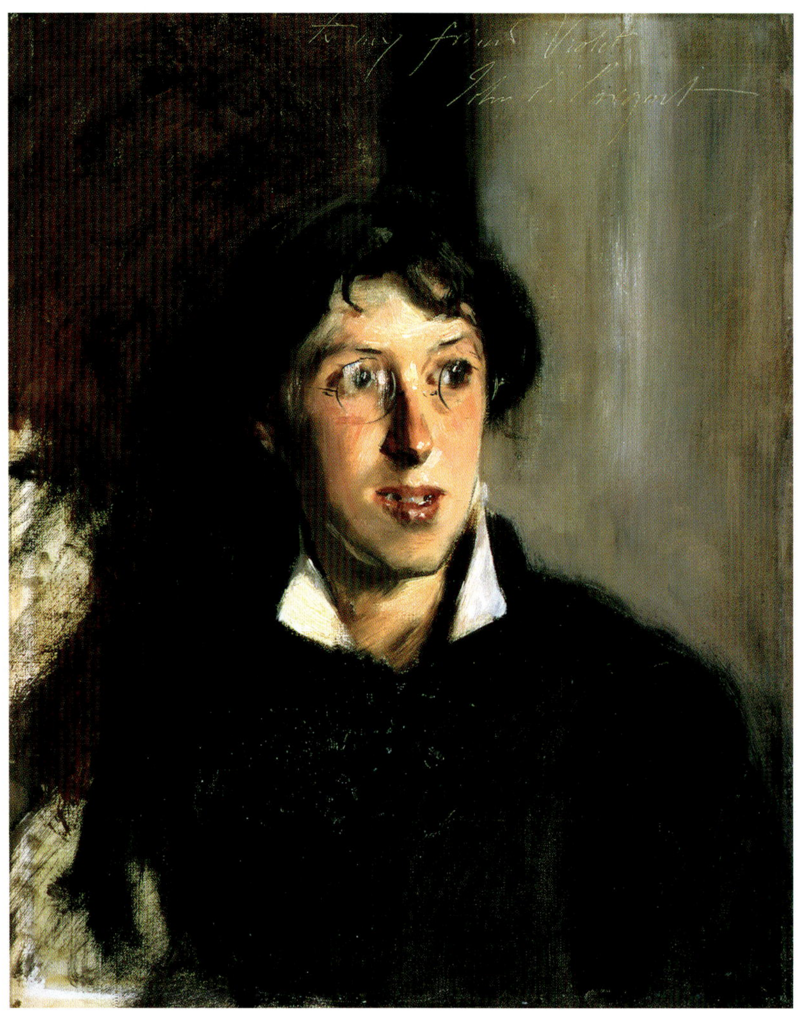

Plate 43
John Singer Sargent
1881
Vernon Lee
Oil on canvas. 53.7 x 43.2 cm (21⅛ x 17in)
Tate Gallery, London

like things, that is to say, my likings are preferences for the qualities that I can enjoy." No doubt there was an element of defensive bluster in her attitudinising, and perhaps Marie saw the person behind the dual identity. She was capable of throwing herself in to relationships, and of remaining faithful to the initial impulse.

Marie Stillman offered Vernon Lee – a young woman "of extreme vulnerability when her passions were aroused"[2] – the stable warmth of a more mature personality without offering the most remote threat; she was anything but *bohéme*. For Marie, starved of the emotional support that a more conventional marriage might have provided, their understanding matched her instinctive closeness with the absent Lucy Madox Brown, now married to William Michael Rossetti. Lucy, who was Marie Spartali's dearest companion of her own generation, had put aside painting after her marriage, the arrival of her children and in declining health, to find satisfaction in writing; she became an effective and radical champion of women's rights to education and suffrage. In her combative character and intellectual vigour she had therein much in common with Vernon Lee.

Marie Stillman's latent feminism was of a different order to Lucy's. She had been brought up in an enclosed family environment surrounded by the evidence of wealth. Educated at home to a high degree of accomplishment, yet divorced from acquaintance with the realities of the world beyond, her feminist sympathies were more instinctive than intellectual. Vernon Lee brought her in to closer acquaintance with a number of leading feminist figures. Marie already knew Annie Cobden – a daughter of the anti-Corn Law reformer Richard Cobden – in London; she too lived for a time in Florence in the via Lamarmora – Janey Morris stayed with her there in 1881 – before her marriage to T J Cobden-Sanderson, the craftsman-bookbinder, founder of the Doves Press and William Morris's neighbour in Hammersmith. The composer Ethel Smyth, a radical suffragiste who was imprisoned for demonstrating for women's rights, whom Marie Stillman first encountered as a visitor to Vernon Lee in Florence, was later a neighbour in Frimley when the Stillmans retired to England; Marie remained a close friend with both Ethel and her sister, Violet Hippisley. Sympathies aside, Marie Stillman could never have become a committed campaigner for equality for women, since she believed, and argued with Lucy Rossetti, that the responsibilities of motherhood and homemaker should come first (she also thought that the young should be chastised for bad behaviour, a view which scandalised Lucy) and, broadly, she considered it right that men should control their families. In her own context she placed the family before her painting, even though her work was important to their income. Nevertheless, she enjoyed the company and shared the aims of the strong women she admired.

Born to English parents, Violet Paget spent most of her life on the Continent: first in France – she was born near Boulogne – and then in Italy. On the death of her first husband, Matilda Adams had married Henry Ferguson Paget – erstwhile tutor to her son, the invalid poet Eugene Lee-Hamilton. Matilda and Henry went on to have one child, Violet, whom Matilda tirelessly groomed to seek a reputation as a successful intellectual. The family were on close terms with the Sargents, originally from Philadelphia, and at the age of thirteen in Rome Violet Paget had made a pact with her young friend John Singer Sargent – he was the same age – that if he would become a painter, she would become a writer. Adopting the persona of Vernon Lee she wrote on a wide range of subjects in art and literature, and was soon known as a controversial commentator on the literary scene. Mannish and peering – she was extremely short-sighted – Vernon Lee complemented her notable scholarly skills with an acid tongue and a comprehensive disdain for social niceties that resulted in a catalogue of personal disputes: "...she is a bright, gifted, abrupt woman... and so untidy and *negligée* with all that sense of beauty. Ouida[3] hated her," wrote Walburga, Lady Paget.[4] Though she lacked the manners considered acceptable in society,

Vernon Lee was a valued contributor to the intellectual circles of ex-patriate Florence and a fixed point on the itinerary of well-connected visitors. Her serious work was widely well-regarded, and she wrote extensively and perceptively on the art of writing and the morality of art itself. Along with her friend and mentor Henry James she was one of the first to write criticism of fiction, to analyse technique, to examine the psychology not only of the writer and his characters but of the way in which the reader responds to the novel.[5] In a lighter moment she wrote a puppet play for Bella and Effie Stillman, *Il Principe delle Cento Zuppe* (1883).[6]

Early in the New Year, 1880, the Stillmans moved again, to 14 Via Alfieri, which remained their home until they left Florence. William had again been unwell with chest problems. Marie worked at the easel as she did every possible moment; it was her private world: "Mrs Stillman has just sent all the way from Florence to borrow your old olive green velvet dress which I painted in that old fiddle picture.[7] She tells me that Stillman is on his legs again and instantly off to do some excavations. She seems to be worked off her legs to judge by the account she gives," Rossetti wrote to Janey Morris.[8]

The *atelier* in which Marie Stillman had her studio overlooking the Arno also housed the studio of another expatriate Pre-Raphaelite, John Roddam Spencer Stanhope. Spencer Stanhope, the grandson of the Earl of Leicester, was an early pupil of George Frederic Watts. As one of Rossetti's Oxford Union painters in 1857, the friend of Ford Madox Brown, William Morris and Ned Jones, and a co-founder of the Hogarth Club in 1858, Spencer Stanhope enjoyed impeccable Pre-Raphaelite credentials. In 1859 he married Elizabeth – Lilla – Wyndham-King (granddaughter of Turner's patron, the 3rd Earl of Egremont). Their London home was Campden Hill House; although Philip Webb designed for them a splendid country home, 'Sandroyd' at Cobham, Surrey, with spectacular views over the rolling North Downs, asthma drove Spencer Stanhope to Florence to spend the winters (from 1873) at his Villa Nuti at Bellosguardo overlooking the city from the west. G F Bodley painted frescoes there, and Spencer Stanhope painted the *Resurrection* triptych for Bodley's Anglican Holy Trinity Church in Florence. Marie Stillman first met him almost by chance: "Mr Stanhope has a studio next to ours. I never saw him in England, have only as yet met him once, is he a friend of yours?"[9] she asked Ford Madox Brown. It is surprising that Marie Stillman should meet this habitué of Little Holland House for the first time on the threshold of a studio

---

Plate 44
Marie Spartali Stillman
1884
Madonna Pietra degli Scrovigni
Watercolour, gouache and gum arabic. 78.5 x 61.1 cm (30⁹⁄₁₀ x 24in)
Exhibited: Grosvenor Gallery, 1884; Liverpool, Autumn 1884
National Museums, Liverpool (The Walker)

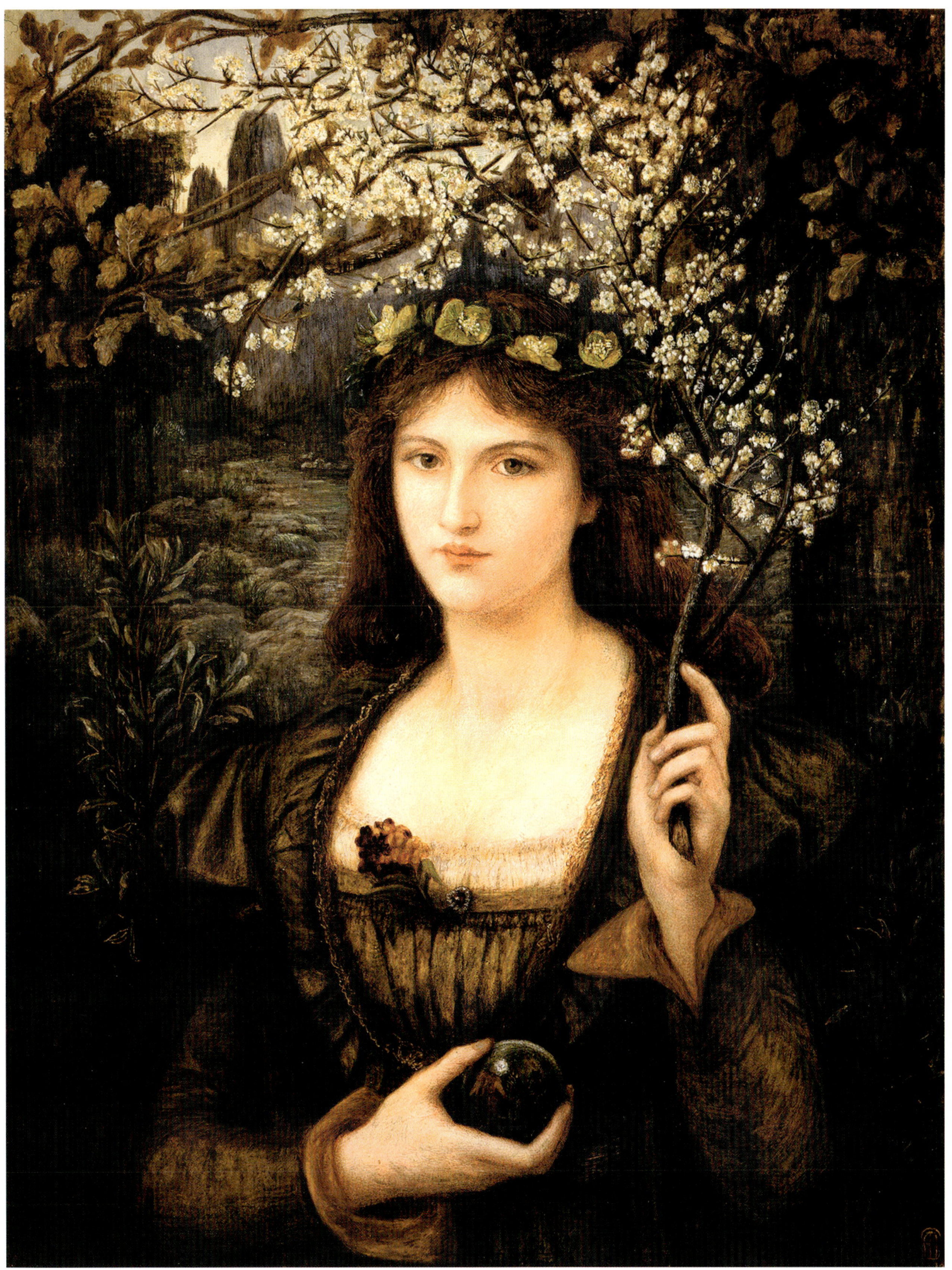

in Florence, a measure of the confined social life outside the Greek community of the unmarried daughters of the reserved Spartali family.

The Florentine expatriates divided broadly on national lines: English and American. For the most part the Stillmans's circle in Florence was from the English colony or among those Anglophile Americans who were prominent in artistic circles. There was a fair degree of overlap, the outcome of shared interests and, in William Stillman's instance, his acquaintances in American arts circles. Married to a Greek, born to English citizenship, Stillman never forgot that he was an American citizen and a Yankee to boot. The famous "literary generation" in Florence, the Brownings, the Trollopes and the Hawthornes, had for the most part been supplanted by younger writers. The quarrelsome poet Walter Savage Landor was dead; Shelley drowned; Browning had returned to a fellowship at Balliol; and Samuel Hawthorne was back in Concord; but there were others to succeed them.

Among the leading members of the American *coterie* was James Jackson Jarves, the self-taught critic and writer on art who had settled in Florence for his health in the early 1850s, and whom William Stillman knew well and hated better from their earlier hostile encounter over the sale of Jarves's collection in the United States. Characteristically, Stillman almost immediately became involved in another confrontation, which eventually reached the correspondence pages of the American periodical, *The Nation*.

While maintaining to Charles Eliot Norton: "Jarves and I are excellent friends and he often comes to me for advice and opinions," Stillman showed no hesitation in denigrating him: "Jarves... called yesterday. He has got a Pollaiuolo, fresco, for the NY Museum and some other fragments paid for by Vanderbilt and to be presented with the collection of Old Master drawings of last year. It is curious how he grows in to an authority on art when in fact he is of an extraordinary incompetence of judgment… I never knew anyone whose opinion was worth less." Stillman's rancour was born as much of envy of Jarves's increasing acceptance among the leading figures in the American museum and academic art world as of his success as a dealer: "He made in commission on the S Donato sale not less than $10,000! I am not envious or avaricious... but when I think of what even a small part of that amount would have been to me, paralysed by debt and over brain worked year after year I feel as if it were of no use studying and ripening one's judgment to be fit to have an opinion when

---

Plate 45
Marie Spartali Stillman
1879
Gathering Orange Blossoms
Gouache on paper. 78.7 x 61.9 cm (31 x 24⅜in)
Exhibited: Grosvenor Gallery, 1879; Liverpool 1879
St Lawrence University Permanent Collection. Gift of the family of Owen D Young

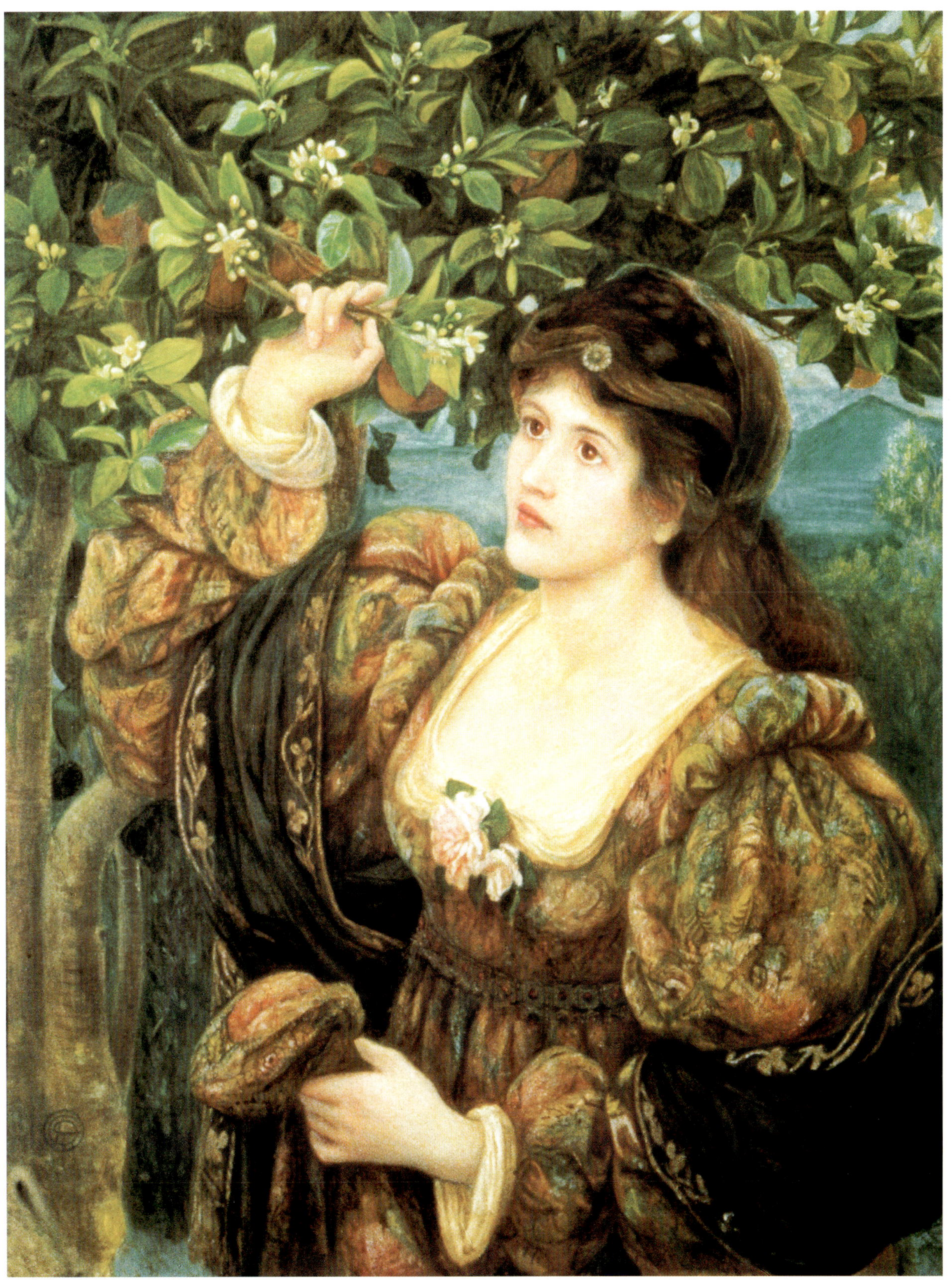

one who has no potentiality of forming opinions has such a position… It would all be merely ludicrous to me if it were not that I feel myself competent to fill adequately such a function which seems needed by the American public and yet nobody will accept my services as a gift."[10] Stillman's disclaimer does nothing to hide this naked display of jealousy. His views had matured since 1855 – he later admitted that *The Crayon* was 'somewhat crude and puerile' – but the animosity remained.

The long-time Florence resident Bella Duffy, with whom Marie took up a friendship that began in London and was to last well over twenty-five years, was one of the Stanhopes's dearest companions in Florence and, like them, she divided her time between Italy and a home in London. The authoress of a *Life of Madame de Staël* and the distinguished historian of *The Tuscan Republics,* long in the making and published in 1898, Bella Duffy was almost inevitably one of the group of artists and writers who might be found at Vernon Lee's *conversatziones*; but she was also acclaimed as a leading figure among the expatriates for her crusading for the conservation of Italy's architectural heritage. Allied to Spencer Stanhope and Fairfax Murray she was a great Anti-Scrape campaigner and was thereby comrade and confidante to a wide range of fellow campaigners (whom Marie Stillman knew first in London), among them Philip Webb – architect to many of the Holland Park circle – George Price Boyce, Edward Burne-Jones, and William De Morgan. In Florence they fought losing battles against the demolition of part of the Bigallo and the Mercado Vecchio. Then there was Janet Ross, the meticulous historian of the Medici, who lived on the Lungarno Torrigiano and later at Poggio Gherado, and who was once described as a somewhat formidable person… alarming if roused, with her determined jaw, white hair and beetling black brows; Ross's lasting achievement was her book of recipes, *Leaves from our Tuscan Kitchen*, published in 1899 and still in print.

There was John Addington Symonds, the first modern historian of male homosexuality, working on his account of the *Renaissance in Italy* and translating Benvenuto Cellini's autobiography; and who wrote of Marie Stillman's beauty, ironically encapsulating the intellectual scene in the Florence of the day: "There is the Pitti, the Uffizi, the Bargello, the Accademia! There are the churches. There is [Pasquale] Villari to talk to & Miss Paget to quarrel with & Mrs Stillman to admire."[11] Algernon Swinburne, another of Marie's Cheyne Walk companions, was unenthusiastic about Symonds's obsession with classical male beauty and dubbed him "Soddington Symonds"; Henry James met Symonds in London in 1877 and summed him up as "a mild, cultured man with the Oxford perfume".[12]

Notwithstanding Symonds's open homosexuality – he went about Florence with a good-looking gondolier he had brought with him from Venice – he and his wife had three daughters.[13] Catherine Symonds became a dear friend of Marie Stillman. Symonds was rather less an admirer of Vernon Lee than of Marie Stillman, writing on one occasion to inform Lee: "I feel you imagine yourself to be so clever that everything you think is either right or valuable. And your way of expressing yourself is so uncompromising that your belief in yourself grates upon my sense of what is just and dignified. It is possible to be frank without being flippant, rude or patronising. You can be firm without posing as an oracle – I cannot help thinking that you would be really greater and more effective if you were (to use a vulgar phrase) less cocksure about a heap of things..."[14] Marie phrased her objections in a more sympathetic but no less firm fashion: "Accept your friends as they are. Don't expect them to attain your own ideal of friendship. It makes me quite nervous to read your severe judgement of Mme L V. You are so young and impetuous and devoted yourself that you are not indulgent enough to those who are toned down." It was a timely rebuke that Lee failed to take to her heart, or perhaps failed to grasp.

Fairfax Murray, who described himself as "hedge-hoggy and armadillo-ish",[15] nevertheless knew a wide range of artists, bibliophiles and those of like mind in Florence. Among his acquaintances there was Henry Roderick Newman, an Anglophile New Yorker; they gravitated towards one another through a shared interest in early books and the Pre-Raphaelite school and "spent many hours scouring the small Florence antique and bric-a-brac shops where one might still find hidden treasures..."[16] With Fairfax Murray's assistance Newman gathered a choice collection of primitive Italian masters, which adorned his studio walls for many years, and an important group of 135 fourteenth-century illustrated books.

In the late 1860s, Newman had abandoned thoughts of a career in medicine in order to paint and soon came under the influence of Thomas Charles Farrer who had studied under Ruskin at the Working Men's College in London. Newman joined the Association for the Advancement of Truth in Art whose members became known as the American Pre-Raphaelites. He found there a companion in Charles Herbert Moore, who later succeeded Charles Eliot Norton as Director of the Fogg Art Museum in Boston. Ruskin involved him, by letter, in recording the buildings in Florence that were being destroyed in the name of progress. It was a relationship that Newman greatly valued, albeit conducted mostly at a distance – they met only in 1880 when Newman was invited to Brantwood – acceptance by the Professor being the culmination of his earliest ambitions as a Ruskinian naturalist painter. He went so far as to issue his *Letters from Professor Ruskin* as a kind of prospectus, an advertisement derided by his fellow artists, and no one was sorry when Ruskin, as he was apt to do, turned abruptly against him.[17]

Henry Roderick Newman was not a popular figure with his American compatriots. His success in selling his work, which some thought outmoded, aroused a good deal of envy. His manner was considered somewhat removed, his persona rather too carefully crafted, his affinities too markedly Anglophile. Marie was on friendly terms with his wife, Mary Watson Willis, but not it seems with Newman himself. The reason can be attributed with some certainty to William Stillman: his view of Newman, the man and his work, was unremittingly hostile.

Stillman had been an enthusiastic promoter of the values of the American Pre-

Raphaelites in his earlier days as an aspiring painter; it was his painting trip to Switzerland with Ruskin in 1860 that had shown him that he lacked the defining talent to be a great artist (or, as he preferred in his autobiography, that Ruskin destroyed). It still rankled. Newman's new-found encouragement from the Slade Professor was all that was needed to rekindle his hostility. Stillman was, moreover, keenly jealous of Newman's success. Writing to Charles Eliot Norton, William Stillman remarked: "I hear Newman has been out to America this year, with all his drawings, a malignant and intolerable nature, bad artist and worse man... I never knew him to speak well of anyone, not even of Ruskin who seems to have been weak enough to praise his childish work... And he has pupils! – he who can neither draw a chair correctly or put the simplest building in Florence in good perspective or paint a buttercup in shadow. I feel no courage to paint and no enthusiasm to write and willingly drop back in to my newspaper correspondence which is at least paid for and soon forgotten."[18] It was not atypical of Stillman's vendettas, fuelled by self-reproach.

William Michael Rossetti was in Florence in June 1880; his opinion of Newman's work was remarkably similar, though conspicuously without malice: "His works are sound, tasteful and very faithful and want a little force, particularly in chiaroscuro. I found Newman a very prepossessing man, with a refined, self-possessed but rather retiring manner." Unusually, James Jackson Jarves was of a similar mind to William Stillman and published an article in the *New York Times* in which he wrote of Newman's work as "a passing type of American art, for the fading out of which the country should feel grateful as a healthful symptom of its art progress."[19] Newman accomplished the unlikely feat of uniting Stillman and Jarves in a single point of view, though the fragile unanimity thus achieved was not to last.

William Stillman's combative temperament was to bring him in to conflict with almost everyone he encountered on his infrequent returns to Florence; while Marie's every new acquaintance turned to warm friendship. Vernon Lee referred to him as 'Old Gibbet';[20] he was an unrepentant skeleton at every feast he attended. It is, however, worth remarking the wide circle of acquaintance that William enjoyed as the founder of *The Crayon*. Eugene Benson, an American artist of vague Pre-Raphaelite inspiration, like many of his compatriots, oscillated between Florence, Rome and Venice during these years. The Stillmans regularly encountered him, though particularly later in Rome where he was a member of Giovanni Costa's circle of Etruscans.[21] Frank Duveneck was another painter of the younger American set. Trained initially in his native Cincinnati, he studied the Old Masters in Munich and settled in Florence for a time before returning to America to a career as a notable bravura portrait painter. Marie Stillman fell in love with Florence, and Florence was the root, stem and branch of the friendships that she enjoyed until the end of a long life or until others left the stage.

Friendships between members of the expatriate communities and their Florentine neighbours were often sorely tested. Vernon Lee alienated Pasquale Villari and his wife, Linda White Villari, friends both of hers and the Stillmans, by writing a slashing critical review of his three volume *Life and Times of Niccolò Machiavelli*. Such was Lee's insensitivity that she could not comprehend that her comments were the reason that the Villaris were no longer on speaking terms with her. In the confines of the small Anglophone community of Florence, the rift was the cause of much embarrassment. Marie was an intimate of Lee and a close companion of the Villaris. The Villaris's goddaughter, Zina, married to the painter William Hulton, was a good friend of the Stillman daughters and they spent much of their time together, both in Florence and, during summer, in Venice where both families would go to escape the oppressive heat. William Stillman, for his own part, found something of a fellow soul in Pasquale Villari, a companionship reminiscent of his bond with Louis Agassiz and James Russell Lowell, which was later renewed in Rome when Villari became Minister of Public Instruction in 1891 and later President of Italy.

In the autumn, the gossipy attention of the Holland Park Greeks shifted to Christina Cahen d'Anvers. Aglaia Coronio wrote to Rossetti: "I have just heard that Christina – Marie Stillman's sister – is seeking a divorce. Did you know that horrid little Jew, her husband?" "I had not heard of the Countess's projected divorce," he replied, "from what her sister said I should judge it high time; but between such an odd pair, will it not be difficult for a court to adjudicate?"[22]

A few days before Christmas 1880, William Michael Rossetti received a visit from Mrs Euphrosyne Spartali: "Mrs Spartali called to inform us that Effie has had a very dangerous typhoid fever but seems to have taken the right turn now... Stillman is going to Greece, Crete or somewhere; will have £40 a month. I don't fully understand about this."[23] Two days later, William Michael Rossetti and Lucy dined with the Spartalis "... a family party including only the two sons and their wives, and Theodore Ralli and his wife... Strati says that Stillman started for Crete last Thursday – he is joined with others in an archeological investigation but of what nature I did not rightly gather. Apparently a good deal of touring, yachting and other such pleasuring cd come within the limits of the scheme."[24]

Visitors to Florence provided particularly agreeable interludes in the claustrophobic social and intellectual round of the small Anglo-American community, and could always be assured of a warm welcome.

Janey Morris spent the winter 1880-1 in Italy, staying at the Villa del Cavo in Bordighera near to the Howards who were at Oneglia. "Most beautiful, olives, lemons and oranges everywhere – blue sea and such sunsets,"[25] she wrote to Dante Rossetti; from there she travelled to Florence. Before she set out she wrote to Rossetti for Marie Stillman's address: "Will you give me Mary Stillman's address? I should like to call on her and see her happy face in her Florentine home, I have never seen the children either..."[26] During her two-week visit to Florence in April, Janey Morris stayed with Bella Duffy, visiting Marie and her children at the new apartment in the via Alfieri on March 28. The two 'stunners' had been acquainted for fifteen years or so; from the time of this visit she and Marie enjoyed a closer bond that was unbroken in Janey's lifetime. "I was very glad to hear so good an account from you of Mrs Stillman and her family. I always thought them extremely charming girls, and Lisa was almost grown-up when I last saw her..."[27] Rossetti wrote in April. Marie also introduced Vernon Lee to the most famous Rossettian muse of all, an occasion that was to have regrettable consequences. Lee was well aware of the value of acquaintance with Janey Morris as an entrée to London's aesthetic circles and she was at pains to obtain an invitation to visit her in London later in the year.

The artist Henry Holiday who, like Fairfax Murray, had worked for Morris in the early 1870s as a glass-painter – his wife was one of the Firm's embroiderers – came to Florence to capture the authentic background detail in his historical masterpiece, *The Meeting of Dante and Beatrice*[28] set on the Lungarno degli Acciaiuoli, looking towards the Ponte Vecchio. Vernon Lee arranged for him to visit the *Biblioteca Nazionale* archives where he learned that in Dante's time the Lungarno was paved in brick; he set out immediately for Siena where the Campo is paved in brick in order to capture this authentic detail. Oblivious to ironic comment, he made a detailed model of the houses on the opposite bank of the Arno on his return to London, which he then photographed to be sure that he achieved the correct perspective in his background. Marie Stillman sat to Henry Holiday for a portrait which he titled *Veronia Veronese*. Vernon Lee briskly dismissed it as "a vile caricature".[29]

Walter Crane returned to Florence to visit his fellow Pre-Raphaelite and old friend, John Roddam Spencer Stanhope and his wife Lilla at the Villa Nuti and Marie Stillman; it was the first occasion on which Walter Crane had met the Stillman girls. Lisa was now a tall, graceful sixteen-year-old whom Crane later recruited for his 1885 tableau of *The Art of Italy*.

Another frequent visitor to Italy, Henry James combined the perennial search for inspiration for plots and characterisation with the art of being an amiable and cultivated guest. He was welcome company in a number of American expatriate houses and aristocratic palazzos in Venice, Florence and Rome, and enjoyed a wide circle of acquaintance in all three cities. In Florence Henry James, the collector of prominent people, permitted himself the pleasure of being himself collected by the Pagets. He was acquainted with the Newmans, the Stillmans – Marie he met often in London – William Dean Howells and the rest of the literary American circle around Constance Fennimore Woolson in whose Villa Bricherieri-Colombini James worked while in Florence.[30] He seems not to have met his fellow American expatriate Edward Augustus Silsbee, whose story would later inspire the central character in James's novel, *The Aspern Papers*, although in London he knew Harry Buxton Forman, another player in the real-life drama that gave him his plot.

Buxton Forman was the Comptroller of Packet Services of Her Majesty's Royal Mail,

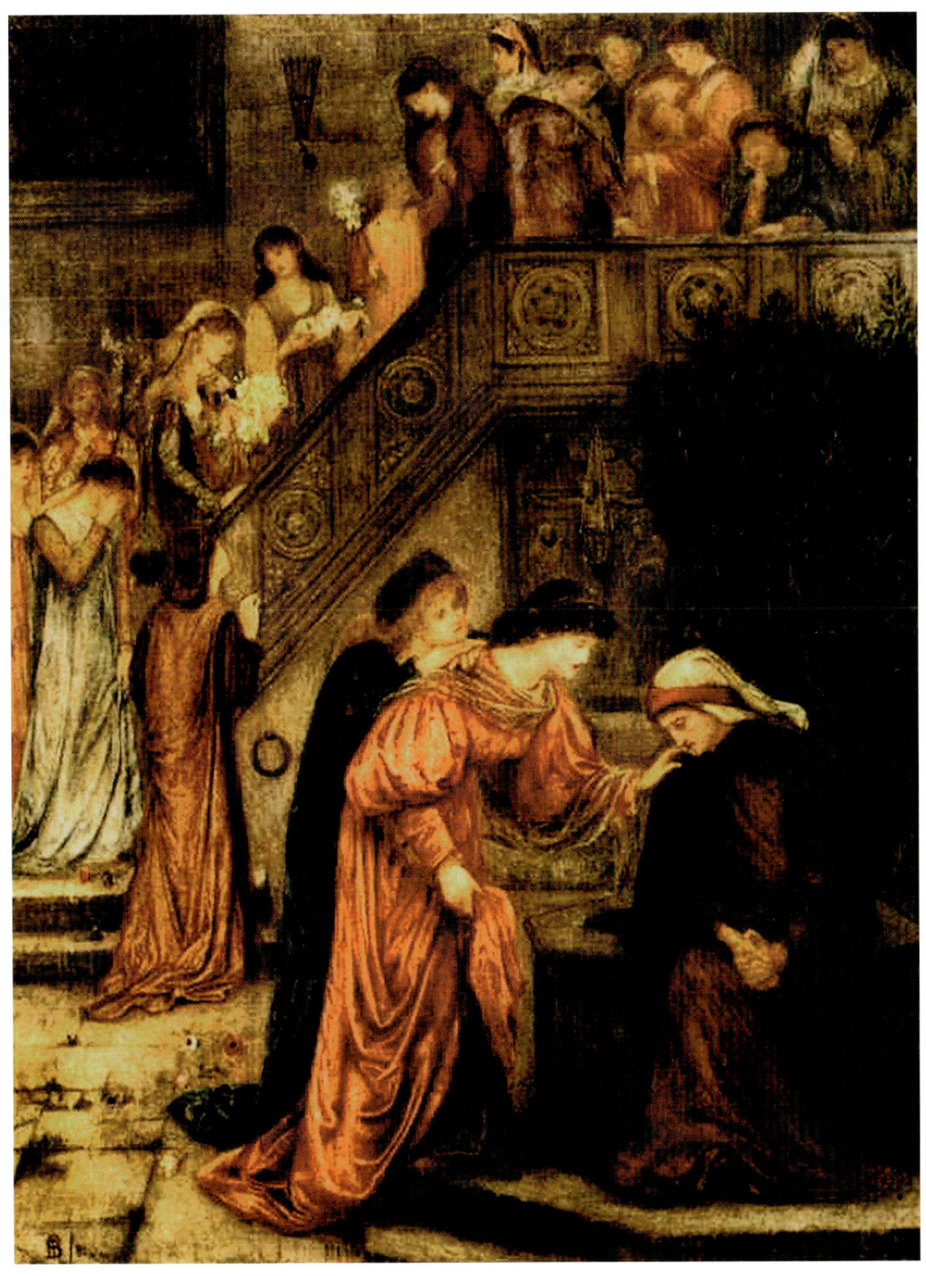

Plate 46
Marie Spartali Stillman
1880
Some Ladies of her Companionship (a scene from Dante's *Vita Nuova*)
Watercolour and bodycolour. 78.1 x 60.3 cm (30¾ x 23¾in)
Exhibited: Royal Manchester Institution, 1880; Grosvenor Gallery, 1881
Private Collection

employment that he combined with literary scholarship and the sale of rare books, autographs and manuscripts – larded with forgeries – in partnership with Thomas James Wise; both he and Wise were passionate admirers and avid collectors of the work of Percy Bysshe Shelley who had drowned at La Spezia in 1822.[31] Claire Clairmont, once Shelley's lover and the mother of Byron's daughter Allegra, had died in 1879, in Florence. She had lived out her days in relative seclusion with her maiden niece Paola and their lodger, Edward Augustus Silsbee. It was well-known that Claire Clairmont treasured a collection of some 50 of Shelley's letters to her, as well as more than 100 from Mary Shelley. Silsbee, a former Salem sea captain and Boston art critic, was determined to possess them, and had at one time travelled to London to ask William Michael Rossetti to remove any mention of their existence from the preface of an edition of Shelley's poems he was preparing. Buxton Forman was equally anxious to acquire them and he commissioned Henry Roderick Newman to act on his behalf, a task that he turned over to Fairfax Murray, while he got on with painting the fatal bay of La Spezia.[32] Paola demanded Silsbee's hand in marriage as the price of selling him the letters, when he demurred she accepted Murray's bid. Eugene Lee-Hamilton told Henry James the story: "Certainly there is a little subject there: the picture of the two faded, queer, poor and discredited old English women – living on into a strange generation, in their musty corner of a foreign town with these illustrious letters as their most precious possession. Then the plot of the Shelley fanatic – his watching and waiting – the way he covets the treasure... the general situation is in itself a subject and a picture."[33]

James was travelling with Hamilton Aïdé, the very model of cultured and wealthy company he delighted in attracting; "... an aesthetic bachelor of a certain age and a certain fortune, moving apparently in the best circles and living in sumptuous apartments," James had once told his mother.[34] Aïdé wrote dreadful verse and the lyrics for some sentimental songs that attained considerable popularity in America, but his principal occupation was knowing people and lavish entertaining in the best taste. He worshiped at Marie Stillman's shrine as only a confirmed and polished bachelor could do, and was deeply fond of her in a humorous way.

John Ruskin made his last, halting visit to Florence in September 1882, accompanied by his secretary and, later, biographer W G Collingwood, and called on Fairfax Murray to arrange a further series of fresco copies for the Guild of St George. Perhaps fortunately, William Stillman was in the Balkans at this time. During his stay Ruskin was introduced to Esther Frances Alexander (1837-1917) whom he immediately renamed 'Francesca' by which name she is generally known today. Francesca Alexander was the first of the American painters from nature to come to Florence. William Stillman, himself among the earliest of Ruskin's American followers, had known the Alexanders in Boston. He wrote of Francesca in the *Critic* that when she first began to draw her father had said: "...her ways were her own, and that she must follow them out by her own light. He would not interfere. That she has done so, her work shows;

execution, qualities of texture, manner of working and of regarding her subject, all are sui generis."[35] The Alexander family journeyed to Florence in 1853, and although they returned to Boston for one more winter and frequently visited the United States, Italy soon became their permanent home. Through the friends and associates of her painter father, Francesca Alexander attracted commissions from wealthy and influential patrons, the money from which she invariably gave to destitute Italians. "Unlike his other American followers, Francesca Alexander does not appear to have been influenced by Ruskin at all. Even before Ruskin heard of Alexander, she was greatly celebrated. In 1874 the poet James Russell Lowell composed a sonnet praising her; Frederic Leighton admired her work."[36] Ruskin too was enchanted by Francesca and her work; he arranged the publication of *The Roadside Songs of Tuscany* with her sensitive illustrations. They formed a close and lasting friendship that was broken only by his final collapse.

In April 1883 Marie Stillman was one of 24 American nationals to sign a petition addressed to the Secretary of the Treasury in Washington protesting against the tariff on works of art imported from Europe. They argued that the signatories were willing to compete on an equal footing "with their European counterparts and that nationality should not be a consideration in admitting art into the USA." It began: "We the undersigned American artists residing in Florence Italy," an indication of the extent to which Marie Spartali Stillman, Greek by blood, British by birth and an American citizen by marriage regarded herself as an American artist, and the United States as her principal marketplace.

The Stillmans remained in Tuscany during the summer of 1883, leaving Florence for the last time only in November. Vernon Lee, on her way to London met the Stillmans at Pistoia on a train in June; she wrote to tell her mother to expect to see Marie at least at Bagnio di Lucca[37] where she took the children to avoid the oppressive heat of Florence. In London, Lee visited the Russell Barringtons and G F Watts, where she encountered Mary De Morgan "of whose odious identity you have heard me speak, odiouser than ever since her brother's engagement to Evelyn Pickering."[38] She was invited to Holiday's studio "which is somehow made like a portable bath and turns in to a drawing room, music room etc thanks to a complicated system of hinges – with plaster casts draped in tissue paper and Liberty silk, full of weird people, women in cotton frocks of faded hues, made wide at the hips and tight at the feet like turkish trousers, v.aesthetical. Annie Cobden-Sanderson was there and, to my joy, Mrs Morris. She certainly is magnificently beautiful."[39]

There was a notable addition to the American expatriates in Florence in 1883, Daniel Willard Fiske (1831-1904) who numbered the Stillman family among his earliest companions there; William he already knew from his two years of service as attaché to the American legation in Vienna from 1861 where he was appointed in the same round of Civil War diplomatic postings that sent William Dean Howells to Venice and Stillman to Rome. A distinguished authority on Icelandic literature, translator of the ancient Icelandic sagas, and a former Professor of Linguistics at Cornell University where he once had taught ancient Persian, Willard Fiske was a gracious and unassuming host whose friendships reached well beyond the American colony. In 1880 he had married Jennie McGraw who was terminally ill with tuberculosis, and on her death in the following year he inherited her sizeable fortune, the cause of much bad blood between him and the University who believed that they would benefit from her estate. Fiske severed his ties and retired to Florence. (When he died in 1904 Fiske left more than half-a-million dollars to Cornell; he is buried there beside his wife Jennie.)

In Florence he settled in to a quiet life at the Villa Forini, playing chess, collecting early books with the help of Fairfax Murray, who gave him three early editions of Petrarch and bought pictures on his behalf, and surrounding himself with the less fractious elements of the ex-patriate community, American and English alike. He failed however to solve the forgotten rules of the Viking board game of *hnefatafl,* about which dispute continues. Both Marie and William were welcome visitors and when the Stillmans had moved to Rome and he to the Villa Landor, once the home of the poet, Marie continued to visit him there and paint in the extensive gardens.

Willard Fiske's letters to his mother, give an interesting picture of the life of a wealthy expatriate.[40] "On Wednesday I now expect to go out to Ponte a Sestaione, where my friend, Mr Stillman, with his delightful family, has a villa for the summer…his place is high up among the Appenines, two hours by rail and then two hours by carriage from Florence," he wrote in August. In September he wrote to Charles Warner: "One day Stillman and I went up a thousand feet higher to Abetone at the summit of the Modenese pass and lunched with Mrs and Miss (Francesca) Alexander – the latter being just now Ruskin's pet craze… People are beginning to come back to the city. The Stillmans (I am more than ever in love with the large, languishing eyes of Mrs S.) return the coming week, and the Russell Sturgises a day or two later." Russell Sturgis, architect, critic and writer, was a founding member of the Association for the Advancement of Truth in Art in 1863, the editor of the Association's magazine *The New Path* and a dedicated Ruskinian all his life. Russell Sturgis and his family spent the next four years in Florence: "The Russell Sturgis family came last night, and the Stillmans reach here tomorrow," wrote Fiske. His next letter said: "Mr and Mrs Stillman have returned and spent all last evening here, they expressing great admiration of my books and bindings. We read over together the remarks of about a dozen American journals on myself, Mr Stillman's comments adding an extra element of amusement to their perusal... Mr Fairfax Murray, the artist, the Stanhopes (a very pleasant English family) and one or two other friends, besides the Stillmans, are back from the mountains, so that I don't lack visitors."

Entertaining was not confined to the intellectual questions of the day: "Today the Stillmans all lunched with me. Two lunch patios of 10 people in 2 days! You see I am getting better. Today's lunch was as follows: – 1. Oysters in the shell. 2. Consommé a la reine soup; 3. Galantine of chicken; 4. Filet of beef a là chateaubriand; 5. Roast partridge on toast; 6. Mayonnaise of tomatoes; 7. Pineapple cake; 8. Cheese; 9. Magnificent grapes, pears, peaches, figs & fresh Engl. Walnuts; 10. Coffee. I had the curiosity to ask the butler for the bills of yesterday's lunch. They were less than 5 dollars… today's lunch was a little different from yesterday's and cost not quite so much… the Stillmans leave this month & I shall miss them greatly."

By the summer of 1883, William and Marie Stillman had reluctantly concluded that their Florentine idyll must end; there was no work for William in Italy and, in a period of relative stability in the Balkans, *The Times* had no present need of his freelance correspondence. The family stayed on through October: "Among the callers this week have been Mr Couper, an American sculptor, and Mr Fairfax Murray, an English artist, both very pleasant fellows. Mr Stillman comes out almost every evening, and yesterday I made a very agreeable call on Mrs Stillman at her studio."; early in November: "In the course of the afternoon many people dropped in (including the Stillmans, the Viscount Debe, Count De Gubernatis, Mr Murray, the painter, etc.) Mr Stillman goes to Leghorn tomorrow, and sails for N.Y. the day after. I am very sorry that he is to leave Florence… I have enjoyed him and his pleasant family more than anybody else here, and they will be a loss to me. Mrs Stillman and the children go to visit her father – a Greek merchant in London…"; and by the middle of the month they were gone: "Mr Stillman has sailed from Palermo for N.Y., and I miss him greatly."

The ever-faithful Lucy and William Michael Rossetti were on hand to welcome Marie on her return; William noted in his diary: "We called on Mrs Stillman at the Shrubbery; she seems to me darker than she used to be. Her husband and Lisa are in America where they wd remain for a year or so, then both return. Bella, Effie and Michael at the Shrubbery, but Effie is soon to be sent to a boarding school in England. Marie is quite attached now to Italy as a place of permanent residence but she thinks that she and the family will soon be leaving Florence and living in a villa on the outskirts... Effie is a sweet-looking, handsome tall girl, Michael very tall and boy-like for his age (5) – both of them seem to take after their mother principally..."[41]

The dream of a villa overlooking the city was not be. The Stillmans were never to return to Florence as their home. William and Marie had spent little more than half of their time in Florence together. Their decision to leave the city marked the end of an era and the beginning of a further period of separation.

CHAPTER THIRTEEN

MISS BROWN

Vernon Lee made the first of many adult journeys to England in June 1881, staying with her passionate love, Mary Robinson, and Mary's sister Mabel, in the family house in Gower Street. This was the year of Gilbert & Sullivan's *Patience,*[1] the ironic celebration of aestheticism, with its 'greenery-yallery' anti-hero and a chorus of young ladies dressed in Lazenby Liberty silks, on the suggestion of Luke Ionides. Agnes Mary Frances Robinson (1857-1944), was a scholar, poetess and biographer, the translator of Euripides, dedicatee of William Michael Rossetti's *Rossetti Family Letters* and author of *Grands Ecrivains d'Outre Manche; Les Brontë, Thackeray, Les Browning,* and of *Rossetti.*

With "no claims but her precocious literary reputation",[2] Vernon Lee was able to gain access to the more exclusive Pre-Raphaelite and aesthetic centres such as the homes of the Madox Browns, the William Michael Rossettis, and Kelmscott House, where she was welcomed by Janey Morris; at Oxford she made the acquaintance, through Marie Stillman, of Walter Pater. Richard Garnett of the British Museum and John Singer Sargent took her to meet Edward Burne-Jones and the Cobdens. William Michael and Lucy Rossetti introduced her to Edmund Gosse, the actor-manager Johnstone Forbes-Robertson, William Morris's friend the author Andrew Lang, D S MacColl, and Leslie Stephen. Evelyn Pickering took her to the Royal Academy. The idea of a contemporary novel about the aesthetic movement was already taking shape in Lee's mind, and she busily gathered material about the style and characters of the artistic and literary circle in to which she plunged herself.

"Mary [Robinson] gave old Madox Brown a last sitting for a portrait of her in chalks; just on the same non-resembling system as Mrs Stillman's portrait of Zina,[3] and indeed much more like Zina than Mary. The idealistic tendency of this portrait is, I fancy, characteristic of this school; he taught Mrs Stillman, a rather prosey, would be amusing old fellow living in a coal black house in a square with trees... as a treat he showed me a picture of his of some Greek women finding the drowned Don Juan, such a false, childishly executed thing..."[4] she wrote to her mother. Lee was welcomed in to the Spartali household at the Shrubbery by Marie. "We are just back from Mrs Stillman's where we lunched. A dismal house and her mother a most dismal and tragic creature. Mrs S very friendly but is extremely depressed; her little boy has been suffering from alarming fainting fits..."[5] she added. Visiting Janey Morris at Kelmscott House she found that "... the room was furnished like an extremely dingy sacristry with faded bits of old Italian furniture. A thick-set, shock-haired bearded man, powerful, common rather like a railway porter or bargee and not unlike a sort of grizzled Charles Grant was introduced to me as Mr Morris. Mrs M had on the usual crinkled white garb with a gold string around the waist or absence of waist; more beautiful and grand perhaps than in Florence. She was very lazy and friendly and asked me to call again," as Lee wrote that evening to her mother.[6] It is not hard to imagine why Vernon Lee was later so cordially disliked by so many of those upon whom she had imposed herself.

In June 1882, Vernon Lee again visited London. By the time of this second visit her characterisations had taken a sharper turn and her observation of the aesthetic scene, dutifully reported in letters to her mother, had become more critical. The letters and diary are full of sardonic accounts of the people she encountered: "Then there were Mr and Mrs Richmond Ritchie – she is Miss Thackeray the novelist, he her godson and twenty years younger and she is the thin, sentimental, leering, fleshy idealistic old person who would marry her godson and who seems quite brimming over at the idea of having babies at an age when she ought to be ashamed of it." Richmond Thackeray Willoughby Ritchie (1854-1912) was the son of the Advocate-General of Bengal, from a family distinguished in the Indian administration for three generations. In 1877, the year of his marriage to Anne Isabella Thackeray – the daughter and biographer of William Makepeace Thackeray – he had entered the India Office from Cambridge. "Poor Annie Thackeray," William Stillman later commented, "... her chance, so plain, so much older, of retaining the interest of a young man is precarious... but she should not have received him as a lover without marriage in prospect... if she loved him and refused to marry on account of disparity of age she would probably have ended in becoming his mistress..."[7]

At the time of the encounter with Vernon Lee, Ritchie had already been appointed private secretary to the parliamentary Under-Secretary of State for India and he rose over the years to Permanent Under-Secretary and a KCB. His wife, Anne, was his father's first cousin, and the marriage was notably happy, their critics being proved wrong. Henry James described her at a dinner party at Hamilton Aïdé's in 1879: "...further advanced towards confinement than I have ever seen a lady at a dinner party... exquisitely irrational." James had a soft spot for Mrs Ritchie: "...in whose extreme good nature and erratic spontaneity I find something lovable, even touching – she has minimum common-sense but quite the maximum good feeling,"[7] as he had once written to his mother. Her husband, ill-mannered and taciturn he thought, "improved on acquaintance". Also present was "the adorable little Mrs Ritchie, wife of Miss Thackeray's boy husband's eldest brother, not of commanding intellect but charm of countenance and an intensity of feminine sweetness." Marie and William Stillman's daughter Effie would marry William George Brookfield Ritchie, William Irvine Ritchie's first son.

Anne Ritchie's father, the novelist, was another born in Calcutta where his father died of lingering fever in 1815, the year of Waterloo. Anne's sister, Minnie, was married to Sir Leslie Stephen, the first editor of the *Dictionary of National Biography* (to which Anne contributed the biography of Elizabeth Barrett Browning); after Minnie's death in 1875, Stephen married the widowed Julia Duckworth, whose late husband had been a Hampstead physician who had held a medical post with the East India Company. Julia was the daughter of the sixth Pattle sister, and niece of both Julia Margaret Cameron and Sara Prinsep; with Stephen she had two daughters, Virginia [Woolf] and Vanessa [Bell].

The remarkable homogeneity of the families linked by their service in India – the Pattles, Prinseps, Hays, Ritchies, Camerons and Thackerays – was recreated in London in 'Aunt Sara' Prinsep's Little Holland House circle. The literary lions that she hunted included Alfred Tennyson, Henry Taylor, Browning and a quizzical George Du Maurier, writer and *Punch* cartoonist; she captivated her delicate resident artist, G F Watts. They in turn extended her embrace both to the artists centred on Watts's friend Ford Madox Brown's *coterie* in Fitzroy Square, to Rossetti, William Morris and Burne-Jones. Her neighbours, the great Greek families – the Ionides, the Cassavettis and, through them, the Spartalis – enjoyed the devoted following of the artists and writers of the day. It also ensured that this quite small group dominated literary circles, that they met often and that all knew one another and one another's business. Vernon Lee found her way to the heart of this circle through the kindness of only a handful of well-intentioned friends who would later regret it. "Mrs Stephen seems to have heard a good deal about me from Mrs Stillman,"[9] she noted complacently to her mother.

She visited the Shrubbery once more and "saw the Stillmans at the great ostentatious, Jewy house of the Spartalos [sic]... Mrs Stillman was tolerably well and in good spirits, but very miserable about the want of sun..."[10] and, with Mary Robinson, dined with William and Lucy Rossetti. The Stillmans were the only other guests: "Oh what a grimy, filthy aesthetic house... I shuddered to sit down in my white frock..." When, at William Graham's house, Lee saw Rossetti's painting of Alexa Wilding she mistook it to be of Marie, moving her to further flights of intemperate comment: "... a caricature with a goitry throat, red hair and German housemaid sentiment, called *Veronica Veronese*[11] and others mainly of Mrs Morris making her look as if her face were covered in ill-shaven stubble and altogether repulsive. To make mere painted, diseased harlots of women like Mrs Stillman and Mrs Morris requires a good deal."

Miss Brown, Vernon Lee's *roman à clef* of the aesthetic movement, was published in London in November 1884. It was with acute embarrassment that Marie Stillman and Henry James found their friends, including some that they had been at lengths to introduce to Lee, easily recognisable and woundingly portrayed. The dedicatee, Henry James, dubbed it "a deplorable mistake"; he had, though, earlier given the author some encouragement: "Henry James takes a most paternal interest in me as a novelist and says that Miss Brown is a very good title and that he will do all he can to push it on," Vernon Lee wrote on another occasion.[12]

The story is a Victorian Pygmalion legend set in the aesthetic circles of Florence and London. The poet Hamlin takes the lovely young Miss Brown, a servant whom he encounters in Italy, in to his house to educate with the idea in mind of marrying her; she is at first awed and willing, but later realises that Hamlin and his friends are disgusting and corrupt. Finally she agrees to marry him in a despairing effort to reform him. It is a flawed first novel that might easily have been ignored were it not that aspects of the principal characters were taken from life, thinly disguised and unmistakable. Lucy and William Michael Rossetti, who had generously entertained Vernon Lee, appear as Mr and Mrs Spencer, a nobody with a "lovable, laughable little woman" of a wife, interested only in her children and the Pre-Raphaelites; Lucy's father, Madox Brown becomes the elderly Pre-Raphaelite painter, Andrew Saunders. Mrs Argiropoulo is surely a composite figure from the Ionides and 'The Duchess', Euphrosyne Cassavetti; the reverent hush as Euphrosyne Argiropoulo takes her place at the piano with her sister can only be a reference to Christina and Marie Spartali. Miss Brown herself, like Jane Burden, is a social inferior, married to Hamlin in the same spirit of courtly love that William Morris displayed; the description of Miss Brown is unerringly one of Janey Morris: "...large wide-opened eyes of strange dark-greyish blue, beneath heavy masses of dark, lustreless hair, crimped naturally like so much delicate black iron wire, on a narrow white brow." Oscar Wilde naturally features, "...a Japanese lily bobbing out of the button-hole of his ancestral dress coat"; Algernon Swinburne and Alfred O'Shaughnessy can be found in the character of Cosmo Chough. Dante Gabriel Rossetti, recently dead, was the model for Walter Hamlin, the poet and painter, the aesthete in decline. There were competing claims of identification with certain composite characters, but all were agreed in feeling insulted.

Two letters to Marie's close friend make her distress clear: "I was so very sorry you had so accurately described Mrs Morris because I am sure she will feel much pain in being in evidence for every one must recognize her and she has suffered so much from being stared at and remarked and now she is so sensitive and suffering that she will feel it all the more."[13] Two weeks later she wrote again: "Your novel has been very much read and I heard it on all sides severely criticized, I cannot say how painful it has been to hear many of the comments, all the more so that it was impossible to feel or to say that you were altogether unjustly treated. There are several characters too easily recognizable, they will naturally object to be held up to ridicule and their friends are indignant. I am sure Miss Brown will cause you many 'dispiaceri' and altho' I know you love polemics and are indifferent to criticism I feel that you have done yourself great injustice and you will one day regret this work."[14] Years later in 1893, Henry James, writing to his brother who was visiting Florence, issued "a word of warning about Vernon Lee because she is as dangerous and uncanny as she is intelligent, which is saying a great deal... she is far and away the most able mind in Florence..."[15]

Chapter Fourteen

A Time of Misfortune 1884-1885

The years 1884 and 1885 were to be, perhaps, the most dispiriting of Marie Stillman's life. She was 40 and now divided her time between The Shrubbery and her father's properties on the Isle of Wight. Life in her parents' households was one of comparative ease, but the stresses of living as a permanent house guest with four young children took its toll. Her work suffered, while William found the going in America no less hard. "Mrs Stillman has just given Lucy that Venetian early picture of hers to which Nolly [Madox Brown] wrote a sonnet inscribed on the frame[1] ... Says that her husband, still in America, with his eldest daughter, writes from time to time in a dispirited tone..."[2] William Michael Rossetti noted in his diary.

The summer nevertheless passed agreeably enough. Vernon Lee was in London in June, forgiven at least by Marie: "In the afternoon, M[ary Robinson], John [Singer Sargent], Evelyn P[ickering] etc at Mrs Stillman's, sitting on the grass, discussion, fantastic, weird, curious, cigarettes, Beaudelaire..." she told her mother.[3] William Michael Rossetti, who saw another side of Lee's character, remained politely hostile: "Mary Robinson, Violet Paget and Mrs Stillman dined with us. Mrs S has had bad news from the IoW of her mother, sick with rheumatic fever... Miss P wishing to see some of Gabriel's works I showed her as much as time would allow of drawings and photographs. She frequently expressed admiration but I doubt she cares for the works as much as so many people do..."[4]

John Singer Sargent wanted to paint Marie's portrait. He "...would have stopped in London all winter if necessary... she looked most beautiful the other day in my studio, in large folds of black, with her pale face...",[5] but she would not sit. Vernon Lee was present at a tea party in July at Sargent's Chelsea studio at which she and Mary Robinson, together with Marie Stillman, Matthew Arnold's two daughters, Theodore Watts-Duncan, D S MacColl, Henry James and Walter Pater were among the guests.[6] "Mrs Stillman met Mme Villari and me and gave us lunch at Simpson's in the Strand, and boldly took us in to a shop to buy cigarettes..." she reported some days later. William Michael Rossetti "went to an afternoon at Mrs Robinson's; Effie Stillman there looking 17 tho' she can hardly be 12½ – the first time I meet her in general company. Was introduced to Henry James who has a fine face and serious tone..."[7]

In America, William Stillman's *Report on the Cesnola Collection* for the Trustees of the American Numismatic and Archeological Society was completed before he left New York in July, and published in October 1885. General Luigi Palma di Cesnola – he had awarded himself the rank of General in recognition of some distinguished soldiering during the Civil War – was the first Director of the Metropolitan Museum of Art, from 1879 until his death in 1904. Born in 1832 at Rivarolo, Piedmont, Cesnola was educated at the Royal Military Academy, Turin (1843-48). He served in Italy's wars of independence and his country's contingent in the Crimea before emigrating to the United States in 1860. When next year the Civil War broke out, Cesnola made his mark as a cavalry colonel with the Union Army. In 1865 he was appointed U.S. consul to Cyprus, in the same distribution of favours that saw William Stillman's appointment to Rome, where he remained for 11 years. With a *firman* from the Turkish authorities allowing him to excavate throughout the island he gathered an astonishing collection of some 35,000 objects of classical antiquity – vases, bronzes, seals and jewellery dating from between 3000 BC to 200 AD – the greater part of which was acquired by the New York Metropolitan Museum of Art in 1872-3.

Cesnola's military bearing, the swirling cavalry cloak, the drooping walrus moustache, the sharp eye and pince-nez, marked him out as a soldier of fortune rather than archaeologist, and the purchase had many opponents. As parts of the collection were put on display, it became clear to scholars that recourse to dubious re-assemblies in the name of restoration had marred many of the artifacts, while evasions about the location of finds and unreliable record-keeping provided further ammunition to his detractors. In August 1880 Gaston Feuardent of the long-established numismatists Rollin & Feuardent in Paris published an article in which he voiced mounting doubts about the collection, suggesting that Cesnola's report of his excavations might be fraudulent, or a gigantic hoax perpetrated at the expense of serious scholars throughout the world. In the libel action, which not surprisingly ensued, the jury failed to agree and legal proceedings languished.

In February 1885 the Society commissioned William Stillman to report independently on Cesnola's finds. It is open to question whether or not Stillman had found an opening to settle an old score, and whether he approached the Society or they him. The probability is that he volunteered his services. It is no reflection on the impartiality of his findings to speculate that it would not have escaped Stillman's notice that Cesnola had attained wealth and position from his posting to Cyprus as Consul, while he himself continued to make a precarious living as a journalist following his posting to Rome in a similar rôle. At any rate, here was an opportunity to demonstrate his own scholarship and acquaintance with the antiquities of the region, and Stillman set about his task with all the zeal of Hercules cleansing the Augean stables. The *Report of W J Stillman on the Cesnola Collection* was published privately by the Society in October 1885; thirty-three pages of closely-reasoned argument found heavily in favour of Gaston Feuardent.[8] Stillman did not renew his membership of the Society. Cesnola continued as Director of the Metropolitan Museum until his death. Neither party withdrew.

In October tragedy enveloped the Spartali family in the first of a series of misfortunes. Lucy Rossetti wrote to her husband: "I had a letter from Marie yesterday telling me of her sister's sudden death somewhere in the Tyrol, her husband, brother and eldest boy had just left her to go to Vienna and she was alone with her youngest boy and an English maid – they had no particulars, the brothers had gone to fetch her remains to England for the funeral."[9]

"Lucy wrote me this morning that the Countess de Cahen [sic] has died suddenly in the Tyrol. I fear that this will be a severe blow to her parents, esply her mother whose health has long been extremely frail," William Michael Rossetti noted in his diary.[10] Marie wrote to Ford Madox Brown from the Shrubbery : "I knew you would sympathise with me in this sorrow and I should have written to tell you about it, only I know that dear Lucy would not fail to do so and that you would know how very painful it is to repeat the little there is to be told... my brother-in-law has written to say he may come over to see Mother and bring the children for a few days shortly." William, she said, would sail for the United States from Liverpool on Wednesday 22nd October, and they hoped to spend a day in Manchester to see the frescoes: "I trust he will not come before the 23rd but if he should appear or announce himself I should have to give up my own plans as this meeting will be extremely painful to Mother ... [who is] very unwell and quite broken down by grief at times."[11] It was later put about that Christina Cahen d'Anvers had died in childbirth; the unhappy truth is that she died, whether or not accidentally, of an overdose of chloral at the tragically young age of 38. Surrounded by luxury and attention, cared for by Marie and Demetrius, protected by the husband she had sought to divorce, she was unable to live with her addiction. She was buried in the Greek Cemetery at West Norwood.

There was to be no respite for Euphrosyne and Michael Spartali. In January 1885 Michael Spartali was formally declared bankrupt. William Michael Rossetti and Lucy were once again at the family's side: "We were very greatly concerned a couple of days or more ago to hear that Spartali's firm had failed for something like £600,000; an utter crash affecting several persons for whom we entertain a more or less warm regard. Since then I have seen Mrs Stillman various times; she bears the blow admirably. But I have not seen Mr and Mrs Spartali. They expressed the wish the other day that Lucy and I would lunch with them today. The general aspect of the handsome, showy house is as yet unchanged tho' I understand that all will be sold off within a month or so. Mrs Spartali who has always been very attentive and complimentary to me looks very worn and ill; and in fact, besides the great shock and the preceding death of her daughter, the Countess E de Cahen, she suffers terribly from neuralgia. She began speaking to me (we were alone at the time) about the failure, but Spartali entering we left off the talk and never resumed it. Spartali looks unhealthily pale and older than he did but his manner is brisk, energetic and cheerful, and I think does him much credit. He talked away volubly on all kinds of subjects, often with a touch of pleasantry and plenty of laughter, but never touched once on his misfortune. The two sons and their wives (all equally ruined except Mrs Demetrius who has her own money[12]) were present; Lisa Stillman, a splendid girl 5'11½" high was at lunch; Bella, Effie and Michael were seen by me after in the schoolroom. Stillman, so Marie informs me, has made a good deal of money lately, writing in American journals. He may soon be leaving America and coming back to London, first perhaps visiting Cyprus."

William read the news of Michael Spartali's bankruptcy on the wire before Marie was able to get a letter to him and he cabled immediately his readiness to return. With little that he could do except offer his support, Marie urged him to remain there. Lisa had recently returned to her step-mother. "She lately had 3 weeks of backwoods life along with her father in some wild part of New York State – their only companion was a guide and they hardly saw a human creature. Lived entirely on fish (river shark) and potatoes. She relished the life much,"[13] Willam Michael Rossetti noted in his diary.

As always, Marie shared her thoughts with Ford Madox Brown: "I felt so much touched by your thinking so kindly of us when you heard of my Father's failure... A dreadful disappointment to him after 55 years of hard work; up to the present moment his courage and cheerfulness have not failed him and he appears to have great hopes of starting afresh when all this is cleared up," she wrote. Her mother was, she thought: "...reconciled to this misfortune (but) she seems to brood over her troubles and always to find them more difficult to endure." The house and property at Rylstone were, at least, in her mother's name and could not be touched by creditors.[14]

Marie called on Lucy early in March. "She says her father's affairs are now provisionally settled. Ralli and other friends advanced £30,000. This enables Spartali to pay 4/– in the pound and the creditors of his London House have accepted this comfort, but his Marseilles house remains over for some future arrangement… at any rate it wd seem that come out of the fiery ordeal with wonderfully little scathe; I am heartily glad of it,"[15] noted William Michael Rossetti in his diary.

After a year in New York working on the *Evening Post*, William Stillman returned to England towards the end of July 1885. Ford Madox Brown, having completed his murals for Alfred Waterhouse's gothic Manchester Town

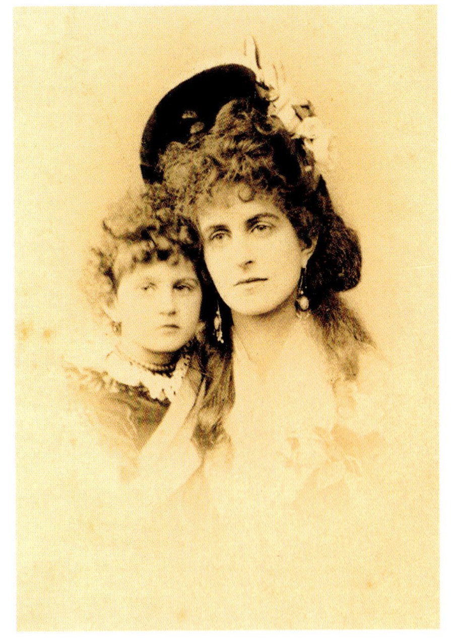

Plate 47
c.1877
Christina, Comtesse Cahen d'Anvers (née Spartali)
with her first son, Rodolphe
Cabinet portrait
Private Collection

Hall, was about to start work on eight immense murals for the Manchester Jubilee Exhibition building. Marie and William wanted to go up to Manchester to see Madox Brown and the paintings: "...but William has had to go to Paris, Bella and Effie go to boarding school – I shall have to stay with them until the last, poor children."[16] George Du Maurier met William Stillman in London for the first time. His comment, to Henry James, was representative of many: "I was much interested to see what kind of man it was who as a poor and middle-aged widower married the most beautiful woman I ever saw against her parents' consent, and still keeps her, apparently, in a state of adoration."[17]

The immediate cause of Spartali's failure was described in *The Times* as "unwise speculation in grain on the Alexandrian market". William Stillman had heard another account: "... a leading cause of his bankruptcy was the treachery and dishonesty of Barsani [sic], Mrs Spartali's brother who, being dispatched to Alexandria to see after a debt of some £100,000 owing to Spartali, compromised the matter for £60,000, put that sum in his pocket and has never turned up since. Stillman considers it almost impossible to probe the real facts."[18]

Michael Spartali was at the same time battling with the very Government to which he had contributed so much of his personal wealth, time and energies in support of the 1864 Greek insurrection in Crete against their Turkish overlords – almost twenty years earlier. He had been deeply involved in supplying arms to the rebels through his network of merchant contacts. Some of this *matériel* was procured with Greek Government money; more was provided on credit out of his own pocket. Spartali & Co had funded the design and building of two gunboats on the lower Thames, two further ships (one of which sank in the port of Liverpool and became the subject of litigation over insurance) and the construction of a coastal fort and its armament at the mouth of the Dardenelles; there were large sums involved, and he had first requested repayment in 1873.

The delay was politically motivated and the issue fuelled by a personal antagonism. At the time of Michael Spartali's bankruptcy Charilaos Tricoupis was the Opposition leader. In December 1876 the Greek chargé d'affaires in London, John Gennadius – who considered that as the accredited envoy of his government he took precedence over the Consul General in representing the interests of the Greek expatriate community – had clashed with Michael Spartali over the formation of a committee to speak for Greek interests in London to the British government. In 1881, they had again fallen out after Gennadius insulted Demetrius Spartali and his wife, the former Virginia Ralli, at a private reception. When Tricoupis had formed a new government in March 1882, he had transferred Gennadius to a post in Vienna. Gennadius appealed to Theodor Deligiannis, the new leader of the Opposition, who warmly carried on the feud for his own political reasons.[19]

Tricoupis was once more out of office between 1885 and 1886. During this crucial period Government auditors made the timely 'discovery' of Spartali's alleged accounting 'errors,' declaring that a number of payments due to Spartali were unsupported by the endless paperwork much loved by Greek bureaucracy. A brief Ministerial enquiry, which did not trouble itself with the irksome business of asking for his explanation, concluded that a complex fraud had been perpetrated. The Government next sequestered the bank accounts of his business in Athens, and the resulting financial problems eventually brought him down. In the months that followed, Tricoupis's political and personal enemy Deligiannis was able to make considerable capital out of the former Prime Minister's relationship with an alleged swindler who was accused of embezzling vast sums of taxpayers' money. *The Times* correspondent William James Stillman was accused of meddling, and it was not until early in 1889 that Tricoupis was able to put a Bill through the Greek parliament – not before there were fisticuffs and handguns flourished on the floor of the Assembly – authorising payment of the greater part of Spartali's claim.

No sooner was this managed than one of the previous creditors who had settled for 20 percent in 1885 claimed the balance and the matter went to court. Spartali assigned his interest in the money due to him to the British Government and diplomatic pressure was brought to bear on the Greek Government. Eventually a committee set up to determine the Greek Government's liability found for him and awarded him the then considerable sum of 335,110 drachmas. Most but not all of the monies due to him would finally be returned in July 1893; Michael Spartali had disbursed the monies 28 years earlier.[20]

Michael Spartali's bankruptcy compelled him to sell up in order to pay his creditors; his financial situation left him unable to maintain the £400 pa he had settled on Marie ten years earlier.[21] William Rossetti recorded in his diary that Marie's parents had found a house "to remove to when they leave the Shrubbery. It is in a new part of the Kensington-Brompton area and will (as I gather) form a very commodious residence. Mrs Spartali will bring away from the Shrubbery such furniture as she chooses."[22] The Stillmans too were obliged to find another home: four weeks later, Marie wrote to Ford Madox Brown from 46 Wellington Square, Oxford: "William has been advised to send in his name as a candidate for the Slade Professorship," adding sadly, "the Shrubbery furniture and effects have all been sold this week."[23] The vacancy in Oxford was created by John Ruskin's second resignation from the Slade chair; the post went to Marie's friend Sir William Blake Richmond.

A chastened Vernon Lee, who had completely miscalculated the effect that *Miss Brown* would have on her reception, returned to London in June 1885. While she moderated her tone in public, her acute observation was still in evidence in her letters to her mother: "Did I tell you that Mr Stillman is one of the candidates for the Slade Professorship, left vacant by Ruskin? One of the others is Pater, who certainly ought to get it but certainly, I think, will not. The Stillmans are going to the country tomorrow..."[24] There were, however, brief visits to London. Lee gave a small reception at the house of Mary Robinson's mother in Gower Street in July; Marie Stillman, Henry James and the Forbes-Robertsons were among those invited. "Yesterday Mrs Stillman came looking really lovely, much less thin & more beautiful than I have seen her for a long while. Then Henry James and Gurney. James is v. friendly with that curious mixture (I should think) of absolute social and personal insincerity & extreme intellectual justice and plainspokenness. He seems to think that John [Singer Sargent] is in a bad way; since Mme Gautreau women are afraid of him lest he should make them too eccentric looking..."[25] "Excepting the Rossettis, everyone has got over Miss Brown. Mrs Stillman wrote me a sweet letter asking me to go and see her in Devonshire,"[26] she added in a further letter.

Walter Crane's tableau of *The Art of Italy*, devised for a Grand Costume Ball at the Institute of Painters in Water Colour, was patronised by the Prince and Princess of Wales, and was among the most brilliant events of the 1885 season. Lisa appeared alongside W A S Benson and various members of the Crane family. Marie attended a rehearsal, and described the event in a letter to Bella and Effie at school, her last written from the Shrubbery: "Mr Crane's frame is a Renaissance triptych so [here she included a diagrammatic sketch showing figures and three arches labelled 'Venice', 'Florence', and 'Rome'] with the figures inside and a few outside: there are too many people for the beautiful scenery to be seen and Lisa's head is only above the others and very little of her dress will be seen." The *Daily Telegraph*, however, was effusive in its compliments: "Here was viewed a Florentine garden such as Rossetti might have imagined... and among the ladies of Florence grouped in this picture, which might have been conceived by Cimabue himself, appeared Boccaccio's *Fiammetta* in the charming person of Miss Stillman," – fast becoming a family tradition.

The Morrises lent Kelmscott Manor to Marie and William who joined her there for a short holiday with Michael. Marie kept Bella (16) and Effie (12), then both still at boarding school, close to her by letter: "Dearest children, we are very sorry we shall none of us be with you for the concert but it was scarcely worth while to leave this lovely place a week earlier and it would have cost us much money too remaining in town. We are coming up on the 14th and going away a few days later but our plans are not yet properly made and I will write and tell you when we know. I hope you will get the flowers Tuesday morning and that they will be fresh and please you. Effie was right about the forget me knots [sic]. We gathered them along the river and I cut all the flowers just before post time. Are not the white moss roses sweet. How I do wish you could see this old place. It is simply perfection. The field beyond the garden is full of elder trees in full flower and the scent of the blossom and the new mown hay fills the house. It is most delicious ...

"Your father was very unwell all thro' this week and I have been very anxious indeed and feel tired and worn from sleeplessness and worry. So sorrow pursues one even in this peaceful nook and tones down all ones enjoyment. I feel old and haggard again. I hate the thought of starting again on our wanderings and leaving this home like place. When oh when shall we have a home. It is all as much in the clouds as ever and I frequently lose heart... Mico races about after the chickens when lessons are over but he is very troublesome over his reading and writing and quite consumes me with rage and indignation... I hope dear children you won't feel lonely on Tuesday. Remember how much better it is for us to be here. I do hate the town and the general scramble so much.

Your very loving mama Marie."

Marie's portrait of her son Mico, painted at this time, shows a very demure young

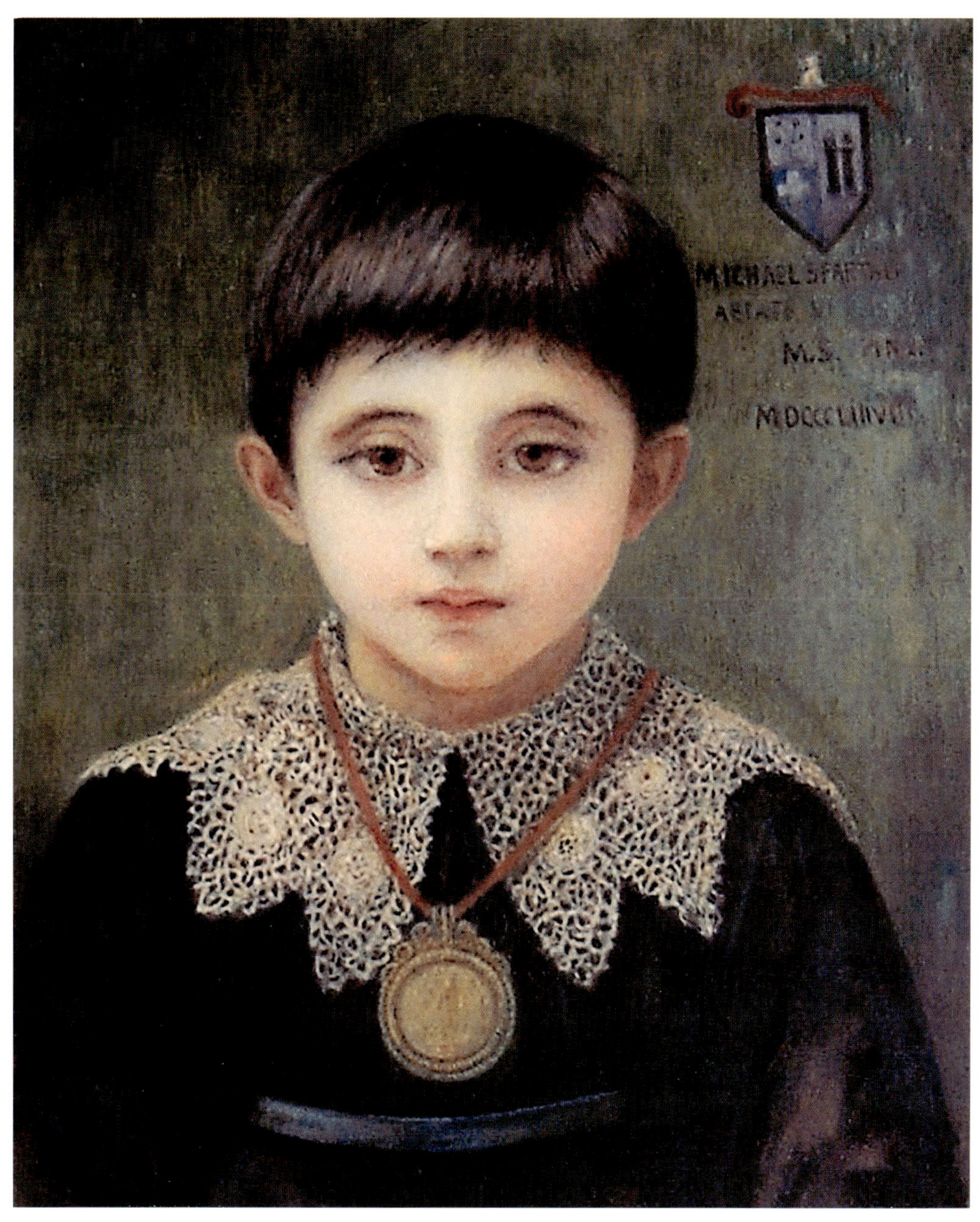

Plate 48
Marie Spartali Stillman
1884
Portrait of Michael (Mico) Spartali Stillman
Watercolour on paper. 38 x 31.5 cm (15 x 12⅖in)
Exhibited Royal Society of Painters in Watercolours, 1884
Private Collection

fellow, standing, gazing up at the artist with big, dark eyes and an expression of angelic patience. He is dressed in a smartly-tailored black velvet suit with silver buttons and a immense, six-pointed white lace collar which Marie Stillman has rendered with all the skill of a Hals. William Stillman's illness at Kelmscott follows the invariable pattern of his adult life; exertion and solitude followed by illness, mostly chest problems – pleurisy and pneumonia – and nervous exhaustion.

Too soon it was time to leave the calm of life at Kelmscott: "Dear Girls," wrote Marie, "I am so glad you have been having a pleasant week and that the concert went off so well. We are leaving here tomorrow. I cannot tell you how sorry I am to be going: it is such a treat to have a large roomy house all to oneself and to do as one likes and not to be hurried or flurried and not even to hear a train. The haymaking has been delicious. It is over now but the white lilies are just bursting into bloom in large clumps in the garden. Your father was in town for two days this week to see Mr Marshall, and I had a very reassuring letter from him. Your father returned on Thursday here and we have since been out in the skiff several times. The banks of the river are bright with wild flowers, quite blue with forget me nots all along; it is rather difficult to get them or I should have sent you more ..."

The older children were included in the discussion of possible plans for the family's uncertain future: there was no regular employment for William Stillman in prospect and it was certain that he must live by the pen as a freelance journalist. The principal question was where he would be best placed to find writing work, and the possibility of a family return to Italy was in the air. William Michael Rossetti recorded in his diary: "[Stillman is] somewhat pulled down with a cough…wishes to spend the next few days with his family in some cheap country retirement. This conflicts with Mrs Stillman's views who wd have like to have found for herself and Lisa a suitable house and studio in the Kensington neighbourhood and to make the best of her opportunities as a painter. What will actually ensue seems rather uncertain."[27] William's view on a suitable place from which to decide on their next move prevailed. "Stillman called on me at Som. Ho. being up for a few days from his present home, half a house in Exmouth."[28] Marie was ever willing to subordinate her wishes to those of her husband and it was September before they returned to London.

William Stillman accompanied the Rossettis to a meeting of the Society for Protection of Girls from Prostitution. William Michael was on the platform, his wife Lucy being an ardent feminist, determined to end a scandal that Parliament seemed equally determined to overlook. W T Stead was amongst the crusaders; now Editor of the *Pall Mall Gazette*, he tirelessly exposed the traffic in young girls in his journal. To prove his case, he bought from her mother for £5 one Eliza Armstrong – a virgin of thirteen – leaving her first with the madam who had been his go-between. He then quickly put her in to the safe-keeping of the Salvation Army, having demonstrated that he could, had he been so minded, have lodged her in a brothel to be kept at his disposal. For this he was charged and found guilty of abduction, and he was jailed for three months in Holloway, emerging as a popular (if engagingly idiosyncratic) hero; he wore his prison uniform every year on the anniversary of his release and sported a fur hat, caught mice which he enjoyed grilled on toast – apparently much taken by reading of this in an account of the Paris siege of 1870 – and enthused over a scheme for distilling gold from seawater. Stead later became a fervent spiritualist who numbered Catherine the Great among his intimate friends, and he perished – having foreseen his end – on the maiden voyage of the *Titanic*. For all his eccentricities he was a dedicated reformer who succeeded in bringing the scandal of child prostitution to public attention where others had either failed for lack of a political voice or had chosen to turn a blind eye.

Wilfrid Scawen Blunt[29] and his kindred spirit Bitters[30] were shocked at the revelations in the *Pall Mall Gazette*: "It seems astonishing that an unlimited supply of maidenheads should be forthcoming at £5 to £10," Blunt noted in his diary.[31]

In September 1885, William Michael Rossetti noted in his diary that the Stillmans were "about to move in to a house in the further part of Kensington with a good studio, rent £90 per annum.[32] Mrs Stillman says her husband ought not to go out again as correspondent to E Europe, and that he might just now have a good opening – his health no longer being strong enough, as proved by more than one experience, for such work. We mean to consign to Mrs S for the present those articles once belonging to Gabriel that are now warehoused in the Bedford Pantechnicon. This was Lucy's idea and I think a very good one; it will save us the warehouse rent, provide well for the articles and please and accommodate the Stillmans."[33] At this critical point in the Stillmans's financial affairs, *The Times'* Rome correspondent died; William Stillman was appointed to the post in May 1886. "Fairfax Murray says that Stillman is now definitely appointed correspondent in Rome with off-excursions to Greece – salary £600 which Murray regards as equal to £800 in London. This is excellent news,"[34] recorded William Michael Rossetti.

William's appointment at the age of 58 as *The Times'* correspondent in Rome and Athens, the first permanent salaried post of his career, tempered the loss of Marie's allowance. It also marked the beginning of another long separation. It was decided that Bella and Lisa should accompany their father to Rome, where Bella would help him in his art historical research and where Lisa was to continue her art studies under Ernest Hébert at the French Academy; the two younger children, Effie and Mico, would continue their schooling in England. Marie remained in England until mid-November 1889.

Chapter Fifteen

3 Challoner Street, 1885-1889

The twelve years between William Stillman's appointment to Rome and his retirement in 1898 are high among the mysteries of his relationship with Marie, from their defiant marriage in the face of parental disapproval and the disbelief of friends, through financial difficulty and separation due to William's work as a foreign correspondent, to the relative security of his new, salaried appointment based in a city that afforded them the chance to be together as a family under one roof. Instead they were together in England for less than a month between July 1886 and the middle of October 1889; nor did Marie travel to Italy.

William Stillman was no longer away from home for months on end, reporting on insurrections in far away places in conditions of great personal danger and discomfort; his work now lay daily close at hand. He had leisure to write. His features would later appear in several of Marie Stillman's later works painted in Rome. In spite of this, they spent almost half of the Rome years apart; the choice was Marie's, in part in order to give the younger children a degree of stability and to attend to their education in England. Marie was also the mainstay of her parents, who were devastated by the death of Christina and financially disadvantaged during the long drawn out recovery from her father's bankruptcy. Seeing little of William Stillman, they were completely reconciled with their daughter, and much of her time was spent caring for them on the Isle of Wight. It is clear also that both Marie and William considered Rome a good deal less congenial than the Florence that Marie loved above all cities, and that William would have preferred to be based in Athens were it not for his health.

It has been suggested that the marriage was not entirely happy; but it may be closer to the truth that William Stillman's unpredictable and peripatetic trade, and his deep-seated inclination to find refuge in solitude, had in the past precluded the sharing of a conventional life. Now that the opportunity was theirs, the need had passed. News of friends and items of common interest passed between them and through the children in complete, if distant, amity. No recorded word of reproach passed Marie Stillman's lips nor can any be found in her surviving letters, no matter the problems she encountered and overcame, mostly alone. She accepted the life she had chosen; any regrets remained scrupulously private. They had become old friends.

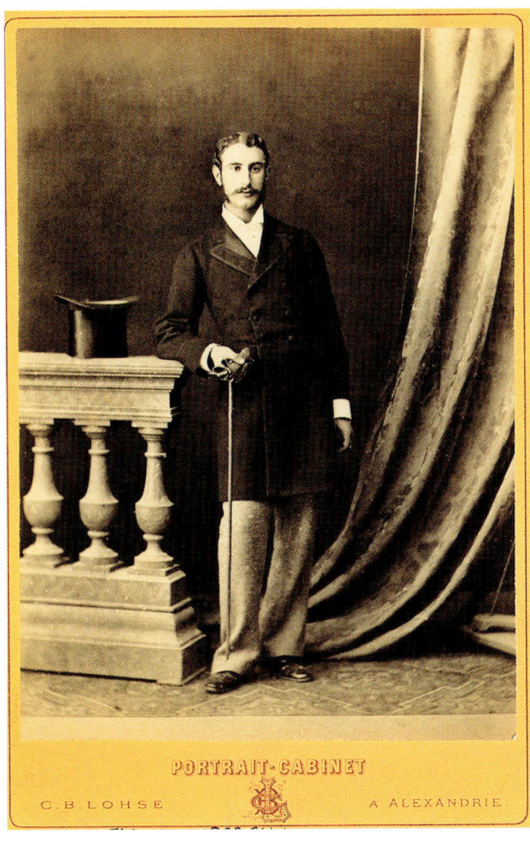

Plate 49
c.1878
Eustratius Spartali (Strati)
Carte de Visite

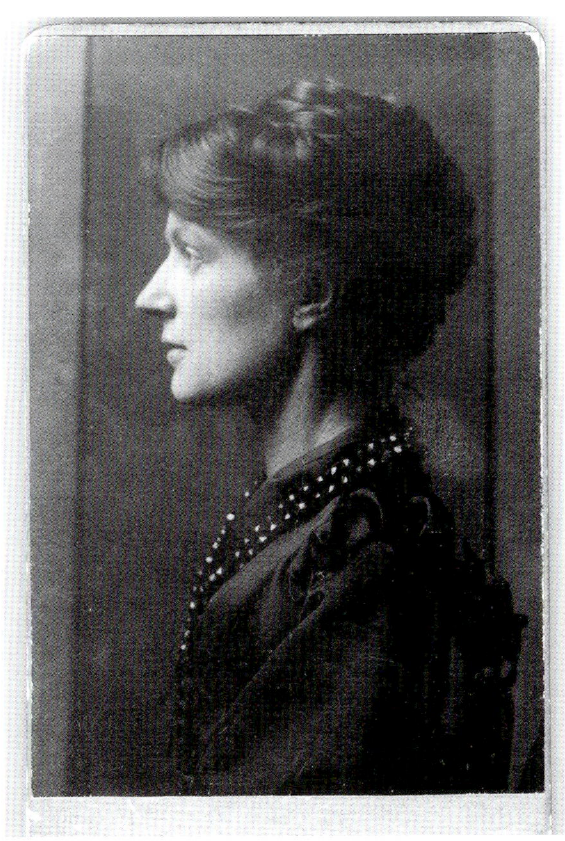

Plate 50
Eveleen Myers
c.1889
Cabinet photograph of Marie Spartali Stillman
Private Collection

In March 1886, Marie was at the bedside of her dying sister-in-law, wife of her youngest brother Eustratius; Olga Spartali, the beautiful daughter of Sir John Antoniadi of Alexandria, was 28 and they had been married just 6 years. Strati, Eustratius Heracles Spartali was a stock-jobber who lost the greater part of his inheritance in the Spartali bankruptcy, though they continued to live in Eaton Square up to the time of Olga's death. After the crash Strati severed his ties to the family – except with Marie who acted as the conduit between him and their parents – and he lived in a boarding house near Victoria Station, at 21 Denbigh Place, London, guarded by the landlady, Miss Emma E. Spencer. He never remarried, and lived to his 80th year; members of the Stock Exchange recalled that 'a talk with Mr Spartali was as good as a tonic.' He was one of the indispensable eccentrics who give the City its flavour.

Arriving in London in June 1886 for what had become an annual visit, Vernon Lee stayed with the Stillmans. She was soon involved in an intensive round of calls, parties and dinners. "Mrs Stillman took Mary and me to Hamilton Aïdé's. He has beautiful rooms overlooking the park in Queen Anne's Mansions which look like a model prison... Zina [Hulton], Mrs van Rensselaer, 'the eternal Mrs Eliot,' Lady

Archie, and Alice [Abadam, Lee's Jamaican cousin] were there." She was pleased to be invited by "the relenting Rossettis – in spite of Miss Brown, Mrs R has invited me to tea,"[1] she wrote to her mother. At tea with the Paters, she again demonstrated her chronic relish for gossip: "It appears poor Mrs Morris is perfectly miserable at her husband's socialist doings and has vainly done all she can to keep her daughter May out of the company of Morris's scallywags; and now May has engaged herself to a man who even the socialists think a tarnished person and who talks of 'splitting the throats of the rich.'"[2] (To the contrary, Janey Morris's letters to Wilfrid Blunt demonstrate a keen interest in William Morris's political activities.)[3]

Lee also called with Marie on Sir Frederick Burton who, as it happened, was out, and arranged to stay for two days with Lady Wolseley, the wife of the victor at Tel-el-Kebir, accompanying Lisa there. Later in June Lee wrote again: "The Stillmans are v. sweet, all of them, and it is delightful to be in their house. Lisa and Bella are delightful girls in v. different ways. Bella has turned out v. solid and hard-working. She is going to begin teaching at Chiswick High School. H Aïdé called on me and asked me to come for a day or two with the Stillmans to his home at Ascot..."[4] Later that month, Fairfax Murray dined at Mrs Stillman's with Vernon Lee and Mary Robinson.[5]

William Stillman left for Rome to take up his appointment as Vernon Lee and Lisa set off to visit Hamilton Aïdé, "a funny little man" she wrote on her return, "like a carefully clipped poodle. He is decidedly intelligent and has seen a great deal of the world. I have for him (who savours lion-hunting) the attraction of being a demi-semi lion and a friend of Mrs Stillman whom he many times tried to marry and still faithfully adores. Lisa is a delightful young woman. She is probably going out to her father in Rome or Athens this autumn & I should be truly grateful if she might be asked to stay for a few days in Via Garibaldi."[6]

The waspish Joseph Lindon Smith, an American landscape artist known generally as 'Zozo', was touring Europe in the spring of 1886, scouting for pictures for Mrs Isabella Stewart Gardner's collection at Fenway Court, Boston. He was accompanied by Denman Waldo Ross, an amateur artist and collector, and Ross's cousin Louise Nathurst.[7] (William Stillman knew Mrs Gardner and may also have met Zozo in America.) Writing to his mother from Venice, Zozo mentioned having had tea with "Mr & Miss Stillman" while in Rome: "On Wednesday evening [March 16] Denman, Louise and I went to Mr Stillman's to tea – at half-past eight – having received the invitation that morning – we had the most delightful evening. Mr Stillman was very pleasant and talked and showed us lots of interesting things, Greek coins etc. In the last 'Century' he has an article about Greek coins – very fully illustrated – and we had the pleasure of seeing a number of the original coins. He was very very interesting, I say, but he was simply nil, side of his charming daughter [Lisa], who is with him now. She is the most beautiful girl I ever saw, everyone who sees her (male and female alike) goes wild over her, and it is no wonder. You can't keep your eyes off her, she is so beautiful. Besides great and unusual beauty, she possesses other charms. She is bright and pleasant and draws extremely well. She showed us some of her work, and there was a good deal of very good work in what she showed us.

"Her mother [sic] is a great beauty, lives in London most of the time and paints very well I believe. She has been painted over and over again by Rossetti and Burne Jones – friends of hers and Mr Stillman. The daughter too – has posed often for artist friends – and they all are lucky dogs – I would be only too pleased if I could get the chance to paint or even make a drawing of her head. We may meet them in Venice, she said she and her father thought some of going there this Spring if war is not declared – in which case her father would have to go at once to Athens, as he is correspondent for the 'Times.'" He added a note in the margin: "Mrs Stillman was Greek, Denman tells me."[8]

Arriving in London in April, the three American visitors called on Marie and Fairfax Murray. Murray, whose home and family remained in Florence, was himself more often in London and a frequent house guest of the Stillmans, using Marie's studio until he became domiciled in Holland Park Studios in 1887. Denman Ross recorded his impressions of their meeting: "Went in the afternoon to see C F Murray (3 Challoner St, Barons Court, West Kensington, the house of Mr Stillman). He showed us some of his pencil drawings very fine and his oil pictures very bad (Rose Madder and chalk.) Saw also a lot of Burne Jones things and some of Rossetti's [illegible] mss. Mr Murray is a great collector of Rossetti's things. Saw sketches for the picture 'Found', very striking and pathetic but [illegible] no draughtsmanship — no technique."[9]

Zozo Smith also recorded their visit in his diary: "This afternoon Miss Nathurst and I went to see Fairfax Murry [sic], a pre-Raphaelite painter whom D had met in Florence. We saw a big picture[10] he was at work on and it was perfectly dreadfull [sic]. I never dreamed that things could be allowed to be done in such a vile way and be called 'Art' and yet this man exhibits his trash along with Jones, Rosetti [sic] and those other chaps and they have some followers."[11]

Louise Nathurst kept her own journal: "Saturday morning at home, afternoon went with D[enman] and S[mith] to the Stillmans – where we had a most awkward time in passing from reception room through dining room containing Mrs Stillman and seven or eight young women and children – all very aesthetic – after arriving in the studio we were placed before Mrs Stillman's picture[12] of fourteen sex-less men or young women leaning [? 'beaming'] over a broad stone wall, so poor in colour and so bad in form that we were speachless [sic] or when we did, speak – not-quite-the-truth. We came away sadder and I hope wiser. I felt as if I had waisted [sic] some precious London time — but the impression of house – and people – and burnt beans – is something not to be forgotten."[13]

On Sunday morning, 18 July the year before, William Morris had addressed an outdoor meeting in Bell Street off the Edgware Road. He was summoned two days later for obstructing the highway, and fined a shilling and costs. Morris seized this opportunity for satirizing the authorities. His interlude *The Tables Turned, or Nupkins Awakened* was produced on 15 October 1887 at the Farringdon Road office of the Socialist League for the benefit of the Socialist League paper *The Commonweal.* Morris himself played the part of the Archbishop of Canterbury, called as a witness for the defence in a police prosecution of a member of the Socialist League on a charge of obstruction and riot. George Bernard Shaw said he had never been present at such an overwhelmingly successful first night.[14] Marie was there, having purchased twelve tickets for the performance.[15] As always she was closely in touch with events in the circle without taking a leading rôle, a loyal supporter of friends and causes.

The early months of 1888 brought nothing but problems: in February Marie's son, Michael, fell ill; she wrote of her concern to Ford Madox Brown: "I could not write yesterday because till quite late friends were calling to enquire about Michael... my dear boy has been dangerously ill with a very violent attack of typhoid fever – Sir A Charles... saw him a week ago and told me he thought it very improbable that he could recover – but ever since then he has been mending – we are now at the 17th day and his strength is well maintained so that we have every hope of his recovery. He is no longer delirious and looks again his dear self – it has been a terrible time for me and from the first I understood how violent the fever was – for ten nights I could not sleep at all... I only let William know when there seemed so little hope." Until Michael's illness Marie had been working hard at her easel: "I have been painting on quite a small scale and I think you would like my work this year – I hope so as I always think of you when I paint and would rather have your approval than anyone else's. Lisa and William have got on well in Rome this winter. Lisa is a great favourite there. I hear she paints regularly at Costa's studio – I am glad because she does not work by herself, she gets easily discouraged."[16] Later in the month Lucy Rossetti was badly shaken in an earthquake while resting in San Remo, where she had gone in the hope of alleviating the symptoms of the tuberculosis that was slowly taking her life; she had to spend the following night in the open, which aggravated her

---

Plate 51

Marie Spartali Stillman

1884

By a Clear Well, Within a Little Field

Pencil and watercolour heightened in gold and white on paper. 54.6 x 48.3 cm (21½ x 19in)

Pre-Raphaelite Inc., by courtesy of Julian Hartnoll; Bridgeman Art Library

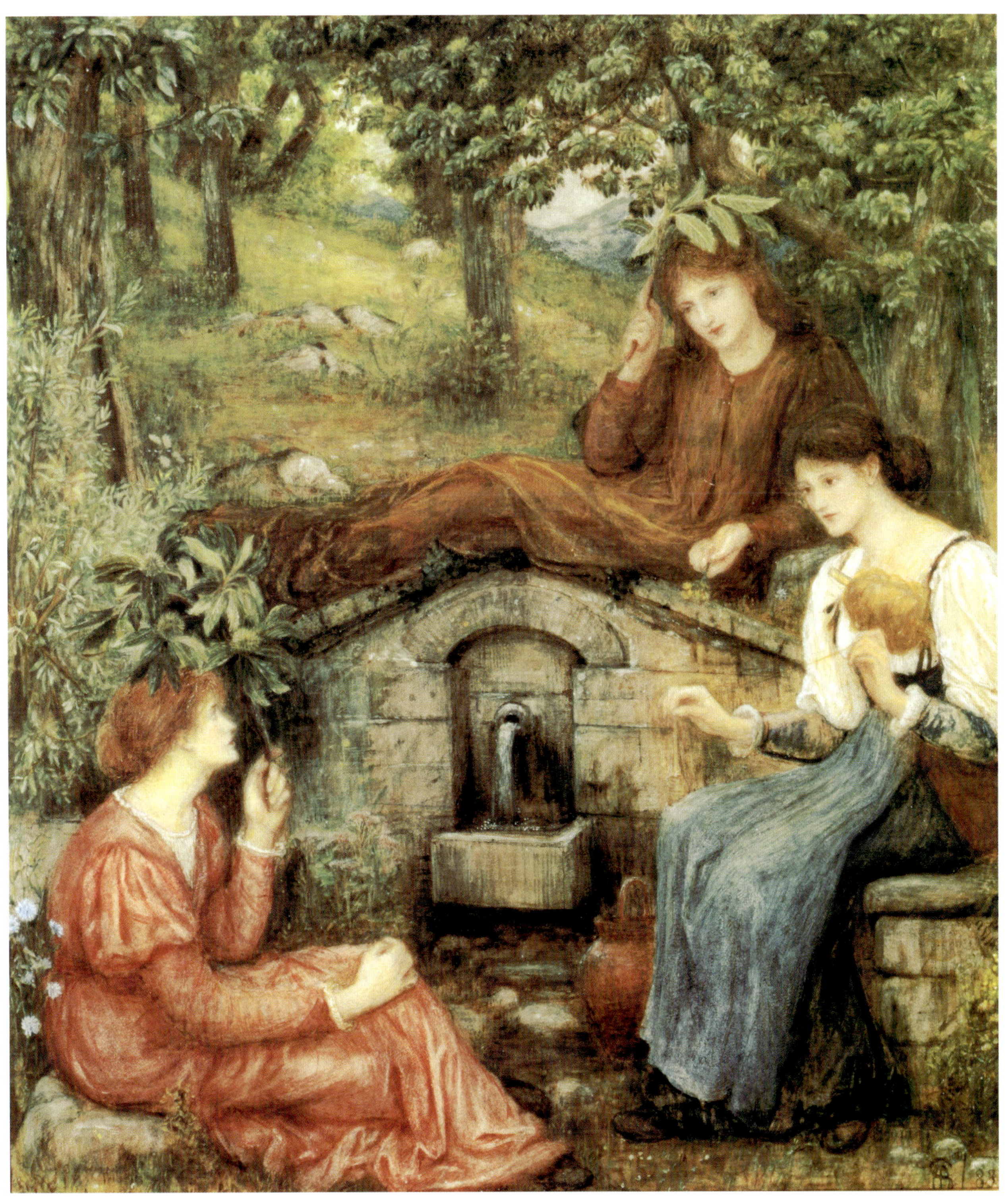

condition further and forced her to leave for Dijon where she rested before resuming her way back to England.

Ford Madox Brown was a welcome guest when he could be persuaded to leave his work on the Manchester Exhibition frescoes. Marie Stillman had heard from Mathilde Blind that he would be in town; many of his old friends were anxious to see him again – the Edward Burne-Joneses had particularly asked if he was coming down. It is clear from her next letter that Ford Madox Brown was determined to avoid socialising on his short visit to London but that he would be very glad to spend a quiet evening with his former pupil and long-time friend Marie Stillman; he suggested Thursday 4 April. It is probable that he wanted to distance himself from Mathilde Blind, or at least to avoid the family squalls that had marked their equivocal relationship of previous years. "Mr Fairfax Murray will be our permanent guest for the next month so he will of necessity be here..."[17] Marie cautioned him.

Mathilde Blind (1841-1896), the daughter of a Mannheim banker named Cohen, was adopted by the socialist and revolutionary republican Karl Blind – whose name she took – who had been forced to leave Germany in the Year of Revolutions and, when the Commune was crushed in 1871, Paris likewise. She was a poet, a radical feminist and writer, an intense woman of demanding and passionate temperament and one of a circle that embraced a number of politically active women who included George Eliot and Lucy Madox Brown. Blind soon made herself emotionally indispensable to Ford Madox Brown, "establishing an extraordinary ascendancy"[18] over him; he in turn tirelessly promoted her work to anyone who might prove sympathetic. (They did not include among their number Dante Gabriel Rossetti who refused to have anything to do with her.) In happier times Lucy had made a striking, if somewhat academic, portrait of her in red, black and white chalks.[19] When Madox Brown had fallen ill in the winter of 1882 matters had reached a crisis point; the suggestion that Mathilde should accompany him during his proposed convalescence by the sea had caused a clash between Madox Brown and his daughters Lucy and Cathy.[20] The question was resolved only when an irate Madox Brown left suddenly for Manchester to resume his work on the Town Hall murals.

Edward Burne-Jones painted the third version of *Danaë* or *The Brazen Tower*, shown at the opening exhibition of the New Gallery in 1888, Marie Spartali having modelled the head of Danaë. The story is of Acrisius, King of Argos who, being warned by an oracle that his daughter Danaë would kill him, had built a brazen tower in which he imprisoned her. Here she was seduced by Jove who appeared as a shower of golden coins; their love-child Perseus killed his grandfather in an accident, fulfilling the prophecy. Danaë watches as the soldiers build her prison. The series derived originally from the illustrations that Edward Burne-Jones made for Morris's *Earthly Paradise* and the choice of Marie Spartali as his model was a delicate tribute to her refusal years before to contemplate confinement in an arranged marriage. It is

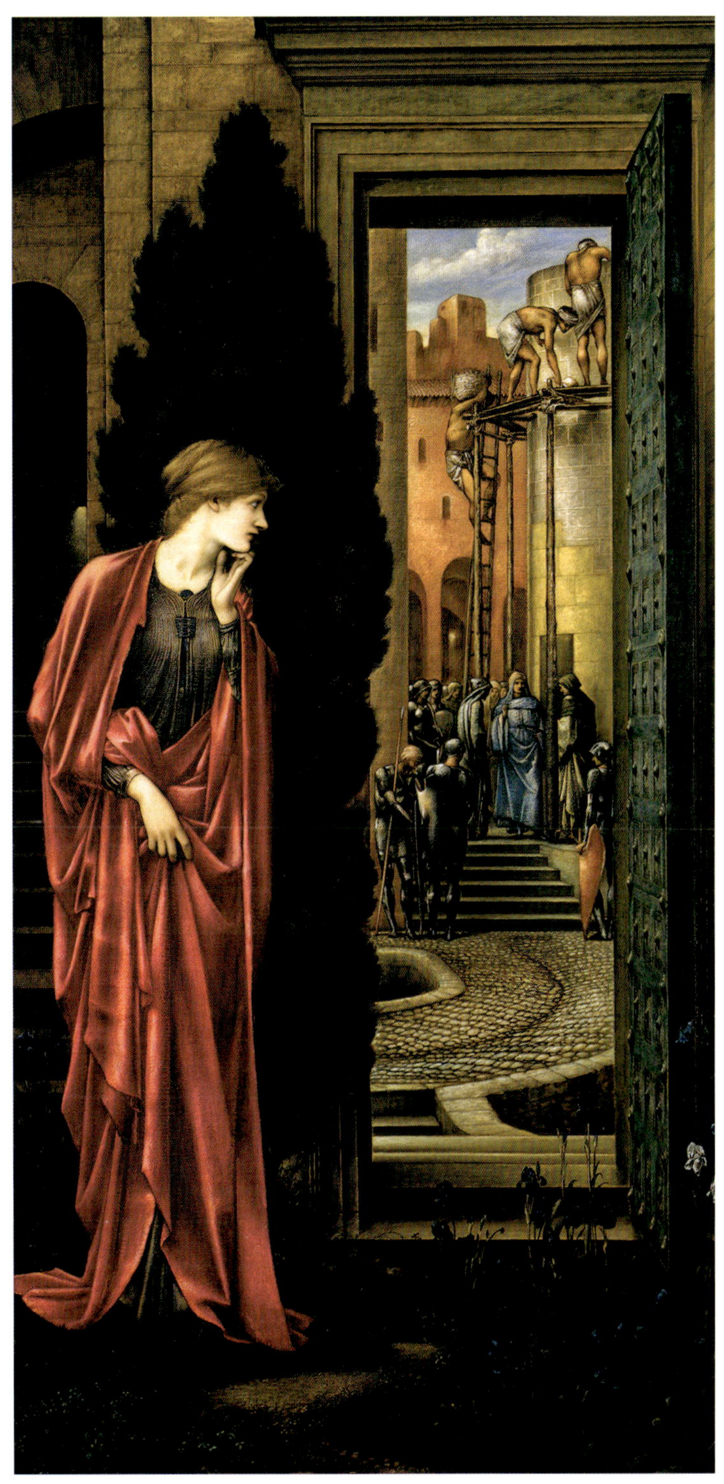

Plate 52
Edward Burne-Jones
1888
Danaë or *The Tower of Brass*
Oil on canvas. Signed 'EBJ' and dated. 231 x 113 cm (90 9/10 x 44½in)
Exhibited: New Gallery, 1888 and 1892-3
Glasgow Museums, Art Gallery and Museum, Kelvingrove

perhaps the truest likeness of her either by Burne-Jones or Rossetti. She was by now 44 years of age and the image is rather an account of her beauty than a portrait at that date; but it was seen at the time as faithful as well as lovely, and it is clear that she had lost none of her clarity of features or her poise. His unfinished portrait of Marie also dates from this time.

Marie Stillman exhibited her own *Dante at Verona* and *My Sister Rachel* at the opening exhibition of the New Gallery.

Marie continued to be closely involved in the art issues of the day, and the circle of artists – now in their late middle years – who had formed the Little Holland House circle so fondly nurtured by Aunt Sara. "Mrs Stillman dined with us. She means to abandon the Grosvenor Gallery and Sir Coutts Lindsay and to exhibit at the New Gallery conducted by Hallé and Carr. She says that at the Grosvenor her direct relations were all with Hallé and not with L[indsay]. She seemed to regard L's prospects as far from good,"[21] William Michael Rossetti noted in his diary. Ford Madox Brown refused to make the break: "I feared you would not want to support the New Gallery," Marie wrote.[22] William Michael Rossetti recorded in his diary that he had visited Marie: "...to see her pictures intended for the Carr-Hallé Gallery. Dante at Verona (from Gabriel's poem) pretty but wanting in energy. Rachele (also a Dante subject) one of her best productions. The Hancocks and the De Morgans arrived while I was there."[23] Excitement in Rome was intense: "Please write & tell us about the P[rivate] V[iew] of the New Gallery," Lisa wrote to Effie.[24]

Effie was noticed for her beauty and attractive personality as she accompanied her mother; William Stillman's letter to Effie on the occasion of the New Gallery opening conveys his habitual distaste for enthusiasm: "I have received the papers with the accounts of your success at the private views and the very funny confusion between you and Lisa. That surprises me more than your success for I do not see how it is possible for anybody to mistake two people of so different a build for each other. But don't let the newspaper compliments turn your head for they are not worth much as compliments – no more than their criticisms of pictures. You are so tall that if you lose your head you might catch an awful fall and the play is not worth the candle."[25] Ever the stern father, always the fear that inevitable heartbreak must follow incautious happiness.

Marie Stillman was unmistakably the outstanding figure of every artistic gathering, garden party, Academy or gallery opening, dinner or opera she attended throughout the six years that she was resident in London, the years between her time in Florence and Rome. "Another beautiful and picture-like head is Mrs Stillman's, so familiar in Mr Burne-Jones's pictures; she looks at the Academy like a figure from one of the artist's canvasses, as she stands clad in a black and gold matelassé cloak reaching to her feet in straight folds, her hair gathered in a great mass at the back of her head and held up by a comb, and a wreath of green leaves on her brow,"[26] read

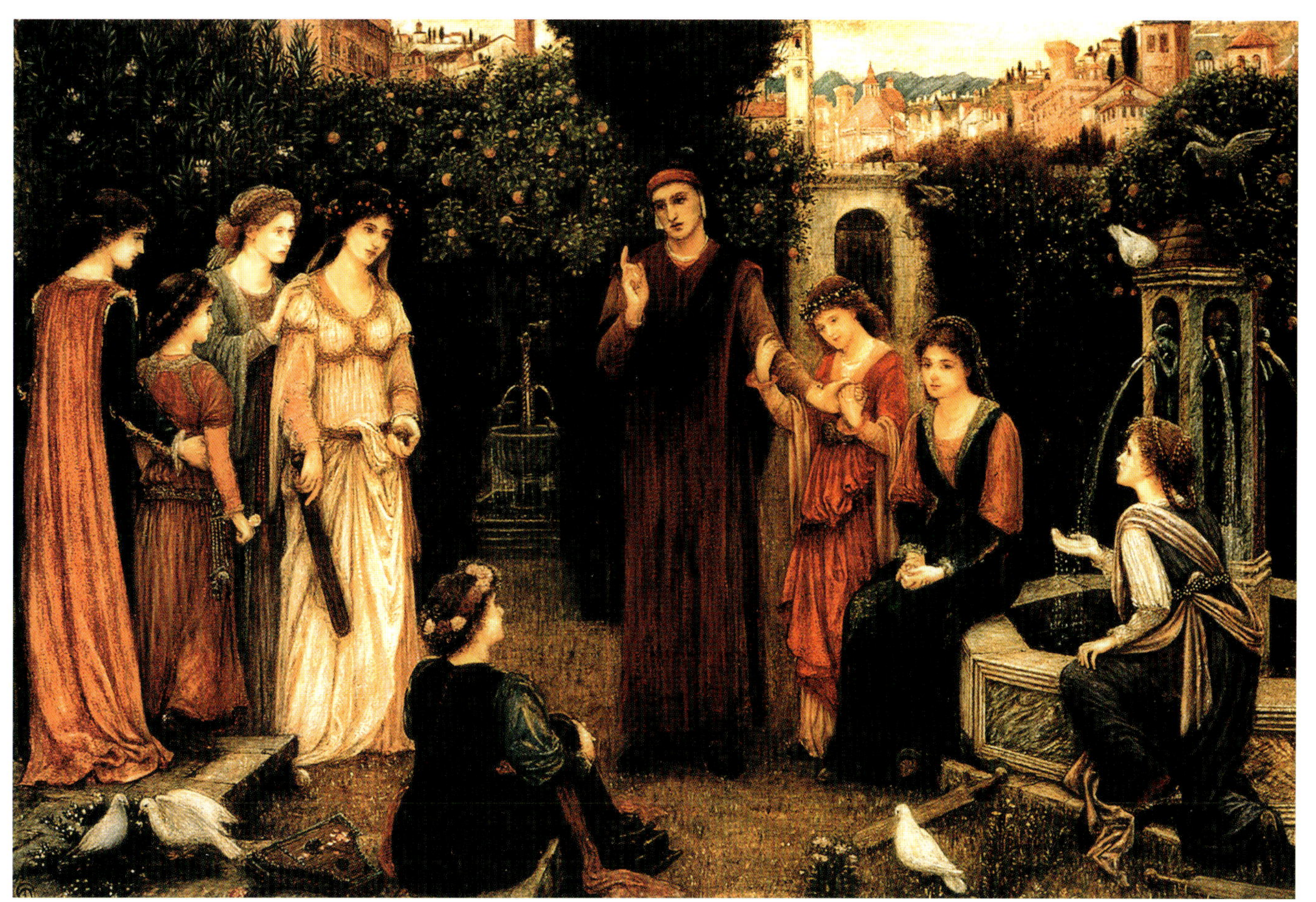

Plate 53
Marie Spartali Stillman
1888
Dante at Verona
Gouache and watercolour on paper. Initialled 'MS' and dated lower left. 49.5 x 73.5 cm
(19½ x 28⁹⁄₁₀in)
Exhibited: New Gallery, Liverpool, Autumn 1889
Private Collection

the report in the *Illustrated London News* after one such function. Alice Comyns-Carr, a frequent visitor to the Grange, described a Sunday afternoon tea party at the Burne-Jones's that summer: "...tea under the mulberry tree... the same people came Sunday after Sunday and the party generally consisted of George Howard [afterwards Earl of Carlisle], the beautiful Mrs Stillman who, though a painter of some note herself often posed as Burne-Jones's model, and Mrs Burne-Jones's two young sisters..."; after another literary gathering she noted: "Last night I enjoyed myself immensely at the Richmonds – Marie Stillman and Mrs Morris sat in that wicker bower, Henry James was there, and Andrew Lang..."[27] Annie Ritchie wrote to her sister in India: "At the New Gallery there is a very fine picture of Burne-Jones's – 'Perseus and the Dragon' – which Mr Richmond was looking at, but I couldn't help wishing that he could have had better snakes to paint from... the snake is all in scallops. Mrs Stillman and Effie were the two prettiest people there, and so beautifully dressed, Gladstone was there looking very, very pale and vigorous, doing the rounds with Charlie Hallé."[28] Alice Comyns-Carr spoke for all: "Mrs Stillman, in whom there never was, or could be, any age at all but merely a change in the type – once a dryad, now a sibyl – greets me with her gently emphasised voice..."[29]

Effie, who was pretty and popular with the younger members of the circle, was often to be seen at garden parties given by the leading artists, their patrons and friends that summer. The surgeon John Marshall was an habitué; over the years G F Watts, Ford Madox Brown, Lucy, Nolly Madox Brown and Dante Gabriel Rossetti were under his care, Burne-Jones consulted him about his depression and rheumatism, and he was also both the Spartalis's and the Stillmans's family doctor in London. Marshall in addition held the post of Professor of Anatomy at the Royal Academy Schools. His daughter appears from her diaries to have been a shrew of singularly unattractive disposition, and a xenophobe to boot; she was certainly out of place in the *milieu* of artists and patrons that her father frequented, and in particular seems to have resented the wealth, culture and attractiveness of the Greek community. "I do heartily object to the aesthetics, but otherwise it was not bad," she recorded after a Burne-Jones garden party, "...under the apple trees whose branches interfered considerably with my comfort, a ghastly & aesthetic company was assembled. We knew a good many folks including Mrs Stillman & Effie, who *is* a telegraph pole, Mrs Morris (who looks like a maniac) & her eldest daughter (who is out and out the ugliest person I ever saw,) Mrs Coronio (looking awful!)." Maria Zambaco she characterised as "meretricious, and so ugly", a curious judgment on Burne-Jones's stunning muse. The 'telegraph pole' remark seems to have gone the rounds, becoming a 'lamp-post' on the way. Years later, Maisie Ionides wrote to Effie Stillman: "It has been very dark lately and we all long for a 'lamppost' to brighten and cheer us."[30]

Miss Marshall was equally trenchant about another aesthetic garden party, at the Holman Hunts: "Found the usual gathering of artistics more or less loathly, but leavened with some fairly clean & respectable folks ... poor Mr Hunt looks pale & old, and his wife in an awful embroidered garment of dubious cleanliness, looks untidy and gaunt. Spoke to Mr Wm Rossetti, who was wandering around with his solemn little family... I spoke to Mrs Stillman & Effie, and was introduced to Mr Strudwick who was unexpectedly un-aesthetic in appearance & manner. Plain & pleasant, in fact... The 3 Morris women looked more witch-like than ever. We left about 6.40 or so. Not even as amusing as the Ionides." She did, in fact, usually derive some mild entertainment from her visits to members of the Ionides clan. But she summed up her attitude after another garden party, at the Coronios's: "I like to see these queer folks now & then, but I do not like Greeks, and never shd. They are a set of 'furriners' of doubtful cleanliness."

Wilfrid Scawen Blunt had visited Marie Stillman's friends, Rosalind and George Howard at Naworth Castle in February 1883 where he found Rosalind "wholly occupied in converting the local town to Teetotalism". In August of that year, Janey Morris was the guest of Rosalind and George Howard, meeting Blunt – one of the most dedicated serial fornicators of the Victorian era – for the first time, he "having been specially invited for the purpose by Mrs Howard".[31] It is not clear how soon

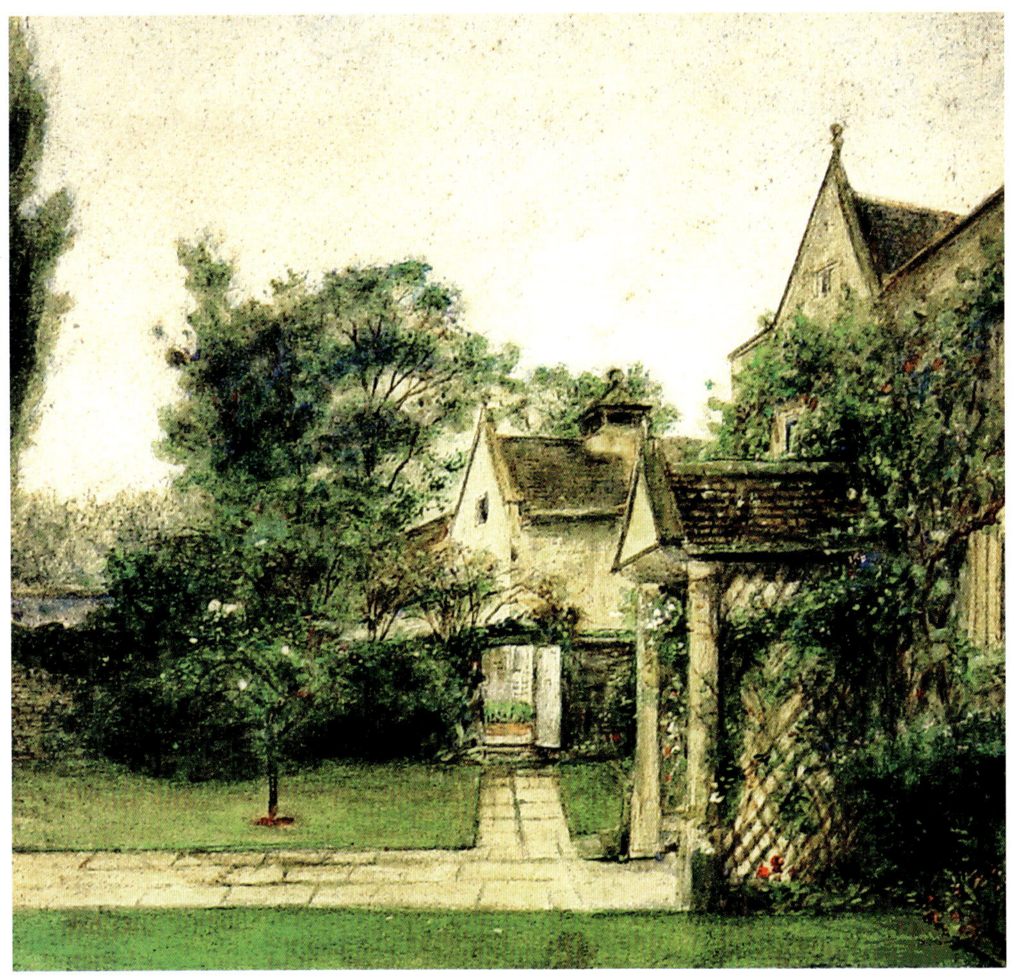

Plate 54
Marie Spartali Stillman
c.1888
Sir W B Richmond's Garden at Beevor Lodge
Watercolour. 21 x 23.9 cm (8¼ x 9½in)
Private Collection

Blunt and Janey Morris became lovers, though her visit to Crabbet Park, Blunt's Sussex estate, in July 1884 is both a possible date and in keeping with Blunt's many seductions there.[32] "... I *did* enjoy my visit to Crabbet very much but it is so many years since I have made a little visit anywhere that I felt rather shy with you. Please believe that I enjoyed myself only too much, I am often amazed at the capacity for enjoyment still left in me, and I have never felt it more strongly that in your house. I should like to come again some day if you will have me," Janey wrote.[33] Whatever the date and whether or not intentionally, Janey seems to have encouraged Blunt to try his fortune with Marie. Early in October 1888 Janey wrote to Blunt: "... I sent a telegram asking you for Saturday. Mrs Stillman and her daughter [Lisa] are here, no one else..." He appeared at Kelmscott with some alacrity, to William Morris's irritation.[34]

Marie's beauty and poise struck the expected note. In December she wrote to thank Wilfrid Blunt for the gift of his poems written during his two month's imprisonment in Kilmainham Gaol, Dublin for breaking the law on public meetings in support of Irish Home Rule: "I received four days ago your beautiful poems In Vinculis. How very kind of you... they seem to me so full of noble thoughts and pure faith expressed in exquisite form..."[35] Is there a trace of irony apparent in the compliment? Blunt was in the meantime enquiring of Janey (by now from Athens) where Marie was to be found: "... I have not even seen Mrs Stillman who is I imagine quite enslaved by Michael, home for his holidays,"[41] she replied. He was to wait for a year before they met again, at Kelmscott once more, where Marie was staying with Lisa and Effie. Blunt left Kelmscott in a hurry to follow Marie to Cambridge where she went on to visit John Henry Middleton; together they examined the Morris & Co. windows in Jesus College and Blunt noted that Marie Stillman was "the most beautiful woman that ever lived or ever will live in the world, though she can't be less than 45".[37] When Wilfrid came to say goodbye Marie scolded him for his love-letters: "You must not talk to me of such things and you must not look at me as you do."[38]

Maria Zambaco was a frequent visitor to Challoner Street. Marie Stillman had been best-maid at her wedding to Dr Demetrius Zambaco in 1861, and they remained close friends throughout the years that followed their youthful appearances with Aglaia Coronio as the Three Graces of Tulse Hill and Little Holland House. Maria Zambaco returned to Paris in October 1872, a year after her passionate affair with Edward Burne-Jones had reached its unhappy climax; she was living there in November 1877 when Marie Stillman visited her (Dante Rossetti wrote to Janey Morris that Marie Stillman had told him of "Mary Z. and her little pseudo-husband… painting Ned Joneses without number"[39]) and in 1878 when William Morris and Fairfax Murray met Edward Burne-Jones who was paying her a covert visit. Breaking with this second lover, Maria Zambaco returned to London around

1882 to study with Alphonse Legros who had been appointed Professor of Etching at the Slade in London in 1876; she was an accomplished sculptress and her portrait medals include a sensitive likeness of Marie Stillman, dated 1886, and now in the British Museum. Exhibited at the Royal Academy in 1887, the portrait medal has the name and date MARIE STILLMAN/MDCCCXXXVI/M T Zambaco; the reverse bears the legend 'sine macula' – without blemish – and the madonna lily, an apt comment on the character of the sitter and a pun on the symbol of the Virgin. An earlier portrait medallion of a young girl, also in the British Museum, made in 1885 and exhibited with that of Marie Stillman, bears a striking resemblance to the young Effie Stillman, who was 13 at this time.

From the time of her return to London, Maria Zambaco had occupied a studio in Campden Hill Gardens; in November 1888 the studio next to hers was occupied by Edward Burne-Jones who was working on his final great canvas *The Last Sleep of Arthur in Avalon*, which he had begun in 1885, too large, it was said, for the garden studio at the Grange. This recourse to the Campden Hill studio raised doubts as to whether the affair of twenty years earlier was really forgotten. "When M.[ama] & I went to her studio in Campden Hill Road the other afternoon, & found it all shut up, a man offered to ring the bell for us, and while waiting, he volunteered some information. There are only 2 studios side by side, and one is Mme 'Zambago's (like lumbago!) & the next Mr Burne Jones's, 'Royal artist' added our informant with a flourish. Now knowing that BJ. has a large studio at the Grange, & that Mme Z. did not know we knew of her studio there, (wh. P[apa]. found out by many enquiries at her former rooms,) & remembering the set out there was between them before, it looks very odd! I feel quite disgusted to think that she is going on agn. in the old style. It is a shame! If I were Mrs B.J., I wd. soon have her wig off!! P.[apa] actually mentioned the man's remark when he & M.[ama] called at Shepherd's Bush to Mme Z., who looked uncomfortable, wh. I don't wonder at. How very inopportune! – I don't like the look of it at all,"[40] the acerbic Jeanette Marshall – the unmarried daughter of John Marshall, physician to many of the Pre-Raphaelites – confided to her diary in November. All the same, when the sculptress paid the Marshalls a visit at Savile Row six months later, she was once again received as though the question had never arisen.

Vernon Lee met Maria Zambaco at Challoner Street in November: "I like being with Mrs Stillman... Mrs Sambako [sic], whose daughter is married in Tangiers, says there is no danger there..."[41] she wrote to her mother. However, by the late spring of 1889 Maria Zambaco, long since divorced from Dr Demetrius Zambaco, had moved again, to Athens, apparently with a young lover; William Stillman, Lisa and Bella were frequent visitors to her house there, and she brought in a number of portrait commissions for Lisa. "Lisa has another commission for a portrait and a friend of Mrs Cassavetti [Zambaco] has proposed to her to take one of the unoccupied rooms in her house to draw in as she cannot do anything in the rooms where she is living. Mrs Cassavetti has been very kind to Lisa and Bella, and would be to me if I had anything which she could do for me. As for the rest of the Greeks, they give me as little trouble as I do them for I see very little of them and I shall be very glad when the time comes for us to go back to Italy,"[42] William Stillman reported to Effie. (In 1891 Marie Stillman told Ford Madox Brown that Maria was once more in Paris to marry 'the young man there was so much fuss about when they were in Athens'. She went back to Athens in 1906 and in 1912 returned to Paris for the last time; she died there in 1914; her married name was Mary Sios.)

In the New Year of 1889 Bella was with her father at Agrigento in Sicily, taking notes of his observations on the great complex of 5th century Greek temples, described by Pindar as 'the most beautiful city of mortals'. From March to June they were joined by Lisa in Athens. In April, William had written to Effie to say that, as Marie had now decided definitely not to come out to Rome for the summer, "we shall not pass the summer together as I hoped we would."[43] The separation was not to his liking; Marie was still reluctant to commit to life in Rome. Bella and Lisa returned to Rome with their father by way of Venice and the Italian Alps. In May, from Cadore, William wrote peevishly to Effie, lamenting the decline of standards of their hotel: "There are lots of Jews there and the service is not so good as it was in the old days." To stay lower down in Recoaro, where the baths had been recommended, it would cost twice as much, which they could ill afford, William lamented: "...it is a heavy item if we all go over ten pounds a month, & we can't stand it..." The letter also contained surprising news of Lisa, which he appears not to have first given Marie: "Did she tell you that the Héberts want to adopt her? I don't know but I shall advise her to accept but as she is of age she has no need to ask my permission. They have no children and Mme Hébert is as fond of her as if she were her own child apparently. They agree perfectly and old Hébert who is cross to everybody is always amiable to her, and for her sake to Bella and me. If it were not for Bella being alone I think I should advise her to go but, as no one wants Bella, and I can't leave her alone when I go off on journeys for The Times and cannot afford to take her with me I don't see how I can spare Lisa." William Stillman was at this moment suffering from gout, habitually despairing, and feeling lonely. He ended: "Love to Mamma and all the rest of the people who care for it."[44]

Bella, now a few months short of her 21st birthday, seemed for a while destined for the rôle of the good-hearted, essential daughter who stayed at home to make certain that the meal was on the table, the sick attended, the household accounts kept; and indeed she fulfilled that function with grace and good humour for a number of years. She sat for hours at the bedside of William Davies – poet and supportive friend of the demented painter James Smetham, of Burne-Jones, Janey and Rossetti – who lay dying in Rome after a stroke, "the nicest, cleverest, and

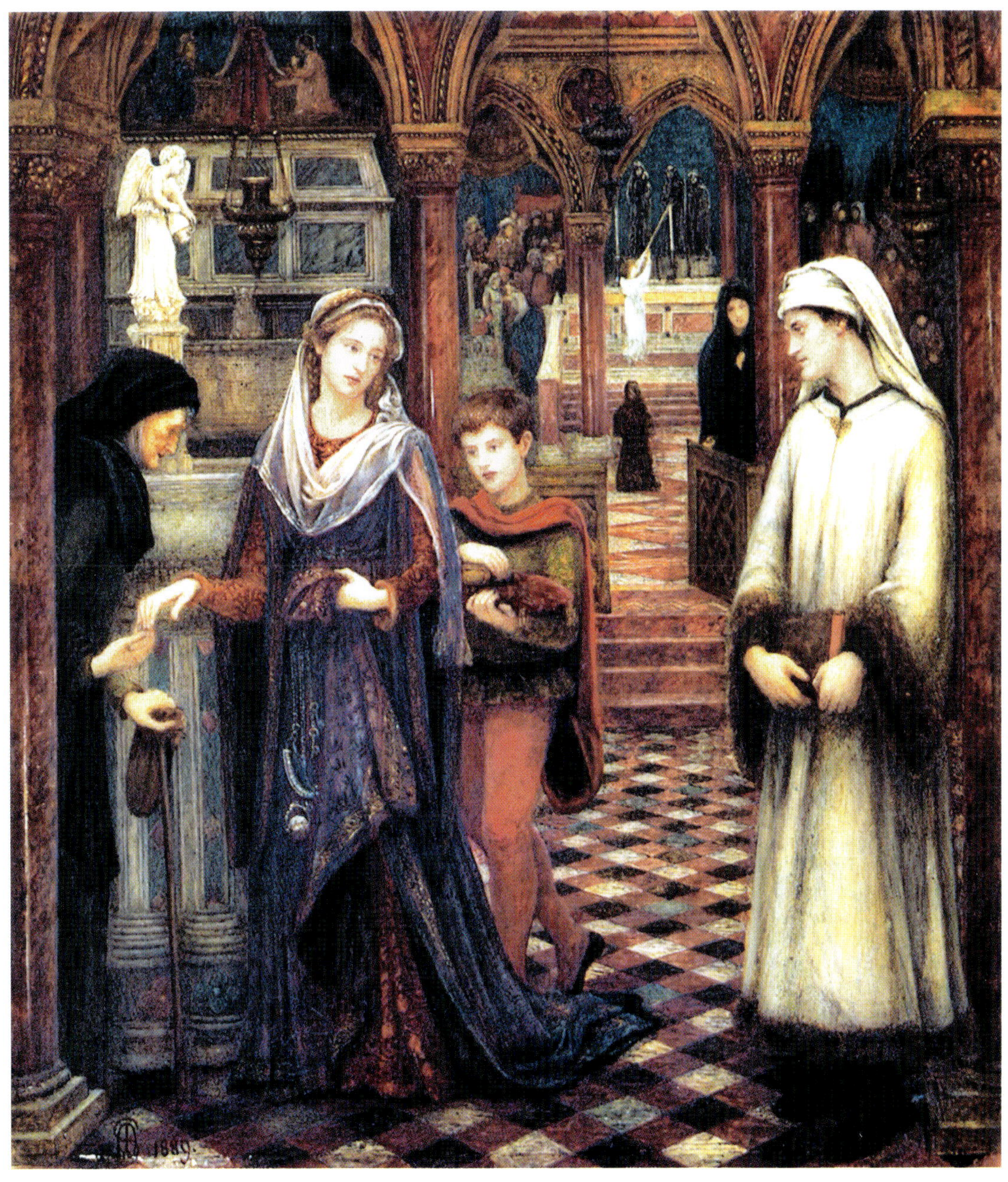

Plate 55

Marie Spartali Stillman

1889

The First Meeting of Petrarch and Laura in the Church of Santa Chiara at Avignon

Watercolour on paper. 56 x 48 cm (22 x 18⅞in)

Exhibited: Liverpool, Autumn 1889; New Gallery, 1890

Courtesy of Peter Nahum at the Leicester Galleries, London

comfortablest of men". Bella had been a baby of less than a year when her mother committed suicide, and she was thought to be dangerously ill in the year Marie and William married. Thus she slipped in to the part of the much-loved problem child early in life, an image that her father seems to have carried with him. Marie was as deeply fond and protective of Bella as of the other children; and together they were intimately concerned for one another's feelings, a happily close-knit family. They were, nevertheless, individuals. Bella was physically shorter than either her elder sister Lisa or her younger half-sister Effie, less immediately outgoing, less strikingly lovely, but the more intellectual; she claimed little artistic talent. She was, instead, highly literate, a cultured and knowledgeable researcher for her father's antiquarian interests and articles, and – a jewel in a writer's household – a typist. If, as William Stillman crushingly put it, "no-one wants Bella", it was to a large degree because of her loyalty; he had made her indispensable, and it was to be three years more before she made her brief escape.

Marie Stillman's remaining time in London proved to be one of her most productive creative periods, her work including the best known of her pictures, *Messer Ansaldo Showing Dianora his Enchanted Garden*, which she exhibited at the New Gallery in 1889, and *The First Meeting of Petrarch and Laura,* which was shown at Liverpool that year. Her family were not neglected. Marie Stillman was a vigilant mother, watching intently over the development of the girls; Effie received regular formal tuition in drawing from Fairfax Murray in London. Back in Rome, Effie continued her studies at the French Academy under the sculptor Charles Desvergne, a winner of the *Prix de Rome,* on the recommendation of Ernest Hébert, the Director and an intimate of the Stillmans; Lisa had studied drawing under him. Fairfax Murray later warned Marie that Effie would spoil the *mestiere* sculpting medallions of her friends.

Marie was also very much the responsible elder daughter following her father's bankruptcy in 1885 and their moves, first to the Brompton Road and, in August 1889, to 42 Earl's Court Square: "Dearest Girls, You must not think that I have let the grass grow under my feet ... I have seen only Murray of our friends because on arriving in town Monday I drove straight to his studio and sorted books until 7pm,

---

Plate 56
Marie Spartali Stillman
1891
Cloister Lilies
Watercolour and gouache
Exhibited: Liverpool, Autumn 1892
Ashmolean Museum, Oxford

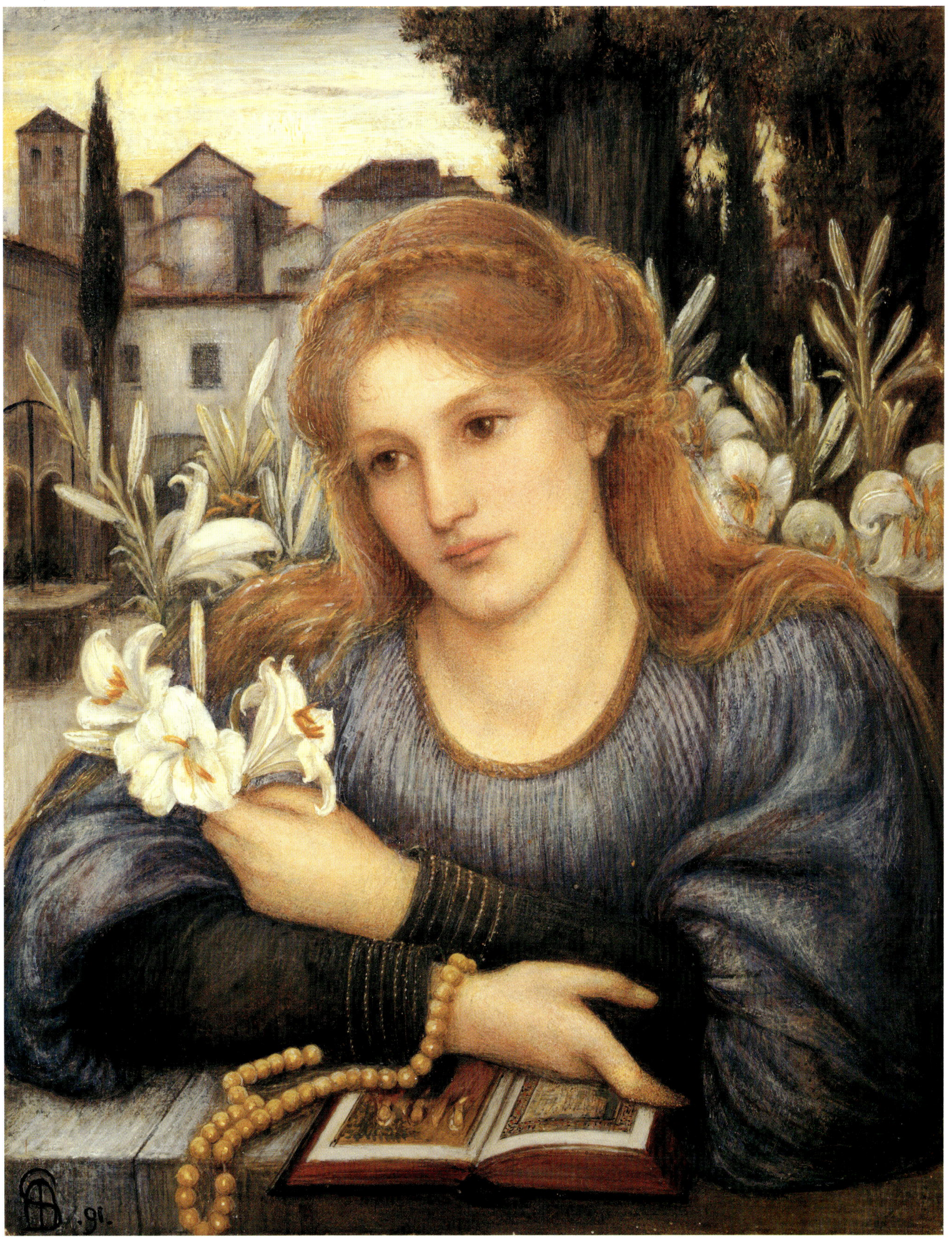

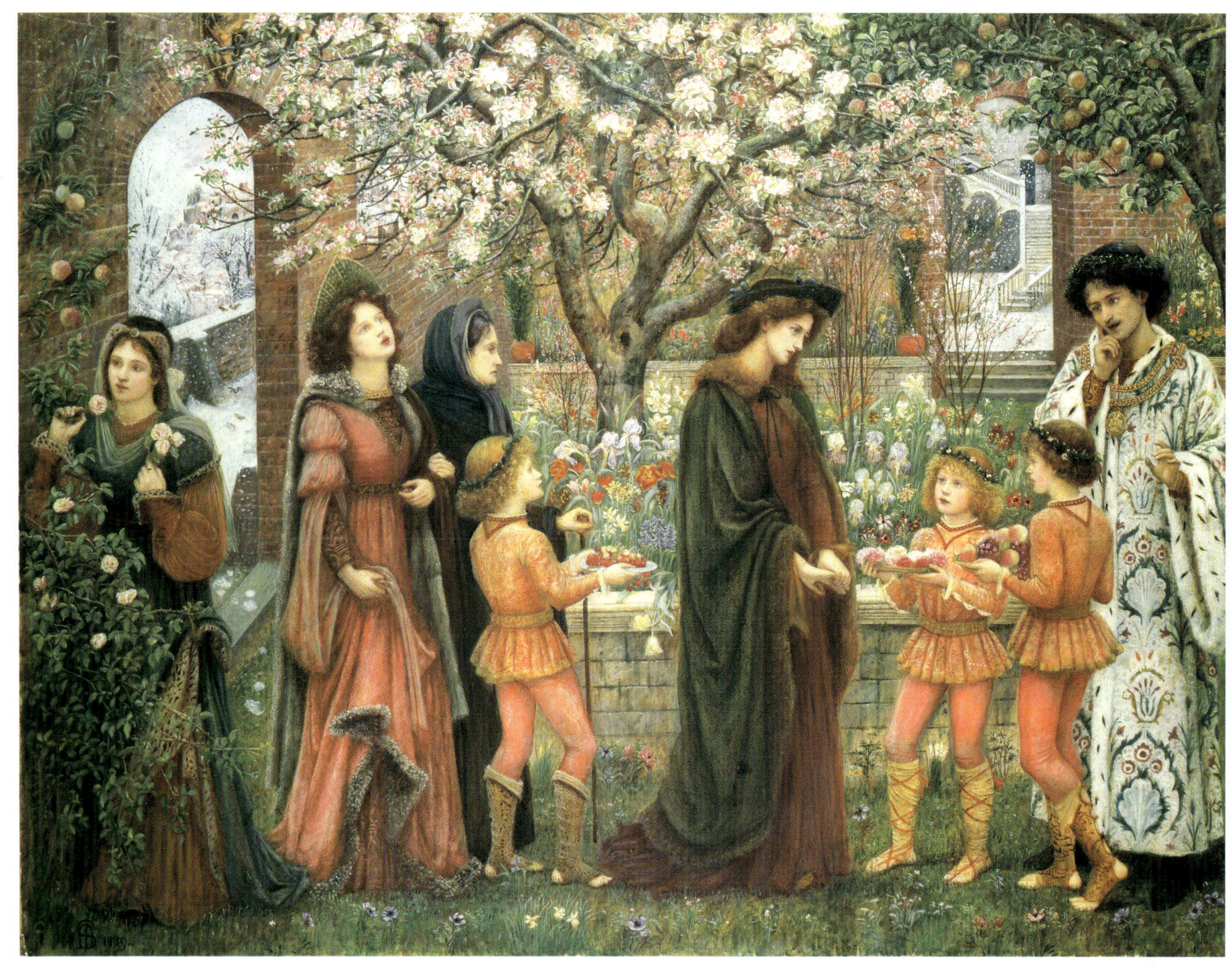

Plate 57
Marie Spartali Stillman
1889
The Enchanted Garden of Messer Ansaldo
Watercolour and bodycolour on paper. Initialled 'MS' and dated lower left.
72.3 x 102.8 cm (28½ x 40½in)
Exhibited: New Gallery, Liverpool, Autumn 1889; New Gallery, 1890
Pre-Raphaelite Inc., London, by courtesy of Julian Hartnoll; Bridgeman Art Library

and all day yesterday I was there with a man to lift boxes... this house is a very pretty one but too crowded with furniture for the size, just the sort of house we like with pretty nooks and corners and plenty of oak paneling, looking out on to trees both ways... Michael I find much improved, he is looking well – he is thin, he is sensitive, but we shall never see him otherwise – he seems to me less excitable than of old and much more reliable, he reads very nicely and is anxious to get on with French. Mr Middleton has asked us, Mico, Lisa and me to spend three days at Cambridge... Strati has just returned from abroad, he is looking very well and is as incoherent as ever, I am afraid he has a screw loose..."[45] Marie reported to Bella and Lisa.

With her parents settled in Earls' Court, Marie steeled herself to join William in Rome. "I shall go to Worthing in another ten days – I do not expect to be in town till October. I have a large placard on the house which proclaims it to be let furnished or un-... I shall do my utmost to sell out as soon as possible and go to Rome, William is very far from well... They are returning to Rome [from Cortina] to stay with the Héberts..." she wrote to Vernon Lee.[46] William Stillman was increasingly pressing, writing to Effie from Rome: "I hope that Mamma will not insist on letting the house as a necessary condition of coming out speedily because I must soon go out to Greece again, and I do not like to leave the girls... if I may judge from her way of talking about it she is not so anxious to come as we are to have her come..."[47] Marie was indeed hesitant to leave London for Rome as she confessed to Charles Fairfax Murray and the Burne-Joneses. Mico, now 11 years old, was left behind to continue his schooling in the care of one Miss Cave in Hampstead, to Marie's great distress. She set out for Rome in the middle of October.

Edward Burne-Jones wrote to her in December: "You would laugh with that incredulous laugh of yours if I told you how dolefully I passed the street that led to your house and how vacant and empty the neighbourhood feels now you are gone – but it is quite true nevertheless and in spite of incredulous smiles – a great deal has gone out of the lives of your friends now you are gone – we all say it and we all feel it and are quite honest about it. Nothing has happened since your going – it has been a good November, warm and not very dark until this week. I have worked pretty hard – set all my pictures of Briar Rose, for one thing, to see how they look together – and I think they will do and four weeks of work will finish them. What a relief it will be when they are finished and I can forget them. Agnew came the other day to see them for the first time and seemed mightily pleased – but many a time I have wished you could come in and cheer me about them and say soft, comforting things such as help a painter far more than judicious criticism."[48]

Chapter Sixteen

The Parnell Affair

William Stillman had been with Marie on leave in England for three months from October 1887 when he resumed his official appointment as *The Times* correspondent in Rome and Athens. "It is anything but a subject of congratulation to me as I feel the responsibility of the family more and more as they grow older and more individual," Marie wrote to Ford Madox Brown in February 1888.[1] It is perhaps the only instance where Marie spoke of her feelings about their many enforced separations. William was for his part equally reluctant to go back; before April 1888 was out, Bella – who was as usual managing the household – wrote to Effie from 44 via Gregoriana: "... Papa has Mr McDonald's permission to take as much holiday as he needs. He is depressed by the sirocco..."[2]

Stillman now represented *The Times* in Rome in a political climate less friendly to Britain. Almost thirty years earlier, Francesco Crispi, the Italian Premier, had been amongst the most ardent of Mazzini's revolutionary supporters; but as Crispi's political career developed he became increasingly authoritarian, and such diplomatic skills as he might once have possessed were by now wanting. He was touchy, uncompromising and dictatorial, having taken the portfolios of Interior and Foreign Affairs in addition to the Premiership. William Stillman, who knew Crispi better than most despite his disdain for the press, was able in time to gain a semblance of trust and personal access, describing him as an "absolutely honest and patriotic statesman, the first since Cavour".

In Athens, William Stillman's return coincided with Charilaos Tricoupis's regaining the premiership for the fourth time as Greece teetered on the verge of war with Turkey, with a combined fleet of the Great Powers blockading Piraeus. While Tricoupis had been out of office, the Greek army was virtually out of political control, rashly stirring the sentiment for war by provoking isolated border incidents against neighbouring Bulgaria. Stillman, who had contracted a severe bout of typhoid and had been unable to cover the work of the border commission for *The Times*, now played a dramatic diplomatic hand at the eleventh hour; acting on the personal authority of Tricoupis, he undertook the task of persuading the British Ambassador, Lord Baring – who was convinced that the Greek Government remained bent on war – that the army would be brought to heel. While Baring cabled this urgent intelligence to London for transmission to the Sublime Porte (the government of the Ottoman Empire), Stillman dramatically rushed from legation to legation to call for diplomatic pressure on both sides to withdraw.[3]

The incident highlights Stillman's propensity for involving himself in affairs of which he should properly have been an impartial observer. He used his rôle of journalist as judge and jury with keen personal convictions, just as he had as a diplomat pursued his own beliefs rather than followed his government's instructions. Representing *The Times,* Stillman was perceived as *de facto* a representative of the British Government, while his justified regard for Tricoupis (and the fact of his being Michael Spartali's son-in-law) embroiled him in Greek domestic politics, without in any way serving Spartali's cause, which still dragged on, and he was lampooned in the Athens press. His reward, as he would record later in his autobiography, was a serious bout of "nervous prostration and acute dyspepsia... by strict diet and activity limited to early morning and afternoon I weathered the summer, but each return of the heats during the succeeding six years brought me a relapse; so I paid a high price for my involvement in Greek politics."[4] Stillman was "compelled to leave Rome by a recurrence of the malady acquired in Athens" and, instead, he spent three summer months of 1888 in the United States on a delicate investigation for *The Times,* which was threatened by a serious legal challenge.

Charles Stewart Parnell, a Westminster MP and President of the Irish National Land League who had become the accepted leader of the Irish nationalist movement in the early 1880s, had been arrested with other Irish leaders in October 1881 and the League suppressed. Gladstone, who supported Home Rule but could not get a Bill through Parliament, came to a limited agreement with Parnell in March 1882 and a programme of reform under the Land Act of 1881 was cautiously resumed. Lord Frederick Cavendish was sent to Ireland as Chief Secretary to begin a new era of peace, but on 6 May 1882 – the day he arrived – he and his Under-Secretary T H Burke, were assassinated in Phoenix Park, Dublin by members of a Fenian secret society. Parnell publicly condemned the murders, but *The Times* published a series of articles, 'Parnellism and Crime', in which the Home Rule leaders were accused of involvement. *The Times* produced a number of facsimile letters, allegedly bearing Parnell's signature, that purported to show that Parnell knew of the plan and had condoned the murders; Parnell immediately sued the paper for libel.

William Stillman had warned McDonald that the letters were forgeries but *The Times* believed it was on firm ground. One of the original letters, purportedly from Parnell to an Irish-American named Sheridan, was thought to be in his possession in America where the Home Rulers received considerable financial support; Stillman was dispatched to obtain it if possible. He first attempted to enlist police help but found that the New York police were Fenian sympathisers to a man – with the corrupt support of the Irish Tammany bosses – so that he became immediately a marked man. At length, with the help of a private detective, he located Sheridan in Nevada. It was soon clear that as well as Stillman, Sheridan was himself under police surveillance and thus of Irish Nationalists. Though willing to sell, Sheridan feared for his life and Stillman's. No contact could safely be effected.

William Stillman returned instead to his haunts of thirty years before in the Adirondacks, where he was shortly surprised to be joined by an Irishman with a rusty firearm who announced himself as a hunter. He had been sent to watch William Stillman and after several whiskey-fuelled days, admitted his rôle and warned Stillman that he was in danger of his life. On the advice of the British Consul in New York Stillman returned quietly to London where, despite his lack of success, the paper considered that his exposure of police corruption in New York merited a bonus; from now on they paid his rent in Rome, the only salary increase he received in ten years. His cloak and dagger undertaking was, at least from the practical point of view, as Ruritanian a failure as his mission to Budapest for Lajos Kossuth in 1852. His capacity for attracting farce remained undiminished.

In February 1889, a Special Commission investigating the charges made against Parnell examined a witness, Stewart Piggot, who admitted to having forged the letters; he fled to Madrid, where he shot himself. William Stillman nevertheless took the view that the substance of the letters, if not the fact, was 'genuine', that Parnell was therefore guilty as charged and thus on balance *The Times* was right to publish. His sanguine expectation that what he saw as the underlying truth would prove more powerful than the matter at trial was soon dashed; the costs of the case, which the paper lost, were so great that there was for a time considerable doubt as to the survival of *The Times*.

He was back in Italy by mid-August 1888. With Bella and Lisa he passed the remaining summer weeks with Giovanni Costa and his wife and family, which now included a daughter Rosalinda, named after Rosalind Howard, at San Felice close to Terracina. Then, late in the autumn, with Lisa, he travelled back to London for consultations with Stebbing, the Assistant Editor of *The Times*, and they remained there with Marie, Effie and Mico for three months. Bella stayed in Rome, "of all deadly toad-in-a-hole places this is the most that way..." she confided in a letter to Effie.[6] She was learning the new Pitman method of shorthand and typing and, of greater concern, she needed a copy of *Mrs Beeton*, urgently.

November 1888 saw Lisa about to join Bella and her father in Rome. Bella wrote to Effie: "I shall be doubly glad to be with her again; first because I have been literary and archaeological so long that I feel that a good gossip would purify my blood. Papa does not see things in a frivolous light, and my small attempts at flippancy and sarcasm are but frigidly received... My second reason for wanting Lisa is that she has all my clothes with her." Travelling with Father was clearly not meant to be lightly undertaken or enjoyed to excess. In mid-November 1888, William Rossetti noted in his diary: "...a largish gathering at the Stillmans prior to the departure of Stillman and Lisa for Rome. They may first stay a while in San Remo or Florence."[7] Another year would pass before Marie joined them in Italy.

Stillman was now 61 but he could not contemplate retirement for lack of funds to support his family. He wrote to Effie in March: "I hope we shall be able to spend the summer together in Italy in some mountain district as it may be the last I shall spend in Italy. I am getting old and the climate of Italy does not agree with me. Until I got to Athens I had not slept more than one night in a month without chloral and not more than half-a-dozen nights since I got back from England without either chloral or supposal; and then I do not like to risk changing the home when my health may give out any day and I obliged to give up my position... until that question is settled the home in London must be kept up. I hope that Mama will succeed in letting it for a while so that you may all come out for a change but as things stand now it is impossible to make any radical change... I have little time to write, without the typewriter I could never get through the work I have to do, though The Times does not print any of my letters..."[5]

In fact, *The Times* foreign and editorial staff were beginning to recognise that Stillman's personal views led him on occasion to editorialise when factual reportage was needed. (He developed a complicated system of signatures to his correspondence that was intended to distinguish between his opinion, his secondary sources and reports of his own observation and interviews.) They stood by him during several bouts of illness when they needed coverage, and his superiors in London who had the task of re-building the paper's reputation and readership saw that the time was not far ahead when he would be ready to retire. For all that, they were ever ready to acknowledge the importance of his wide-ranging contacts in government, and that his constant search for the truth maintained both his own reputation, and that of *The Times,* with his sources in government. McDonald, the Manager of *The Times* died in December 1889, the loosening of 'a personal tie.' There was no material change in William Stillman's relationship with the paper, but in the ensuing re-organisation he was offered the choice of representing the paper either in Greece or in Italy rather than continue his roving assignment. He chose Rome for family and health reasons, though he considered this a great sacrifice since he much preferred Athens.

Chapter Seventeen

Marie in Rome 1889-1896

Marie found Rome uncongenial, just as she had feared: "... I feel I did well to come here and that gives me courage – there are very few people who attract me in any way here, there are so many uninteresting sticklers to etiquette and such etiquette!"[1] she wrote to Fairfax Murray in November 1889. Her circle of friends in Rome was very similar in nature to those of her days in Florence: Linda and Pasquale Villari, now Minister of Public Instruction, Giacomo Boni, once Ruskin's young associate in Venice and now the Superintendent Architect of the Ministry under Villari, the Costas, Wolfgang Helbig, the Director of the German Archaeological Institute, and his wife Nadine, a concert pianist and pupil of the Abbé Listz,[2] Richard Norton, Charles Eliot Norton's son and the Director of the American School of Classical Studies in Rome, Prince Ouroussoff, the Russian Minister whom she had known for ten or more years, and Giovanni Cavalcaselle, the art critical writer.[3] Both of Lucy Rossetti's children, now grown up, were in Rome and married. Life continued against the background of personal tragedy – the decline and death of Bella's husband John Henry Middleton, the deaths of Ford Madox Brown, Lucy Madox Brown Rossetti, Marie's brother Demetrius and William Morris, and the severe illness of Vernon Lee – and the day-to-day routines of the household; and of working daily at her easel. In the same letter to Fairfax Murray she wrote of meeting Mme Helbig "sitting in her garden one glorious day. She talked so well and so convincingly on many subjects, I was very much fascinated by her. Lisa thinks her not sincere... I like her immensely and I am sure she is a good friend for she spoke so cordially of people we knew.

"I am, I confess to you, very much disappointed with Lisa's work. She begins things excellently well, works rapidly and surely up to a certain point, and when it comes to finishing she destroys everything good and the whole thing gets in to a dreadful mess. I believe that pastel work is very bad for her. I do not think that she learnt anything at the Academy – I should not say this to anyone but you. It is so disappointing that she does not seem to have any plans for work beyond any head which is wanted. Her skill in beginning is very remarkable and she gets such pure, fresh colouring in the early sittings – the later stages are all the more unexpected..."

In December, the Stillmans were visited by Wilfrid Scawen Blunt and his wife Lady Anne who were on their way to their stud at Sheykh Obeyd where they bred Arab horses; he duly reported his impressions to Janey Morris.[5] Blunt's pilgrimage to Rome was made in a markedly half-hearted endeavour to regain his lost Catholic faith – a nod towards the unlikely possibility of heavenly triumph over the temporal odds. Rome was also conveniently *en route* to Naples where they would take the steamer to Egypt. He toyed with the idea of turning his back on his adulteries and reclaiming his belief while admitting to Cardinal Manning and – with remarkable candour – in an audience with the Pope that he must place himself in God's hands since he lacked the will required to reform himself. He went daily to Mass, visited the Torrigiano statue of St Peter, kissed the toe, and waited for a sign that would not come, fearful that it might. That penance behind him, he proceeded as before, dreaming of another amorous siege with the delicious anticipation of capitulation, complacently prepared to hazard his hopes of salvation once again. "Instead I cling the closer to my past life... love is to me what a dram is to a drinker." He had a design in mind. His passionate affair with Janey Morris had reached its zenith in the summer as her breathless letters testify: "I can't write you a letter my soul is in too great a turmoil... Whether it will ever calm down again Heaven only knows..."[6] They were already moving gently towards a deeper friendship, though the flame was not yet extinguished; it was October 1890 before he noted in his diary: "I spent the day yesterday with Mrs Morris, the last I fancy in a quite intimate way – she felt this and said it, and I did not contradict."[7] It was a redeeming feature of Blunt's adulterous liaisons that so many later grew in to true affection. Janey, and perhaps John Henry Middleton whom Blunt had met that May at Kelmscott, had stirred his memories of Marie Stillman's beauty of character and bearing: "He speaks of them with enthusiasm as the two noblest women in the world..."[8] Blunt recorded in his diary. Janey, at least, anticipated his reaction to this new temptation: "I want much to hear if you saw Mrs Stillman often and if you saw any places in her company and what you thought of the girls..."[9] she wrote to him.

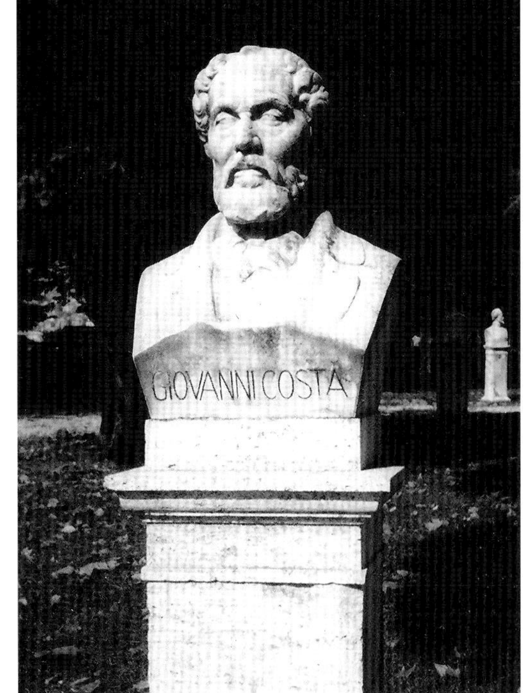

Plate 58
Giovanni Costa, artist and patriot, founder of the Etruscan school of landscape painters: statue at the Garibaldi Monument, Rome

"Lunch with the Stillmans. She was looking lovely. I could be really in love with her if it were of any use. I am sure she likes me but it is not a thing within the reach of fortune. I wish I had met her 10 years ago. Stillman is more agreeable than I expected to find him and the two eldest girls are pretty and all three clever," he reported to Janey, who responded: "I am glad you liked Mr Stillman, you are the first man I have ever heard say a good word for him, I always say his greatest crime is in having so beautiful a wife... I should like to have seen all you very tall people standing together in one room. As if I *could* leave off writing to you. What put such an idea in to your head? It must have been a little turned through seeing so much of Mrs Stillman."[10]

Blunt diligently recorded the downward progress of his penitence in his diary. A week later he went again to the Vatican, and "afterwards to see Mrs Stillman. I found her alone... I talked to her for an hour about Rossetti and many other things and I still thinks she likes me, I didn't ask her, I hardly know why, and I feel quite foolishly about her and could sit listening to her voice and looking at her eyes for days together without going further. She is like a woman in a dream whom one feels, if one moved or touched her, would change in to something less beautiful. Going away I kissed her hand... It is agreed we should meet again, perhaps tomorrow. How foolish this all is, yet how sweet. Rossetti <u>must</u> have loved her. She told me that he corresponded with her once when she was in Florence and that his letters were full of wit and fun. She burnt them, foolish woman." Blunt, in his fascination with Rossetti's poetry, and with his prurient interest in the sexual minutiae of Rossetti's relationships, pictured himself in the guise of Rossetti's *alter ego*.

After three days of anticipation, Blunt again "went to see Mrs Stillman. She was with all her family and I think she looks best with them. She is a dear woman..." The following day they visited the Sistine Chapel. "She and I drove in an open fly with a white horse (omen of fortune) – we talked of Rossetti. She told me she knew him first two years after his wife's death when she used to sit to him as model... She saw him constantly in his later years when all his other women friends had left him. I told her of my foolishness about her, for I really love her with all my soul. All my pious thoughts have vanished, how will it end?"

Bella, Effie and Lisa called on the Blunts next day, and Lisa commenced a portrait of Judith, the Blunts's daughter. Wilfrid Blunt noted privately in his diary that the drawing was "at one moment perfectly lovely but has been spoiled since", echoing the concern that Marie had expressed to Fairfax Murray just one month earlier.

Another letter from Janey arrived in Rome: "... I quite agree with all you say about the Stillman family, Mrs S is not approached by the girls in any way, although I am fond of them all. The thought of America being her last resting place is too monstrous, I won't believe in such a fate for her." For Wilfrid Blunt the visit to Rome was coming to an end and with it his fevered hopes of a liaison with Marie Stillman, as he noted in his diary in December 1889: "It is agreed that we are to correspond but beyond that nothing."[11] Marie may not have been entirely displeased with the effect she had innocently created and they parted on good terms; but she would scarcely have been flattered that he imagined that she might so readily surrender.

They continued to write; unfortunately his letters do not survive, but hers show unmistakably that they enjoyed an easy friendship, and offer a glimpse of her characteristic wry humour and strength of will: "... No doubt [Lisa] has been telling you of a plan she has been cherishing of spending a winter in Paris and working at a French atelier. She has just proposed this to us but her father will not hear of it... we have a nice sunny little apartment and I am quite content, it is a great happiness having Michael here. I laughed much at your postscript, I only begged you to try and think a little better of me than to believe I had a taste for futile compliments. I am very glad to hear from you when you are serious,"[12] and next month: "I am very much perplexed by the arrival of a young Irish sculptress utterly deaf who was most unexpectedly left on my hands... When the young lady arrived I found there was no way of communication except writing and that not a word of French or Italian did she know. The good people of Dublin, who had given her a Prix de Rome allowance and insisted on her coming here, awarded her the modest sum of £100 a year with which she is to get instruction, models, food, lodging and to send home to Dublin an immortal work of art... curiously she has a strong brogue and I fear I have caught it. This grafted on to my poor pronunciation will make me also unintelligible..." William was obliged to ask Lord Dufferin, the British Ambassador, to call on the committee in Dublin to allow their protégé to spend her allowance in eight months, lest she starve. "Lisa is still in England..." Lisa was enjoying her escape hugely, and was spinning out her freedom for as long as she could.

Marie stayed in close touch by mail with her many friends in London: "The influenza when it left, left also a doleful legacy in the way of melancholy, such as I have never known before," wrote Edward Burne-Jones. "For many weeks I was a hopeless about all things as if a great and terrible misfortune had happened, and could see no light or brightness anywhere, and went about like a forlorn spectre; but this is all very slowly mending. People say I ought to be glad to be forced to rest but that is a height of philosophy I cannot attain to, any more than a man in Newgate might be glad of seclusion."[13]

Early in the New Year 1891, William became involved in his last act of diplomacy on the world stage. On 15 October of the previous year a group of *mafiosi* in New Orleans had gunned down Police Chief Hennessy; he had recently cabled the police chief in Rome for dossiers on known *mafiosi* wanted back in Italy. They were apprehended on 'information received' and at their trial a judicious distribution of bribes had ensured that the jury found the murderers not guilty. This so enraged the citizenry of New Orleans that the defendants were re-arrested on related charges and removed to the Old Parish Jailhouse on Bienville Street. Two days later a lynch-mob stormed the prison and shot, hanged or simply beat to death sixteen of the nineteen Italians. As one New Orleans paper, *The Item,* had it: "The military precision, skill and rapidity with which the prison was stormed and taken, the care exercised to do no harm except to the guilty parties, the wonderful forbearance of the angered populace, all are commended: while no complaint is uttered against the officials for their failure to interpose resistance to the avengers of outraged justice." The Italian government however, viewed the matter in a different light and Baron Forva, the Italian ambassador, was instructed by the Foreign Minister, Antonio Starabba, Marchese di Rudini, to lodge an official protest in Washington.

Rudini was twice the Italian Premier. He had joined the revolutionaries of 1860 and, in 1864, following the Piedmontese annexation, he was appointed Mayor of Palermo. In 1869 he served briefly as minister of the interior before entering parliament, where he in time became a leader of the Right. By 1891 he was Foreign Minister in Crispi's administration. The political temperature in Rome was hostile to the government and Rudini decided that decisive action was needed to demonstrate the will to act in Italy's interest overseas. The New Orleans martyrs would be avenged and the newspaper that described the *mafiosi* as "...Sicilians whose low, receding foreheads, repulsive countenances and slovenly attire proclaimed their brutal nature..." would be humbled.

If Stillman's account is to be accepted there now followed possibly the most breathtakingly foolhardy episode in the history of Italy's foreign adventures. Rudini ordered the Italian Navy to prepare a battle fleet to sail for New Orleans to shell the town. The news reached William Stillman through a friendly contact in Crispi's private office and, seeing it as his duty as a friend of Italy and an American citizen to act, he rushed without delay to the Minister for Public Instruction, Pasquale Villari, his long-time friend from Florence, to urge him to put an end to this desperate undertaking. (He also found it necessary to point out that the Mississippi was insufficiently deep for the draught of a battle cruiser and that, in addition, the massacre was subject to Louisiana State law, and was not therefore a matter for the Federal authorities; there were, he emphasised, no grounds in international law for shelling the United States.) Together with Villari, by now thoroughly alarmed, Stillman dashed off to find Crispi who intervened with Rudini. An international incident of dramatic impact and wider consequence had been halted by Stillman's personal intervention. War was once again averted in an afternoon. Eventually, President Benjamin Harrison went before Congress on 19 December, 1891 to deplore the outrage in New Orleans, and compensation of $25,000 for relatives of the murdered men was authorised.

In May 1892, Effie was in England where Lisa joined her; Bella wrote to her sisters: "... as to the £20 Father owes me, I cannot ask for it. We are in such low water here that unless The Times sends Papa somewhere we shall not leave Rome... the

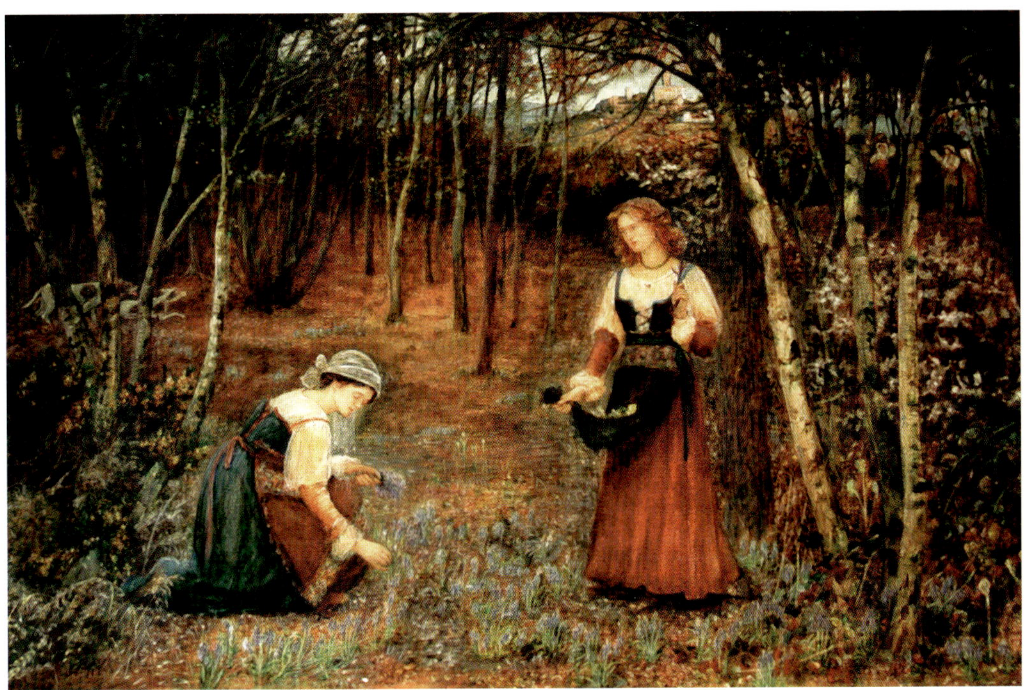

Plate 59
Marie Spartali Stillman
1893-94
Early Spring in Umbria
Watercolour and gouache. 46.5 x 54.6 cm (18⅓ x 21½in)
Private Collection

Costas are going down to Bocca d'Arno till the end of the month – the Doctor thought it might do Mico good, so I am off tonight..." Costa wrote to his daughter in Rome from Bocca d'Arno for "the cartridges and revolver that Stillman gave me", having taken up target shooting under Stillman's influence. "Firearms have always been a passion with Stillman, and they typify his spiritual combativeness, his readiness to engage in controversy, which, after all, is perhaps only one manifestation of the Yankee impulse to propose an 'improvement' on everything under the sun."[14]

The Stillmans – Marie, William, Bella and Mico – spent some happy weeks in August and September in Perugia on the estate of Count Rossi-Scotti, another of Giovanni Costa's followers and a keen painter. They were joined there by Sir William Blake Richmond and Lady Richmond, and in September by John Henry Middleton. There Marie whiled away the hours painting in the extensive gardens of the Rossi-Scotti villa outside the town walls, with the sweeping views towards Assisi and Lake Trasimene, overlooking the high road from the Porta Pisana that leads to Monte Luce.[15]

During the last week in September, Bella wrote to her sisters in great excitement: "all upside down and mixed up", she announced that John Henry Middleton, the Slade Professor at Cambridge, had asked her to marry him and that she had accepted him. Middleton was then 46 years old and had been a family friend for some years;

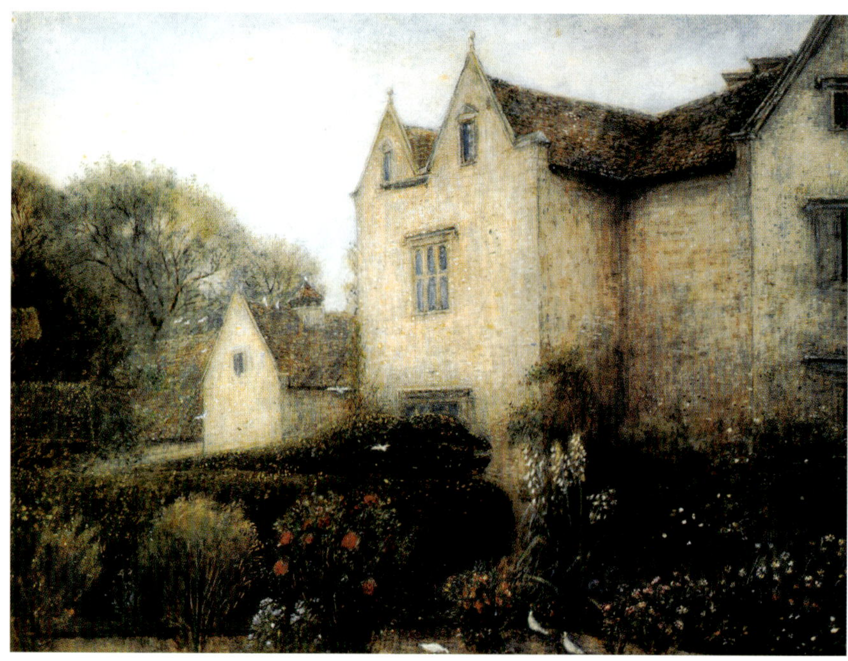

Plate 60
Marie Spartali Stillman
undated
Kelmscott Manor
Watercolour. 33 x 47.6 cm (13 x 18¾in)
Exhibited: New Gallery, 1906
Wightwick Manor, The Mander Collection (The National Trust)

he had been a friend of the Morrises for twenty. Born in Darlington, the son of an architect, in 1846, he lived as a child for a time with his parents in Naples before returning to school in England. At Oxford he suffered an acute nervous breakdown, which prevented his taking his degree. Middleton spent years recovering at home before setting out on a period of adventurous, solitary travel, which took him to the celebrated Mohammedan university at Fez where he studied Platonic philosophy and where he gained admission to the Great Mosque disguised as a Muslim pilgrim. He achieved an exceptional knowledge and understanding of the history of mediaeval art and architecture in his travels and, unexpectedly, turned up as a traveller to Iceland in 1871 as a passenger on the *Diana,* the ship that carried Charley Faulkner and William Morris to Reykjavik on their second Icelandic journey. (Faulkner, who was an Oxford mathematical don as well as a partner in Morris, Marshall, Faulkner & Co., knew Middleton from his time at Exeter, Morris's college). May Morris "often wondered why Mr Middleton went to Iceland. He was not particularly bound up in things of the North, he detested cold as a cat does, yet there he was, utterly unprovided with the ordinary traveller's outfit; he had no comforts, positively nothing, as though he had just fallen down from the moon."[16]

Middleton turned to architecture, joining his father's practice and later working under Sir Gilbert Scott; but it was clear that the academic life was better suited to his

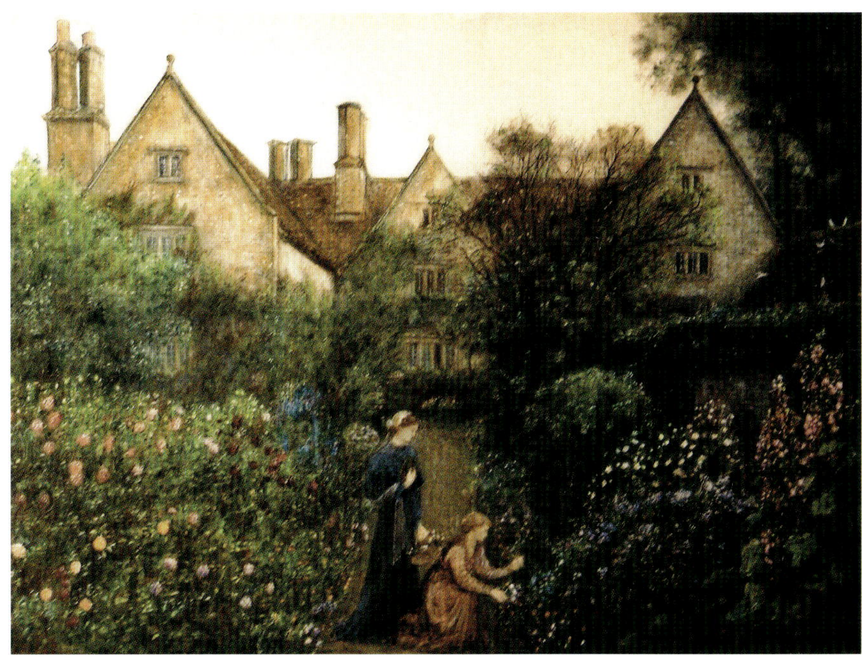

Plate 61
Marie Spartali Stillman
1902
The Long Walk at Kelmscott Manor
Watercolour. 15.5 x 21.7 cm (6⅒ x 8½in)
Private Collection

highly-strung temperament. He became one of William Morris's closest friends, Morris particularly appreciating his connoisseurship in early manuscripts, rare books and oriental carpets, and enjoying his quirky humour and ascetic mannerisms; at the time of his appointment to the Slade Professorship he was photographed, thin and monkish, wearing a black skull cap, his long face adorned with "a thin woeful-looking beard".[17] Academic honours followed; Fellow of King's in 1888, Director of the Fitzwilliam Museum in 1891, D Litt. in Cambridge in 1892 and, in the year following his marriage, Doctor of Common Law at Oxford at the age of 47. From 1893 until his early death in 1896 he was the South Kensington Museum's director.

"He [Middleton] has been sweeter and kinder than anything all the time he has been here, and I have liked him more than ever; but I did not think it meant anything – till this morning. He says it is a long time since he has felt so, and that last year when he rowed us up the river he could hardly keep from asking me; but he thought it would be wrong, because he is twenty years older than me. He was talking about me to Mrs Morris, and she advised him to come, and made him take courage. I am so glad. I should never have thought I could feel as I do."

By the middle of October they were back in Rome to prepare for the wedding. "Thank you for your kind congratulatory letter," Marie wrote to Wilfrid Blunt: "It is such a rare thing in our family that anything pleasant and unexpected should happen that it requires the sympathy of friends to reassure one that it is not merely a dream. I never expected that either of my girls would ever marry anyone I liked, they have all so frankly assured me that our likes and dislikes are so very different... Mr Middleton is so good and reliable & Bella's being settled in England will prevent the others from desiring to go to America – America has always been a red rag to me. Michael seems to feel deeply injured by Mr Middleton's wishing to marry his sister, he had supposed that his sisters were his own property and his surprise and sorrow to learn that this was not the case is very amusing..."[18] John Henry Middleton and Bella Stillman were married in December 1892. Marie wrote to Blunt: "Effie has made a fine medallion of Anne Thackeray Ritchie. The girls are pained at Bella's departure, the more so since she seems so happy to leave us." In March 1893, Bella and her husband were at Kelmscott, while Janey was in San Remo.[19]

Not long after the couple's return from their honeymoon in Italy the *Westminster Gazette* reported "strange rumours afloat about recent blunders at the (South Kensington) Museum... perhaps the appointment of Professor Middleton will put an effectual stop to such alleged scandals."[20] The faction-riven management was accused of a number of poor decisions on acquisitions, and the appointment of John Henry Middleton was seen as a hopeful augury; but he quickly found his position undermined by persistent political battles. The highly-strung Middleton found this intolerable, despite the warmth and tenderness of his late marriage and the arrival of their daughter Peggy, and he fell in to a nervous depression. He took leave of absence on health grounds, and for more than a year he was resting, much of the time at Kelmscott.

Lisa joined them at Kelmscott during August 1893.[21] "We have Lisa with us now to Jenny's joy... Lisa began a drawing of me in the summerhouse, she did a very good one of me two years ago, it was not quite finished, but very like; now I hear she has lost it... Mrs Stillman arrived in London on Sat: and went to the Isle of Wight on Sunday, where she will stay some time."[22] Janey Morris reported to Wilfrid Blunt. Marie arrived at Kelmscott in August.[23] "We have had Mrs Stillman for a short visit – she is leaving England early in October, and I fear I am not likely to see her for years..."[24]

There were more terrible times in store. On 6th October 1893 Ford Madox Brown died at 1 St Edmund's Terrace, Primrose Hill. Georgiana Burne-Jones, William Holman Hunt and Arthur Hughes were among the mourners at a secular service led by Moncure Conway. Madox Brown's daughter Lucy – Mrs William Michael Rossetti – Marie Stillman's closest friend and ally from the earliest days and a witness at her wedding to William Stillman, was unable to attend. She was travelling to Italy, dreadfully ill with tuberculosis, which had first struck in 1885. Lucy had been advised that the cool air of Pallanzo on Lake Maggiore would be most beneficial for her tortured breathing, but finding little relief there she moved on, first to Genoa and then to San Remo where she put up at the Hotel Victoria. She died there on 12th April 1894.

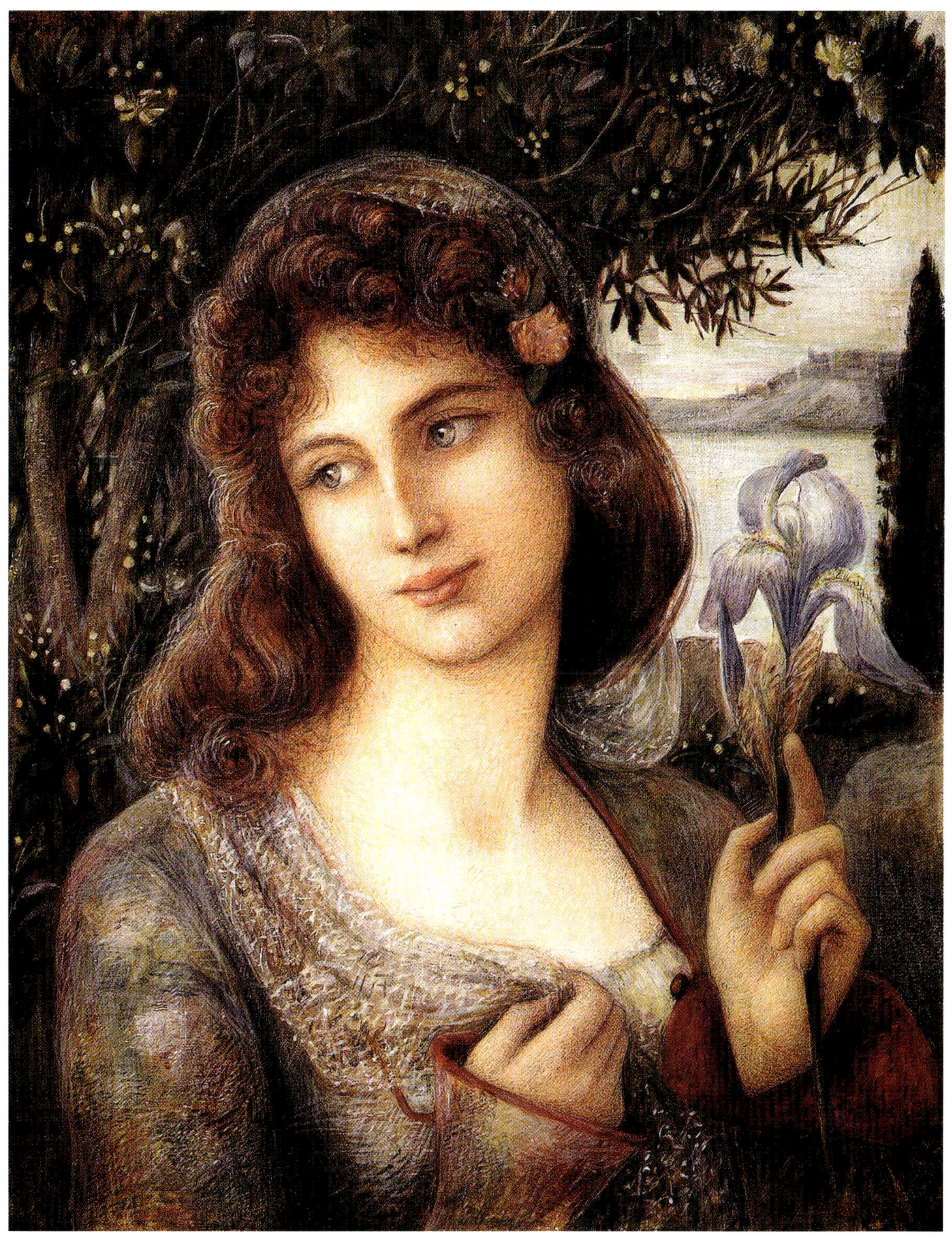

Plate 62
Marie Spartali Stillman
1894
Portrait of Giorgia Costa
Pastel on board mounted on panel. 47.5 x 39 cm (18 11/16 x 15 3/8in)
Private Collection

Marie's beloved brother Demetrius had died in London on 4th April.

Bella, her husband and their baby Peggy were back at Kelmscott[25] in July 1894, as Janey Morris reported to Wilfrid Blunt: "Mr Middleton is so very ill, hopelessly to my thinking – he is out of doors all day, walking and resting at intervals, he does not appear to be suffering so much as in London but there is so little life in him, Bella reads to him several hours a day, he sometimes dictates a few letters to her and is quite exhausted afterwards – he appears to have lost interest in most things except wife and baby – I perceive clearly that nothing will induce him to seek help apart from them... Mrs Stillman will arrive in England this day week."

Marie was in England for two months, much of which she spent with her aging parents: "... My visit here has been very happy and restful in the Isle of Wight where I spent a whole month with my Mother and Father," she wrote to Vernon Lee, adding, "... I hope to meet my husband and Mico at Basle and then we go to Zurich and spend a few days with Michael before leaving him at school – we think it will be better for him though it will be a very hard wrench to have to go away and leave him – he too hates the thought. Dr Middleton is not much better – he suffers constantly and that makes us all sad – Peggy is a very fascinating little minx and rejoices her mother's heart... the picture you gave me has been much admired, it is supposed to be a Bonifazio – Villegas and Costa have been much excited about it... I have had news of you from Miss Duffy who has been so cordial and kind to me... Yr affectionate, Marie Stillman."[26] To Cathy Heuffer – Madox Brown's elder daughter – she said: "Dr Middleton is better but still very far from well – I feel much disturbed at the slowness of his recovery..."[27]

James Darmesteter, the husband of Vernon Lee's *amour* Mary Robinson and Marie's friend in Florence, died in October. In November, Marie again travelled to London. "To National Gallery where I encounter Mrs Stillman – she is attending some invalid relative here, Stillman nr Basle, not well. Middleton ordered abroad owing to overwork."[28] William Rossetti recorded in his diary. Janey kept Blunt informed: "...news of Mr Middleton still in Rome – but I gather that he is in reality very little better than when he left England – the

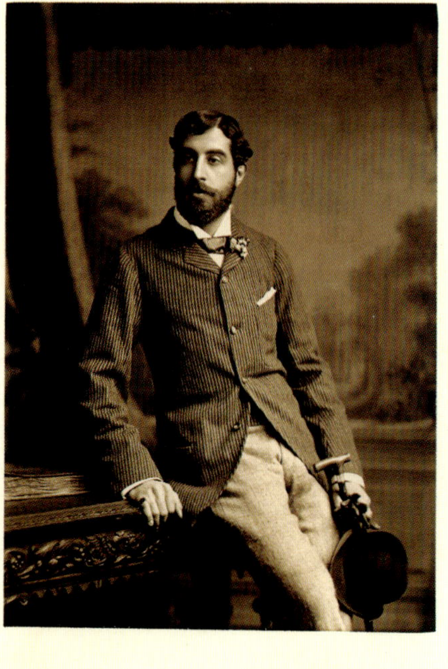

Plate 63
Demetrius Spartali (Demi) Carte de visite
c.1880

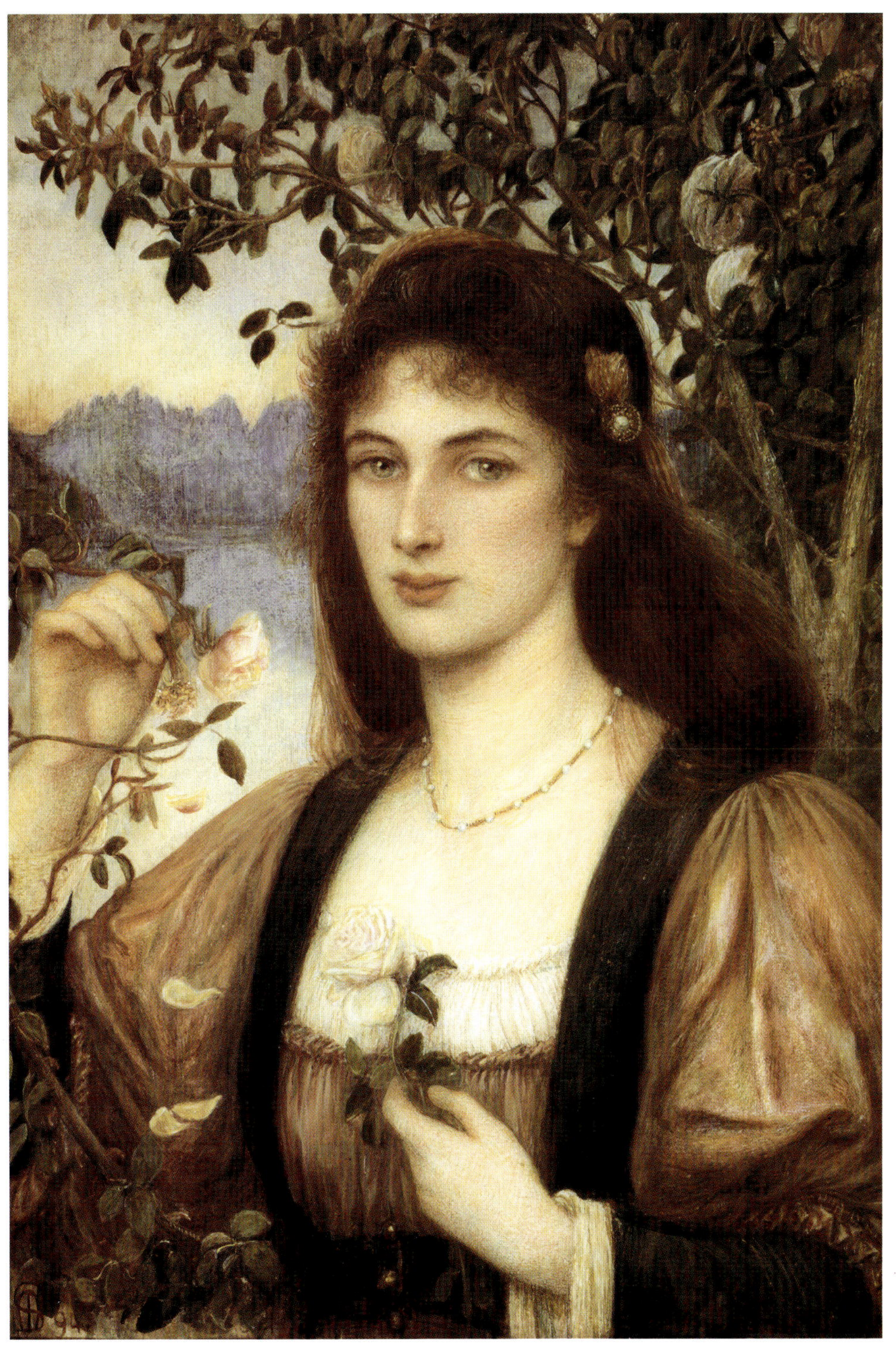

Plate 64
Marie Spartali Stillman
1894
A Rose from Armida's Garden
Watercolour and bodycolour on paper. 64 x 42.5 cm (25⅜ x 16¾in)
Exhibited: New Gallery, 1894; Liverpool Autumn, 1894
Courtesy of The Maas Gallery, London; Bridgeman Art Library

head-trouble still goes on, which is after all the chief thing – he talks of returning to London early in March, I hope however that he will be dissuaded from this which should I think be fatal to him..." she wrote in February 1895.[29]

Early in 1895, Marie wrote to Cathy Heuffer apologising for her infrequent letters, she had been ill over Christmas she explained. William, she added, was suffering from a bronchial attack, and her little grandchild, Peggy, also. Although he had spoken of a return to England in the previous March, John Henry Middleton was still in Rome in June 1895. That summer he gathered his resolve and returned to work at the South Kensington Museum. It was clear to his colleagues that he was still far from recovered and, indeed, failing once more to manage the stresses inherent in his situation, though he carried on in to the New Year. In June 1896 came news of Middleton's death.[30] He had been discovered unconscious with a bottle of laudanum and a glass beside him, and he died hours later. The inquest verdict was of Accidental Death but it transpired in evidence that he had been a morphine addict since his breakdown with 'brain fever' at Oxford.

Contemporary comment suggests that Middleton was thought by some to have committed suicide. Wilfrid Blunt noted in his diary for 17 June 1896: "He was a morphine addict, having taken morphine for twenty years. He is a great loss or has been rather, for he has been dead to the world and his friends for something like two years."[31] The problems of drug abuse are not a modern phenomenon. Rossetti's trouble was chloral. [James] Thomson's trouble was alcohol. With [William] Burges – occasionally at any rate – it was opium.[32] "Yes, I knew of Mr Middleton's habit, I discovered it soon after we first knew him, he nearly killed himself then. I wonder Bella ever left the bottle within his reach..."[33] Janey mused to Blunt.

It was a sad end to a marriage that should have brought happiness and heartsease to two people who, for all their assembled talents, were somehow adrift in life, a miserable end to a scholar and traveller of great erudition and perception, and a fascinating and amusing companion of wide-ranging interests to those he allowed to know him well. Chief among them was William Morris, who had delighted in his company for 25 years, and who was himself in the closing months of his remarkable life. News of Middleton's death was kept from Morris until he had boarded the train

---

Plate 65
Marie Spartali Stillman
1894-5
A Florentine Lily
Gouache and watercolour on paper.73.5 x 43.5 cm (28 15/16 x 17⅛in)
Exhibited: New Gallery, 1895
Private Collection

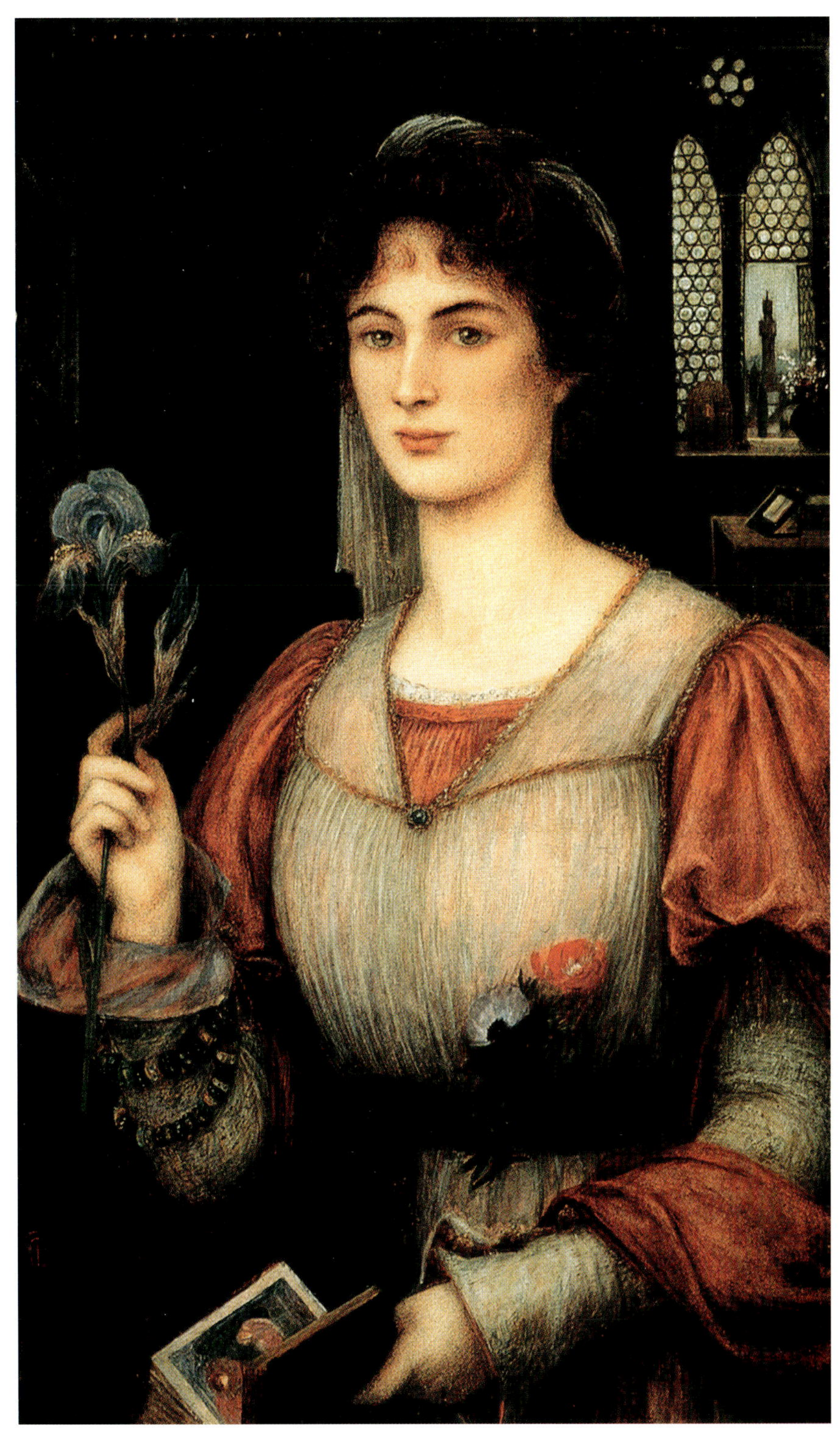

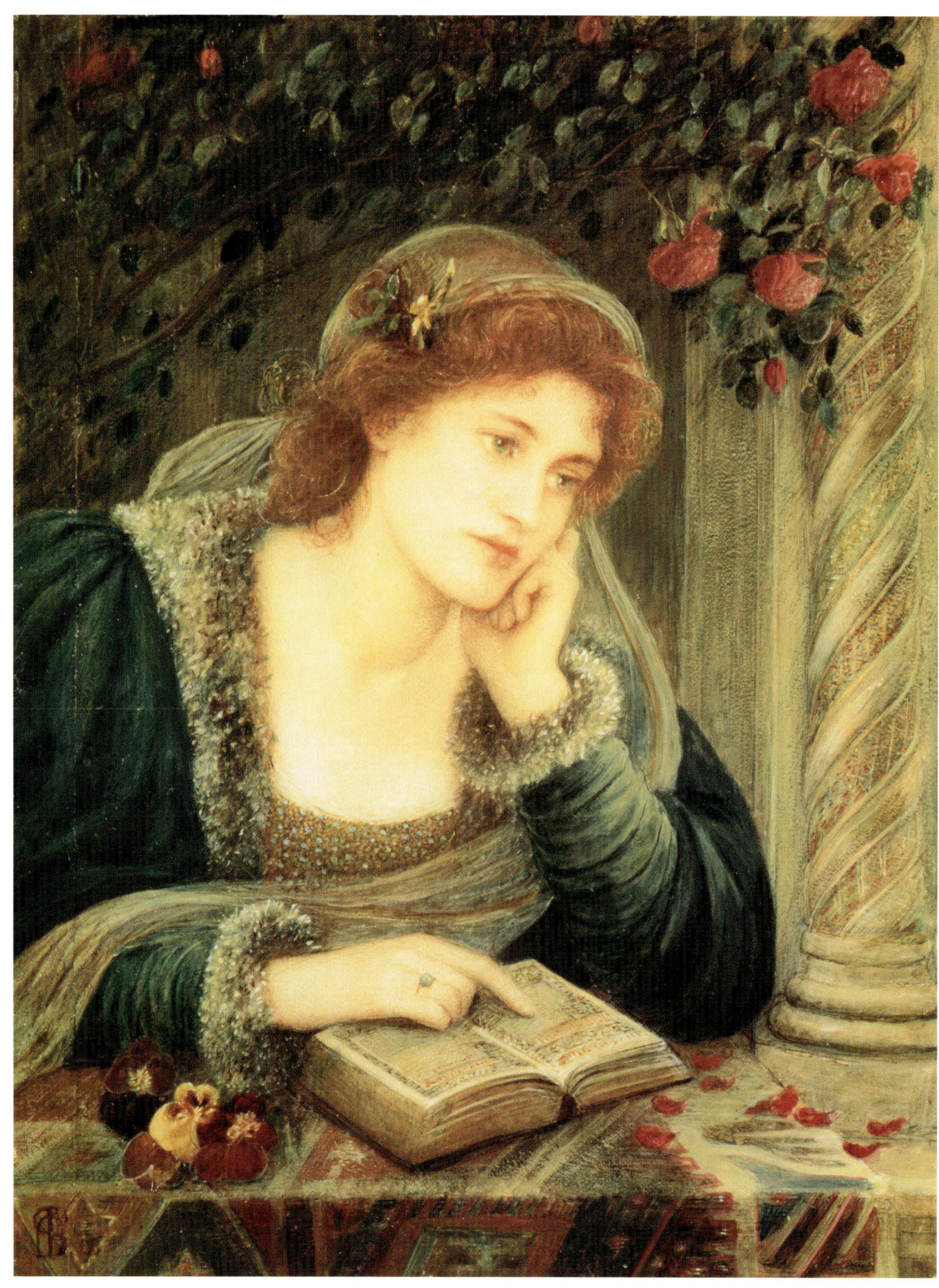

Plate 66
Marie Spartali Stillman
1896
Beatrice
Watercolour on paper mounted on panel. 57.6 x 43.2cm (22 11/16 x 17in)
Exhibited: New Gallery, Liverpool, Autumn 1896

to Folkestone, where it was hoped he would regain his strength; he was deeply depressed to learn of the passing of his once-ebullient friend.[34] On the 6th October William Morris was laid to rest in the churchyard of the simple, 12th century village church at Kelmscott.

However, the Rome years were a productive period for William Stillman; when he was not engaged in reporting for *The Times* he wrote numerous articles and contributed to collected works including *The Old Rome and the New, and Other Studies* in *The Decay of Art,* in which he hid none of his taste for debate: "There can be no doubt that the Greek sculptors never worked directly from nature. We know the same to be true of Michael Angelo, and in all the work of the great painters of the Italian schools we find unmistakeable indications that they did not work before nature. Not only is this the immutable law of all great art, but I maintain that the scientific study of nature, whether as anatomy, geology or botany, is obnoxious in a high degree to the development of great qualities of design." Houghton Mifflin had published *In the Steps of Ulysses, with an Excursion in Quest of the so-called Venus of Melos* in 1892, the outcome of his Aegean expedition ten years earlier. He wrote the text for a book of wood engravings, *Old Italian Masters*, by Timothy Cole, who also wrote engraver's notes on the illustrations. The work is collected from a series of articles in the *Century* magazine, and, unconventionally, includes a number of additional notes by Fairfax Murray on Duccio, Simone Martini and Giorgione, amplifying and at times disagreeing with Stillman's conclusions. His most important work of political history, *The Union of Italy 1815-1898*, also dates from this period. In all, William Stillman published more than 130 articles, book reviews and letters to the press during his time in Rome, in addition to his correspondence for *The Times.*

His delight in controversy was in evidence when the young Bernard Berenson was worsted in an attack on Stillman's article on Tintoretto's *The Apparition of St Mark* in *The Nation* in 1893.[35] Berenson sought to dismiss Stillman's qualifications as critic by asserting that the painting was in Milan and not in Venice, implying that Stillman had neither examined the picture nor knew anything of Tintoretto's style and work. Stillman took some pleasure in pointing out that Berenson had confused the Milan *St Mark* with the *Apparition of St Mark*, that the picture was by Domenico Tintoretto, the great Jacopo's son, that it was indeed in Venice, and in casting doubt on the depth of Berenson's knowledge of Venetian Renaissance art.

At home together, William Stillman had posed for Marie. Her painting of *St Francis on his Deathbed* bears a label on the reverse stating that W J Stillman posed for St Francis, Michael Spartali Stillman for the priest, and Bella, Effie and Lisa for the female attendants. Now that Ford Madox Brown was dead, Marie turned regularly to Edward Burne-Jones for advice, discussing her work and sending him her early sketches and ideas: "I LOVE HELPING YOU and it is kind of you to pretend that I can. Send me over tracings later on for final correction and warnings..." he had

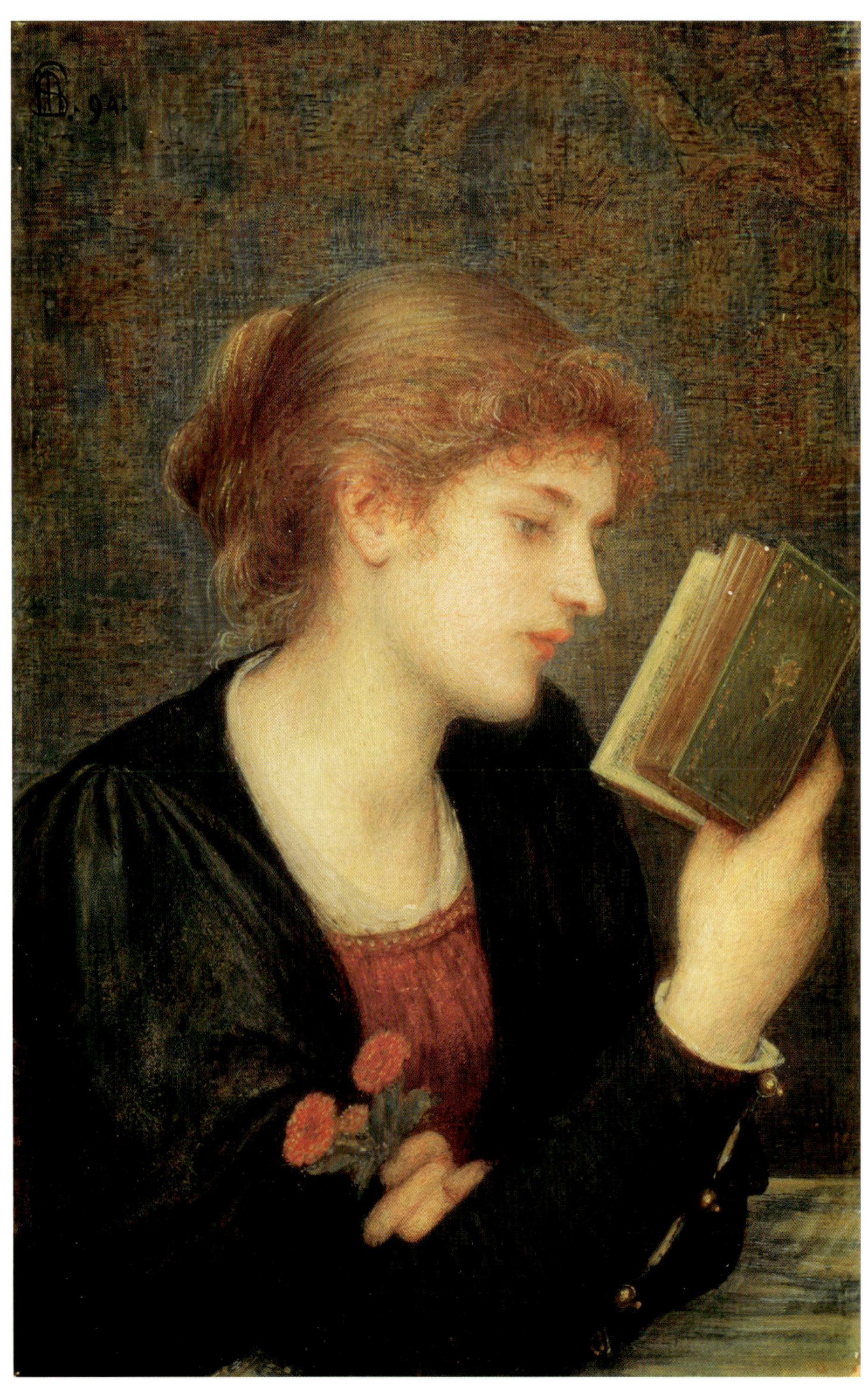

Plate 67
Marie Spartali Stillman
1894
Love Sonnets
Watercolour on paper mounted on panel. 44.1 x 27.9 cm (17¾ x 11in)
Exhibited: New Gallery, 1894

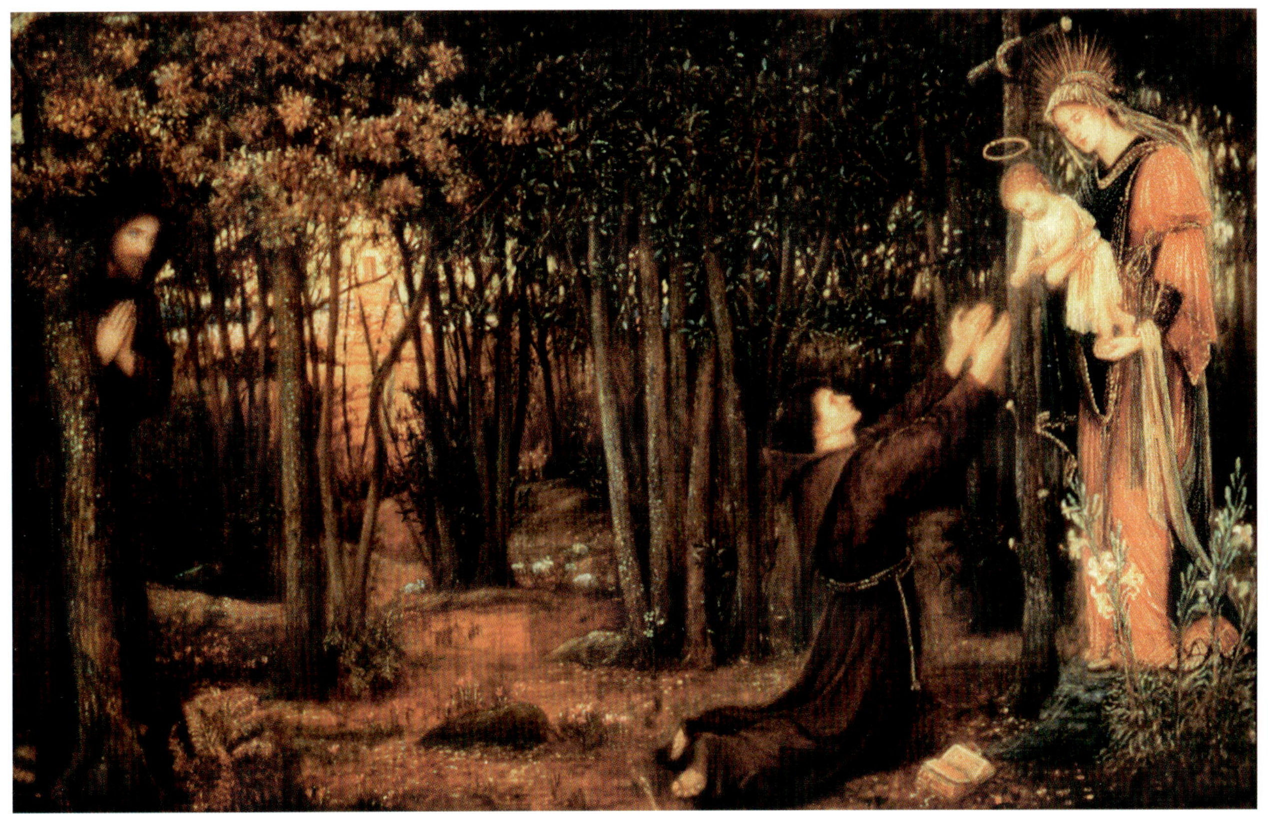

Plate 68
Marie Spartali Stillman
1892
How the Virgin Mary Came to Brother Conrad of Offida and Laid Her Son in his Arms
Watercolour, bodycolour and gold paint. 49.5 x 80 cm (19½ x 31½in)
Exhibited: Liverpool, 1892
Wightwick Manor, The Mander Collection (The National Trust)

written when she was working on *How the Virgin Mary came to Brother Conrad of Offida and Laid Her Son in his Arms.*[36]

Summers were spent away from the oppressive heat of Rome, at Costa's villa at Bocca d'Arno, in the hills above Florence or Cortina, and in England. The spring of 1897 was typical of the manner in which the family dispersed over the summer months: "May is rushing along and we must soon turn away from Rome and go northwards," Marie wrote to Vernon Lee. "Could you have me about the 7th? As yet my plans are chaotic... Many, many thanks my dearest Vernon, I am so full of the pleasure of our day at Hadrian's Villa – I have had you so little to myself on your visits here..." To Fairfax Murray she wrote of a short visit to the Fiskes in Florence and to see his wife Angelica, after which she would take Ida[37] to Davos to go into the care of nuns there who look after invalids. Fairfax Murray had promised to contribute to the cost, as had Mrs Symonds who was reluctant to take Ida in to her household on account of the contagious nature of her illness, presumably tuberculosis.

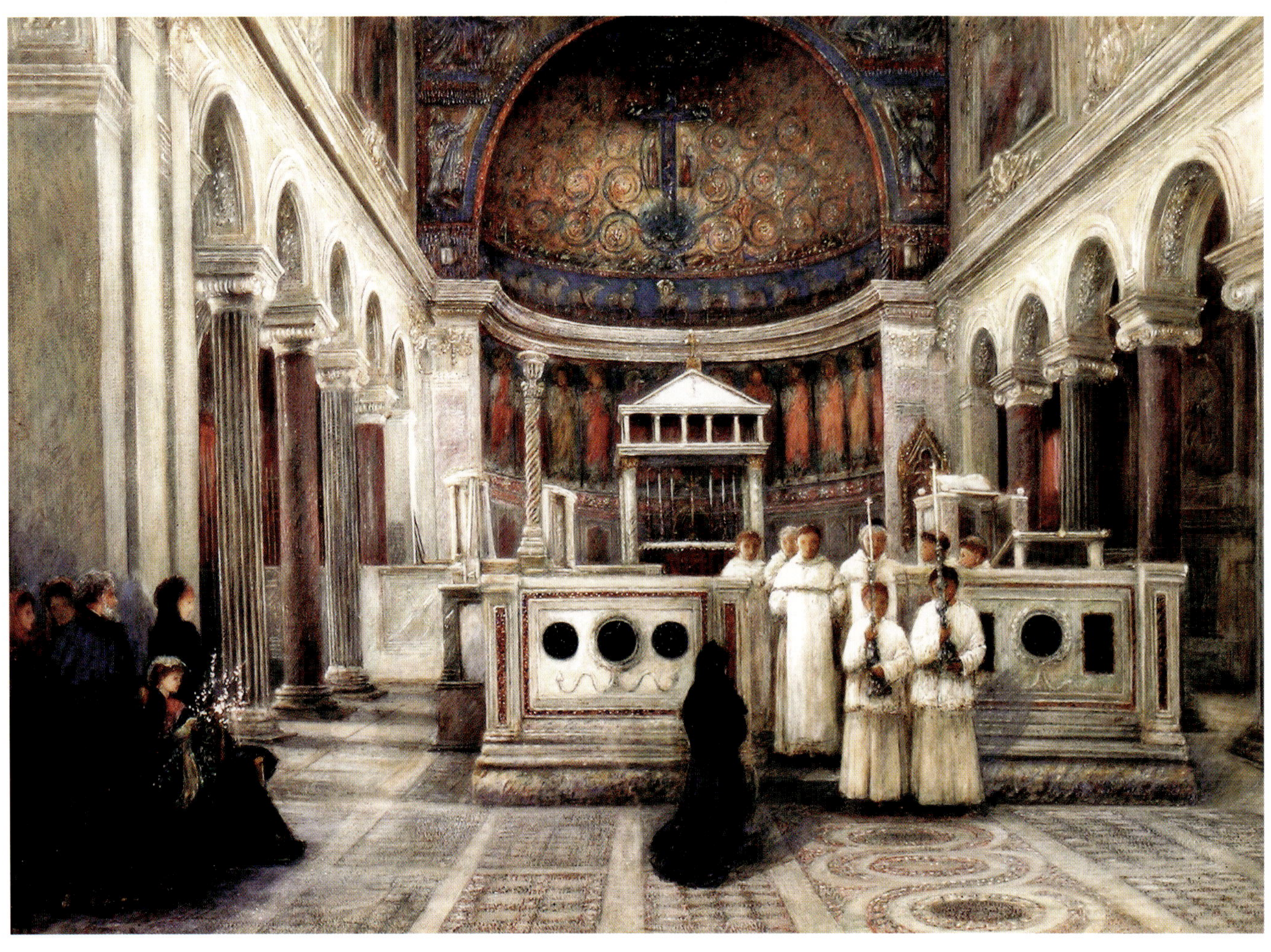

Plate 69
Marie Spartali Stillman
1897
After Vespers in San Clemente, Rome
Watercolour and gouache on paper
Private Collection

Plate 70
Marie Spartali Stillman
1893
Saint Francis on his Deathbed
Watercolour and gouache heightened with gold paint. 48.2 x 80 cm (19 x 31½in)
Exhibited: New Gallery, 1893
Private Collection

The priest, kneeling, is modelled by Michael Stillman, St Francis by William James Stillman, the three attendants by Lisa, Bella and Effie Stillman

"We arrived here safely and not too tired yesterday afternoon... A snow storm covered the flowery meadows with a thin white veil which this morning's sun has already dissipated. The air is very exhilarating but quite cold. I never saw such masses of flowers as on the ascent from Klosters – pansies and forget-me-nots, yellow and orange poppies, campanulas and yellow ranunculas all in patches of intense colour... We had a hearty welcome from the girls and Mrs Symonds – their house is quite beautiful... No wonder they keep on their house here... Yesterday as I got out of the train I was astonished to find my tall boy waiting for me, his Father had telegraphed him to be there... I was so grieved to leave you dearest Vernon so full of anxiety – I do hope that the consultation with the doctor will at least lead you to having confidence in the treatment Kit is to undergo... My little Ida feels so much better, she breathes more easily and rejoices in the cold, I have seen the room for Ida at 5½ per day and with the nuns..."[38] Marie wrote to Vernon Lee.

In September, Marie joined Janey Morris at Kelmscott.[39] It was time to leave Rome. "Mrs Robinson tells us that Stillman, on the grounds of health, has now given up his Italian correspondence for The Times and has re-settled in England, living with his daughter Mrs Middleton who is fairly well-off,"[40] William Michael Rossetti added to his diary.

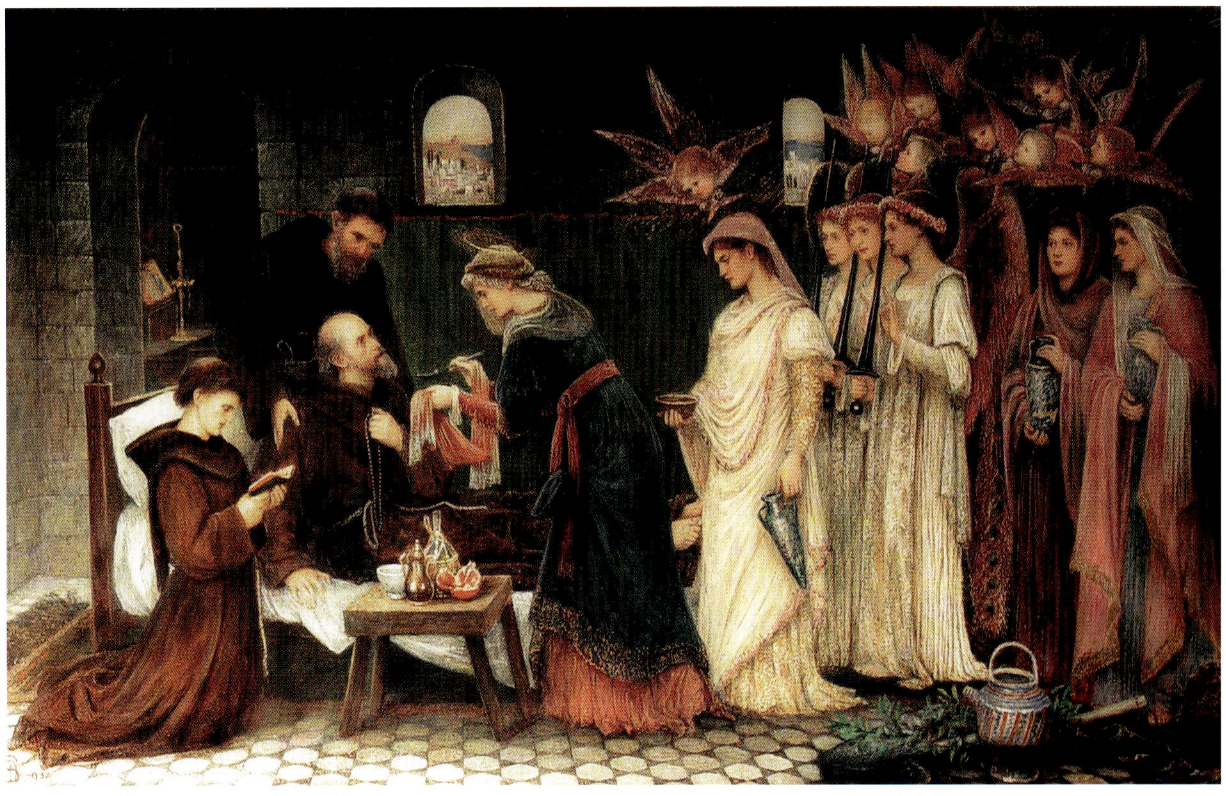

Chapter Eighteen

The Closing Years

William Stillman retired on a pension from *The Times* in 1898 and the family moved to Frimley Green in Surrey. Settling in to his longed-for retirement, William contemplated the Surrey woodland around them with a degree of calm. Marie as always managed the day-to-day tribulations of setting up yet another home; the builders remained in possession after months of work and she dealt with the adjustments to life that all expatriates encounter when they finally return to the country they think of as home. She was now 55 and perhaps a little more tired than she had anticipated. William summed up his satisfaction in a letter to W J Stebbing of *The Times,* describing "a little house in the pine woods which furnish these heated days a most grateful shade all round us. It is almost like being in the backwoods of America again... I doubt I shall ever leave the place for more than a day or two while I live, and as Bella owns it I shall ask her to let me be buried in the wood at the back of the house where at present I spread food for the squirrels... it is a five roomed cottage befitting my state of retirement, quite shut in by trees to remind me that I am no longer part of the active world..."[1] "You must let me know when you can come and stay with me, do not come and go hurriedly but rest here a little in peace,"[2] Marie wrote to Vernon Lee from Frimley in July 1898, "The older I grow the more averse I am to hurry, I find people in England so terribly overcrowded with engagements one does not enjoy the restful side of friendship, so many things seem indispensable which are not thought of in Italy... There is nothing very salient here, one feels dropped in the wood and here one might starve if you did not spend time and trouble in getting things to eat – I shall before long get in to the ways of the place – William seems really quite content here so I do hope everything will go smoothly. I fear Bella's house is very fatiguing, the up-hill and up-stairs quite does for me..."

Lisa, Effie and Mico spent time in the United States, Effie working on a series of American portrait medallion commissions at a farm near Boston. Michael Spartali Stillman, Mico, who was destined to remain in America, entered the office of the leading New York architects McKim, Mead, and White; William and Marie had found that it required too great an outlay to train in England. McKim's were engaged at the time in the design of J Pierpont Morgan's Murray Hills mansion between Madison and Third Avenue, today's Morgan Library, completed in 1903.

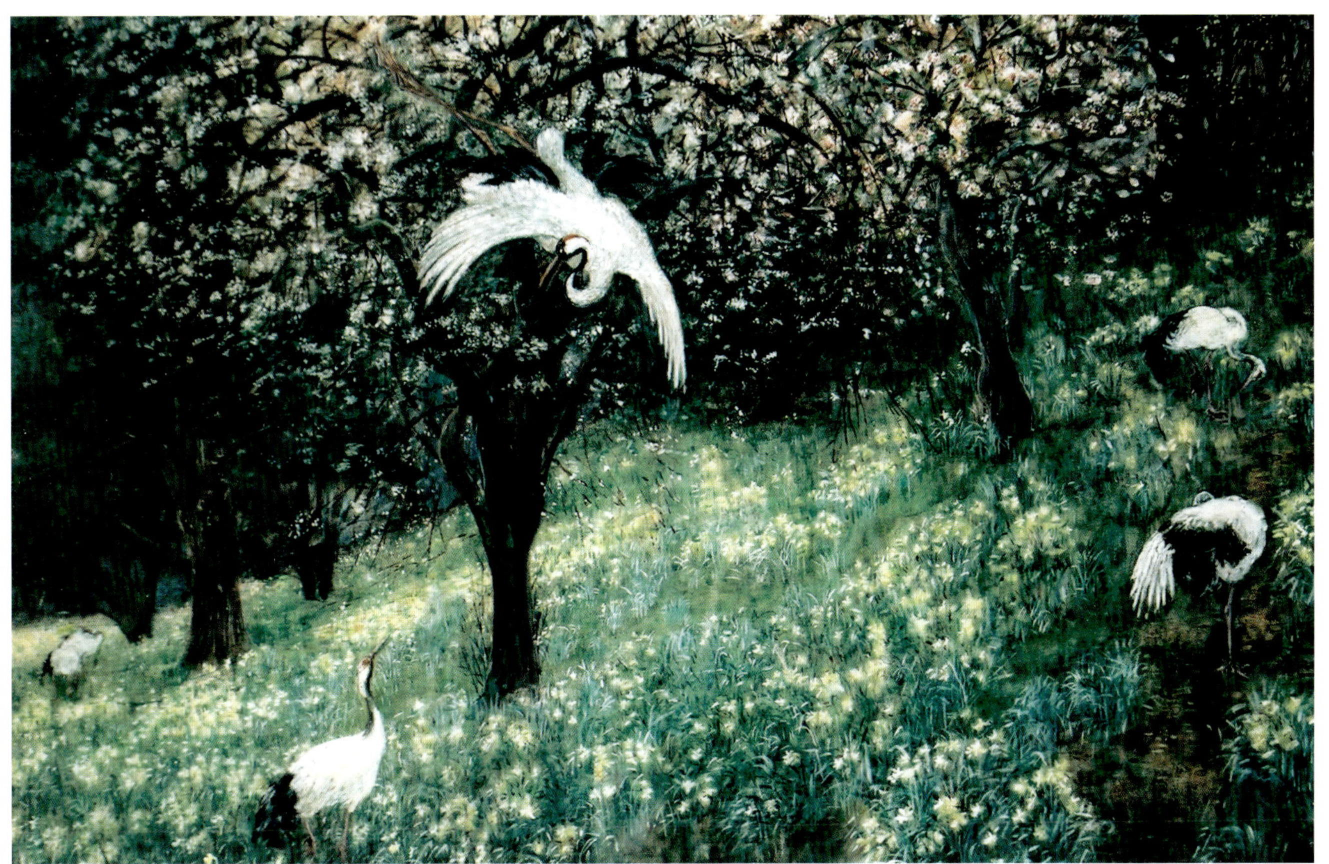

Plate 71
Marie Spartali Stillman
undated, possibly c.1903
White Herons
Watercolour and gouache on paper
Private Collection

Michael worked also on Penn Central station, designing the lettering and frieze over the entrance; by a curious co-incidence, it fell to his son, William James, jr., a civil engineer, to pull down the façade he designed when the Madison Square Garden complex was built over the station.

Marie continued to visit her parents on the Isle of Wight, and paid a short visit to friends in Florence: "I am painting Effie watering lilies in the cypress garden of the Villa Landor at Florence. We have stayed there with Professor Willard Fiske and I studied it with the intention of a picture last time I was there."[3]

William Stillman completed his *Autobiography of a Journalist*, his last words on his working life, background and outlook; he laid down his pen. The record is remarkably short of any personal history, of mentions of Marie and his family or of any sentiment. Partly this may be ascribed to reticence born of his solitary nature, but it surely reflects Marie's own personal reserve too: "It has always been my practice to destroy all letters. I have seen so much mischief come from letters found after people are dead. But altho' I do not very clearly remember dates I will try to jot down some remembrances of those days for Ford in case they may serve him..."[4] she had recently written to Cathy Heuffer.

Janey Morris continued to keep Wilfrid Blunt informed, writing to him in July 1898: "I passed Easter with Mrs Stillman in Surrey and had a very pleasant visit though I could have wished for more warmth. The woods come up right to the back of the house and squirrels leap about all day and look delightful, it is almost as good for Mr Stillman as being in the backwoods..."[5] William Michael Rossetti visited in November 1898, noting in his diary: "Mrs Stillman (whom I had not seen since about August 1894) wrote to me the other day inviting me down to their house... I fixed to come today but only for one afternoon. Went, and was much pleased to renew my old friendship with her and her husband... [she] is still handsome and gracious, tho' there is a little more evidence of age than when I saw her last; she must be I believe, fully 56. Stillman looks old in point of wrinkles, parchment skin etc., and his great height shows less than of yore; he did not however seem much amiss and says that since he settled in England his very persistent and some alarming bronchitis has not recovered... the house, Deepdene, (bought by Bella Middleton) is not a big one but pleasantly home-like amid well-wooded grounds of fair size. Stillman who is a great patron of squirrels has hung some trees with boxes wherein nuts are deposited. Mr and Mrs Spartali are still living in the IoWight. They have no London home now."[6]

Towards the end of 1900 the Stillmans made a new acquaintance who would later become a confidante and friend to Marie, and a collector of her work. This was Samuel Bancroft Jr., Fairfax Murray's American industrialist client who had commissioned a copy of Effie's Bayard bust in 1898. "It was a great satisfaction to make your acquaintance for we had heard of you for many years from Effie, Mr Murray and Richard Norton..." Marie wrote after his visit to Frimley. At the beginning of the New Year 1901, Bancroft wrote, thanking Marie for a photograph of Dante Gabriel Rossetti's portrait of William: "I have had within the last few days two notes from Lisa who seems too busy to come down from Beacon Hill yet, and who seems to be having a happy busy time on that empyrean height."[7]

In a long letter in reply, Marie Stillman reflected on the past year and the old century. William had been ill: "Certainly we did not start the new century well, more's the pity since having had a large slice of the old century we are entitled to a very small slice of this one." Bancroft had sent her an article on Rossetti by Miss E L Carey in reply to a hostile comment on a Rossetti drawing he owned and that she had countered in a piece in the *New York Times*: "I can fully appreciate Miss Carey's difficulties with the mass of irrelevant correspondence already printed to deal with, and heaven only knows how much more to come, and all those ill-natured books, W B Scott's, Hall Caine's, Prinsep's and others. I can understand also that anyone with a New England conscience can scarcely grasp the nature of the artistic temperament and its impulses – always indulged in – its want of responsibility. For my own part, Miss Carey seems to explain away any qualities short of heroic in Rossetti and to make too many excuses for any deficiencies – we ought to accept a man of genius with all his faults and be thankful ... those who knew and loved him in those bright days when he was quite himself were under the spell of his splendid and imperious personality..."[8] This is the clearest insight in to Marie's outlook towards the artist she revered above all and who returned her understanding with affection and admiration for her beauty and bearing. Aware and tolerant of his foibles, unsurprised by words and actions that were far removed from her own, gently quizzical but always sympathetic to the his creative animus.

William's *Autobiography* was published. "Rec'd Stillman's Autobiography. G is treated in a discerning manner, Christina in a highly sympathetic one,"[9] Rossetti noted in his diary. By March 1901, William Stillman was seriously ill once more with a pulmonary infection. Bancroft saw Lisa and Michael in New York and found them "very much worried"[10], Marie wrote in reply to Bancroft: "Your kind letter found us all in the greatest anxiety for after all those weeks of watching William does not seem to be improving at all, his weakness increases and the cough has diminished very little. The Doctor has told us frankly that it is all a question of food and that if William is able to go on taking as much as he does he may recover but at his age it was always doubtful... he has suffered terribly, he never realised poor fellow that anyone could be so full of pain and discomfort... I have hope that the Dr does not know the vitality of the American constitution – without hope life would be intolerable – I cannot cable any comforting report to Lisa and Michael yet. I am so pleased that you care to have my picture 'Loves Messenger'."[11]

In May Marie wrote again: "... William is still very very ill, coughing away and still in bed... the doctor finds him improving, but... I do not feel satisfied about him – we have had so many relapses. Effie is here gardening... the strain of all this most painful time has told on her more than any of us, we are all looking forward to Lisa's return and to news of Michael; I am glad to hear that Michael is really happy and identifies himself and means to remain there and find work. England is too crowded, there is no room for the young people not backed by capital..."[12] A few days later: "My husband has been very ill again... Lisa is on her way home and I am glad indeed for probably her return will brighten up William and she will have much to tell him about old friends and about Michael. I do hope the boy will get on and not weary of plodding away at his office..."[13]

"I learn that the steamer 'Eagle Point' is in the Delaware and I suppose the picture will be here in the next few days. I enclose my cheque for £100.00 and I hope that 'The Messenger of Love' will be a constant confirmation of its name between us..."[14] Bancroft replied.

On 10 May William Rossetti recorded a visit to the Stillmans: "...to Frimley Green to see Stillman who has been alarmingly ill since January – found him in bed, looking a trifle less ill than I had feared. He conversed readily but in a low voice, a bad form of bronchitis being the essential ailment. Am rather in hopes that he will recover from this attack, but the outlook is far from cheering. Was much pleased to talk with Mrs Stillman, Bella and Effie and also a pleasant American lady who is visiting. Saw Bella's daughter who is aged I suppose about 6. Bella is in good looks and seems a very agreeable, sensible woman."[15]

William James Stillman died at Deepdene on 6 July 1901, aged 73. "...notwithstanding the long illness, death came on us almost unexpectedly... already so many friends have gone and now this dearest of all companions and friends,"[16] Marie wrote to Samuel Bancroft that very day. A week later Bancroft replied: "The corn was ripe for the harvest." To Fairfax Murray she wrote: "My Dear Friend, William died yesterday, 6th at 5pm he did not know he was leaving us and we had been told only 24 hours before by the specialist. I had fully expected a verdict of death – but did not suspect the moment was so near. I had tried to persuade Lisa and Effie two days before that the case was hopeless, they could not believe Dr Goodheart even... He is to be cremated and buried at Brookwood – Effie has gone to ask a Unitarian Minister to conduct a service... we want it to be what he believed, a future life, a God of love, the laws of nature and not an anthropomorphic Deity. We are not asking anyone. You were of all our friends the one he loved best and who always had a most happy influence on him. The beautiful Turner[17] has been a great delight – his last aesthetic pleasure, it has been opposite his bed all these weeks... I will soon bring it to your house and tell you anything you like to ask. Yours affectionately, Marie Stillman."[18]

"Am very sorry to see in the paper the announcement of Stillman's death – sorry for him and still more so for Marie. This has been about my best day for sciatica,"[19] William Michael Rossetti, now 72 himself, noted in his diary. *The Times* obituary (9 July) commented: "Perhaps his material prosperity and success might have been more signal had his taste and gifts been fewer. Certainly his life would have been less full and the man less engaging."[20] William Michael Rossetti captured the spirit of his friend William James Stillman in an obituary in *Some Reminiscences*: "In temperament, in his attitude to the inner and outer things of life, Stillman had more of the man of genius than the man of talent. In actual mental endowment and

---

Plate 72
Marie Spartali Stillman
1885
Love's Messenger (Persephone Umbra, revised background 1895)
Watercolour, tempera and gold paint on paper mounted on wood. 82.9 x 67 cm (32⅝ x 26⅜in)
Exhibited: Grosvenor Gallery, 1885; Philadelphia, 1901
Bancroft Collection, Delaware Art Museum

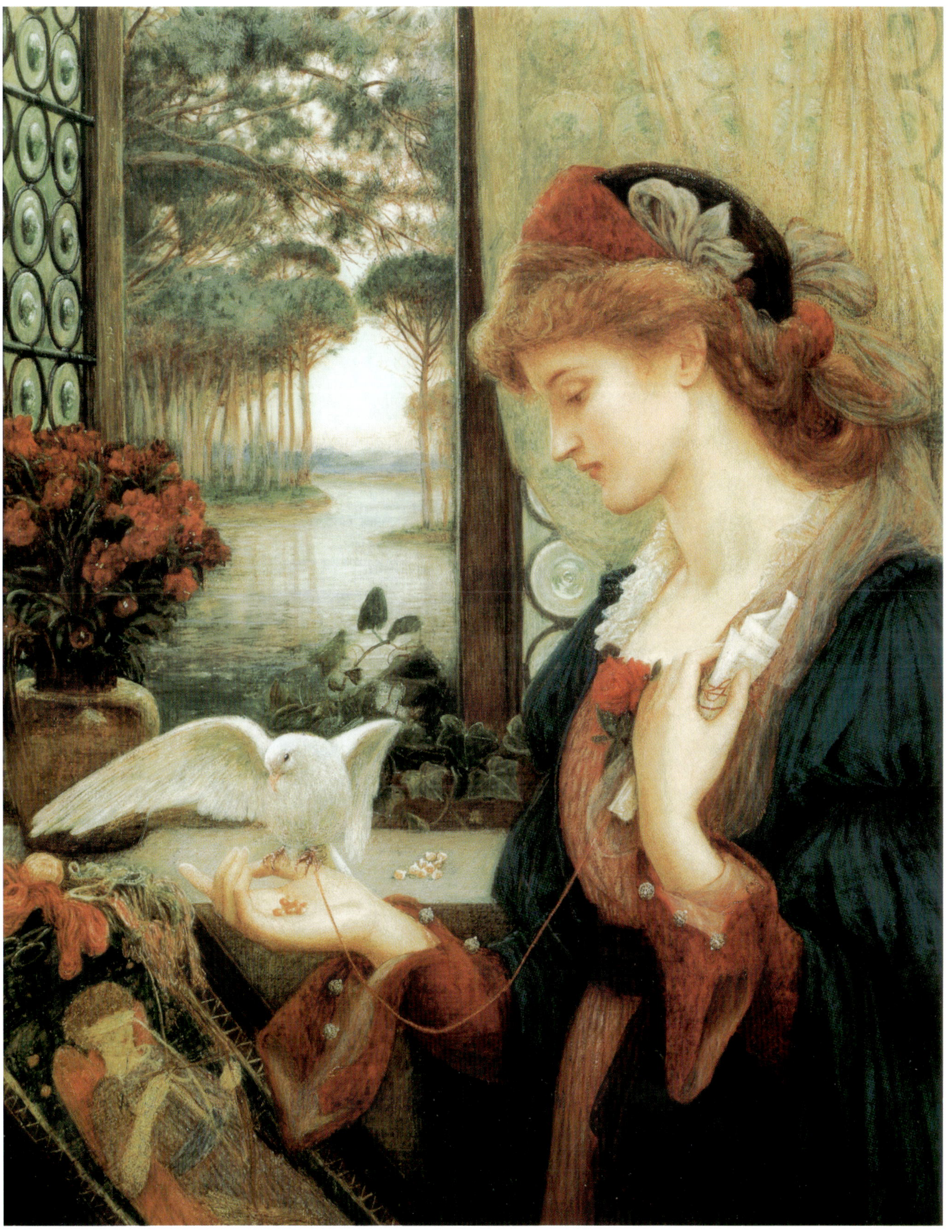

outcome the reverse was the case. He did not possess genius but his talents were authentic and versatile, and so was the course of his life. His Autobiography of a Journalist is in many respects an interesting book... it gives a true insight in to a character and career, and the mainsprings of both."[21] Stillman had been fearless but not brave, self-centred without selfish intent, self-absorbed and unable to express the warmer of his emotions, a legacy from his troubled, constrained childhood.

In October Rossetti noted in his diary: "... went to see Mrs Stillman – all the family were in the house from time to time, Bella and her daughter, Lisa and Effie. With Mrs Stillman and Bella I had a good talk about Stillman's last days. The end came rather sooner than had been expected but was near the last clearly announced by a physician called in to consult. Stillman seemed to have little pain in the last 2 or 3 days. Much pleasant talk on less sorrowful subjects. Mrs Stillman will continue living principally at Deepdene, seeing also a good deal of her parents in the Isle of Wight; they are both well and cheerful at present – ages 84 and 76 (higher than I thought.) Lisa looks handsome, quite as much so as ever I knew her: Effie has a strained and nervous look and voice..."[22]

In December, Marie wrote to Vernon Lee: "I was glad to get a letter from you, I had been intending to write... You would know without telling how things are... I do not feel capable of talking much – I am very glad to be allowed to stay on here,

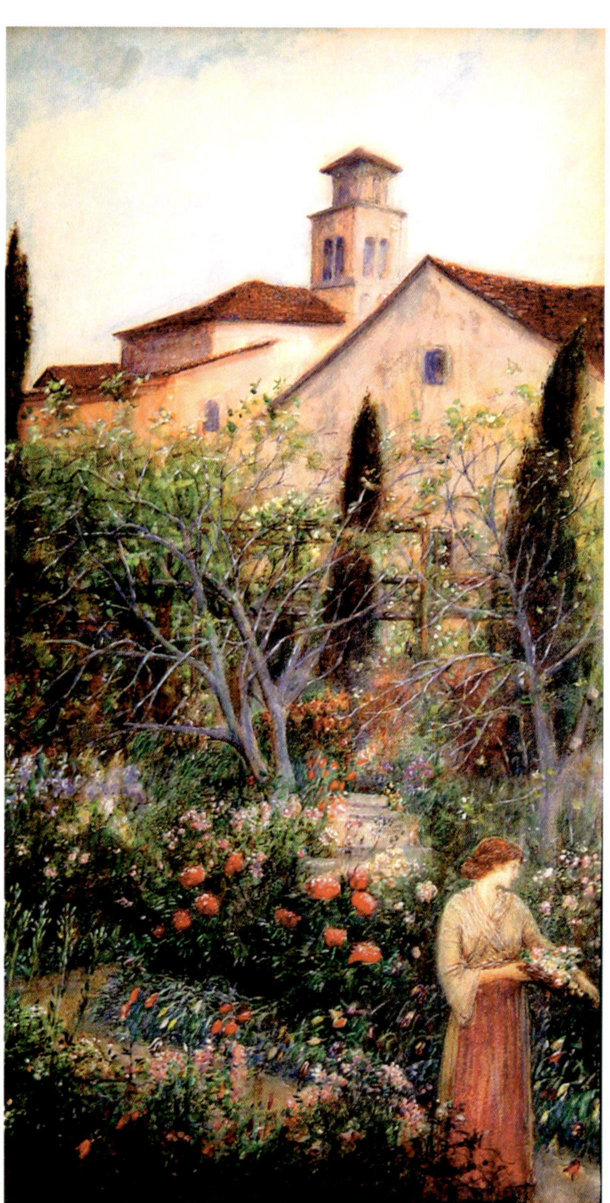

Plate 73
Marie Spartali Stillman
1903
Lady Radnor's Garden on the Guidecca
Watercolour
Exhibited: Oehme Gallery, New York, 1908
Private Collection

Bella has been more than generous in all the arrangements she has made for me..."[23] Marie lived on for 26 years after her husband's death; they had been married for 30 years. She continued quietly about her life, increasingly devoted to her children, her step-children and grandchildren, but still unmistakeably her own person.

In May of the following year she was in Rome with Bella, Peggy and Lisa. William Michael Rossetti was there too, staying with his daughter Helen Maria Madox Angeli[24], he noted in his diary: "...the rest of the day passed in a visit to Mrs Stillman. Mrs Middleton and her daughter[25] present and we met Lisa as we descended the stairs." By June 1902, Marie was back in Frimley, awaiting a visit from Vernon Lee: "Violet Hippisley wants you to come and hear Ethel Smyth's opera on 11th July or 15th at Covent Garden[26] ... the garden here is a mass of weeds – but I must tear myself away and try not to come back for some time – it does not do to attach oneself to places or things – it is too much luxury."[27] With the death of William Stillman she became a dependent – strong-minded and self-motivated certainly – but nevertheless reliant on Bella in particular since she owned the house at Frimley; the only capital in the family came from the widowed Bella's marriage to John Henry Middleton, and that needed to be eked out carefully, supplemented by the occasional sale of a painting.

Ethel Smyth was a neighbour in Surrey. An imposing figure in tweed Norfolk jacket and breeches, "a woman of boisterous vitality who fell prey to inconvenient passions for persons of both sexes", she was a composer of considerable stature in a Brahmsian manner. Later Dame Ethel, she was a close friend of Emmeline Pankhurst and her daughters Sylvia and Christabel; not surprisingly in a strong character of her Sapphic inclinations she was an ardent suffragette, which contributed greatly to the difficulty of getting staged performances of her work. Her *March for Women* received its most notorious performance in Holloway prison in 1912 when Ethel Smyth and over 100 suffragists, including Mrs Pankhurst, were serving two months' imprisonment. Ethel Smyth conducted the suffrage battle anthem with her toothbrush from the window

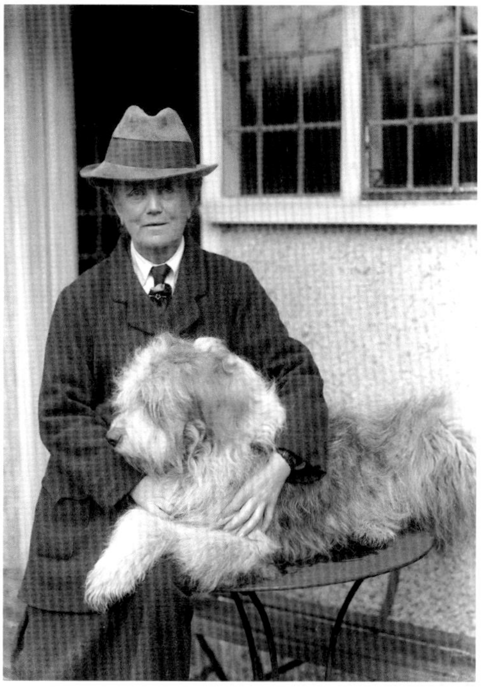

Plate 74
Dame Ethel Mary Smyth (1858-1944), composer and suffragist, by Bassano
National Portrait Gallery, London

of her cell overlooking the prison yard.

A favourite of Vernon Lee from her many visits to Florence, Ethel Smyth also provides us with a perceptive view of Marie Stillman's dearest remaining friend. "... I believe the tragedy of her life was that without knowing it she loved the culte humanly and with passion; but being the stateliest, chastest of beings she refused to face the fact or indulge in the most innocent of demonstrations of affection, preferring to create a fiction that these friends were merely intellectual necessities. One day in an extra-expansive mood I gave her a parting hug myself, and though she bore it with courtesy and kindness, I felt I had committed a solecism."[28]

That July, Marie's childhood friend Aglaia Coronio committed suicide in grief over the death of her daughter Calliope. In August Marie visited Janey Morris at Kelmscott.[29] In September she was staying with her parents on the Isle of Wight: "I had thought of going to Orvieto with Rodolphe [Cahen d'Anvers] for October but he has been sent to Bukarest so he can't take a holiday this year – for my own part it is rather fortunate for I want to get in to regular working habits... I have agreed to take part of Effie's studio for a few months to be in London a good deal."[30] She had also found time to paint a picture of *St Francis Blessing the Pigeons He has Freed*, exhibited at the New Gallery, now unlocated.

For the next few months she divided her time between Bella's house in Frimley and her parents' property on the Isle of Wight. In March 1903, she wrote to Lee from Sandford: "I have been at Niton with Mrs Morris who was ill and now she has left and gone to her home..."[31] Then, in the summer of 1903, Marie returned to the States for the first time since 1871. "I am much disappointed to find that you are coming late to England for I am going to America the 2nd week in July," she told Vernon Lee early in June. "I fear I shall find Michael much changed and it will take some time to get acquainted again, it is desirable that I find what chances of work he has there and many things I can never know if I remain quietly here – it is not a journey that in itself tempts me..."[32] Marie joined Michael in New York on 27 July after a short stay with Grace Norton in Boston, following an unusually rough summer passage from England: "We left Liverpool in the rain and the wind came up before we reached Queenstown," she wrote to Fairfax Murray, "so that we had an uncomfortable three days and there could be no thought of sitting on deck – Saturday the sun shone... I was beginning to think a better time was in store for us when a fog came up and persisted for five days and nights till we got in sight of Cape Cod lighthouse... the quarantine officers had gone by the time we reached Boston so we had to wait on board until the next morning... it was good luck for me to have Sally Norton on board. I carried the picture on land safely and got it out of customs on bond by showing the consular declaration to one of the officers known to Prof. C E Norton."[33] Marie was delivering J M W Turner's *Devonport and Dockyard* to the Fogg Museum, Fairfax Murray's gift in memory of William Stillman.

She passed the rest of the summer with Mico at Cornish, New Hampshire, in the artists' colony that formed around the sculptor Augustus Saint-Gaudens. Saint-Gaudens, born in 1848 in Dublin, Ireland, studied classical art and architecture in Rome and became an avid supporter of the American Academy there, where William Stillman first met him. Saint-Gaudens first came to Cornish in 1885; the studio he built there became the centre of a group of assistants and established artists who followed Saint-Gaudens and became known as the "Cornish Colony".[34] The painters Maxfield Parrish, Thomas Dewing and Kenyon Cox, the dramatist Percy MacKaye, and the architect, Charles Platt, and sculptors Paul Manship and Louis Saint-Gaudens, his brother, were prominent members of the community there. When the following year the studio burned down, Michael Stillman moved to Cornish to assist Saint-Gaudens with the redesigned structure, the 'Studio of the Caryatids', and he stayed on to rebuild there. Saint-Gaudens died in Cornish in 1907 and with him the artist colony gradually departed.

Marie became closely involved with the sale of Giovanni Costa's estate in Rome in 1903. Costa had died the previous year and his widow was relying greatly on Marie and Lisa to guard her interests from a host of would-be buyers who were interested only in giving the least possible money for valuable works. Marie did what she could by letter from America; among those to whom she appealed for advice and assistance were two friends of hers and of Costa's: Sir W B Richmond and George Howard.[35] Back in England she wrote once more to George Howard, asking him to contribute his memories of the painter and to select the pictures to be published. Olivia Agresti – Dante Gabriel Rossetti's niece – W B Richmond and Mrs Corbet were writing and seeking further material, and she asked if Howard's daughter Lady Mary Murray would add her record of Costa's talk. [36]

For a time Marie became an itinerant in her husband's land, visiting his relatives and straining every sinew to find work for Michael who was unable to flourish creatively in the dry, hierarchical atmosphere of a major architectural practice. In September she was in Plainfield, New Jersey with her niece, Mrs Myers. In October Bella wrote to Vernon Lee to say that Marie was in New York with Michael and not able to anticipate returning before mid-December, determined to introduce Michael to contacts whom she hoped would help him to find work. Samuel Bancroft had become a fast friend and confidante; William Michael Rossetti published *Some Reminiscences*, which he dedicated to the Stillmans. "I have burrowed a bit in to W M Rossetti's new book," Bancroft wrote, "and in spite of your being the Dedicatee I must tell you what a friend of mine said of his work – 'it is like the Hawthorne children, when they ran dry one would say to another, 'come, let us dig up father'." "I laughed much," she replied, "at what you told me of the Hawthorne children – feeling as I do about publishing people's private letters and having expressed myself very frankly to WMR, I was surprised at his wishing to dedicate the volume to William and me – William wanted us to accept the dedication so that is why my name is there, much as I disapprove of such books, and this one is such a salad of things the public cannot care about..."[37] In November Marie was able to arrange an exhibition of her work at the Curtis & Cameron Gallery, Boston; among the works shown were *Dante with Beatrice on All Saints Day* (Grosvenor 1881, unlocated) and *The Enchanted Garden of Messer Ansaldo* (New Gallery, 1889), which was sold to T E Stillman, thereby disappointing Samuel Bancroft who had hoped to buy it.

Once again, New York proved a better market place than Rome or London: "I went yesterday to see Ms Alfred Collins about exhibiting my pictures here at her studio Carnegie Hall Room 90... I heard from Doll & Richards of the sale of two – the Wedding from the Vita Nuova and Manor... I consider myself in luck, for on Tuesday the St Francis Legend of the 2 Monks was carried away from here for a birthday present..." The fatal modesty was ever present. "I was also very much encouraged by my visit to Wilmington and seeing my poor little pictures in such good company in your beautiful home, for I have felt in these latter years that painting pictures that nobody wants is a selfish enjoyment and I should have done better in scouring floors and mending stockings in the good old fashion..."[38] she wrote to Bancroft.

There was no respite from domestic problems on her return to England early in1904: "I have had a very anxious time since I returned to these shores... I was recalled by the illness of Effie who had pleurisy and until quite recently I feared it had left some delicacy of the lungs... Effie is engaged to be married to Mr William Ritchie, a young barrister,"[39] Marie reported to Vernon Lee in February 1904. Effie was married to William George Brookfield Ritchie, barrister-at-law, at the Church of Our Lady of Victories, High Street, Kensington. William Ritchie was the brother of Sir Richmond Ritchie, whose wife – Anne Isabella Thackeray before her marriage to her godson – was a notable member of the literary and artistic circle surrounding Little Holland House in the 1870s and '80s which maintained the bonds between the families of Anglo-Indian and Greek descent that played so great a part in the arts of Victoria's England in to the next generation.

Marie kept at her painting, sometimes using it as protection from the outside world, as she wrote to Bancroft in September 1904: "I have been painting gardens all summer and now I have taken up a large watercolour of the subject from the St Francis Fioratti, the Wolf of Gubbio... I keep quietly at work all the while I am here, I am too tired to take part in society – I am often in the Isle of Wight with my parents. I was asked to design a memorial window for Vassar College..."[40]

William Stillman's life-long belief that God would always provide at the appropriate moment proved illusory with his parting. Money was short, and the familiar recourse to Marie's easel could not alone bring in the funds for her daughter's wedding. Sadly, Marie Stillman parted with one of her few remaining personal treasures from a crowded life. She was now 61 and had been widowed for over a decade. Nearly thirty-five years before, on the threshold of Marie's controversial marriage to William Stillman, Euphrosyne Cassavetti – Maria Zambaco's mother – had commissioned a nude portrait of her daughter, *Venus Epithalamia*, by her lover Edward Burne-Jones, as a wedding present for the Stillmans. The painting shows Maria Zambaco in the foreground pensively watching a passing procession of singers, the *epithalamia* whose duty it was to sing outside the house of the newly married, from behind the cover of a pillar. Fairfax Murray arranged the sale of the original painting to Agnew's; years later he bought it back at Christie's and passed it to his friend and client, the American collector Grenville Lindall Winthrop.

Years later, Marie wrote to Gladys Norton: "I am glad to know that Mr Grenville Winthrop possesses that delightful picture I so much loved and prized. Burne-Jones painted it for my wedding present from Mrs Cassavetti. Mrs Cassavetti was so much pleased with it that after giving it to me she begged to have it back to get it copied for herself and Mr Fairfax Murray made the copy which I used to see in her bedroom. The year Effie, Mrs Richie [sic] was married I had to sell this most beloved picture to give her a trousseau and to pay for other necessary things. It was a terrible wrench, but I had nothing else of value and I required the money – it was bought by the Agnew firm."[41]

Marie's latent feminism became more overt: "... how splendid of Annie Cobden to go to prison for the cause – we ought all to be ready to endure prison and death for our convictions but very few are not afraid of hardships... there are others ready to be imprisoned for Ireland and the Education Bill but I am told it would be bad legislation to take count of these devotees to ideas – I am sure and have been told AC's imprisonment has excited many to join the cause and to work for it..."[42] she wrote.

Her children and a growing number of grandchildren remained the focus of her life. "... Lisa is still in Rome, I hope you will see her on her way through Florence – my daughters are all devoted to you as you know – Michael's news is of the birth of a little daughter we heard by cable. He has not yet found sufficient work to support himself comfortably and fortunately his wife has a little of her own and is a very clever manager and does everything herself – they are content and happy – I hope it will be well for them..." she told Vernon Lee.

In 1908, Marie Stillman returned to New York: "I wish I knew of a dealer in New York who would undertake to sell my pictures as I should like to withdraw them from Doll & Richards in Boston, but I don't know how to set about it," she wrote to Samuel Bancroft in February. Back from the East Coast in May, Marie reported to Vernon Lee that she had: "left Michael much as I found him – alas – and I felt I had no power to alter anything, so after doing what I could, I returned to try my hand again at more gardens as they seem to please the sort of public who can pay for them."[43] Marie, in the midst of her own money problems, was working hard to send money to Michael.

In November 1908 she was able to tell Bancroft: "I shall be in New York for a fortnight from the 1st at 18 East 66th St until the 7th and then at 414 W 20th St till the 14th and then here till January. I have a little exhibition at Julius Oehme's 320 5th Avenue which will open next Saturday and last 3 weeks, and I hope you may be in New York before it is over..."[44] she wrote to Bancroft late November. The catalogue included several of her major works, exhibited in London in the 1880s, a reminder of the difficulties she faced in selling her paintings in Europe.

Effie's developing career had taken her to the States. She had first exhibited at London's New Gallery in 1892 and, thereafter, annually until 1907, with the exception of 1905 – the year of her marriage; her work was also shown at the Royal Academy in 1897. Most of her known works are on an intimate scale in the form of busts, statuettes, reliefs and medals.[45] Her first breakthrough as a sculptress came at short notice, in 1897. Thomas F Bayard, the US statesman who had served as Secretary of State during Cleveland's first presidency of 1885-9 was appointed to the post of Ambassador to the Court of St James in 1893. Before his departure from Britain in 1897, the American Society of London held a dinner at which they presented him with an awesomely eccentric loving-cup in the form of a silver-gilt pumpkin mounted on the backs four eagles, wings outstretched in flight, surmounted by allegorical figures of America and Britannia with hands linked, carrying palm fronds and their arms blazoned on shields beside them, the whole topped by a bust of Bayard executed by Effie. When Bayard died in September 1898 Bancroft set about canvassing subscriptions for a statue of Wilmington's famous son and asked Effie to submit a design.[46] Effie's macquette was exhibited at the New Gallery in 1900 before it was sent to America. Delayed by other work, competing schemes, uncertainties over funding and endless prevarication by subscribers, as well as her own engagement and marriage, Effie did not complete her work on the Bayard memorial until 1906. It was finally placed in position early in 1908. "Did I send you a photograph of the Bayard statue as it stands?" Bancroft asked Fairfax Murray, adding a little wistfully, "... I am rather proud of it."[47]

The Bayard memorial was to be Effie's only major work. Untimely death cut short a career of immense promise. Weakened by the birth of her third child, Euphrosyne Stillman, Mrs W B Ritchie, died on 18 August 1911, age 39, from heart failure resulting from tuberculosis; she left her husband and a young family of three children.

Not long after Effie's unexpected death Marie wrote to Vernon Lee: "I knew that you would be so grieved for us. I can't tell you as the days pass how more and more

I feel how great my own loss is in not being able to look forward to seeing Effie – she was so happy and fortunate that the thought of that contented family always did me good – now my heart is always aching thinking of them all – William [Ritchie] especially for the loss is for him the most bitter and he has been so brave and good, so resigned and unselfish – we can ill spare her, but had she lived she could never have been happy, her life would have been tormented with illness and invalidism – so she died, happily without knowing. Bella has probably written to you about it – I had no idea she was ill (beyond weakness) till the morning she died. Bella only understood the day before so it came quite suddenly and I still feel quite dazed. She looked radiantly happy when dead and that brought me some comfort in my sorrow and I always believe that the soul lives on after this life – so the loss is ours. Those little boys are too young to remember Effie but they needed her wise discipline – what we can do for will be done, but no one can be what their mother was for them… your loving friend Marie Stillman." That Christmas she wrote again: "It was like you dear Vernon to know how painful the feste are to me – I have these 10 years since William's death been away from my dear ones in London, always here [Stanford] and twice away in America – but Effie knew how I thought of them and used to write all about her little surprises for the sisters and the children and of their fun... I miss her just now very keenly but I am looking forward to seeing those dear little boys with Bella in another week or so – Bella is admirable with them and they trust her and find such ready sympathy with them about their little troubles. Dear Vernon, I am poorer than ever – the picture dealer who sold my pictures in New York died over a year ago and I have not even sought to do anything with my work which for many years has made things easy for me about money..."[48] She was now 67 and tiring; the loss of an adult child being, perhaps, the least tolerable tragedy of old age.

Effie's children now became a much-loved part of Bella's household. "Those most darling boys are now with Lisa in Sussex, they are the very light of our life, they are very happy children. Willie and Jackie too always talk of Effie and remember many incidents in their days with her – Willie feels she can't return here but they will go to her – Jackie always hopes she will come back to them and questions me when I have been away as to whether I shall see her..." Her mother was now 88, Marie was 68 and tired, living much of the time on the Isle of Wight looking after her parents; "Here everything is as before, Mother is very very deaf and is now losing her eyesight... it is sad to grow old like that..." Bella took over the Ritchie family as Marie had taken over William's orphaned children. They shared a larger house, 19 Ashburn Place, in Kensington. Marie and Lisa moved there too. Perhaps because of an unhappy love affair, Lisa remained for years unmarried, and poured her creative effort in to writing poetry.

Euphrosyne Spartali died at 88 on 11 September 1913, at Monterey, their house in

Shanklin, Isle of Wight. The funeral service was conducted in the Greek Orthodox rite by the Archimandrite, Agathanopolos Moschovakis from the Greek Church in Moscow Road, and she was interred in the churchyard at Godshill, close to another Spartali property, Sandford House. Michael Spartali died on his 95th birthday, 12 January 1914, also at Monterey; the funeral was again led by Archimandrite Moschovakis. Michael was interred beside his wife at Godshill.

War came. Henry James took tea with Marie Stillman at 19 Ashburn Place.[49] In New York Michael Spartali Stillman enlisted in the American army and served in Italy for a time before being invalided out. Architectural commissions were few and far between in the war years, and he ran an interior design and furnishings business, The Kelmscott Decorating Company, from his architect's practice in partnership with his wife Evangeline, and later his cousin Florence Stillman. 'Our charge for *Decorating* and *Furnishing* and the purchase of *Antique Furniture, Pictures, Rugs* and in fact anything required in the household is *Ten Per Cent* on the cost,'[50] proclaims a company handbill of the time.

Charles Fairfax Murray died on 25 January 1919, breaking 50 years of close friendship; Marie Stillman was at his bedside. William Michael Rossetti died two weeks later.

After the war Vernon Lee returned to Settignano for the first time in 5 years. "How glad I was to get your postcard and to know that you are settled happily in your own home again – it was a great relief to my mind for I feared that you would find your servants very difficult to manage after years of complete mastery of the situation, and I wondered how the refugees had dealt with your house... I have just had 15 pictures packed to send to N York to Michael – they had been standing about here for 5 years all but the flower groups which I did in the Spring..."[51] Marie wrote to her in October 1919.

Walter de la Mare talked with Marie, now 76, at Alecco Ionides's house in the summer of 1920; she was, he recalled, the last surviving person to know and remember Christina Rossetti.

Over the years Marie and Vernon Lee exchanged little scraps of the events of their circumscribed lives; in 1922 Marie wrote: "We had a very dull Xmas for Lisa, Jack and Dick had to be away from here as their school had chicken-pox – so Lisa had them at Camber where she had taken a house of Mrs Dew Smith[52] for three months – I went there on 28th December, it was intensely cold and so windy, not a tree to be seen nor even a shrub, nothing but sand-dunes, a more desolate outlook I never did see – the wind and cold reduced me to complete inactivity and depression, I could only sit by the fire and read Henry James's very last novels which I found very fatiguing and uninteresting to my astonishment – and also his notes on French authors which I very much enjoyed. Peggy is settled in her home near here and Bella is constantly over there or going about with her so in reality they are more together than when Peggy lived at home..."[53]

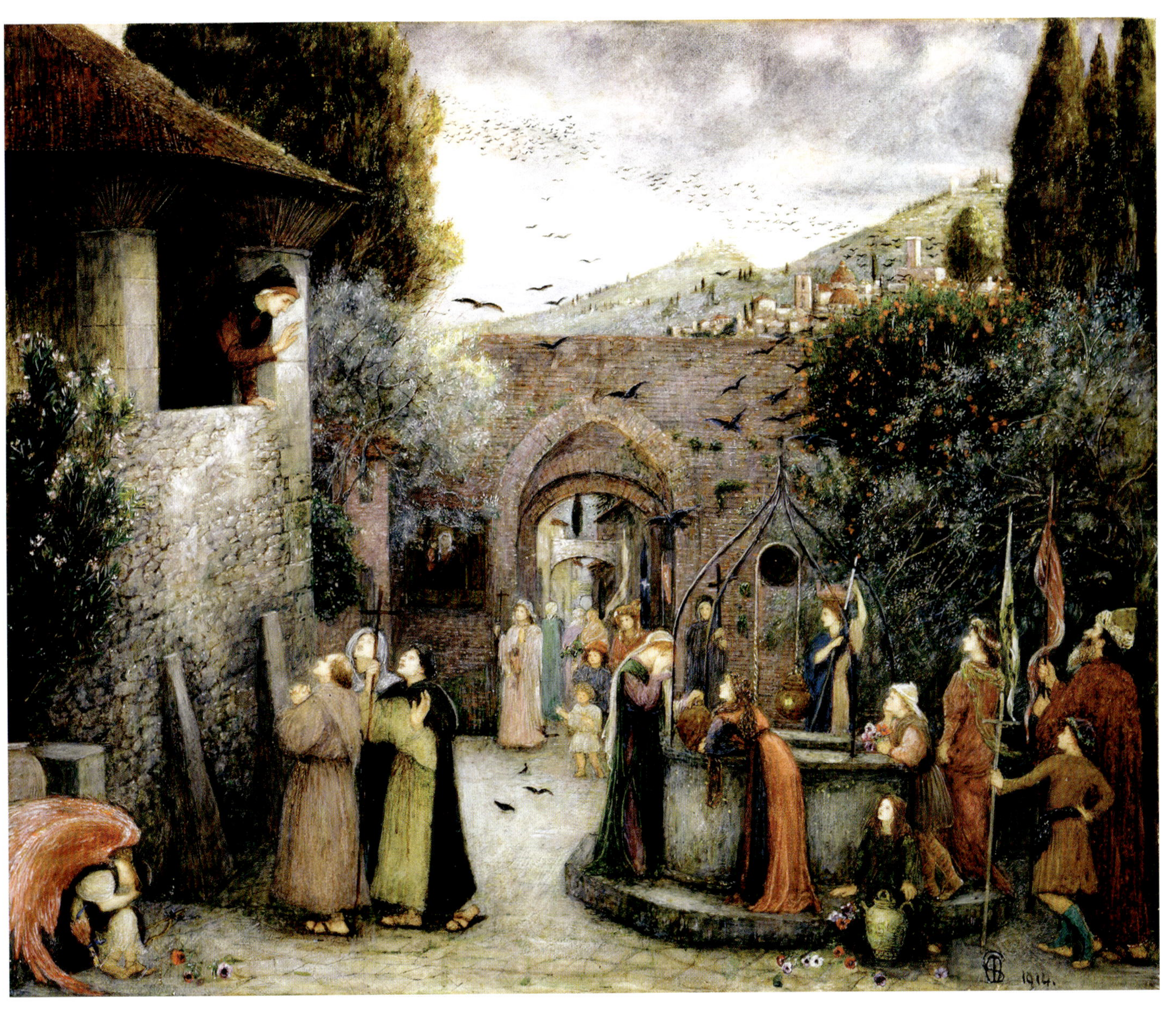

Plate 75
Marie Spartali Stillman
1914
The Pilgrim Folk
Watercolour and gouache on paper. 56.7 x 70.4 cm ($22\frac{5}{16}$ x $27\frac{11}{16}$in)
Bancroft Collection, Delaware Art Museum

They were both growing old. In June 1924, Marie wrote: "I have been thinking of you all these weeks and I was very much grieved to hear of your suffering and the loss of your hair. I have been very ill or I should have written before – I have made you this boudoir cap as you may find it useful when you don't have your hat on – I could have made it prettier with 'colifichets' of divers kinds but I know your severe tastes... Your old and true friend Marie Stillman."[54]

Marie Spartali Stillman died on 6 March 1927 at her home in London, a few days short of her 84th birthday. "Her two stepdaughters, who were in all but blood, true daughters to her, were with her to the last, and she was laid to rest beside her husband at Brookwood. Her wonderful beauty was enhanced by a total and almost equally wonderful absence of self-consciousness; and it was combined with perfect frankness and simplicity and with an indomitable spirit. Affectionate, and yet subtly malicious, radiating rather than exerting an indefinable and insuperable charm, she retained throughout her life a delightful girlishness. Not only her own children and grandchildren, but those of her friends, found in her almost a contemporary of their own and one with whom they could be, and were, immediately and spontaneously intimate,"[55] read her obituary in *The Times* (8 March 1927).

Bella's tribute in her letter to Vernon Lee on 16 March was the most moving and deeply felt: "Dearest Vernon – indeed you must keep a place in your heart and not let us slip – we miss Mama so much that we <u>cannot</u> let any of those who loved her to forget us. It felt as though music that had accompanied us from the beginning had just died away in to empty silence, as though the fire on the hearth had gone out, leaving the house so cold. And yet, her going was so triumphant, so like herself, that one could not wish her to be still exposed to the risk of deterioration – which she so triumphantly escaped. There is something in her death of the quality of John Sargent's; I feel as though she had conquered old age and won eternal youth. Partly the marvellous beauty of her, lying there like an empress, so sweet and serene, makes one almost glad. I only regret that Michael was too late for that exquisite and comforting sight and that you, Emily and Violet should not have this picture to remember." To this, Lisa added: "Bella has said what we all feel. Dearest friend, I can only send my love, Lisa."[56]

We catch a last glimpse of Lisa in July 1939; she went to Kelmscott one last time to buy a memento of her family's connection with the old house at the sale of the remaining contents. May Morris had died in October 1938, and she was followed in March by her companion Miss Lobb. When war came, Lisa left her home on the coast and went to live with her niece, Effie's daughter Peggy. She died in a nursing home in Wandsworth, on the outskirts of London, on 11 February 1946; she was 82. Bella, for more than sixty years the mainstay of the family, outlived her sister and died on 15 August 1948 at the age of 80 in Chelsea, living in the home of her nephew, Effie's son Richard; she had been 52 years a widow and had lost her beloved step-mother, Marie, 21 years earlier.

Mico's final years were overshadowed by the death by drowning of his 17-year-old son 'Midie' – Michael – in an accident on the Hudson River at Woodstock when the ice on which he was walking broke up under him. Mico's devoted wife Evangeline suffered a stroke soon after and was left an invalid; Mico died at Northfield, Mass. in 1966, his eighty-ninth year.

It is easy to think of Marie Stillman as English, the land of her birth; but she came from an intrinsically Greek family who spoke Greek at home, as she did with her parents. As the wife of an American citizen, she carried an American passport. In later life, warmly involved with the children and delighting in young people, Marie Stillman was also lonely. Her affection for Vernon Lee was once expressed in near-Sapphic terms; as a widow a more mature love remained. She was attracted to forceful, blue-stocking women such as Barbara Bodichon, Lucy Madox Rossetti, Annie Cobden-Sanderson and Ethel Smyth, all of whom she admired and perhaps she shared many of their convictions; but she never stepped outside the rôle of wife, mother and painter. She was surprisingly timid, a characteristic confirmed by a strong sense of propriety.

The closeness of her relationship with William remained a mystery to many of their friends. His abrasive, Yankee personality was far from universally applauded by those who knew him as Marie's husband. She discerned in him warmth and a degree of caring that was largely unseen by others; few of her friends were also his. It was a durable marriage, conceived in passion, strengthened by difficulties that would have daunted a lesser woman, ending in regard and mature friendship.

Envoi

Marie Spartali Stillman, the Artist

Marie Spartali Stillman's career as a painter – her early determination to make her way as a serious professional artist, her consistent productivity and the considerable qualities of much of her work – are less well-known than might reasonably be expected. Her output was remarkable, some 170 known works (and others in all probability lost to record), in a career spanning her early pictures, first exhibited in 1867 to her last major exhibition in New York in 1908. She continued to paint diligently almost up to her death at the age of 83 in 1927.

There is a handful of work that is widely known from reproduction and exhibition, from the early *The Lady Prays – Desire*[1] of 1867 to *Cloister Lilies*[2] of 1891 by way of *La Pensierosa*[3] (1879) and *Messer Ansaldo Showing Dianora his Enchanted Garden*[4] (1889) and it is on these few paintings that her standing currently rests. There are periods when the quality of her work can be related to her personal circumstances, discernable influences at certain stages of her career – the Florentine years in particular – and evidence of growing assurance in her technique and handling of groups of figures. The range of her genre subjects – following her early close involvement in the Rossetti circle when she largely abandoned semi-autobiographical Greek themes for the tales of Dante and Boccaccio – nevertheless remained limited over the span of her career of more than 40 years as an exhibiting artist. The stories from the *Fioratti,* the 'little flowers' of St Francis, came late with her time in Rome, but she returned to Dante for her last major work.

Marie Spartali Stillman was eminently a woman-artist rooted in the mid-Victorian era. The chosen medium for by far the greater part of her work, watercolour or gouache, was for the most part the preference of many other serious women painters of the era (though her friend and contemporary Evelyn De Morgan chose *tempera,* and Emma Sandys worked largely in oils.) Watercolour is intrinsically less well suited to forceful expression or to strikingly dramatic subjects, and Marie Stillman possessed no apparent inclination to paint in oils, nor in a stronger or more stirring vein. The scale of her painting is equally modest; one of the larger of her works (and one of the most successful) is *Messer Ansaldo Showing Dianora his Enchanted Garden*, which measures 30" x 40" (76.1cm x 101.1cm). At no juncture did she attempt to break out from the Victorian mould, for example in the

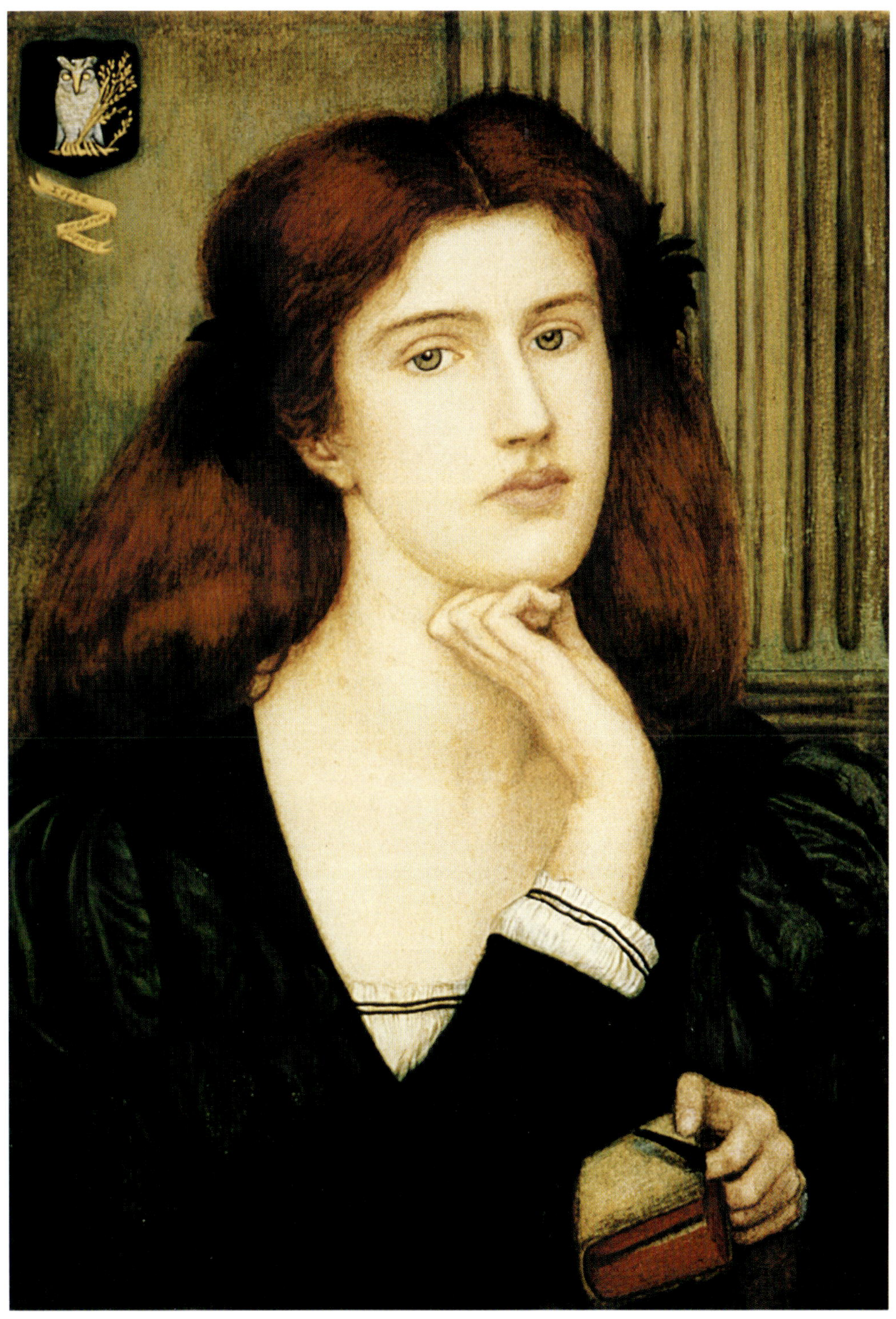

Plate 76
Marie Spartali Stillman
1867, monogrammed lower left
The Lady Prays - Desire
Watercolour with gold paint on paper. 41.9 x 30.5 cm (16½ x 12in)
Exhibited: Dudley, 1867
Courtesy of The Maas Gallery, London; Bridgeman Art Library

modernizing directions taken by women artists such as the impressionistic Berthe Morisot or her exact contemporary, the American Mary Cassatt, both of whose work she knew; or indeed the major canvases of her friend Evelyn De Morgan. She was seldom inclined to move on and always returned to the things she knew best.

From her adolescent years, Marie Spartali was surrounded by a cultivated set of artists such as James McNeill Whistler and Fantin-Latour, and discerning patrons such as the Ionides. She came early in to frequent contact with the group of writers and artists of the Little Holland House circle – Alfred Lord Tennyson, William Makepeace Thackeray and his daughters Anne and Minnie, Julia Margaret Cameron, George Frederic Watts, Dante Gabriel Rossetti, Edward Burne-Jones and William Morris among them – who determined her to paint professionally. She was unusually well-educated and accomplished, ironic and intelligent, but she had still to overcome the rigid social values of the mid-Victorian era; it took considerable ambition and strength of character to prevail against her wealthy father's belief that painting was a genteel accomplishment for a young lady but not a career.

The principal influence on her style and technique throughout her career was the five years she spent as Ford Madox Brown's student alongside his daughter Lucy and, later, the help and encouragement he continued to give her after her marriage. Under his guidance she first exhibited, aged 23, *The Lady Prays – Desire*, a self-portrait on a line of Spencer's *Faerie Queen,* at the Dudley in 1867. Madox Brown's method of teaching was well-suited to her temperament, and it is interesting to speculate what might have been the direction of her work if she had first attached herself to Dante Gabriel Rossetti as his pupil as she, and her father, had hoped. "Ruskin said Mr Brown was equal to Mr Rossetti as a painter, but would probably be superior to him as a teacher... Mr Brown's teaching was as systematic as Mr Rossetti's had been free. Mr Rossetti always objected to students making a firm outline, he wished the work to be free... Mr Brown on the other hand insisted on a firm outline. 'Do not scrabble around in the hope that the effect you seek will appear by chance. Be clear in your own mind and you'll best advance your work.'"[5]

Later, in the 1880s Edward Burne-Jones took up the rôle of counsellor, but it was as the supporter to an established stylist. There is little evidence of mentoring in their correspondence; rather, of the encouragement of a friend and suggestions freely given only when asked. "It is always most flattering to me," she wrote to Samuel Bancroft, "to be taken for a pupil of Burne-Jones for of course I have loved his work of all periods as few others have, and he was always most helpful to me when I was in need of advice about my work, especially these latter years, but it was Madox Brown who encouraged me to become an artist and who taught me to paint. I can never feel sufficiently grateful for his having given this immense interest to my life..."[6]

Her early work under Ford Madox Brown included a number of history paintings on Greek themes of her own choice that reflected two personal preoccupations:

first, that of heroic resistance to oppression and injustice – a matter of immediacy and importance in a household whose wealth stemmed from the Greek trade with countries under Turkish domination and, secondly, that of personal ambition in a male dominated world. There is a strong autobiographical element in many of her early pictures. Marie Spartali was privately educated by tutors chosen for their concurrence with the radical, freedom-loving views of her father, whose own parents had been forced to flee from Turkish persecution in Smyrna when he was a young child. (Muller-Strübing, her mentor in Greek history and philosophy, was an authority on the historical importance of Aristophanes in the political history of Athens, but also a revolutionary conspirator in exile from his native Prussia.)

Subjects included *Korinna the Theban Poetess,* an important icon from Greek cultural history whose philosophic poetry drew parallels between the world of mythology and ordinary human behaviour.[7] Marie identified herself with Korinna, acclaimed as the greatest lyric poet in Greece; "This is a portrait of herself on a moderate scale – good but not elaborate... red drapery," William Michael Rossetti noted.[8] *Procne in Search of Philomela* in 1869 portrayed the woman who was turned in to a swallow.[9] Her 1869 painting, exhibited at the Dudley in 1870, of *Antigone and Ismene Burying the Body of Polynices on the Battlefield,* portrays another Greek heroine defying the orders of King Creon: "Let him lie unwept, unburied, a toothsome morsel for the birds of heaven, and whoso touches him shall perish by the cruel death of stoning." Even more directly autobiographical was *Pharmakeutria, or Brewing the Love Philtre* of the same year, depicting two women casting a lover's spell over their brew. It bears a quotation from Theocritus: "O! Wheel of fortune, draw this man to my house."

During this period she also painted a considerable number of flower pieces influenced by her father's collection of Henri Fantin-Latour's *nature morte,* and small conventional landscapes of scenes on the Isle of Wight where her father owned extensive properties, in the mould of Victorian lady amateurs and artists like Helen Allingham. She also painted more ambitious and successful self-portraits and portraits of her younger sister Christina, perhaps because she lacked access to models.

"She has evinced so much application and artistic expression that one may fairly expect her – even if (like most of her sex) not gifted with a strong eye for form – to continue bringing this quality in to nearer and nearer harmony with her command of colour,"[10] William Michael Rossetti – a friendly but truthful critic – said of her *Brewing the Love Philtre. The Times* commented critically, but to much the same point: "Miss Spartali is probably entitled to the prize for bad drawing... at the same time it would be unfair to deny Miss Spartali the uncommon quality of rich and solemn colour." The question of women's depictions of the human form raised deeper issues than the qualities or deficiencies of Marie Spartali's work.

In the year that she married, the Slade Professor spoke of "the difficulty which has always stood in the way of female students acquiring that thorough knowledge of the figure which is essential to the production of work of a high class." Prevailing proprieties excluded women from drawing from the nude in the life class and thus from tackling figure work with the assurance of men, "hence the timidity of their renditions". From 1871, life classes from the nude model – albeit "half-draped" or heavily wrapped round the middle – were held in a separate room for ladies at the Slade and, by the end of the century, at Royal Academy classes.

The same social conventions inhibited women artists in their choice of subject. It was expected of them that they should confine themselves to uplifting subjects of intrinsic beauty – landscapes and still lifes, scenes of domestic virtue, historical or poetic themes or religious stories. Her work has, nevertheless, a distinctive and instantly recognizable character that derives mainly from her highly personal technique of short, layered brush strokes that is particularly well suited to the lively skin-tones and the velvet bloom of flowers in so much of her work, supported by an

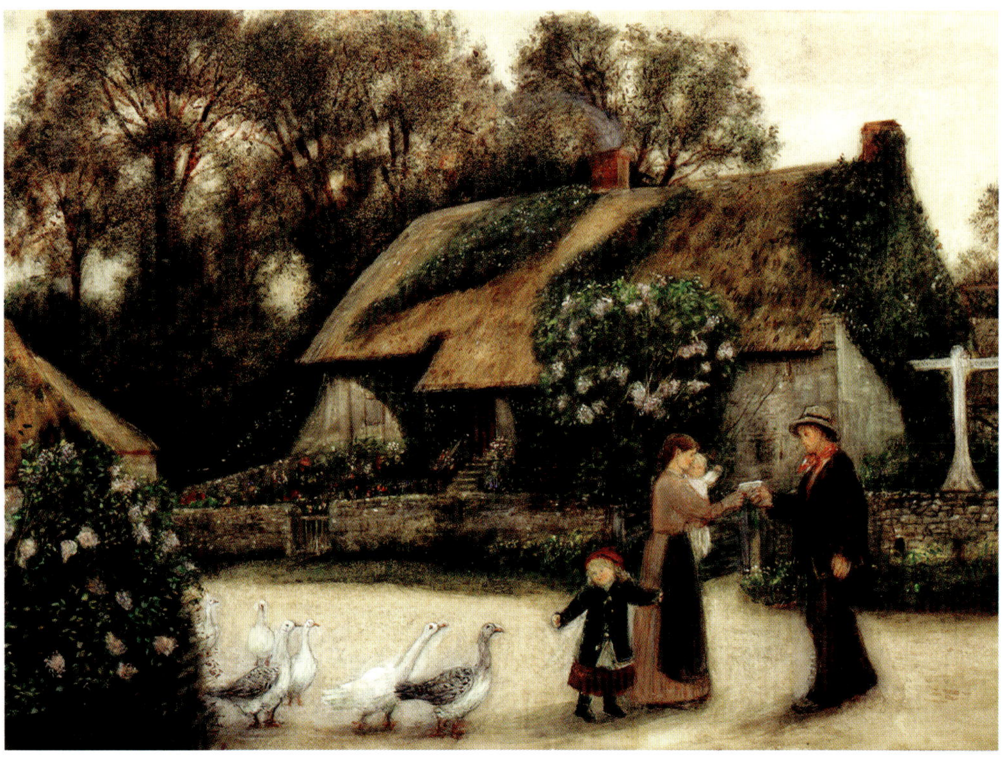

Plate 77
Marie Spartali Stillman
Crossroads at Arreton, Isle of Wight
Watercolour on paper. 30.8 x 43.5 cm (12⅛ x 17⅛in)
Bancroft Collection, Delaware Art Museum

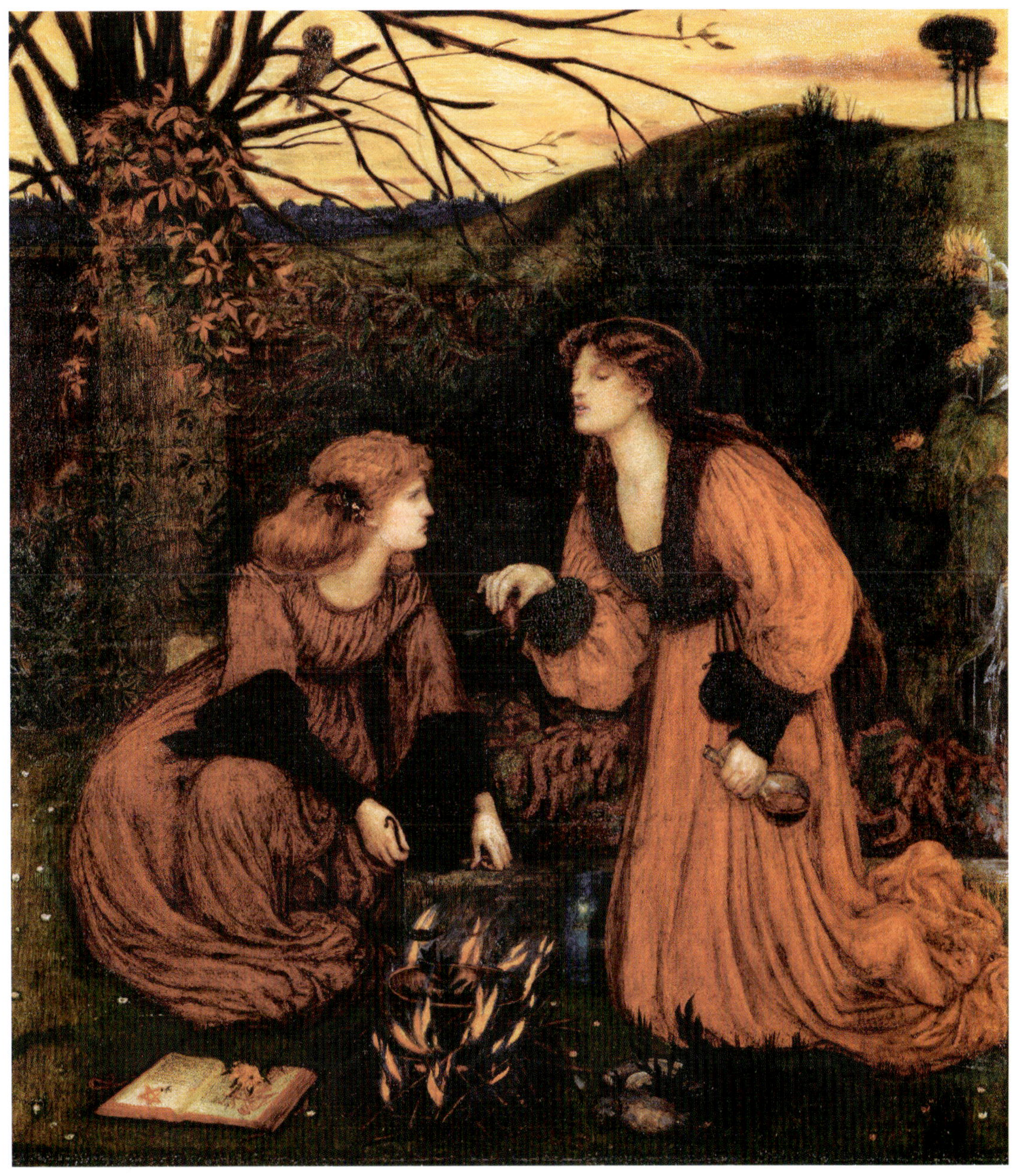

Plate 78
Marie Spartali Stillman
1869
Pharmakeutria or Brewing the Love Philtre
Watercolour, bodycolour and gum arabic on paper laid on panel. 52 x 47 cm (20½ x 18½in)
Exhibited: Dudley, 1869
Private Collection

unerring but restrained colour sense; so that her work is always charming, and often beautiful, far beyond the merely amateur.

Artist and Pre-Raphaelite expert Bennett Siegal describes the way in which Marie builds up her pictures with: "a range of surfaces from solid to transparent by varying the layers of brushstroke... a sense of transparency and depth of surface in most areas due to a complex matrix of successive layers of washes and layers of thin strokes embedded between, and laid upon, the layers of wash colour... reserving the most gestural and dancing wispy light lines for the uppermost layer, as though to apply definition to the very air that clings to the surfaces within the composition, the air between objects in the composition and the air between the viewer and objects. This all serves to soften the overall surface and picture plane.

"...to create a more solid surface, she uses fewer layers of more opaque paint and if there are marks up on the surface as highlights or additional layering, they are closer in value and color to the underlying opaque layer of color. This keeps the surface in that local area more solid in its appearance, although still possessing local highlights, and as a result the viewer experiences a range of surface from highly textured to smooth."[12]

There is ample evidence of a leaning towards feminism and feminist causes throughout Marie Stillman's career, reflecting a robust but non-militant political socialism. She detested the unquestioned expectation that she would make an arranged dynastic marriage, and the broader hostility towards women earning their living independently and taking responsibility for their own lives. Although she rejected the Victorian perception of the woman's rôle as homemaker, obedient wife and chattel she was, nevertheless, ambivalent in her own life, putting her duty and preference as wife and mother before any other consideration. The subjects of many, indeed almost all, of her paintings are women, for the most part single figures; pensive, gentle, and romantic. Her subjects from Dante favour Beatrice. (The *St George*[13] of 1892 is an interesting exception cast, not in the conventional heroic mould, but as a youthful idealist.)

By 1867, Marie Spartali was an intimate of the Rossetti circle and under his influence she gradually extended her range from portraiture and Greek mythological and Shakespearian subjects to include pictures based on tales from Dante Alighieri and Boccaccio, in Dante Gabriel Rossetti's translation. When, as Marie Stillman, she exhibited *By a Clear Well in a Little Field,* her interpretation of Boccaccio's sonnet *Of Three Girls and of their Talk* at the American Society of Painters in Water Color show, "Galaxy", at the National Academy in New York, Henry James reviewed the exhibition in an article 'Some Pictures Lately Exhibited': Marie Stillman 'is a spontaneous, sincere, naïve Pre-Raphaelite' he declared. (She exhibited here also in 1877, 1878, 1883 and 1884, and in addition at the Philadelphia Centennial Exposition of 1876.) Years before she and Henry James became personal friends, he wrote of the 'refinement, the deep pictorial sentiment'[14] of her painting and, crucially,

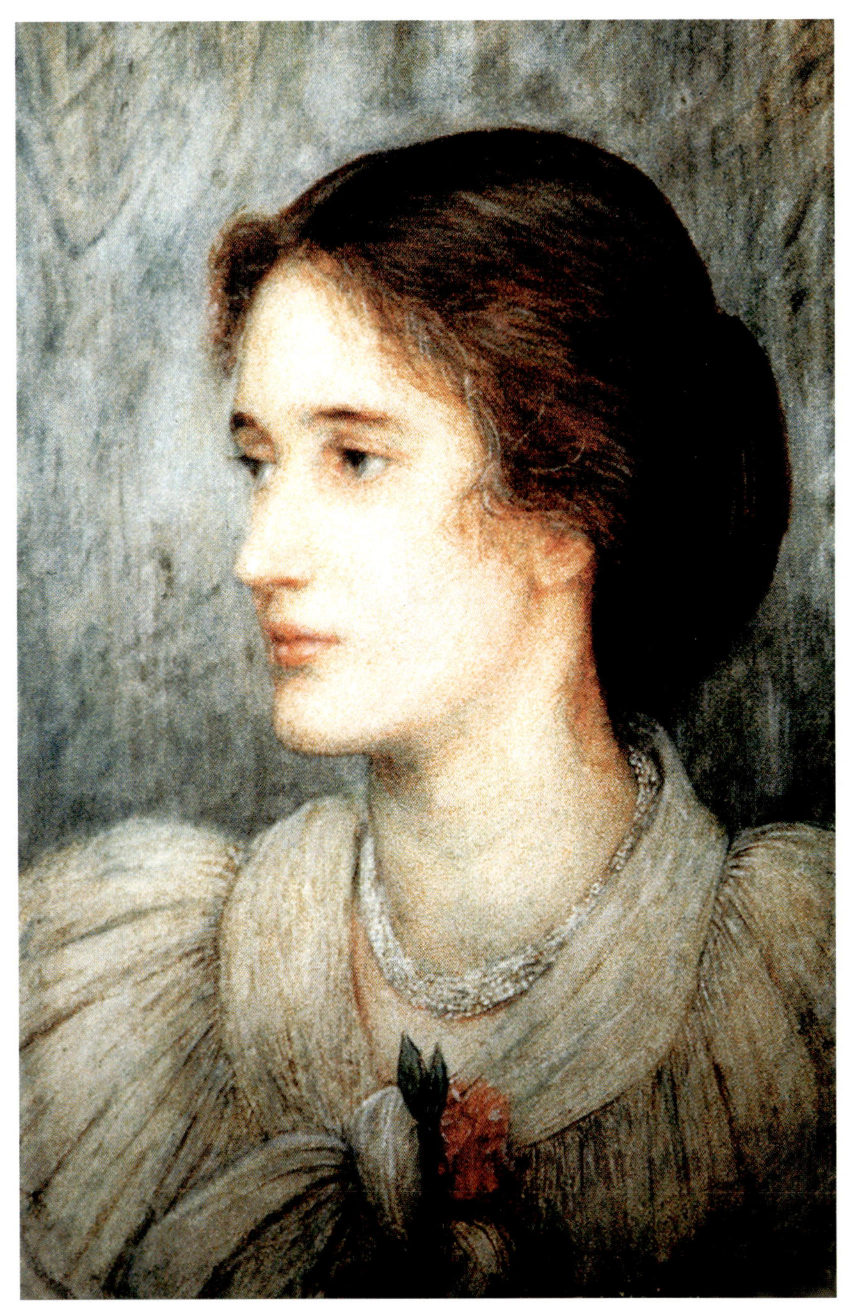

Plate 79
Marie Spartali Stillman
1896
Euphrosyne (Effie) Stillman
Watercolour
Private Collection

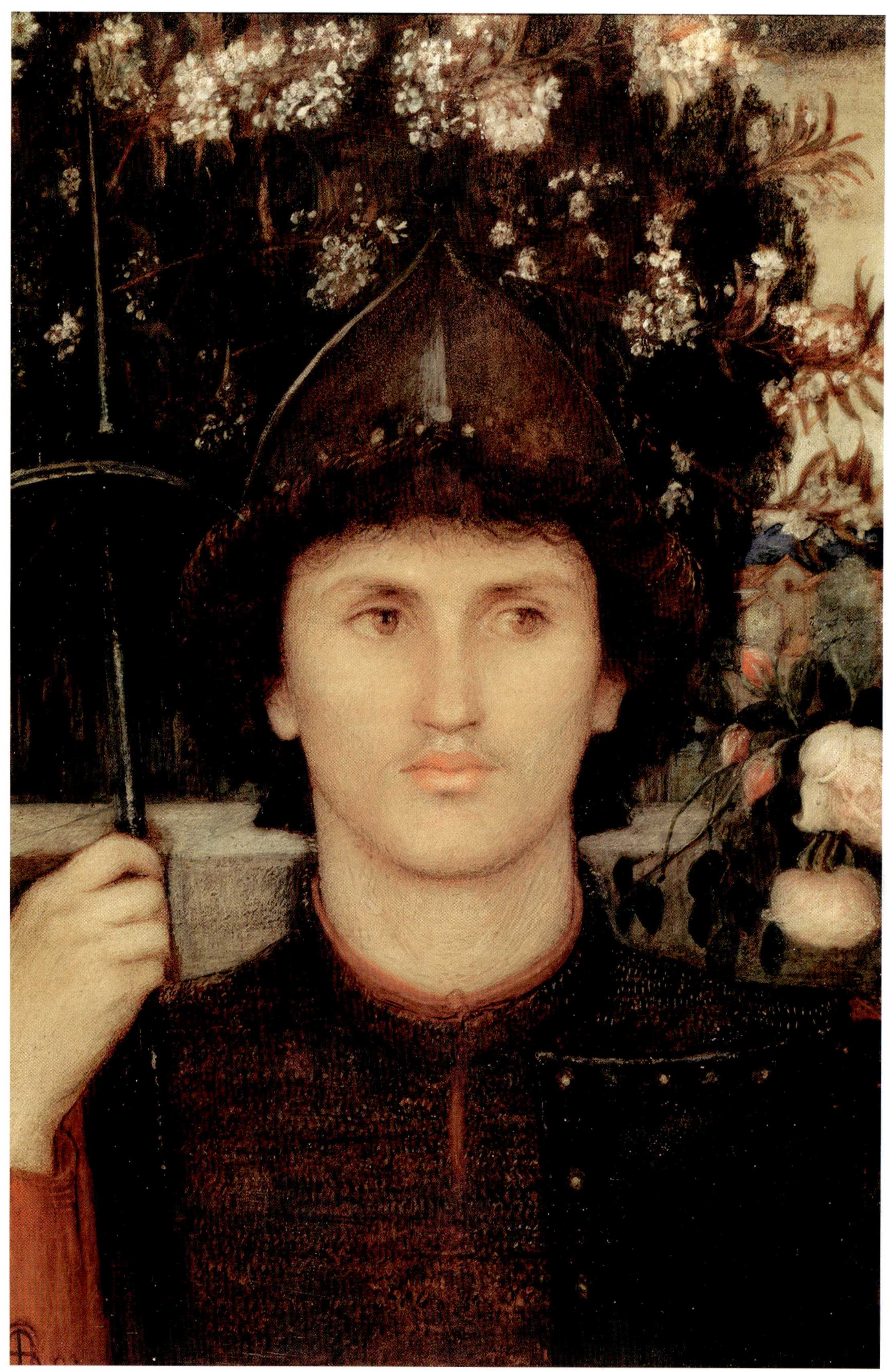

that some evidently more skilful pictures seemed by comparison 'vulgar'.

Critical comment throughout her career followed broadly similar lines. George Bernard Shaw, making his journalistic debut as an art critic in 1885, was of two minds: "More reflective work… is Mrs Stillman's beautifully coloured and carefully finished 'Love's Messenger' tho' the texture of the flesh is a distinct failure."[15] Two years later in 1887 he was commenting: "Mrs Stillman's work... suffers from earnestness and unsparing diligence, much of which is wasted on a system of hatching and stippling that never produces satisfactory results as to texture..."[16] and later that year: "... I doubt Mrs Stillman shows any appreciation of a strong man like Dante by repeatedly painting him as a limp, sprawling, moping mediaeval Mrs Gummidge."[17] Nevertheless, Shaw was to modify this rather severe judgment just a year later, writing: "Mrs Stillman's gift of convincing story-telling – Dante at Verona for example – grows more apparent as the flight of time proves that, in spite of manipulative deficiencies, her pictures have the rare quality of being memorable."[18] William Michael Rossetti's private comment on *Dante at Verona* was "pretty but wanting in energy".[19] Shaw capitulated finally in 1890, writing: "In the days of my novitiate as a critic of painters, I got a wholesome lesson from the works of Mrs Stillman. In a superior manner I pointed out certain obvious technical infirmities in her works, and paid no more attention to them until I began to find as the years passed on, that I always remembered Mrs Stillman's pictures, whereas the impression made by her brilliant, adroit, swift-handed competitors had faded as completely as last year's snow."[20]

Considered as a whole, Shaw's comments on her pictures painted between 1885 and 1889, make a fair if somewhat puffed-up critique of Marie Stillman's work at the height of her powers. Shown at the Grosvenor Gallery, and from 1888 at the New Gallery, they included, in addition to *Love's Messenger* and *Dante at Verona*, *Messer Ansaldo* and *The First Meeting of Petrarch and Laura.*

Following her marriage in 1871, despite the emotional turmoil of her father's rejection, her first pregnancy, her husband's hostility to Madox Brown, and their financial difficulties, there was little sign of any diminution in the number of works she produced. There was, however, discernably an attempt to experiment with a broader range of subjects than before, ranging in the next five years between two Greek mythical pictures, *The Fates* and *Ianthe,* (one of the Oceanides, playmate of Persephone,

---

Plate 80
Marie Spartali Stillman
1892
Saint George
Watercolour on paper mounted on panel. 46 x 30.8 cm (18⅛ x 12⅛in)
Exhibited: New Gallery, Liverpool, 1893
Bancroft Collection, Delaware Art Museum

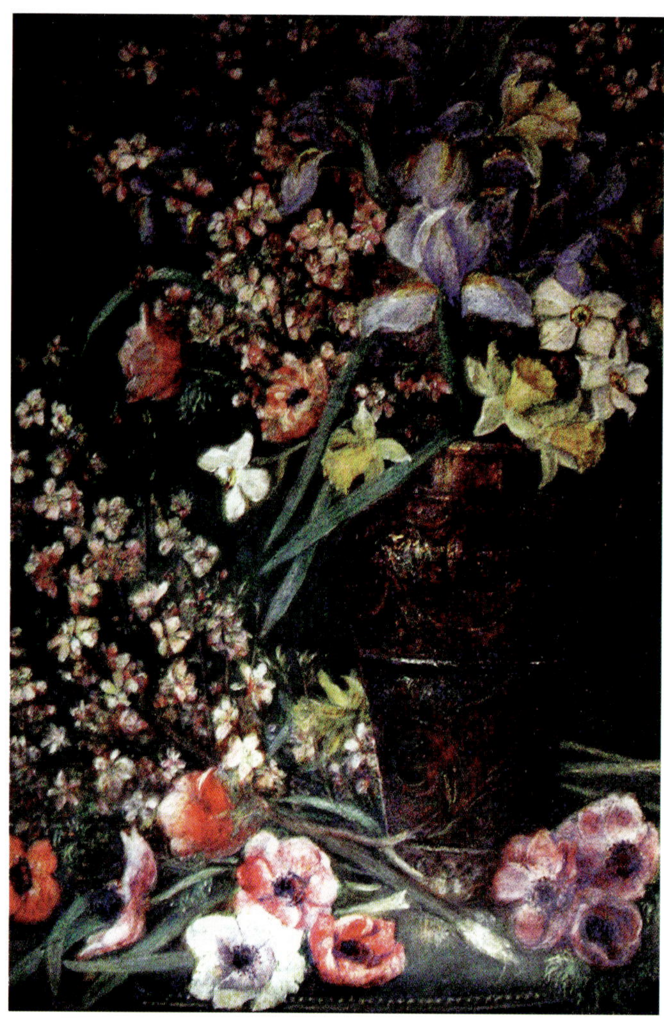

Plate 81
Marie Spartali Stillman
undated
Spring
Watercolour. 49.5 x 33 cm (19½ x 13in)
Exhibited: Oehme Gallery, New York, 1908
Private Collection

Artemis and Athene and the personification of the violet-colouring of clouds, a subject later painted by John William Goodward), and the historical Florentine *Buondelmonte* whose ungallant repudiation of his betrothal to a daughter of the Amidei family in order to marry a beautiful Donati led to his murder on Easter Day 1215, and to the Guelf-Ghibelline struggles that engulfed Tuscany in the 1300s. There were also *Tristram and La Belle Fronde* of 1873 and *Elaine Finding Sir Lancelot Disguised as a Fool,* subjects taken from Tennyson's *Lancelot and Elaine.* Dante Rossetti considered her work had suffered from the turmoil in her life.[21] At least seven fine flower pieces, three exhibited at the Royal Academy of 1875, also date from this period, and it may be supposed that these were primarily intended for the market place.

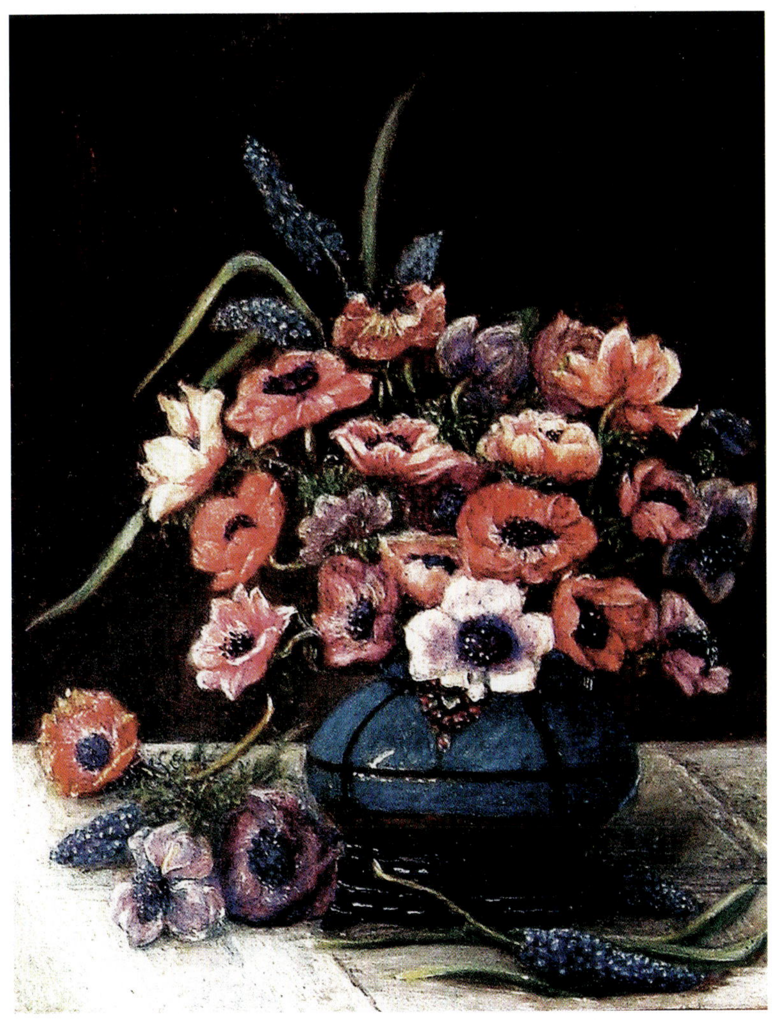

Plate 82
Marie Spartali Stillman
undated
Anemones
Watercolour. 43 x 33 cm (17 x 13in)
Private Collection

In 1878 the Stillman family moved to Florence, and here her work blossomed in technical assurance, and her inspiration became more focused on the Dante and Boccaccio subjects that had so long held her interest *in absentia*. The greater confidence in her work is best seen in four of her most resolved, and best-known, half- and three quarter-length female figures, *Gathering Orange Blossoms, Madonna Pietra Degli Scrovigni, La Pensierosa* – a portrait of her daughter Effie – and *Love's Messenger*. Her subjects from the Italian poets, in particular *The Meeting of Dante and Beatrice on All Saints' Day* and *By a Clear Well, Within a Little Field*, display a firmer grasp of anatomy and greater assurance in the composition of figure groups, prefacing a number of important figure groups in the five years that followed Marie

Stillman's return to London in October 1883. These include *Upon a Day Came Sorrow Unto Me (1887),* a subject from Dante, *A May Feast at the House of Falco Portinari (1887)* and *The First Meeting of Petrarch and Laura, (1889).*

Once in Rome, in the period from 1889 until retirement and the death of William Stillman in 1901, Marie turned mostly to portraits and single three quarter length figures, exclusively of women, including *A Rose from Armida's Garden.*

She achieved another landmark in her career as a painter in 1890, showing her work at the Galleria del Belle Arti in Rome with the international In Arte Libertas exhibiting group. The painters' circle surrounding Giovanni Costa attracted such important Italian landscape artists as Fattori and Maccari, in addition to Costa himself; the group's importance can also be measured by the inclusion of work by Frederic Leighton, G F

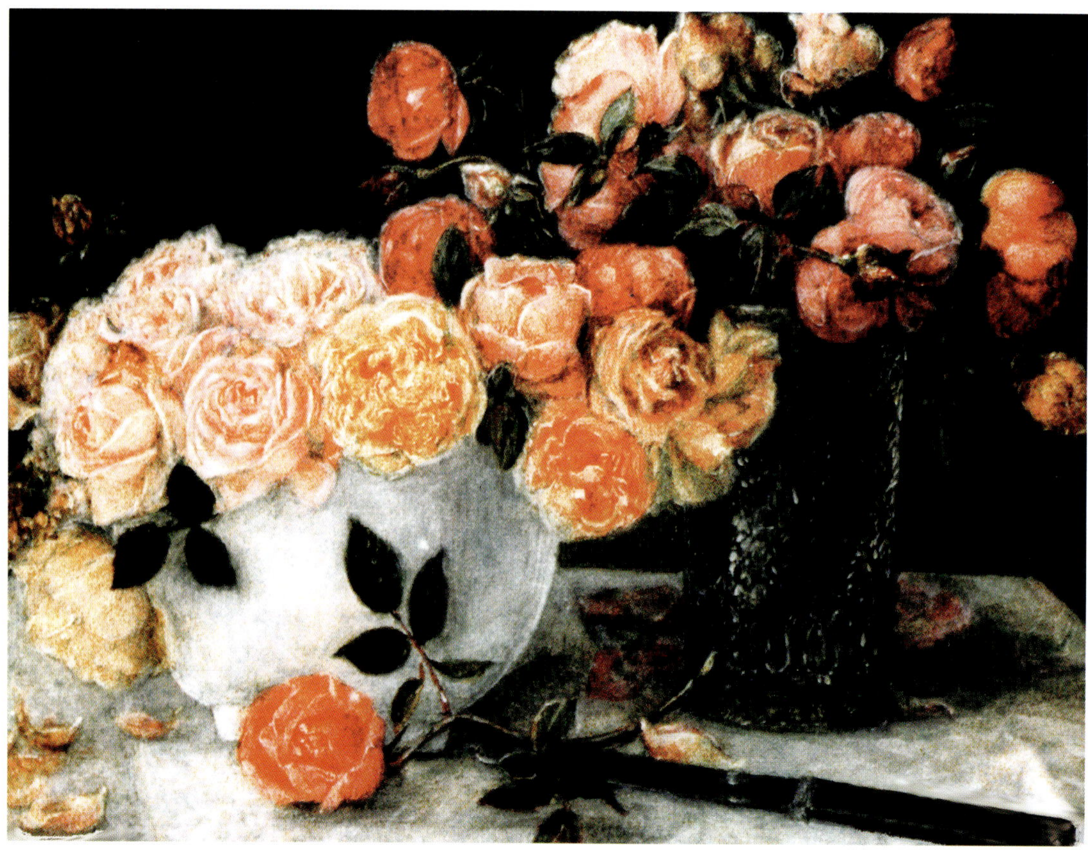

Plate 83
Marie Spartali Stillman
undated
Roses
Private Collection

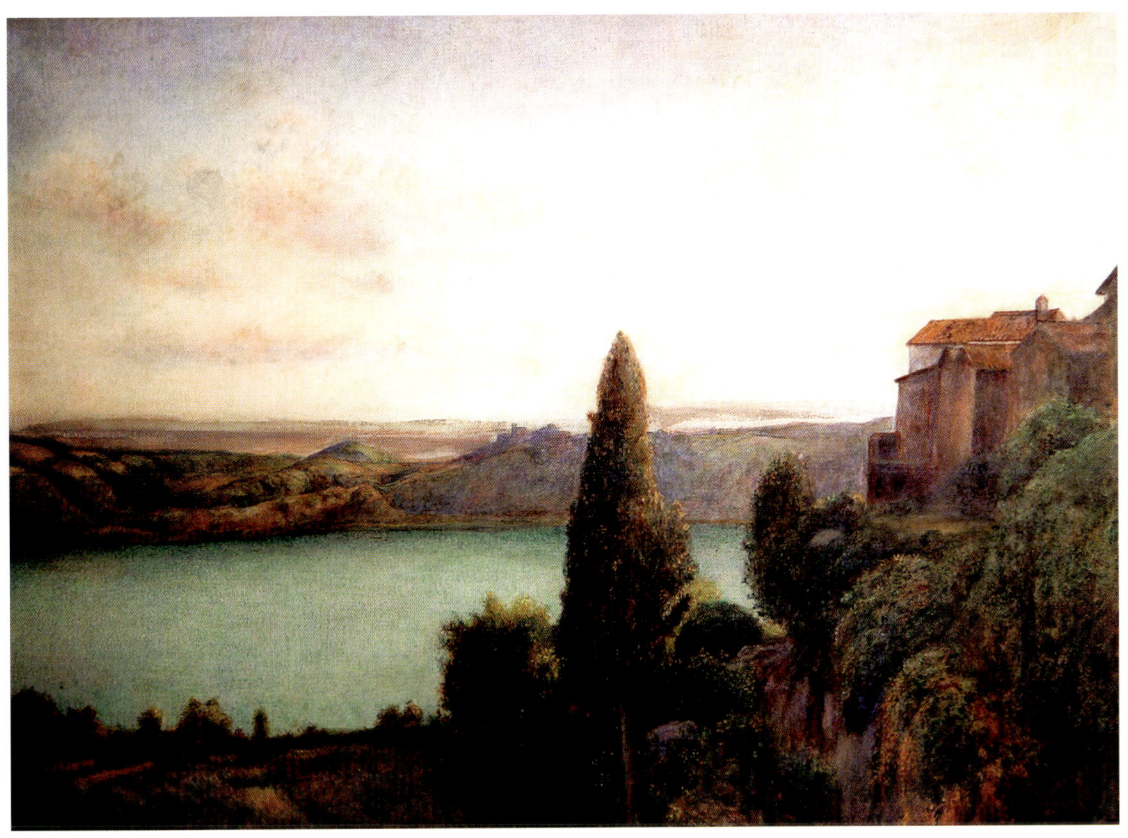

Plate 84
Marie Spartali Stillman
1899
Lake Nemi
Watercolour
Private Collection

Watts, Laurence Alma-Tadema, Puvis de Chavanne, Edward Burne-Jones (who showed his mosaic designs for the American Church in Rome) and George Howard, now the 9th Earl of Carlisle. The landscapes Marie painted in this period show a much matured style and finish, and are clearly influenced by the Etruscans.

She also embarked on a series of genre pictures illustrating the *Fioratti of St Francis*, which she continued after her return to England. Another departure was the copy of a detail from Verrocchio made during a summer visit to England in 1891.

Marie's personality was reticent (despite her mordant wit and the occasional outburst, her "Greek rages") and marked by a certain lack of self-assurance. Janey Morris, her close friend, described her as "timid" when she was in her 50s. Fairfax Murray told his friend William Spanton: "My friend Miss Stillman has ruined her reputation in Rome by running herself down,"[22] an overstatement, perhaps, but containing more than a grain of truth. On selling her picture *Love's Messenger* to Samuel Bancroft she wrote: "... I feel rather anxious to think of my poor handiwork in such splendid company."[23] A letter to Bancroft's secretary is typical of her self-deprecatory way of dealing with admiration: "I wish I could tell you something

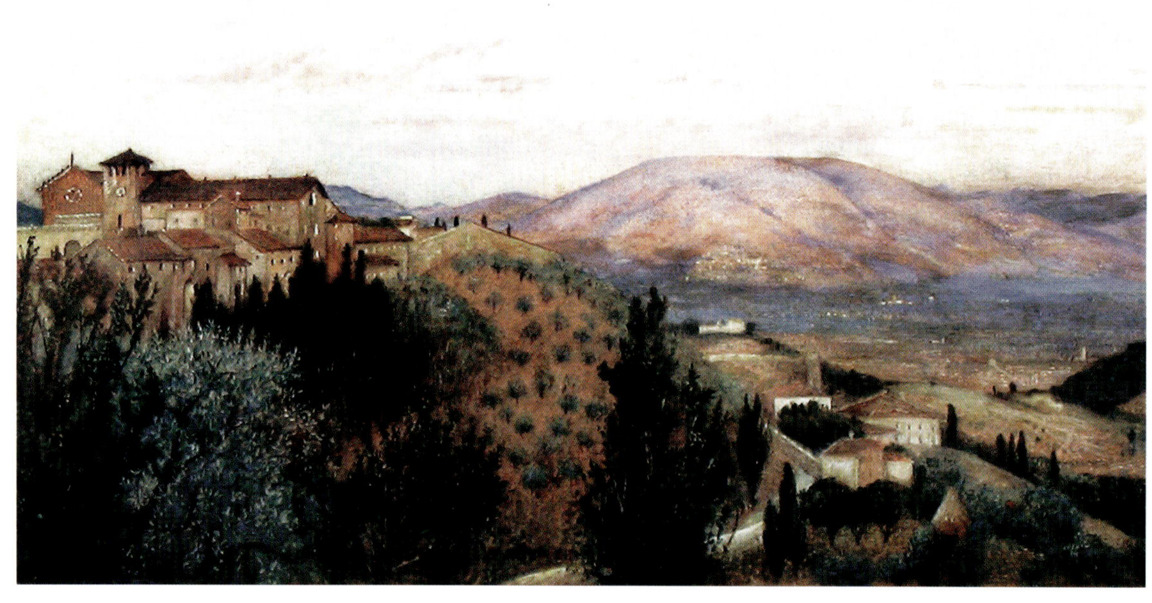

Plate 85
Marie Spartali Stillman
1893
Monte Luce from Perugia at Sunset
Watercolour on paper. 21 x 39.5 cm (8¼ x 15½in)
Private Collection

Plate 86
Marie Spartali Stillman
1893
Cypresses
Watercolour. 16.5 x 34.3 cm (6½ x 13½in)
Private Collection

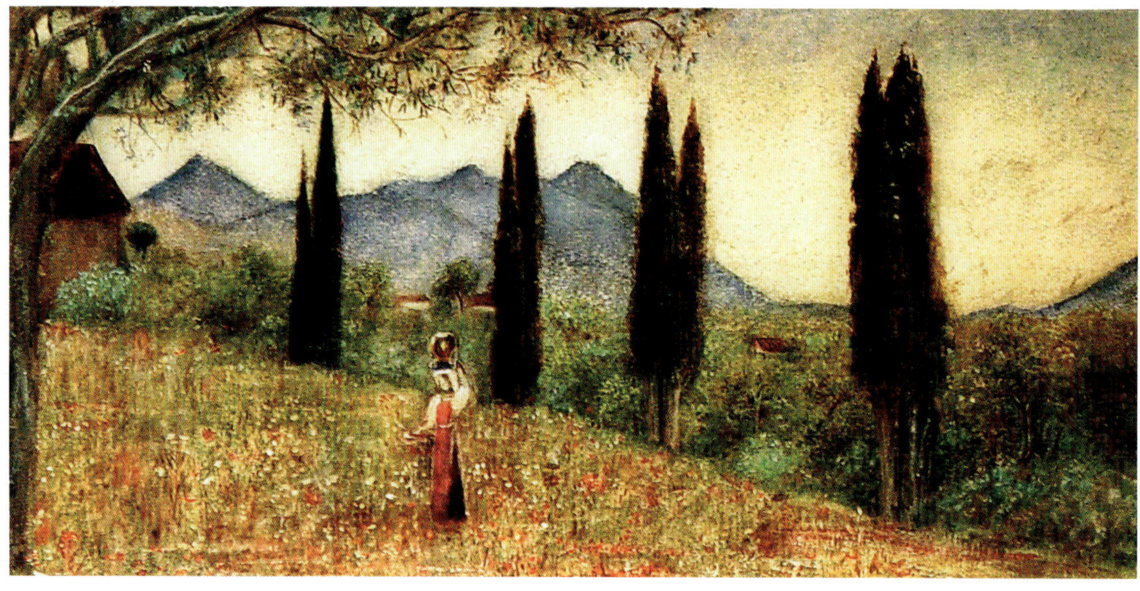

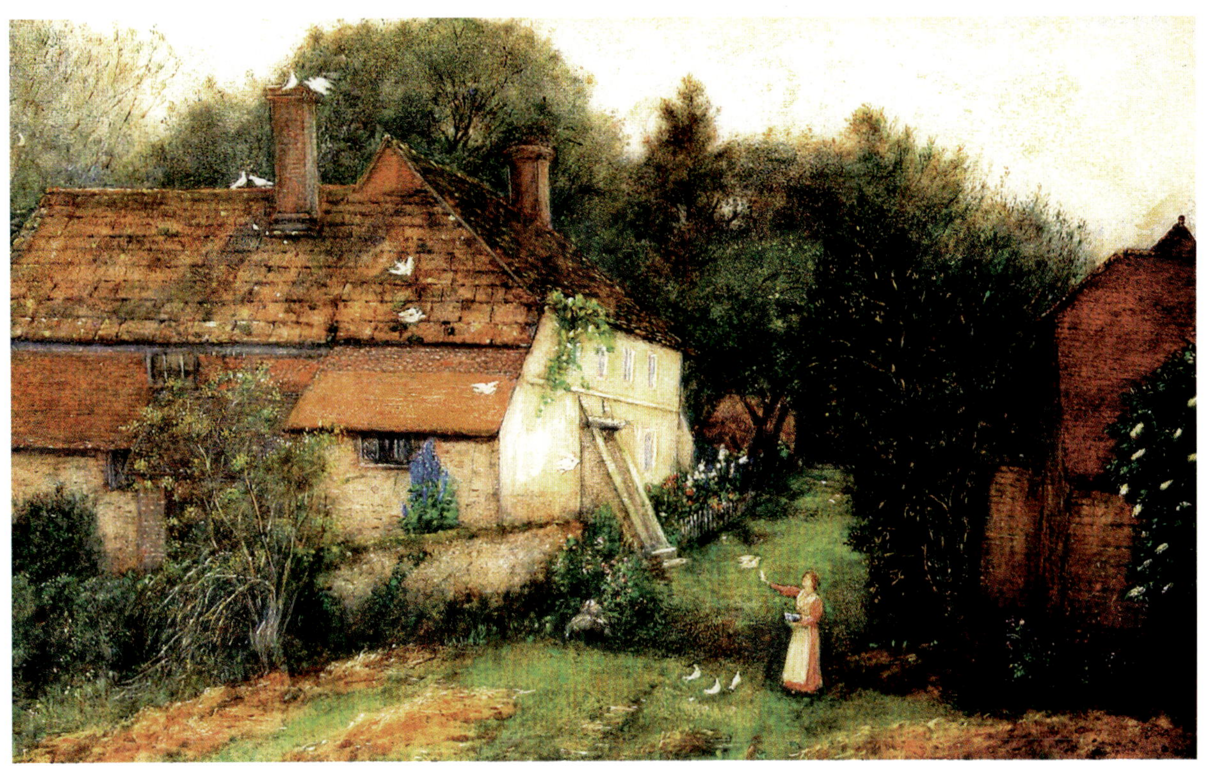

Plate 87
Marie Spartali Stillman
undated
Apse Farm, Isle of Wight
Watercolour. 33 x 53.3 cm (13 x 21in)
Exhibited: Oehme Gallery, New York, 1908
Private Collection

interesting about my pictures at Mr Bancroft's... they are all merely studies of heads done for the pleasure of painting. I cannot now recollect dates but I believe I generally sign and date my pictures in the corner, some I forget to, it doesn't seem to matter..."[24] The obscurity in this comment is deliberate; she painted not only for the release she found in painting, but also because any income derived from selling her work was important to her family's modest finances. The flower-pieces she produced tended to sell better than more ambitious work and she continued to create a steady flow of these pictures – of consummate skill and pleasing appearance – to satisfy this market after her husband's death.

Marie Spartali Stillman's reputation as a painter has recently been revived, partly as the result of her being swept along by the feminist movement of the late 20th century, which has included her among its icons alongside such women artists as Evelyn Pickering, Kate Bunce, Joanna Boyce, Emma Sandys and Rebecca Solomon, and partly the consequence of critical reassessment of her work and the reappearance of some of her best work in the salerooms. She may now be seen as a more significant artist than has heretofore been understood; the crucial lack of confidence and her unwillingness to promote her work remain the most potent factors in her relative neglect.

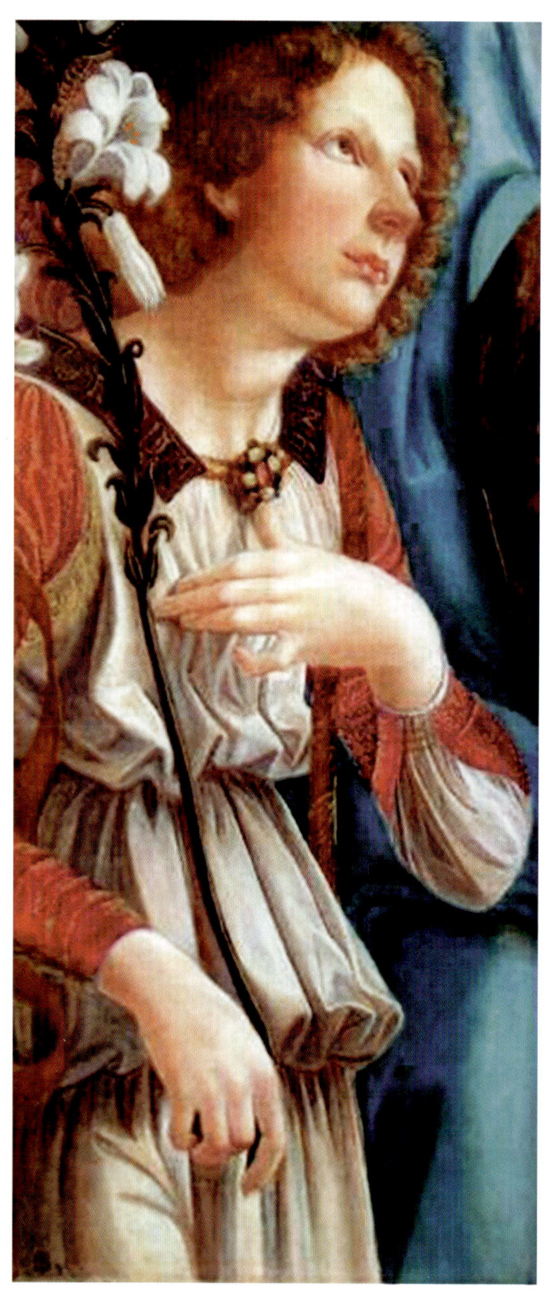

Plate 88
Marie Spartali Stillman
1891
Copy of a detail from *Virgin and Child with Two Angels* attributed to Verrocchio, National Gallery, London
Watercolour
Private Collection

ENDNOTES

Introduction

[1] *London Meteorological Observer*, Campden Square, 10 April 1871: Meteorological Office Archives
[2] Registrar, Chelsea 1a 471 June 1871, ONS
[3] Kate Courtney, *Diary*, 23 July 1892. Courtney Collection vol XXVI ff 157-8; on the marriage of her sister Beatrice Potter to Sidney Webb: see Pat Jalland, *Women, Marriage & Politics*, p40
[4] William James Stillman to Ford Madox Brown,11 April 1871. Ford Madox Brown papers, National Art Library, MSL 1995/14/105
[5] Dante Gabriel Rossetti to Charles Eliot Norton, 11 April 1870. William Michael Rossetti (ed), (1903), *Rossetti papers*, Sands
[6] Marie Spartali Stillman to Samuel Bancroft, 6 July 1901. Delaware Art Museum, Bancroft Archive Box 16

Chapter One: The Greeks in London

[1] William Michael Rossetti, *Diary*, 26, 27 & 29 January 1885. Angeli-Dennis Collection, University of British Columbia
[2] Du Maurier, Daphne, (ed), (1951), *The Young George Du Maurier: A Selection of his Letters 1860-1867*, Peter Davis: London
[3] Jeanette Marshall, *see*: Schonfield, Z., (1987), *The Precariously Privileged, A Professional Family in Victorian England*, [based on *The Diaries of Jeanette Marshall*], Oxford University Press, p86
[4] Spencer, Robin, (1999), *After the Pre–Raphaelites: Art and Aestheticism in Victorian England*, n.43, Manchester University Press, p83
[5] Charles Fairfax Murray, *Diary*, 1886. Collection Frits Lugt, Paris
[6] Pennell, (1908), *Life of James Abbott McNeill Whistler*, Heinemann, p118
[7] Ionides, Alexander Constantine, (1927), *Ion, A Grandfather's Tale*, Cuala Press: Dublin
[8] Notes written by Madame Legros for the authors of an unpublished Life of Alphonse Legros, L A Legros, her son, and J Clement-Janin, Ms 470, Collection Doucet, Bibliothèque Nationale, Paris
[9] John Marshall, 1818-1891, was Lecturer in Anatomy at the Government Schools of Art & Design from 1854-1874, appointed Professor of Anatomy at the Royal Academy Schools 1873, Professor of Clinical Surgery at University College Hospital 1866, Council member of the Royal College of Surgeons 1873 and President from 1883, and President of the General Medical Council 1887
[10] Adelaide Sartoris (née Kemble), 1814-1869, art critic; sang Bellini's *Norma* at Covent Garden in 1841; married E J Sartoris
[11] Hallé, Charles, (1909), *Notes from a Painter's Life*, John Murray: London

Chapter Two: Little Holland House

[1] Dakers, Caroline, (1999), *The Holland Park Circle, Artists and Victorian Society*, Yale, p21
[2] Gersheim, Helmut and Alison, (1963), *Creative Photography from 1826 to the Present*, Wayne State University
[3] Robertson, W Graham, (1931), *Time Was*, Hamish Hamilton: London
[4] Robertson, W Graham, *ibid*
[5] Robertson, W Graham, *ibid*
[6] Pennell, (1908), *Life of James Abbott McNeill Whistler*, Heinemann, p118
[7] Ionides, Alexander Constantine, (1927), *Ion, A Grandfather's Tale*, Cuala Press: Dublin
[8] Murray, Janet, *Strong Minded Women and other lost voices from nineteenth-century England*; see also Schonfield, Z, (1987), *The Precariously Privileged*, A Professional Family in Victorian England, OUP
[9] Dante Gabriel Rossetti to Ford Madox Brown, (nd). Doughty & Wahl, ii p525
[10] Ford, Ford Madox, *Memories and Impresssions*; [appears to be] an edited version of *Ford Madox Brown: A Record of His Life and Works*. Longmans, 1896
[11] Dante Gabriel Rossetti to Frederick Leyland, (possibly c.1870). Francis Fennel (ed), (1978), *Rossetti-Leyland Letters* **18**, Ohio

Chapter Three: Marie Spartali and the Rossetti Circle

[1] Dante Gabriel Rossetti to Ford Madox Brown, 29 April 1864. Doughty & Wahl, ii p528
[2] Charles Fairfax Murray to A C Benson. John Murray, (1924), *Memories and Friends*
[3] Stillman, William James, (1901), *Autobiography of a Journalist*, Houghton, Mifflin: Boston, ii p476
[4] Du Maurier letters 244, NAL MSL/1976/5451
[5] Worcester Art Museum, Massachussetts
[6] Pennell, (1908): *Life of James Abbott McNeill Whistler*, Heinemann, i p123
[7] Christie's; 14 November 1999, identified by John Christian as Christina Spartali
[8] Merrill, Linda, (1998), *The Peacock Room, A Cultural Biography*, Yale
[9] Dante Gabriel Rossetti to Ford Madox Brown, 23 February 1866. Doughty & Wahl, ii p673
[10] Holman Hunt, Diana, (1969), *My Grandfather, His Wives and Loves*, Hamish Hamilton
[11] Holman Hunt, Diana, *ibid*
[12] Williams, Montagu QC, *Leaves of a Life*, i pp224-246
[13] William Holman Hunt to F G Stephens, 30 September 1871. Troxell Collection, Box 30, Princeton
[14] Dante Gabriel Rossetti to Jane Burden Morris, 21 July 1869. Bryson & Troxell, (1976), Clarendon, p5
[15] Dante Gabriel Rossetti to Jane Burden Morris, 30 July 1869. *ibid*, p7
[16] Burne-Jones, Georgiana, (1904), *Memorials of Edward Burne-Jones*, Macmillan, i p293
[17] Burne-Jones, Georgiana, *ibid*, i p303
[18] William Bell Scott to Alice Boyd, 2 November 1868. Angeli-Dennis Collection, University of British Columbia
[19] Henderson, Philip, (1967), *William Morris, His Life, Work and Friends*, London
[20] Dante Gabriel Rossetti to Jane Burden Morris, 4 August 1869. Bryson & Troxell (1976), Clarendon, p8
[21] Dante Gabriel Rossetti to Jane Burden Morris, 14 August 1869. *ibid*, p10
[22] Dante Gabriel Rossetti to Charles Fairfax Murray, 7 September 1881. Harry Ransom Humanities Research Center, Austin, Texas

Chapter Four: William James Stillman, Childhood and Youth

[1] Family biographical information is to be found in Mrs Hannah Stillman Bradfield's 'Family History'

[2] Benedict, David, (1848), *A General History of the Baptist Denominations in America and Other Parts of the World*, Colby Lewis & Co: New York, (originally published 1813, Lincoln & Edmonds: London)
[3] Born 11 September 1783, died 16 December 1869
[4] Stillman, William James, (1901), *Autobiography of a Journalist*, Houghton, Mifflin: Boston
[5] Born 20 August 1806, died 1 January 1886
[6] Published posthumously by Paul Stillman, New York, 1864
[7] Stillman, William James, (1901), *Autobiography of a Journalist*, Houghton, Mifflin: Boston, i p28
[8] Stillman, William James, *ibid*, i p63
[9] Stillman, William James, *ibid*, i p64
[10] Stillman, William James, *ibid*, i p110
[11] Stillman, William James, *ibid*, i p115
[12] Stillman, William James, *ibid*, i p130
[13] Stillman, William James, *ibid*, i p142
[14] Stillman, William James, *ibid*, i p213

Chapter Five: The Critic and the Seeds of Journalism
[1] Clarence Cook, (1855) in the *New York Tribune*
[2] Steegmuller, Frances, (1951), *The Two Lives of James Jackson Jarves*, Yale: New Haven
[3] Stillman, William James, (1901), *Autobiography of a Journalist*, Houghton, Mifflin: Boston, i p230
[4] Stillman, William James, *ibid*, i p227
[5] Stillman, William James, *ibid*, i p224
[6] Stillman, William James, *ibid*, i p288
[7] Stillman, William James, *ibid*, i p238
[8] Stillman, William James, *ibid*, i p281
[9] Garrison, Wendell Phillips, (5 September 1893), *Century Quarterly* **Vol 46**
[10] Bagehot, Walter, (1881), *Biographical Studies*. Longmans Green
[11] Stillman, William James, (1901), *Autobiography of a Journalist*, Houghton, Mifflin: Boston, i p298
[12] Ruskin, John, *Works* **XXXVI**, Cook & Wedderburn (eds), (1903), George Allen, p339
[13] William James Stillman to Charles Eliot Norton, 23 March 1865. Houghton Library, Harvard University
[14] Concord Free Public Library, formerly in the collection of Judge Hoar
[15] Ruskin, John, *Works* **XXXVI**, Cook & Wedderburn (eds), (1903), George Allen, p624,
[16] Stillman, William James, (originally published July 1891 in *Atlantic Monthly*, **Vol 68**; republished in 1897), *The Old Rome and The New, Essays*
[17] Stillman, William James, (1901), *Autobiography of a Journalist*, Houghton, Mifflin: Boston, i p327

Chapter Six: Diplomacy
[1] Stillman, William James, (1901), *Autobiography of a Journalist*, Houghton, Mifflin: Boston, i p366
[2] Stillman, William James, *ibid*, i p355
[3] Chadwick, Owen, (1998), *A History of the Popes 1830-1914*, Clarendon
[4] William James Stillman to William Michael Rossetti, 10 June 1864. University of British Columbia
[5] Garrison, Wendell Phillips, (5 September 1893), *Century Quarterly* **Vol 46**, p 658
[6] Stillman, William James, (1901), *Autobiography of a Journalist*, Houghton, Mifflin: Boston, ii p389
[7] Stillman, William James, *ibid*, ii p435
[8] Stillman, William James, *ibid*, ii p455
[9] William Michael Rossetti, *Diary*, 18 April 1867, University of British Columbia
[10] Rossetti, William Michael, (1906), *Some Reminiscences*, Brown: Langham, p342

Chapter Seven: William James Stillman in London, 1869
[1] *Forgetfulness*, exhibited Liverpool 1871; William Michael Rossetti, 24 November 1868. *Rossetti papers*, Sands 1903; the picture was later owned by his daughter Olivia Frances Madox Agresti
[2] William Michael Rossetti, 7 September 1869. *Rossetti papers*, Sands, 1903
[3] Michael Spartali to Ford Madox Brown, 7 March 1870. Ford Madox Brown papers, National Art Library, MSL1995/14/105
[4] Ruskin, *Diaries*, 9 November 1869. Bodleian transcript. MS Eng. Misc. c. 235, 157]
[5] William Michael Rossetti, 20 November 1869. *Selected Letters*, Peattie (ed.), (1990), Penn State University Press
[6] William Michael Rossetti, 15 November 1869. *Rossetti papers*, Sands, 1903
[7] William Bell Scott to Alice Boyd. Minto, W (ed), (1892), *Autobiographical Notes*, Osgood, McIlvaine & Co
[8] Whistler, J Abbott McNeill, *Journal*, 1863, quoted by Henderson (1973) in *Swinburne*, Kegan & Paul
[9] William Michael Rossetti, *Diary*, 1 March 1880. Angeli-Dennis Collection, University of British Columbia
[10] Michael Spartali to Dante Gabriel Rossetti, 22 February 1871. Angeli-Dennis Collection, University of British Columbia, Box 4 Folder 1

Chapter Eight: The Engagement
[1] William James Stillman to Marie Spartali, (nd). Stillman papers, Schaffer Library, Union College, Schenectady, p389
[2] see Newman, Theresa & Watkinson, Ray, (1991), *Ford Madox Brown*, Chatto & Windus; Bendiner (1998) in *The Art of Ford Madox Brown*, Houghton Mifflin: Boston, p36 n53 first doubted the likelihood though later inclined to accept it
[3] Stow Hill papers, House of Lords Records Office
[4] see also Thirlwell, Angela, (2003), *William & Lucy – The Other Rossettis*, Yale: London, p148
[5] Angela Thirlwell has kindly drawn the author's attention to a previously unknown picture by Marie Spartali, *Two Girls and a Peacock*, once attributed to Lucy or Cathy Madox Brown, to which Madox Brown appended some verses; Ford Madox Brown to Lucy (who was staying with Marie on the Isle of Wight), 8 September 1869: "I have also tried my hand at a song to suit Marie's drawing of the girls with the peacock which [Marie?] ought to have written."(UBC Box 5 Folder 4). He had tried it in English, in French as 3 triolets and as a sonnet and he would send all three. Madox Brown was an inveterate versifier, further grounds for doubting a literal interpretation of the courtly sentiments expressed in 'Je te salue, Marie plein de grace'
[6] Ford Madox Brown to Lucy Madox Brown, 29 August 1869. Angeli-Dennis Collection, University of British Columbia
[7] Marie Spartali to Ford Madox Brown, 18 March 1870. Ford Madox Brown papers, National Art Library, MSL1995/14/105/1
[8] Michael Spartali to Ford Madox Brown, 7 March 1870. Ford Madox Brown papers, National Art Library, MSL 1995/14/105
[9] Michael Spartali to Ford Madox Brown, 12 March 1870. *ibid*. MSL 1995/14/105
[10] Marie Spartali to Ford Madox Brown, (nd). *ibid*, MSL1995/14/105/3
[11] Dante Gabriel Rossetti to Jane Burden Morris, 4 March 1870, Bryson & Troxell (1976), Clarendon, p18
[12] Dante Gabriel Rossetti to Barbara Leigh Smith Bodichon. *Letters*, Doughty &Wahl, ii p946
[13] Dante Gabriel Rossetti to William Allingham from Scalands, 7 March 1870. *ibid*
[14] Dante Gabriel Rossetti to F S Ellis, 30 April 1870. *ibid*
[15] William Michael Rossetti, *Diaries*, 25 April 1870, Bornand (ed), (1977), Clarendon

[16] William James Stillman to Marie Spartali. Schaffer Library, Union College, Schenectady, p389
[17] William James Stillman to Marie Spartali. *ibid*, p390
[18] William James Stillman to Marie Spartali. *ibid*, p391
[19] William James Stillman to Marie Spartali. *ibid*, p391
[20] William James Stillman to Ford Madox Brown, 15 March 1870. Ford Madox Brown papers, National Art Library, MSL1995/14/105
[21] Stillman, William James, (1901), *Autobiography of a Journalist*, ii p478: Houghton, Mifflin: Boston
[22] Stillman, William James, *ibid*, ii 478
[23] Marie Spartali to Dante Gabriel Rossetti 1 May 1870. Angeli-Dennis Collection, University of British Columbia
[24] Edward Burne-Jones to F S Ellis, 1886. Fitzwilliam Museum, Cambridge
[25] William Morris to Jane Burden Morris, 15 April 1870. Kelvin (ed), (1987), *Collected Letters of William Morris*, Princeton
[26] Stillman, William James, (1901), *Autobiography of a Journalist*, Houghton, Mifflin: Boston, ii p469
[27] Stillman, William James, (19 March 1898), *Academy*, vol 53 p333,
[28] Ford Madox Brown to Frederick Shields, 10 August 1868. Bell, ernestine (ed), (1913), *Life and Letters of Frederick Shields*. London
[29] Bell, Ernestine Bell, *ibid*
[30] Anon, (January 1880), 'Abuse of Chloral Hydrate', *Quarterly Journal of Inebriety*, **Vol. 4** , pp53-54
[31] William James Stillman to Marie Spartali, nd.. Schaffer Library, Union College, Schenectady, p393
[32] Stillman, William James to Marie Spartali. *ibid*, p393
[33] Stillman, William James to Marie Spartali. *ibid*, p388
[34] Stillman, William James to Marie Spartali. *ibid*, p389
[35] Stillman, William James to Marie Spartali. *ibid*, p389
[36] Stillman, William James to Marie Spartali. *ibid*, p388
[37] Stillman, William James to Marie Spartali. *ibid*, p392
[38] Stillman, William James to Marie Spartali. *ibid*, p393
[39] Minto, W, (ed), (1892), *Autobiographical Notes of William Bell Scott*, Osgood, McIlvaine & Co: London
[40] *Dictionary of Saints*, Penguin, (1995)
[41] Michael Spartali to Dante Gabriel Rossetti, 22 February 1871. Angeli-Dennis Collection, University of British Columbia
[42] Michael Spartali to Dante Gabriel Rossetti, 13 March 1871. *ibid*

Chapter Nine: Marriage

[1] William Michael Rossetti, 1 May 1871, *Diary* 1870-1873, Bornand (ed), (1977), Clarendon, p59
[2] William Michael Rossetti, 21 May 1871, *ibid*, p63
[3] Dante Gabriel Rossetti to William Bell Scott, nd, from Kelmscott Manor. Doughty & Wahl, ii p1139
[4] Morris, May, (1903) *Introduction to Collected Works of William Morris,* **Vol VI**, Longmans, Green & Co: London
[5] William Michael Rossetti, 4 June 1871, *Diary* 1870-1873, Bornand (ed), (1977), Clarendon, p66
[6] Thirlwell, Angela, (2003), *William & Lucy – The Other Rossettis*, Yale: London, p 165
[7] William Michael Rossetti, 29 August 1871, *Diary 1870-1873*, Bornand (ed), (1977), Clarendon, p113
[8] Stillman, William James, (1901), *Autobiography of a Journalist*, Houghton, Mifflin: Boston, ii p487
[9] William Michael Rossetti, 13 October 1871, *Diary 1870-1873*, Bornand (ed),(1977), Clarendon, pp114 and 114Ni
[10] Stillman, William James, (1901), *Autobiography of a Journalist*, Houghton, Mifflin: Boston, ii p491
[11] William Michael Rossetti, 2 November 1871, *Diary 1870-1873*, Bornand (ed), (1977), Clarendon, p122
[12] William Michael Rossetti, 15 October 1871, *ibid*, p115
[13] William Michael Rossetti, 25 October 1871, *ibid*, p118
[14] William Michael Rossetti, 14 December 1871, *ibid*, p138
[15] It is possible that she acquired the habit when recovering from surgery for peritonitis in 1864; John Marshall was a liberal prescriber of the drug
[16] Marie Spartali Stillman to Ford Madox Brown, nd. Ford Madox Brown papers, National Art Library, MSL 1995/14/105/6
[17] Eustratius Spartali, Marie and Christina's brother, the youngest of the siblings
[18] Marie Spartali Stillman to Ford Madox Brown, nd. Ford Madox Brown papers, National Art Library, MSL 1995/14/105/7
[19] William Michael Rossetti, 27 December 1871, *Diary 1870-1873*, Bornand (ed), (1977), Clarendon, p140
[20] Alastair Grieve, (1978), *The Art of Dante Gabriel Rossetti,* Norwich
[21] Private collection. The finished pencil study is in the Delaware Art Museum, 74-49
[22] William Michael Rossetti, 8 January 1872, *Diary 1870-1873,* Bornand (ed), (1977), Clarendon, p147
[23] Marie Spartali Stillman to Ford Madox Brown. Ford Madox Brown papers, National Art Library, MSL 1995/14/105/8
[24] William Michael Rossetti, 9 January 1872, *Diary 1870-1873*, Bornand (ed), (1977), Clarendon, p148
[25] William Michael Rossetti, 24 January 1872, *ibid*, 153
[26] Stillman, William James, (1872), *The Cretan Insurrection 1866-8*. Smith & Elder: London
[27] William Michael Rossetti, 10 March 1872, *Diary 1870-1873*, Bornand (ed), (1977), Clarendon, p176
[28] Dante Gabriel Rossetti to William Michael Rossetti. *Letters of Rossetti, Dante Gabriel,* Doughty &Wahl, 1 iii pp1062-4
[29] (25 November 1872). Henderson, P, (1950), *Letters of William Morris to his Family and Friends*, p 49-51
[30] Dante Gabriel Rossetti, 4 February 1873. *Family Letters*, (1895), Ellis & Elvey
[31] Marie Spartali Stillman to Ford Madox Brown. Ford Madox Brown papers, National Art Library, MSL 1995/14/105/27
[32] William Michael Rossetti, 30 December 1872, *Diary 1870-1873*, Bornand (ed), (1977), Clarendon, p222
[33] William Michael Rossetti, 30 December 1872. *ibid*, p233
[34] Marie Spartali Stillman to Ford Madox Brown. Ford Madox Brown papers, National Art Library, MSL 1995/14/105/29
[35] Ford Madox Brown to Marie Spartali Stillman. WHS36 5 August 1873, Schaffer Library, Union College, Schenectady, NY
[36] Marie Spartali Stillman to Ford Madox Brown. Ford Madox Brown papers, National Art Library, MSL 1995/14/105/39
[37] Wightwick Manor WIG/P/28
[38] Robertson, W Graham, (1931), *Time Was*, Hamish Hamilton
[39] Burne-Jones, Georgiana, *Memorials of Edward Burne-Jones,* ii p39
[40] Marie Spartali Stillman to Ford Madox Brown. Ford Madox Brown papers, National Art Library, MSL 1995/14/105/41
[41] Pennell, (1908), *Life of James McNeill Whistler*, Heinemann, i p179
[42] John Marshall held the posts of Prof. of Anatomy at the Royal Academy and Prof. of Surgery at University College Hospital at this time
[43] John Ruskin to William Stillman, 19 December 1874. John Rylands University of Manchester Library
[44] *Atlantic Monthly*, July 1874
[45] Marie Spartali Stillman to Ford Madox Brown. Ford Madox Brown papers, National Art Library, MSL 1995/14/105/18
[46] Marie Spartali Stillman to Ford Madox Brown. *ibid* MSL 1995/14/105/19
[47] Buckle, G. E., Morison, S., McDonald, I., *et al*, (1935), *History of The Times*, (4 vols). Printed privately: London, ii p367
[48] William James Stillman to Marie Spartali, nd. Stillman papers, p393, Schaffer Library, Union College, Schenectady
[49] Angeli, Helen Rossetti, (1949), *Rossetti, Dante Gabriel - His Friends and Enemies*, Hamish Hamilton: London, p171

Chapter Ten: Corfu

[1] Marie Spartali Stillman to Ford Madox Brown. Ford Madox Brown papers, National Art Library, MSL 1995/14/105/44

[2] Marie Spartali Stillman to Emma Madox Brown. Ford Madox Brown papers, National Art Library, MSL 1995/14/105/12

[3] William James Stillman, (1901), *Autobiography of a Journalist*, Houghton, Mifflin: Boston, ii p562

[4] Marie Spartali Stillman to Ford Madox Brown. Ford Madox Brown papers, National Art Library, MSL 1995/14/105/47

[5] William Michael Rossetti, 20 March 1877, *Diary*, Angeli-Dennis Collection, University of British Columbia

[6] William James Stillman to Marie Spartali, nd. Stillman papers, p451, Schaffer Library, Union College, Schenectady

[7] William James Stillman to W J Stebbing, nd. Harry Ransom Humanities Research Center, University of Texas

[8] Marie Spartali Stillman to Ford Madox Brown. Ford Madox Brown papers, National Art Library, MSL 1995/14/105/14

[9] Dante Gabriel Rossetti. *Family Letters*, (1895), Ellis & Elvey

[10] Dante Gabriel Rossetti to Jane Burden Morris, 2 December 1877. Bryson & Troxell (1976), Clarendon, p22

[11] Dante Gabriel Rossetti to Jane Burden Morris, 19 December 1877. *ibid*, p23

[12] Dante Gabriel Rossetti to Jane Burden Morris, 27 February 1878. *ibid*, p26

[13] Marie Spartali Stillman to Dante Gabriel Rossetti, 3 April 1878. Angeli-Dennis Collection, University of British Columbia

[14] Stillman, William James, (1901), *Autobiography of a Journalist*, Houghton, Mifflin: Boston, ii p626

Chapter Eleven: Florence 1878-1883

[1] Marie Spartali Stillman to Ford Madox Brown, 5 August 1878. Ford Madox Brown papers, National Art Library, MSL 1995/14/105/36

[2] Dante Gabriel Rossetti to Marie Spartali Stillman, 18 June 1878. Harry Ransom Humanities Research Center, University of Texas

[3] Dante Gabriel Rossetti to Frederick Shields, 16 July 1879, *Letters*. Doughty & Wahl

[4] William Michael Rossetti, 6 August 1878. *Some Reminiscences*, (1906), Brown, Langham

[5] William Michael Rossetti, 13 August 1878, *Diary*. Angeli-Dennis Collection, University of British Columbia

[6] Marie Spartali Stillman to Ford Madox Brown, 5 October 1878. Ford Madox Brown papers, National Art Library, MSL 1995/14/105/10

[7] William Michael Rossetti, 27 April 1879, *Diary*. Angeli-Dennis Collection, University of British Columbia

[8] Charles Fairfax Murray to Dante Gabriel Rossetti, 16 June 1879, *ibid*

[9] Dante Gabriel Rossetti to Jane Burden Morris, 16 June 1879. Bryson & Troxell, (1976), Clarendon, p60

[10] Dante Gabriel Rossetti to Jane Burden Morris, 15 August 1879, Bryson & Troxell, (1976), Clarendon, p73

[11] Jane Burden Morris to Dante Gabriel Rossetti, 18 or 25 August 1879, Bryson & Troxell, (1976), Clarendon, p75

[12] Dante Gabriel Rossetti to Jane Burden Morris, 26 August 1879. *ibid*, p76

[13] Dante Gabriel Rossetti to Christina Rossetti. *Letters*, Doughty & Wahl, p2119

[14] Dante Gabriel Rossetti to Theodore Watts-Dunton, 1879. *ibid*

[15] William Michael Rossetti, 9 October 1879, *Diary*. Angeli-Dennis Collection, University of British Columbia

[16] Cormell Price, founder and Head Master of the United Services College, Westward Ho! in Devon was Burne-Jones's, and later William Morris's close friend from their days at Oxford; he is immortalised as the headmaster in Rudyard Kipling's *Stalky & Co*

[17] Dante Gabriel Rossetti to Jane Burden Morris, 9 October 1879. Bryson & Troxell, (1976), Clarendon, p80

[18] 'Abuse of Chloral Hydrate', *Quarterly Journal of Inebriety*, **Vol. 4**, January 1880, pp53-54

[19] Rossetti, William Michael, Introduction to H. T. Dunn, (1904), *Recollections of Dante Gabriel Rossetti*. Elkin Matthews

[20] Marie Spartali Stillman to Dante Gabriel Rossetti, 18 November 1879. Angeli-Dennis Collection, University of British Columbia

[21] Stillman, William James, (1901), *Autobiography of a Journalist*, Houghton, Mifflin: Boston, ii p626

[22] Dante Gabriel Rossetti to Jane Burden Morris, Christmas Eve 1879. Bryson & Troxell, (1976), Clarendon, p86

[23] Philip Webb to Giacomo Boni, 19 December 1882. Webb Archive, Courtauld Institute

[24] The illustrator and engraver H M Paget accompanied William Stillman on his first Aegean expedition for Scribner's

[25] Charles Fairfax Murray to Dante Gabriel Rossetti, 24 April 1880. Angeli-Dennis Collection, University of British Columbia

[26] Dante Gabriel Rossetti to Jane Burden Morris, 14 June 1880, Bryson & Troxell, (1976), Clarendon, p113

[27] Dante Gabriel Rossetti to Charles Fairfax Murray, 7 September 1881. Harry Ransom Humanities Research Center, University of Texas

[28] Charles Fairfax Murray to Dante Gabriel Rossetti, 10 September 1881. Angeli-Dennis Collection, University of British Columbia

[29] General Manager of *The Times*

[30] William James Stillman to Marie Spartali Stillman, 21 August 1881. Stillman papers, 510, Schaffer Library, Union College, Schenectady

[31] Marie Spartali Stillman to Ford Madox Brown, 13 September 1881. Ford Madox Brown papers, National Art Library, MSL 1995/14/105/21

[32] William Michael Rossetti, 27 September 1881, *Diary*. Angeli-Dennis Collection, University of British Columbia

[33] William Michael Rossetti to Dante Gabriel Rossetti, 16 February 1882. Angeli-Dennis Collection, University of British Columbia

[34] William Michael Rossetti, 8 March 1882, *Diary*. Angeli-Dennis Collection, University of British Columbia

[35] Marie Spartali Stillman to Vernon Lee, 16 September 1882. Somerville College, Oxford

[36] Stillman, William James, (1901), *Autobiography of a Journalist*, Houghton, Mifflin: Boston, ii p661

Chapter Twelve: Expatriates, Friends and Visitors

[1] Marie Spartali Stillman to Vernon Lee, 16 September 1882. Vernon Lee papers, Somerville College, Oxford

[2] Smyth, Ethel, (1933), *Female Pipings in Eden*, Peter Davies

[3] The novelist Marie Louise de Ramée; she lived in Pisa

[4] Lady Paget, Walburga, (1923), *Embassies of Other Days*, Hutchinson. The former Gräfin Walburga Ehrengarde Helena von Hohenstahl of Saxony was the wife of Sir Augustus Paget, the British Ambassador in Rome, and a cousin to Queen Victoria

[5] see Colby, Vineta, (1970), *The Singular Anomaly: Women Novelists of the Nineteenth Century*, University Press, New York: New York, p237

[6] see Gunn, Peter, (1964), *Violet Paget 1856-1935*, OUP; reprinted 1975, Arno: NY

[7] *Veronica Veronese*, 1872, Delaware Art Museum 35-28

[8] Dante Gabriel Rossetti to Jane Burden Morris, 29 February 1880. Bryson & Troxell (1997), Clarendon, p106

[9] Marie Spartali Stillman to Ford Madox Brown, 19 January 1880. Ford Madox Brown papers, National Art Library, MSL 1995/14/105/38

[10] William James Stillman to Charles Eliot Norton, 3 October 1880. Houghton Library, Harvard University bMS Am 1088/713741
[11] John Addington Symonds to Henry Graham Dakyns, 27 November 82. *Letters of John Addington Symonds*, Herbert M. Schueller and Robert L. Peters (eds), (1968). Wayne State University Press
[12] Henry James, 28 February 1870, *Letters*, Edel (ed), (1978), Macmillan
[13] Phyllis Groskerth (ed), (1984), *Memoirs, John Addington Symonds*, Hutchinson
[14] Gunn, Peter, (1964), *Violet Paget 1856-1935*, OUP; reprinted 1975, Arno: NY
[15] Charles Fairfax Murray to William Silas Spanton, early 1881. Dulwich Picture Gallery
[16] Leith, Royal W, (1996), *A Quiet Devotion*, New York
[17] Leith, Royal W, *ibid*
[18] William James Stillman to Charles Eliot Norton, 3 October 1880. Houghton Library, Harvard University bMS Am 1088/7137
[19] James Jackson Jarves, 28 April 1881, 'Artists and Art Critics', *New York Times*, quoted by Leith, (1996), *A Quiet Devotion*
[20] Vernon Lee to her mother, 16 June 1881. *The Letters of Vernon Lee*, Willis (ed), p281
[21] Sandra Beresford, (October 1986), *PreRaffaelismo ed Estetismo a Firenze negli ultimi del XIX secolo, in L'Idea di Firenze: Temi e interpretazione nell'arte straniera dell'Ottocento*
[22] Dante Gabriel Rossetti to Aglaia Coronio, 24 September 1880. *Letters* **Vol IV**, Doughty & Wahl, 2335
[23] William Michael Rossetti, 10 December 1880, *Diary*. Angeli-Dennis Collection, University of British Columbia
[24] William Michael Rossetti, 12 December 1880, *Diary. ibid*
[25] Jane Burden Morris to Dante Gabriel Rossetti, 2 February 1881. Bryson & Troxell (1997), Clarendon, p131
[26] Jane Burden Morris to Dante Gabriel Rossetti, 5 March 1881. *ibid*, p133
[27] Dante Gabriel Rossetti to Jane Burden Morris, 28 April 1881. *ibid*, p138
[28] Walker Art Gallery, Liverpool
[29] Gunn, Peter, (1964), *Violet Paget 1856-1935*, OUP; reprinted 1975, Arno: NY
[30] F O Mathiessen & K B Murdoch (eds), (1947), *The Notebooks of Henry James*, OUP
[31] Collins, John, (1992), *The Two Forgers*, Oak Knoll Press: New Castle, Delaware
[32] for Buxton Forman and Henry Roderick Newman, see Leith, Royal W A, (1996), *A Quiet Devotion*
[33] Edel, (1977), *Life of Henry James*, 2 vols, Harmondsworth
[34] Henry James to his mother, 20 May 1877. *Letters of Henry James*, Edel (ed), (1978), Macmillan, p113
[35] William James Stillman, 'Francesca's Country', *The Critic* 12, pp301-302
[36] Leith, Royal W, (1996), *A Quiet Devotion*, New York
[37] Vernon Lee to her mother, 21 June 1883. *The Letters of Vernon Lee*, Irene Cooper Willis (ed), p116
[38] Vernon Lee to her mother, 30 June 1883. *ibid*, p120
[39] Vernon Lee to her mother, 6 July 1883. *ibid*, p124
[40] Willard Fiske papers, Cornell University
[41] William Michael Rossetti, 23 November 1883. *Diary*, Angeli-Dennis Collection, University of British Columbia

Chapter Thirteen: Miss Brown

[1] First performed 23 April 1881 at the Opera Comique, London
[2] Irene Cooper Willis (ed), Introduction in *The Letters of Vernon Lee*
[3] Zina Hulton was Pasquale Villari's god-daughter. William Hulton (1852-1922) was a landscape painter who exhibited at the Soc. Brit. Artists and at the RA 1882-9; he died in Venice 12 February 1922
[4] Vernon Lee to her mother, 16 June 1881. *The Letters of Vernon Lee*, Irene Cooper Willis (ed)
[5] Vernon Lee to her mother, 16 June 1881. *ibid*
[6] Vernon Lee to her mother, 23 July 1881. *ibid*
[7] William James Stillman to Marie Spartali Stillman, 9 August 1882. Stillman papers 451, Schaffer Library, Union College, Schenectady
[8] Henry James to his mother, 20 May 1877. *Letters of Henry James*, Edel (ed), (1978), Macmillan
[9] Vernon Lee to her mother, 22 June 1882. *The Letters of Vernon Lee*, Irene Cooper Willis (ed), p82
[10] Vernon Lee to her mother, June 1882. *ibid*
[11] Delaware Art Museum, 35-28
[12] Vernon Lee to her mother, 11 July 1884. *The Letters of Vernon Lee*, Irene Cooper Willis (ed), p146
[13] Marie Spartali Stillman to Vernon Lee, 12 December 1884. Colby College Archive
[14] Marie Spartali Stillman to Vernon Lee, 27 December 1884. *ibid*
[15] Gunn, Peter, (1964) *Violet Paget 1856-1935*, Oxford UP, reprinted 1975, Arno: NY

Chapter Fourteen: A Time of Misfortune 1884-1885

[1] *Forgetfulness*, 1870, exhibited Liverpool 1871
[2] William Michael Rossetti, 29 May 1884, *Diary*. Angeli-Dennis Collection, University of British Columbia
[3] Vernon Lee to her mother, 16 June 1884. *The Letters of Vernon Lee*, Irene Cooper Willis (ed)
[4] William Michael Rossetti, 14 June 1884. *Diary*, Angeli-Dennis Collection, University of British Columbia
[5] Pennell, E. R. & J., (1908), *Life of James Whistler*. Heinemann
[6] Vernon Lee to her mother, 4 July 1884. *The Letters of Vernon Lee*, Irene Cooper Willis (ed), p144
[7] William Michael Rossetti, 11 July 1884. *Diary*, Angeli-Dennis Collection, University of British Columbia
[8] Adelson, Howard L, *The American Numismatic Society 1858-1958*. p87
[9] Lucy Madox Brown Rossetti to William Michael Rossetti, October 1884. Angeli-Dennis Collection,University of British Columbia
[10] William Michael Rossetti, 30 October 1884, *Diary*. Angeli-Dennis Collection, University of British Columbia
[11] Marie Spartali Stillman to Ford Madox Brown, 4 October 1884. Ford Madox Brown papers, National Art Library, MSL 1995/14/105/22
[12] Demetrius, Michael and Euphrosyne Spartali's third child; married Virginia Ralli, 22 March 1879
[13] William Michael Rossetti, 18 January 1885, *Diary*. Angeli-Dennis Collection,University of British Columbia
[14] Marie Spartali Stillman to Ford Madox Brown, 8 December 1884. Ford Madox Brown papers, National Art Library, MSL 1995/14/105/24
[15] William Michael Rossetti, 19 March 1885, *Diary*. Angeli-Dennis Collection, University of British Columbia
[16] Marie Spartali Stillman to Ford Madox Brown, nd. Ford Madox Brown papers, National Art Library, MSL 1995/14/105/20
[17] George Du Maurier to Henry James, 14 September 1884. Houghton Library, Harvard, quoted by Leonée Ormond (1969) in *George Du Maurier*, Routledge
[18] William Michael Rossetti 2 August 1885, *Diary*. Angeli-Dennis Collection, University of British Columbia
[19] Tricha, Lydia, (1991), *Diplomatia kai Politike: Charilaos Trikoupis-Joannes Gennadios, Allelographia 1863-1894* [Diplomacy and Politics: Charilaos Tricoupis-John Gennadius, Correspondence 1863-1894], Athens
[20] Tsimpidaros, Vasos, (1979), *The Greeks in England*, Athens

[21] William James Stillman, (1901), *Autobiography of a Journalist*, Houghton, Mifflin: Boston, ii p663
[22] William Michael Rossetti, 7 May 1885, *Diary*. Angeli-Dennis Collection, University of British Columbia
[23] Marie Spartali Stillman to Ford Madox Brown, 11 June nd. Ford Madox Brown papers, National Art Library, MSL 1995/14/105/41
[24] Vernon Lee to her mother, 18 June 1885. *The Letters of Vernon Lee*, Irene Cooper Willis (ed), p177
[25] Vernon Lee to her mother, 16 June 1885. *ibid*, p178. Sargent's over-lifesize portrait of 'Madame X,' actually Madame Gautreau, caused a scandal at the 1884 Salon in Paris by the unashamed sensuality of the pose, her stark white skin and revealing dress. It blighted both her reputation and his in Paris. Now Metropolitan Museum, New York
[26] Vernon Lee to her mother, 1 September 1885. *The Letters of Vernon Lee*, Irene Cooper Willis (ed), p179
[27] William Michael Rossetti, 7 May 1885, *Diary*. Angeli-Dennis Collection, University of British Columbia
[28] William Michael Rossetti, 21 August 1885, *Diary. ibid*
[29] Wilfrid Scawen Blunt (1840-1922): diplomat, poet, Arabist and anti-Imperialist agitator for Home Rule in Ireland, Egypt and India; cousin to Percy Wyndham, patron of Philip Webb who built 'Clouds' for him; grandson of Turner's patron the 3rd Earl of Egremont. Blunt was born at the Wyndham family seat, Petworth House
[30] Francis Gore Currie; cousin to Wilfrid Blunt
[31] Wilfrid Scawen Blunt, 7 July 1885, *Diaries*, Fitzwilliam Museum, Cambridge
[32] 3 Challoner Street, Baron's Court, London W
[33] William Michael Rossetti, 25 September 1885, *Diary*. Angeli-Dennis Collection, University of British Columbia
[34] William Michael Rossetti, 27 May 1886, *Diary. ibid*

Chapter Fifteen: 3 Challoner Street 1885-1889

[1] Vernon Lee to her mother, 16 June 1886. *The Letters of Vernon Lee*, Irene Cooper Willis (ed)
[2] Vernon Lee to her mother, 16 June 1886. *The Letters of Vernon Lee*, Irene Cooper Willis (ed)
[3] see Kelvin, Norman, the editor of William Morris's correspondence, in *New York Review of Books*, 18 June 1985
[4] Vernon Lee to her mother, 16 June 1886. *The Letters of Vernon Lee*, Irene Cooper Willis (ed)
[5] Vernon Lee to her mother, 26 June 1886. *ibid*
[6] Vernon Lee to her mother, 29 June 1886. *ibid*
[7] Joseph Lindon Smith (1863-1950) was a pupil of Charles Moore, later the first Director of the Fogg Art Museum, Harvard University. He was closely associated with Mrs Isabella Stewart Gardner. Small in stature, Mrs Gardner called him 'my gnome'. Denman Waldo Ross was an amateur artist and collector, and benefactor of the Fogg Art Museum
[8] Dublin [New Hampshire] Historical Society Archives
[9] Fogg Art Museum Archive, Harvard University
[10] Charles Fairfax Murray, *The Concert*; exhibited: Grosvenor Gallery (1890); 'Pre-Raphaelites and Other Masters', Royal Academy (2003)
[11] Dublin [New Hampshire] Historical Society Archives
[12] Marie Spartali Stillman, *A May Feast at the House of Falco Portinari 1274*; exhibited: Grosvenor Gallery (1887)
[13] Fogg Art Museum Archive, Harvard University
[14] Henderson, Philip, (1967), *William Morris, His Life, Work and Friends*, London
[15] Archives of the Socialist League, 3463.5/2863-5 ad 3456, Internationaal Instituut voor Sociale Geschiedenis, Amsterdam
[16] Marie Spartali Stillman to Ford Madox Brown, 17 February 1888. Ford Madox Brown papers, National Art Library, MSL 1995/14/105/33
[17] Marie Spartali Stillman to Ford Madox Brown, nd. Ford Madox Brown papers, National Art Library, MSL 1995/14/105/46
[18] Newman & Watkinson, (1991), *Ford Madox Brown*, Chatto & Windus, p182
[19] 1872. Now at Newnham College, Cambridge
[20] Ford Madox Brown to Lucy Madox Rossetti, 15April 1883. Angeli-Dennis Collection, University of British Columbia
[21] William Michael Rossetti, 20 February 1888, *Diary*. Angeli-Dennis Collection, University of British Columbia
[22] Marie Spartali Stillman to Ford Madox Brown, nd. Ford Madox Brown papers, National Art Library, MSL 1995/14/105/32
[23] William Michael Rossetti, 24 April 1888, *Diary*. Angeli-Dennis Collection, University of British Columbia
[24] Lisa Stillman to Effie Stillman, 4 May 1888, from 44 Via Gregoriana, Rome. Family papers
[25] William James Stillman to Euphrosyne Stillman, 26 May 1888, from 44 Via Gregoriana, Rome. Family papers
[26] Florence Fenwick-Miller, Ladies Column, *Illustrated London News*, 11 May 1889; quoted by Cherry, Deborah, (1993), *Painting Women. Victorian Women Artists*, Routledge: London, p604
[27] Adam (ed), (1906), *Alice Comyns-Carr, Reminiscences*, Hutchinson
[28] Ritchie, Hester (ed), (1924), *Letters of Anne Thackeray Ritchie*, John Murray: London
[29] Adam (ed), (1906), *Alice Comyns-Carr, Reminiscences*, Hutchinson
[30] Maisie Ionides to Euphrosyne Stillman, nd. Family papers
[31] Wilfrid Scawen Blunt, *Diaries,* Fitzwilliam Museum, Cambridge; see *Jane Burden Morris to Wilfrid Scawen Blunt*, Faulkner (ed), (1986), University of Exeter, p1
[32] Marsh, Jan, (1986), *Jane and May Morris*, Pandora, p192. Marsh makes a convincing case for the later date of the autumn 1888 and that their sexual relationship was short-lived. If so, Janey Morris may have confided in Marie and, in introducing her to Blunt, to have aroused his interest, while simultaneously resolving the dilemma of her infidelity, of which Morris was probably aware.
[33] Jane Burden Morris to Wilfrid Scawen Blunt, July 1888. Fitzwilliam Museum, Cambridge
[34] William Morris to F S Ellis, 8 October 1888. *Collected Letters of William Morris*, Kelvin (ed)
[35] Marie Spartali Stillman to Wilfrid Scawen Blunt, 25 December 1888. Fitzwilliam Museum, Cambridge
[36] Jane Burden Morris to Wilfrid Scawen Blunt, 28 December 1888. *Jane Morris to Wilfred Scawen Blunt*, Faulkner (ed), (1986), University of Exeter
[37] MacCarthy, Fiona, (1994), *William Morris*, Faber & Faber, p 628
[38] Longford, Elizabeth, (1979), *A Pilgrimage of Passion*. Weidenfeld & Nicholson
[39] Dante Gabriel Rossetti to Jane Burden Morris, 2 December 1877. Bryson & Troxell, Clarendon, p22
[40] Schonfield, Zuzanna, (1987), *The Precariously Privileged, A Professional Family in Victorian England*, Oxford University Press
[41] Vernon Lee to her mother, 16 November 1888. *The Letters of Vernon Lee*, Irene Cooper Willis (ed)
[42] William James Stillman to Euphrosyne (Effie) Stillman, 7 April 1889. Family papers
[43] William James Stillman to Effie Stillman, 7 April 1889 from Athens. Family papers
[44] William James Stillman to Effie Stillman, 17 May 1889 from Athens. *ibid*
[45] Marie Spartali Stillman to Bella and Lisa Stillman in Rome, 13 August 1889. Family papers
[46] Marie Spartali Stillman to Vernon Lee, 28 August 1889. Somerville College, Oxford. Ernest Hébert was Director of the French Academy in Rome 1867-1873, 1885 and 1891
[47] William James Stillman to Euphrosyne Stillman, 7 October 1889. Family papers

[48] Edward Burne-Jones to Marie Spartali Stillman, December 1889. Fitzwilliam Museum, Cambridge

Chapter Sixteen: The Parnell Affair

[1] Marie Spartali Stillman to Ford Madox Brown, 17 February 1888. National Art Library, MSL 1995/14/105/30
[2] Bella Stillman to Euphrosyne Stillman, 23 April 1888. Family papers
[3] Stillman, William James, (1901), *Autobiography of a Journalist.* Houghton, Mifflin: Boston, ii p670
[4] Stillman, William James. *ibid*, ii p67
[5] William James Stillman in Athens to Euphrosyne Stillman, 5 March 1889. Family papers
[6] Bella Stillman to Euphrosyne (Effie) Stillman, nd, from 44 via Gregoriana, Rome. Family papers
[7] William Michael Rossetti, 30 November 1888, *Diary*. Angeli-Dennis Collection, University of British Columbia

Chapter Seventeen: Marie in Rome 1889-1896

[1] Marie Stillman to Charles Fairfax Murray, 19 November 1889. John Rylands University of Manchester Library
[2] Formerly the Russian princess Nadejda Schakowskoy
[3] Giovanni Battista Cavalcaselle (1820–97): Italian art critic and writer, who took part in the revolution of 1848 and was exiled to England, where he produced, in collaboration with Joseph A Crowe, their first joint work, *Early Flemish Painters* (1856). Their *History of Painting in Italy* (3 vol., 1864–66) remains a standard work of reference. Cavalcaselle returned to Italy in 1857 and in 1861 was appointed Secretary of a Government commission with the remit of listing heritage works of art to prevent their sale abroad
[4] Marie Spartali Stillman to Charles Fairfax Murray, 19 November 1889. John Rylands University of Manchester Library
[5] see Jane Burden Morris to Wilfrid Scawen Blunt, 1 and 12 December 1889. *Jane Morris to Wilfred Scawen Blunt*, Faulkner (ed), (1986), University of Exeter
[6] Jane Burden Morris to Wilfrid Scawen Blunt, 11 August 1889. Faulkner (ed)
[7] Wilfrid Scawen Blunt, 18. October 1890, *Diaries*, Fitzwilliam Museum, Cambridge
[8] Wilfrid Scawen Blunt, 2 September 1890. *ibid*
[9] Jane Burden Morris to Wilfrid Scawen Blunt, 29 November 1889. *Jane Morris to Wilfred Scawen Blunt*, Faulkner (ed), (1986), University of Exeter
[10] Jane Burden Morris to Wilfrid Scawen Blunt, 12 December 1889. *ibid*; see also *A New Pilgrimage*, (1889). Kegan Paul & Co.
[11] Wilfrid Scawen Blunt, 30 December 1889, *Diaries*, MS 306-1976, Fitzwilliam Museum, Cambridge
[12] Marie Spartali Stillman to Wilfrid Scawen Blunt, 28 December 1890 from 46 via de Fontanella di Borghese. Fitzwilliam Museum, Cambridge
[13] Burne-Jones, Georgiana, (1904), *Memorials of Edward Burne-Jones*, London, vol ii p221
[14] Wendell Phillips Garrison, *Century Quarterly* **Vol 46**, 5 September 1893
[15] Exhibited Oehme Gallery, New York (1908)
[16] May Morris, *Introductions to the Complete Works of William Morris*, i p235
[17] May Morris, *ibid*, i p235
[18] Marie Spartali Stillman to Wilfrid Scawen Blunt, 15 October 1892. *Diaries*, Fitzwilliam Museum, Cambridge
[19] Jane Burden Morris to Wilfrid Scawen Blunt, 11 March 1893. *Jane Morris to Wilfred Scawen Blunt,* Faulkner (ed), (1986), University of Exeter
[20] *Westminster Gazette*, 5 June 1893
[21] Kelmscott Manor Visitors' Book, BL Add. MSS 45.412, British Library
[22] Jane Burden Morris to Wilfrid Scawen Blunt, 17 August 1893. *Jane Morris to Wilfred Scawen Blunt,* Faulkner (ed), (1986), University of Exeter
[23] Kelmscott Manor Visitors' Book, BL Add. MSS 45.412, British Library; also *ibid* p81
[24] Jane Burden Morris to Wilfrid Scawen Blunt, 28 August 1893. *Jane Morris to Wilfred Scawen Blunt,* Faulkner (ed), (1986), University of Exeter
[25] Kelmscott Manor Visitors' Book, BL Add. MSS 45.412, British Library; also *ibid* p82
[26] Marie Spartali Stillman to Vernon Lee from SKM, 21 September 1894,. Somerville College, Oxford
[27] Marie Spartali Stillman to Cathy Heuffer. Ford Madox Brown papers, National Art Library, MSL 1995/14/105/10
[28] William Michael Rossetti, 3 November 1894, *Diary*. Angeli-Dennis Collection, University of British Columbia
[29] Jane Morris to Wilfrid Scawen Blunt, 18 February 1895. *Jane Morris to Wilfred Scawen Blunt,* Faulkner (ed), (1986), University of Exeter
[30] J W Mackail, *Life of William Morris,* **II** p39
[31] Wilfrid Scawen Blunt, 17 June 1896, *Diaries*, MS 306-1976, Fitzwilliam Museum, Cambridge
[32] Crooke, J Mordaunt, *William Burgess*, quoted in Kelvin, Norman, (1987), *Collected Letters of William Morris*, 2 vols, Princeton, vol ii letter 1073 p403n
[33] Jane Burden Morris to Wilfrid Scawen Blunt, 19 June 1896. *Jane Morris to Wilfred Scawen Blunt,* Faulkner (ed), (1986), University of Exeter
[34] MacCarthy, Fiona, (1994), *William Morris*, Faber & Faber, p663
[35] *Nation* **56:11**, 5 January 1893 and **56:178**, 9 March 1893
[36] Edward Burne-Jones to Marie Spartali Stillman. WJS53, Union College, Schenectady: exhibited Liverpool (1892), now Wightwick Manor
[37] Unidentified, possibly Ida Cahen, wife of Ugo Cahen d'Anvers, or Ida Walker, a friend both of Marie Stillman and of Vernon Lee in Florence, see, 11 July 1884, *The Letters of Vernon Lee*, Irene Cooper Willis (ed)
[38] Marie Stillman to Vernon Lee, nd. Somerville College, Oxford
[39] Kelmscott Manor Visitors' Book, BL Add. MSS 45.412, British Library
[40] William Michael Rossetti, 16 November 1897, *Diary*. Angeli-Dennis Collection, University of British Columbia

Chapter Eighteen: The Closing Years

[1] William James Stillman to W J Stebbing. Harry Ransom Humanities Research Center, University of Texas
[2] Marie Spartali Stillman to Vernon Lee from Frimley, 16 July 1898. Somerville College, Oxford
[3] Delaware Art Museum, Bancroft Archive
[4] Marie Spartali Stillman to Cathy Heuffer.
Ford Madox Heuffer (later Ford), was writing a biography of his father-in-law - *Ford Madox Brown: A Record of his Life and Work*, (1896), Longmans
[5] Jane Burden Morris to Wilfrid Scawen Blunt, 16 July 1898. *Jane Morris to Wilfred Scawen Blunt,* Faulkner (ed), (1986), University of Exeter
[6] William Michael Rossetti, 23 November 1898, *Diary*. Angeli-Dennis Collection, University of British Columbia
[7] Samuel Bancroft Jnr to Marie Spartali Stillman, nd. Delaware Art Museum, Bancroft Archive
[8] Marie Spartali Stillman to Samuel Bancroft Jnr, 31 January 1901. Delaware Art Museum, Bancroft Archive
[9] William Michael Rossetti, 24 January 1901, *Diary*. Angeli-Dennis Collection, University of British Columbia
[10] Samuel Bancroft to Marie Spartali Stillman, 23 March 1901. Delaware Art Museum, Bancroft Archive
[11] Marie Spartali Stillman to Samuel Bancroft, 11 April 1901. *ibid*

[12] Marie Spartali Stillman to Samuel Bancroft, 4 May 1901. *ibid*
[13] Marie Spartali Stillman to Samuel Bancroft, 21 May 1901. *ibid*
[14] Samuel Bancroft to Marie Spartali Stillman, 21 May 1901. *ibid*
[15] William Michael Rossetti, 10 May 1901, *Diary*. Angeli-Dennis Collection, University of British Columbia
[16] Marie Spartali Stillman to Samuel Bancroft, 6 July 1901. Delaware Art Museum, Bancroft Archive
[17] J M W Turner's *Devonport and Dockyard*, purchased by Charles Fairfax Murray from John Ruskin's collection, lent by him to William Stillman in his last weeks; now Fogg Art Museum
[18] Marie Spartali Stillman to Charles Fairfax Murray, 7 July 1901. John Rylands University of Manchester Library
[19] William Michael Rossetti, 10 July 1901, *Diary*. Angeli-Dennis Collection, University of British Columbia
[20] *The Times*, 9 July 1901
[21] Rossetti, William Michael, (1906), *Some Reminiscences*, Brown: Langham, p267
[22] William Michael Rossetti, 6 October 1901, *Diary*. Angeli-Dennis Collection, University of British Columbia
[23] Marie Spartali Stillman to Vernon Lee, 12 December 1901. Somerville College, Oxford
[24] She wrote under, and was known by, the name Helen Rossetti Angeli. With her sister Olivia Frances Madox Agresti, she wrote *A Girl among the Anarchists* under the pen name Isabel Meredith
[25] Peggy Middleton, later Peggy Reynolds
[26] The English premiere of Ethel Smyth's one-act opera, *Der Wald* [The Forest], was given at Covent Garden in July 1902; Royal Opera House Archive
[27] Marie Spartali Stillman to Vernon Lee, 26 June 1902. Somerville College Archive, Oxford
[28] Smyth, Ethel, (**1933**), *Female Pipings in Eden*, Peter Davis, on Vernon Lee
[29] Kelmscott Manor Visitors' Book, BL Add. MSS 45.412, British Library
[30] Marie Spartali Stillman to Vernon Lee, 26 June 1902. Somerville College Archive, Oxford
[31] Marie Spartali Stillman to Vernon Lee, 15 March 1903. *ibid*
[32] Marie Spartali Stillman to Vernon Lee, 4 June 1903. *ibid*
[33] Marie Spartali Stillman to Charles Fairfax Murray, nd. John Rylands University of Manchester Library
[34] Dictionary of American Biography
[35] Marie Spartali Stillman to George Howard. Castle Howard Archive, 7 January/11 and 30 August 1904, J92/96.1480-82
[36] Marie Spartali Stillman to George Howard. J92/96.1483-4. *ibid*
[37] Marie Spartali Stillman to Samuel Bancroft, 6 October 1903. Delaware Art Museum, Bancroft Archive
[38] Marie Spartali Stillman to Samuel Bancroft, nd. *ibid*
[39] Marie Spartali Stillman to Vernon Lee, 2 February 1904. Somerville College Archive, Oxford
[40] Marie Spartali Stillman to Samuel Bancroft, 20 September 1904. Delaware Art Museum, Bancroft Archive
[41] Marie Spartali Stillman to Gladys Norton, 9 December 1912. Fogg Museum of Art Archive
[42] Marie Spartali Stillman to Vernon Lee, 9 November 1906?. Somerville College Archive, Oxford
[43] Marie Spartali Stillman to Vernon Lee, 15 May 1908. Somerville College Archive, Oxford
[44] Marie Spartali Stillman to Samuel Bancroft, 29 November 1908. Delaware Art Museum, Bancroft Archive
[45] The author is indebted to Philip Attwood for a detailed account of Effie Stillman's work in *The Medal*, **No 14**, Spring 1989
[46] Samuel Bancroft to Charles Fairfax Murray, 16 June 1898. Elzea, Rowland, (1980), Occasional Paper 2, Delaware Art Museum, n1
[47] Samuel Bancroft to Charles Fairfax Murray, 13 September 1908. *ibid*
[48] Marie Spartali Stillman to Vernon Lee, December 1911. Somerville College Archive, Oxford
[49] Henry James to Marie Spartali Stillman, nd. Za James 55, Yale University
[50] Handbill. Delaware Art Museum, Bancroft Archive
[51] Marie Spartali Stillman to Vernon Lee, 13 October 1919. Somerville College Archive, Oxford
[52] Widow of A G Dew-Smith, a Cambridge friend of John Henry Middleton and partner with Harold Darwin (Charles Darwin's son) in the Cambridge Scientific Instruments Company
[53] Marie Spartali Stillman to Vernon Lee, 3 September 1922. Somerville College Archive, Oxford
[54] Marie Spartali Stillman to Vernon Lee, 20 June 1924. *ibid*
[55] J W Mackail, 8 March 1927, Obituary, *The Times*
[56] Bella Stillman to Vernon Lee, 16 March 1927. Somerville College Archive, Oxford

Envoi: Marie Spartali Stillman, Artist

[1] Andrew Lord Lloyd-Webber collection
[2] Ashmolean Museum, Oxford
[3] Elvehjem Gallery, University of Madison, Wisconsin, USA
[4] Pre-Raphaelite Inc., with Julian Hartnoll
[5] J Philips Elmslie, a Working Men's College pupil, quoted by Ford Madox Heuffer (later Ford)
[6] Marie Spartali Stillman to Samuel Bancroft, 19 September 1903. Delaware Art Museum, Bancroft Archive
[7] Snyder, Jane McIntosh, (1991), *The Women and the Lyre*, Southern Illinois University Press
[8] William Michael Rossetti, 2 November 1869, note on a list of work from Marie Spartali re his intended article in *Portfolio*, 1870. Angeli-Dennis papers, University of British Columbia
[9] Cherry, Deborah, (1993), *Painting Women*. Victorian Women Artists, Routledge: London, p198
[10] Rossetti, William Michael, 'English Painters of the Present Day', *Portfolio* **8**
[11] *see* Marsh, Jan and Nunn, Pamela Gerrish, introduction to *Pre-Raphaelite Women Artists*
[12] Siegal, Bennett, private correspondence with the author
[13] Delaware Art Museum, 74-44, Bancroft Collection
[14] Peter Rawlings, (ed), (1996), *Henry James, Essays on Art and Drama*, Scolar
[15] Shaw, George Bernard, (June 1885), in Annie Besant's *Our Corner*
[16] Shaw, George Bernard,(27 April 1887), *The World*
[17] Shaw, George Bernard, (16 November 1887), *The World*; The painting, *Upon a Day Came Sorrow unto Me*, is at present unlocated. There is an illustration in Bates, Percy, (1899), *The English Pre- Raphaelites*, George Bell & Son
[18] Shaw, George Bernard, (16 May 1888), *The World*
[19] William Michael Rossetti, 20 February 1888, *Diary*. Angeli-Dennis papers, University of British Columbia
[20] Shaw, George Bernard, (April 1890), *Truth*
[21] '... they are not nearly as good in the higher sense as some things she did before her marriage': Dante Gabriel Rossetti to Jane Burden Morris, 19 November 1877, Bryson & Troxell, (1976), Clarendon, p23
[22] Spanton, William Silas, *An Art Student and his Teachers in the 60s*, p83
[23] Delaware Art Museum, Bancroft Archive
[24] Marie Spartali Stillman to Deborah Peacock, 16 June 1906. Delaware Art Museum

Identified Works by Marie Spartali Stillman

Paintings were exhibited from time to time under names attached by the gallery rather than the artist, for example 'St Barbara' as 'Girl with Peacock Feathers,' and as pictures have re-appeared in auction houses their original titles have sometimes been lost or incorrectly identified; this may have given rise to occasional duplication

Picture/Title	Date	Exhibited/Sale
The Lady Prays Desire	1867	Dudley 3rd 1867
Shanklin Chine	1867	
The Pasha's Widow	1867	
The Mystick Tryst	1867	Dudley RA 1870
Korinna the Theban Poetess	1867	Dudley
Christina, Study	1868	
Mariana	1868	Dudley (Oehme 1908?)
Apse Farm, Isle of Wight	1868	Dudley
In the Cornfield/Landscape	1868	Dudley Christie's 4 Nov. 1999
Christina (Portrait of Young Lady)	1869	Sotheby's 14 June 2001
Self Portrait (but probably Christina)	1869	Christie's 4 Nov. 1999
Pharmakeutria *or* Brewing the Love Philtre	1869	Dudley
Nerea Foscari	1869	Dudley 1870 Sotheby's 20 Nov. 1969
Two Girls and a Peacock	1869	
Procne in search of Philomela	1869	Dudley
La Romaunt of the Rose	1870	Dudley
The Eros of Rhodes	1870	Dudley
Forgetfulness	1870	Liverpool 1871 New York Met. 1874
St Barbara, Girl with Peacock Feather	1870	RA 1870 WMR Portfolio 1871
Fear	1870	
Self Portrait, Lady with a Fan	1871	
Buondelmonte	1871	Dudley
Antigone and her sister Ismene on the Battlefield (Burying Polynices)	1871	Dudley
In the Cloisters	1872	
The Fates	1872	Dudley
Ianthe	1872	Dudley 1872 Oehme 1908
A Chaldean Priest (*aka* ? Monk Reading) (*aka* ? Assyrian Monk)	1872	Dudley New York Met. 1874 San Francisco AA 1875
Portrait of a Child	1872	Dudley

On a Balcony	1872	Dudley New York ASPW 1875
Portrait (sitter unknown)	1873	RA 1873 Liverpool Autumn 1877
Sir Tristram & La Belle Fronde (Tristram & Iseult)	1873	RA 1873 New York/ASPW 1875 Philadelphia 1876 Liverpool Autumn 1877
Elaine Finding Sir Lancelot Disguised as a Fool (Sleeping in her Garden?)	1873	RA, New York 1875,'78,'79
Head of Christ	1873?	New York Met. 1874
Self portrait	1874	
Three (3) Flower Pieces	1875	RA 1875
Mona Lisa	1875	Dudley
May Time	1875	Dudley New York/ASPW?
Chrysanthemums & Christmas Roses	1875	Dudley New York/ASPW?
Study of Lilies	1875	Dudley New York/ASPW?
Lilacs and Roses	1875	New York ASPW 1875 San Francisco AA 1875
Ranunculae	1876	
Consider the Lilies (Effie)	1876	RA 1876 Exposition Universelle, Paris 1878
The Last Sight of Fiammetta	1876	Dudley Liverpool 1879
Blossom Time	1877	RA 1877
Roses and Lilies	1877	Grosvenor 1st Exhibition
Portrait	1877	Liverpool Autumn 1878
The Missal	1878	Liverpool Autumn 1878
In the Gypsies's Cave, IOW	1878	Grosvenor 1879 Liverpool Autumn 1879
Gathering Orange Blossoms	1879	Grosvenor 1879 Liverpool Autumn 1879 Sotheby's Belgravia, 1 Mar. 1984
Fiammetta Singing	1879	Grosvenor 1879
La Pensierosa (Effie)	1879	Grosvenor Summer 1880
A Scene from Dante's Vita Nuova (Some Ladies of her Companionship)	1880	Royal Manchester Inst., 1880 Grosvenor 1881 Liverpool Autumn 1881
Portraits of her brothers Eustratius and Demetrius	1879	
Among the Willows of Tuscany	1880	Grosvenor Winter 1880
Female Portrait	1880	Grosvenor Winter 1880
Portrait, MSS's daughter ?	1880	Grosvenor 1881
The Meeting of Dante & Beatrice on All Saints' Day	1880	Grosvenor Winter 1881, Summer 1882 Liverpool Autumn 1882
Crown of Roses	1881	Grosvenor Liverpool Autumn 1882
Flags	1882	Grosvenor Liverpool Autumn 1882
Legend of Fair Women	1882	Grosvenor 1883
The Childhood of St Cecily	1883	Grosvenor, Liverpool

Madonna Pietra Degli Scrovigni	1884	Grosvenor 1884 Liverpool Autumn 1884 Christie's 25 Oct. 1991
By A Clear Well, Within a Little Field	1884	
Portrait, Michael (Mico) Spartali Stillman	1884	Royal Institute of Painters in Watercolour, 1884
Luiza Strozzi	1884	Grosvenor Liverpool, Autumn 1885
Love's Messenger	1885	Grosvenor 1885
Garland Makers	1885	Grosvenor Liverpool Autumn 1887
Upon a Day Came Sorrow Unto Me	1887	Grosvenor Liverpool Autumn 1887 Sotheby's 1 Mar. 1984
A May Feast at the House of Folco Portinari 1274	1887	Grosvenor 1887
Rachel & Leah	1887	New Gallery 1st Exhibition 1887
Mia Suora Rachel	1888	New Gallery 1st Exhibition 1887
Gelsomina	1888	New Gallery 1st Exhibition 1887 Liverpool Autumn 1888
Dante at Verona	1888	New Gallery Liverpool Autumn 1889
Messer Ansaldo Showing Dianora his Enchanted Garden	1889	Liverpool Autumn 1889 New Gallery 1890
The First Meeting of Petrarch and Laura at the Church of Santa Chiara at Avignon	1889	Liverpool Autumn 1889 New Gallery 1890
Petrarch & Laura at Vaucluse	1889	New Gallery Liverpool Autumn 1890
At a Florentine Wedding Feast	1890	New Gallery 1890
Costanza (Zina) Hulton	1890	Liverpool 1891 New Gallery 1892
Alexandra	1890	
Audaces Fortuna Juvat	1891	New Gallery 1891 Liverpool 1892
Dante and Beatrice, scene from the Vita Nuova	1891	New Gallery 1891
Portrait, Irene	1891	New Gallery 1891
Angel (after Verrochio)	1891	
Cloister Lilies	1891	Liverpool Autumn 1892
How the Virgin Mary came to Brother Conrad of Offida	1892	
St George	1892	New Gallery Liverpool Autumn 1893
The Vision of the Good Monk of Soffiano	1893	New Gallery 1893 Liverpool 1893
A Fisherman in an Italian Landscape	1893	New Gallery 1893
Monte Luce from Perugia at Sunset	1893	New Gallery 1893 (?Oehme 1908)
Italian Landscape with Water Carriers (? In the Campagna, Rome)	1893	
St Francis on his Deathbed	1893	New Gallery 1893
Via della Pergola, Perugia	1893	New Gallery 1893 Oehme 1908
Portrait of Giorgia Costa	1894	

Capri	1894	New Gallery 1894 Liverpool Autumn 1894
A Rose from Armida's Garden	1894	New Gallery 1894
Love Sonnets	1894	New Gallery 1894
Afternoon in Colonna Garden, Rome	1894	New Gallery 1894
St Peter's, Rome	1895	New Gallery Liverpool Autumn 1895
Sfera Fatidica	1895	New Gallery 1895 Liverpool 1895 Oehme 1908
A Florentine Lily	1895	New Gallery 1895
Ponte Nomentana	1895	New Gallery 1895
Persephone Umbra (Love's Messenger, revised background)	1895	
Effie	1895	
Beatrice	1895	New Gallery Liverpool Autumn 1896
Il Falco di Messer Federigo	1896	New Gallery 1896
Ciocaro, nr Allesandria in Piedmont	1896	New Gallery 1896
Soracte	1896	
Portrait, Mrs Welbore St Clair Baddeley, Rome	1897	
Fior de Granato	1897	New Gallery 1897
After Vespers in San Clemente, Rome	1897	New Gallery 1897
A Tomb in the Roman Campagna	1898	New Gallery 1898
San Domenico, Perugia from Porto Pesa	1898	
Beata Beatrix	1898	New Gallery 1899
Lake Nemi	1899	New Gallery 1899
Sunset at Anacapri	1899	New Gallery 1899
Via Praenostina, Rome	1900	New Gallery 1902
In the Garden of the Villa Landor	1902	New Gallery 1902 Oehme 1908
St Francis Blessing the Doves He Has Released	1903	New Gallery 1903
St Catherine in her Garden	1903	New Gallery 1903
St Peter's at Rome from the Porta Pinacerea	1903	New Gallery 1903
A Lady of Thoulouse, whom Love doth Call Mandetta	1903	New Gallery 1903
The Legend of St Francis and the Wolf of Gubbio	1904	
Kelmscott Manor	1904	
Kelmscott Manor	c.1904	
William Blake Richmond's Garden	1905	New Gallery 1905
Kelmscott Manor	1907	New Gallery 1907
The Old Barn, Arreton	1907	New Gallery 1907
White Bush with White Roses	1907	New Gallery 1907
Flower Girls at the Fountain of Bacchus, Florence	1907	New Gallery 1907
Arreton Manor, IOW	1908	Oehme 1908 New Gallery 1908
Old Church at Arreton		Oehme 1908
Early Spring in Umbria	1893	Oehme 1908 New Gallery 1893
The Backyard, Kelmscott		Oehme 1908
San Clemente, Rome, May Day at Yaverland		Oehme 1908
By the Waters of Vaucluse		Oehme 1908

The Long Walk, Kelmscott		Oehme 1908
Monte Amiata and the Paglia River from Torre Alfina		Oehme 1908
Dante and Virgil in the Dark Wood		Oehme 1908
Lady Radnor's Garden on the Guidecca, Venice	c.1902	Oehme 1908
The Orchard at Spring Time, Kelmscott		Oehme 1908
The Farm at Arreton		Oehme 1908
The Chapel of the Santissimo, San Marco, Venice		Oehme 1908
Sir Rennell Rodd's Garden, Surrey		Oehme 1908
The Norman Church and Farm Pool at Arreton		Oehme 1908
A Kentish Farm		Oehme 1908
The Piazza San Vio, Zattere, Venice		Oehme 1908
Florence from San Gervasio		Oehme 1908
Portrait, Frances Stilllman	c.1908	
Storrington, Sussex	1913	
The Orchard in Autumn, Kelmscott	1914	
The Pilgrim Folk	1914	
Flowers	1921	
White Herons	undated	
Cherry Orchard in Kent	undated	
(4) Flower arrangements	undated	
Plaiting	undated	
Playing in a Garden (Kelmscott?)	undated	
Dreams of Camelot	undated	
Jolie Coeur (after Rossetti)	undated	
Landscape (Crossroads, Godshill IOW)	undated	
A Summer Day	undated	Newport RI 1924
Lady in a Wood with a Squirrel (Billy & Hans)	undated	
Meadow/woodland with lake	undated	
Autumn Group	undated	
Chrysanthemums & Pomegranates	undated	
Spring Flowers & pic. ? Vaucluse	undated	
Two Bowls of Roses	undated	
Spring Flowers/glass vase, pewter tray	undated	
Autumn	undated	Bonhams 9 Mar. 1904
Fiammetta (Lute Player)	undated	
Legend of St Francis and the Two Monks	undated	

Selected Bibliography

The Greeks

Atkins, Julia, (June 1987), 'The Ionides Family', *Antique Collector* 58 no.6, pp86-93

Butterworth, Dorothea, *Descendants of Constantine John Ionides*. Family tree in National Art Library

Ionides, Alexander Constantine, (1927), Ion, A Grandfather's Tale, Cuala Press: Dublin

Ionides, Luke, *Memories*. Privately published

Ionides, Alexander Constantine, *Ion, A Traveller's Tale*. Privately published

Ionides, Julia, 'The Greek Connection, in Pre-Raphaelitism in its European Context' in *Essays*, Casteras, Susan (ed). Associated University Presses

Leoussi, A, *The Ionides Circle & Art*

Metaxas, K H, (1988), *A Greek Family In Britain*

Marie Stillman 1844-1927

Agresti, Olivia Rossetti, (1904), *Giovanni Costa - His Life, Works and Times*. Gay & Bird: London

Angeli, Helen Rossetti, (1949), *Dante Gabriel Rossetti, His Friends and Enemies*. Hamish Hamilton

Attwood, Philip, (1990), *The Stillmans and the Morrises*, JWMS **Vol IX** i

Baddeley, W St Clair, *Diaries*, Gloucester Records Office

Beresford, Sandra, (December 1986), *PreRaffaelismo ed Estetismo a Firenze negli ultimi del XIX secolo, in L'Idea di Firenze: Temi e interpretazione nell'arte straniera dell'Ottocento*

Berwick, Lady Theresa, Bequest, Papers, Eng Lett. C533 Bodleian Library

Blunt, Wilfrid Scawen, (publ 1919), *My Diaries; Being a Personal Narrative of Events*. Martin Secker: London

Brown, Ford Madox, *Papers*, Box 32, Letters from WMR and WSB

Brown, Hazel, (1992), *Marie Stillman 1844-1927*, Dissertation, Royal Holloway College

Burne-Jones, Lady Georgiana, (1904), *Memorials of Edward Burne-Jones*. Macmillan

Casteras, Susan P & Denney, C, (1996), *The Grosvenor Gallery: A Palace of Art in Victorian England*. Yale University Press

Casteras, Susan P, (1990), *English Pre-Raphaelitism and its Reception in America in the 19th Century*. Farleigh Dickinson University Press

Cherry, Deborah, (1993), *Painting Women. Victorian Women Artists*. Routledge: London

Christian, John, (1984), Exhibition catalogue: 'The Pre-Raphaelites and their Times'. Tokyo 1985

Christian, John, (1984), *Marie Spartali*. Apollo

Clayton, Ellen, (1876), *English Women Artists*. Tinsley Brosthers

Cobden-Sanderson, R, (1926), *Journals of T J Cobden-Sanderson*, 2 vols. Privately published

Colvin, Sidney, (1921), *Memories and Notes of Persons & Places*. E. Arnold

Darbyshire, *Letters to Ford Madox Brown*, Box 4, National Art Library

Du Maurier, Daphne (ed), (1951), *The Young George du Maurier: A Selection of his Letters 1860-1867*. Peter Davis: London

Elzea, Rowland, (1984), *The Pre-Raphaelite Collections of the Delaware Art Museum*. Delaware Art Museum

Elzea, Roland, (Spring 1989), 'Bancroft papers', *Journal of Pre-Raphaelitism & Aesthetic Studies*. pp56-7

Faulkner, Peter (ed), (1986), *Jane Morris to Wilfrid Scawen Blunt*, University of Exeter

Ford, Ford Madox, (1896), *A record of His Life and Work. Longmans*

Hare, Augustus, (ed), (1879), *Life and Letters of Frances, Baroness Bunsen*. Smith, Elder & Co.: London

Henderson, Philip, (1950), *Letters of William Morris to his Family and Friends*. Longmans Green & Co.
Heuffer, Cathy, Stow Hill Papers, STH/BH/2/1, HLRO
Holiday, Henry, (1914), *Reminiscences of My Life*. Heinemann
Ivory, Sarah E, (1983), *The Artistic Career of a Victorian Lady*. St Lawrence University
James, Henry, J L Sweeney (ed), (1956), *The Painter's Eye*. R. Hart Davies
Percy Lubbock (ed), (1920), *Henry James, Letters*. Macmillan
Kelvin, N (ed), (1984-1996), *Collected Letters of William Morris*, 4 Volumes (Vol 1: 1848-1880; Vol 2: 1881-1888; Vol 3: 1889-1892; Vol 4: 1893-1896). Princeton University Press
le Gallienne, R, (1951), *The Romantic '90s*. Putnam
Lee, Vernon, *Vernon Lee's Letters*, with a preface by her Executor, Irene Cooper Willis
Marshall, John, *Autographs*. Exeter University Library
Merrington, W R, (1977) *University College Hospital and its Medical School: A History*
Minto, W (ed), (1892), *Autobiographical Notes of William Bell Scott*, 2 vols. Osgood, McIlvaine & Co
Morris, Jane to Sydney Cockerell, National Art Library
Morris, May to Sydney Cockerell, National Art Library
Morris, May, (1966), *William Morris, Artist, Writer, Socialist*. Russell & Russell: New York, Vol I, p74
Morris, May, (1973), *Introductions to Collected Works of William Morris*. Orlie Editions: New York
Murray, Charles Fairfax, papers, John Rylands, MSS 1281, 1560 als; six letters from Marie Stillman
Obituary, *New York Times*
Obituary, (8 March 1927), *The Times*
Ormond, Leonée, *Vernon Lee as a Critic of Aestheticism in Miss Brown*, Colby Library Quarterly
Ormond, Leonée, (1969), *George du Maurier*. Routledge
Ormond, Richard, (30 December 1965), *Country Life*
Paget, Walburga, (1924) *In My Tower*. Hutchinson: London
Peattie (ed), (1990), *William Michael Rossetti, Letters*. Penn State University Press
Praz, Mario, *The House of Life*. Adelphi: Milan 1964
Prettejohn, E, (ed), (1999), *Art and Aestheticism in Victorian England*. Manchester University Press
Ritchie, Hester (ed), (1924), *Letters of Anne Thackeray Ritchie*. John Murray: London
Robertson, W Graham, (1931), *Time Was*. Hamish Hamilton: London
Rossetti, D G, (1895), *Family Letters*. Boston
Rossetti, W M, 'English Painters of the Present Day', *Portfolio* **8**
Rossetti, W M, (1900), *Pre-Raphaelite Diaries and Letters*. Hurst & Blackett
Rossetti, W M, (1903), *Rossetti Papers*. Sands
Rossetti, W M, (1906), *Some Reminiscences*. Brown: Langham
Rossetti-Angeli Papers, University of Britiish Columbia, Angeli-Dennis Collection (& Bodleian)
Rossetti-Leyland Letters, Ohio 1978
Schonfield, Zuzanna, (1987), *The Precariously Privileged. A Professional Family in Victorian England*. Oxford University Press
Schueller, Herbert M & Robert L. Peters, (eds), (1968), *Letters of John Addington Symonds*. Wayne State University Press
Shepherd, Kristen Adele, (1998), *Marie Stillman*, MA Dissertation, George Washington University
Spencer, Robin, (1990), 'Whistler', *Studio*
Stephens, F G, *Papers*, Bodleian Library
Stillman, Chauncey D, *Impressions of Marie Stillman*. Wightwick
Stillman, Marie to Sydney Cockerell, SCC Papers, National Art Library
Stillman, Marie to Sydney Cockerell, BL Add Mus 52754, British Library
Stillman/Bancroft papers, Box 16, Delaware Art Museum
Stirling, A W M, (1926), *Richmond Papers*. Heinemann: London

Surtees, Virginia, (1971), *The Paintings and Drawings of Dante Gabriel Rossetti*, **2 vols**. Clarendon
Symonds, James Addington, (1920), *Letters*, Lubbock (ed). Macmillan
Symonds, James Addington, (1984), *Memoirs*, Phyllis Groskuth (ed). Hutchinson
The Pursuit of Beauty, (June 1978). Apollo
Thirlwell, Angela, *William & Lucy - The Other Rossettis*. Yale 2003
Troxell, J, (1937), *Three Rossettis*. Harvard University Press
Vance, William L, (1990), *America's Rome*, 2 Vols. Yale
Waterson, Merlin, (1981), *Lady Berwick, Attingham and Italy*. National Trust Studies
Wiseman, T P, (1992) *Talking to Virgil*. University of Exeter Press

William Stillman

Buckle, G. E., Morison, S., McDonald, I., *et al*, (1935), *The History of The Times*. Privately printed: London
Caine, Hall, (1929), *Recollections of Dante Gabriel Rossetti*. Cassell: London
Dickason, D H, (1953), *The Daring Young Men, The Story of the American Pre-Raphaelites*. Indiana University Press
Fiske Papers. Cornell University
Glenny, Mischa, (1999), *The Balkans, 1804-1999*. Granta
Jalland, Pat, (1997), *Women, Marriage and Politics*. Oxford University Press
Miller, Frances, (1974), *Catalogue of William James Stillman Papers at Union College*
Morris, May, (1966), *William Morris, Artist, Writer, Socialist*, vol 1. Russell& Russell: New York
Steegmuller, Frances, (1951), *The Two Lives of James Jackson Jarves*. Yale: New Haven
Stillman Papers, Union College, Schenectady
Tea, Eva Boni, *Philip Webb, Life and Work*
Ulmann S O A, *Rossetti, Stillman and the Union College*, Willowwood mss
Vance, William L, (1990), *America's Rome*, 2 vols. Yale

Publications and articles by William J Stillman

Acropolis of Athens, (1870). F S Ellis: London
Autobiography of a Journalist, (1901). Houghton, Mifflin: Boston
'Billy & Hans', (illus. Lisa Stillman), (February 1897), *The Century*, Vol 53, Issue 4
Cesnola Report, (1885). Thompson & Moreau: New York
Class of 1848, Union College, Schenectady
'DGR & Chloral', *Academy*, v 53.333
'Francesco Crispi', (1894), *The Century*, Vol 49, Issue 2
Herzegovina and the Late Uprising, (1877)
Landscape Painting and Modern Dutch Artists, (1906) by Stillman, Greenshields, Symonds & Ruskin. Baker & Taylor Co.: New York
'Mr Jarves and Mr Stillman', *Nation* 37:250 (Sept 20)
Old Italian Masters, The Century Co: New York
The Cretan Insurrection 1866-8, (1872). Smith & Elder: London
'The Old Rome and the New', (July 1891), *Atlantic Monthly*, Vol 68, Issue 405
The Union of Italy 1815-1895, (1899), Cambridge University Press
'Two European Schools of Design', (July 1874), *Atlantic Monthly*, Vol 34, Issue 201

Miscellaneous

Amor, Anne C, *William Holman Hunt*, Constable
Attwood, Philip, (Spring 1989), *Medals* **No14**
Bendiner, F, (1998), *The Art of Ford Madox Brown*, Houghton Mifflin: Boston
Bland, Lucy, *Banishing the Beast; English Feminism and Sexual Morality, 1885-1914*, Penguin
Brown, Ford Madox, Papers, NAL MSL 1995/14/105
Bryson & Troxell (ed), *Jane Morris and Dante Gabriel Rossetti, Correspondence* Clarendon Press
Burton, Andrew, *Vision & Accident, History of the V&A*

Buxton-Forman, Harry, (1897), *The Books of William Morris*. F. Hollings: London
Cahen d'Anvers, Mme A, (1972), *Baboushka Remembers*. Published privately
Campbell Orr, C, (1995), *Women in the Victorian Art World*, Manchester University Press
Chadwick, Owen, (1998), *A History of the Popes 1830-1914*, Clarendon Press
Christian, John, (ed), *The Little Holland House Album*
Colby, Vineta, (2003), *Vernon Lee, A Literary Biography*, University of Chicago Press
Collins, John, (1992), *The Two Forgers*, Oak Knoll Press: New Castle, Delaware
Constable, W G, (1964), *Art Collecting in the United States*. Nelson: London & New York
Conway, Moncure, (1882), *Travels in S Kensington*, Harper & Bros: New York
Faxon, A Craig, (1996), *Three Rossettis*, Apple Tree Valley
Ford, Colin, (2003), *Julia Margaret Cameron*. Getty Trust
Francillon, R E, (1914), *Mid Victorian Memories*, Hodder
Gunn, Peter, (1964), *Vernon Lee, Violet Paget*. Oxford University Press
Hallé, Charles, (1909), *Notes from a Painter's Life*, John Murray: London
Hare, Augustus, (1884), *Florence*, Kegan Paul & Co: London
Heuffer, Ford M, (1896)*Ford Madox Brown, Life and Work*, Longmans
Horner, Lady Frances, (1933), *Time Remembered*, Heinemann
Hunt, Diana Holman, (1969), *My Grandfather, His Wives & Loves*, Hamish Hamilton
Jackson Lear, T J, (1981), *No Place of Grace*. Pantheon: New York
Jones, Mark Bence, (1982), *The Viceroys of India*. Constable & Co.
Lamont, L M, (1912), *T Armstrong, a Memoir*, Secker
Levi, Donata, (1994), *Cognoscitori, mercanti e amateurs a Firenze nell' Ottocento, La Cultura artistica a Siena nell'Ottocento, Carlo Sisi, Ettore Spaletti*, Pizzi: Milano
Lindsay, Jack, (1991), *William Morris, Life and Works*, Nine Elms
Longford, Elizabeth, (1979), *Pilgrimage of Passion*, Weidenfeld & Nicholson
Marsh, Jan, (1985), *The Pre-Raphaelite Sisterhood*, Quartet
Merrill, Linda, (1998), *The Peacock Room: A Cultural Biography*, Yale
Mills, Ernestine (ed), (1912), *Life and Letters of Frederick Shields*, London
Morris, Jane to Sydney Carlisle Cockerell, National Art Library
Newman, Theresa & Watkinson, Ray, (1991), *Ford Madox Brown*, Chatto & Windus
Paget, Violet, *Papers*, Somerville College
Paget, Lady Walburga, (1923), *Embassies of Other Days,* 2 vols, Hutchinson
Prinsep, Valentine, (May 1892), 'Rossetti and his Friends', in *Art Journal* **54**
Rendall, Jane (ed), (1987), *Equal or Different; Women's Politics 1800-1914*. Blackwell
Ritchie, Anne T, (1873), *Old Kensington*, Smith, Elder
Rothenstein, William, (1931), *Men and Memories*, Faber
Saarinen, Aline B, (1958) *The Proud Possessors*, Random House: New York
Shields, Frederick, *Letters to Ford Madox Brown*, FMB Box 20, National Art Library
Smith, Joseph Lindon, *Diary & Letters to his Mother*; Dublin New Hampshire Archive
Smyth, Ethel, (1933), *Female Pipings in Eden*, Peter Davis
Stirling, A M W, (1922), *William De Morgan & His Wife*, Thornton Butterworth
Surtees (ed), (1967), *Ford Madox Brown, Diaries*, Yale
Surtees, Virginia, (1988), *The Artist and the Autocrat*, Michael Russell
Troxell, J, (1937), *Three Rossettis*, Harvard University Press
Waldron, K, (c.1905), *Two American Women Artists*, photocopy in Delaware Art Museum archive
White, Horatio Daniel, (1925), *Willard Fiske*, OUP
Vicinus, Martha, (2004), *Intimate Friends, Women Who Loved Women*, University of Chicago Press

INDEX

Page numbers in bold type refer to illustrations and captions